Media, Social Movements, and Protest Cultures in Africa

Media, Social Movements, and Protest Cultures in Africa

Hashtags, Humor, and Slogans

Edited by Lungile Tshuma, Trust Matsilele,
Shepherd Mpofu, and Mbongeni Msimanga

LEXINGTON BOOKS
Lanham • Boulder • New York • London

Published by Lexington Books
An imprint of The Rowman & Littlefield Publishing Group, Inc.
4501 Forbes Boulevard, Suite 200, Lanham, Maryland 20706
www.rowman.com

86-90 Paul Street, London EC2A 4NE

Copyright © 2024 by The Rowman & Littlefield Publishing Group, Inc.

All rights reserved. No part of this book may be reproduced in any form or by any electronic or mechanical means, including information storage and retrieval systems, without written permission from the publisher, except by a reviewer who may quote passages in a review.

British Library Cataloguing in Publication Information Available

Library of Congress Cataloging-in-Publication Data

Names: Tshuma, Lungile Augustine, editor, author. | Matsilele, Trust, editor, author. | Mpofu, Shepherd, editor, author. | Msimanga, Mbongeni Jonny, editor, author.
Title: Media, social movements, and protest cultures in Africa: hashtags, humor, and slogans / edited by Lungile Tshuma, Trust Matsilele, Shepherd Mpofu, ad Mbongeni Msimanga.
Description: Lanham: Lexington Books, 2024. | Includes bibliographical references and index.
Identifiers: LCCN 2024024763 (print) | LCCN 2024024764 (ebook) | ISBN 9781666970135 (cloth) | ISBN 9781666970142 (ebook)
Subjects: LCSH: Social movements–Africa, Sub-Saharan. | Protest movements–Africa, Sub-Saharan. | Social media–Political aspects–Africa, Sub-Saharan. | Social media and society–Africa, Sub-Saharan.
Classification: LCC HM883 .M43 2024 (print) | LCC HM883 (ebook) | DDC 303.4840967–dc23/eng/20240603
LC record available at https://lccn.loc.gov/2024024763
LC ebook record available at https://lccn.loc.gov/2024024764

Contents

Introduction: Contesting Africa: A Theoretical Appreciation of Media, Social Movements, and Protest Cultures   1
Lungile Tshuma, Trust Matsilele, Shepherd Mpofu and Mbongeni Msimanga

PART I: SOCIAL MEDIA AND SOCIAL MOVEMENTS   **11**

1. Violence as a Decolonizing and (De)humanizing Force, and Social Media(ted) Protests in Africa   13
   Shepherd Mpofu

2. Disrupting Patriotic Discourse in Zimbabwe: Reading Evan Mawarire's #ThisFlag as Counter-Hegemony   35
   Blessing Makwambeni

3. Testing the Illusory Truth Effect: An Analysis of Comments to Nigerian Army's "Fake News" Tweets on Lekki #EndSARS Shootings   53
   Raheemat Adeniran and Kunle Adebajo

4. #VoetsekANC: (Un)Civil Disobedience as Protest Action in South Africa's Twittersphere   69
   Trust Matsilele and Blessing Makwambeni

5. #EndSARS: The Role of Social Media Influencers in Raising Awareness of Police Brutality in Nigeria   87
   Temitope Opeyemi Falade and Lungile Tshuma

PART II: ONLINE PROTEST STRATEGIES — 105

6 Online Protests and Government Countermeasures in Zimbabwe: A Decolonial Perspective — 107
Tawanda Mukurunge and Lorenzo Dalvit

7 I Don't Pay Hidden Debts: An Analysis of Public Integrity Center (CIP) Digital Communication Campaign in Mozambique — 121
Tânia Machonisse

8 Of Protests and Satire: Representations of #EndSARS Brutality in Selected Nigerian Hip-Hop Music — 139
Ruth Karachi Benson Oji

9 Ironic Activism and Social Justice: A Case Study of Political Satire and Social Media in Zimbabwe — 159
Mbongeni Msimanga

PART III: MEDIA TEXTS PRODUCTION — 181

10 Protesting for Change: Ethopia's Diasporic Media and the Fight for Democracy — 183
Solomon Kebede and Abit Hoxha

11 *Gukurahundi* Memory, Subversive Pleasures, and Protest Cultures in Zimbabwe — 203
Mphathisi Ndlovu and Nkosini A. Khupe

12 Theorizing Graffiti as a Novel Alternative Public Sphere in Zimbabwe's Contested Politics — 219
Nyasha Cefas Zimuto

13 Publishing as Revolutionary Tools from Pre-independence to Post-independence Kenya — 235
Job Mwaura

14 Photographs, Protest, and Memory: A Case of #BlackLivesMatter in South Africa — 255
Lungile Tshuma

Index — 273

About the Editors and Contributors — 275

Introduction

Contesting Africa: A Theoretical Appreciation of Media, Social Movements, and Protest Cultures

Lungile Tshuma, Trust Matsilele, Shepherd Mpofu and Mbongeni Msimanga

Africa has for a long time been characterized by political upheavals owing, arguably, to bad governance, corruption, and authoritarian rule (Branch and Mampilly, 2015; Harsch, 2009; Makumbe, 2005). These upheavals have often led to coups, civil conflicts, and outbreaks of violence along ethnic and tribal cleavages (Sanches, 2022; Posner, 2005). However, it is important to state that resistance against inadequate or corrupt leadership in Africa has a long lineage. Terence Ranger staked out much of the terrain with his *Revolt in Southern Rhodesia* and a widely discussed article in the *Journal of African History,* which argued for a fresh assessment of movements of resistance to the establishment of colonial rule (Crummey et al., 1986, p. 10). Ranger's work mainly looked at the influence of religion as a source of resistance and reaction to colonization. Instead, collective belonging and shared societal interest were some of the key issues that caused the revolt. Thus, the fresh assessment called for a deeper understanding of resistance, as there are no unitary forces but a plethora of reasons and sources of resistance. This is an aspect of dissent from which we build the current volume. In this book, we argue that resistance and social movements are influenced by various reasons and take different forms based on the state of democracy in each community. In most African countries, independence was won through protests and armed struggle. Hence, social movements and protests are not a new phenomenon in African societies, as most were at the forefront of anti-colonial struggles that brought about independence across the continent (Sithole, 1968; Nyerere, 1968).

A clarion call to democratize the continent has dominated the region for many years, as societies feel that their liberators have become tyrants and derailed the train of liberation, democracy, and decolonization while depriving the masses of a decent life. While democracy remains a contested term, protesters have called for an end to state crackdowns on citizens and for free participation in electoral processes (Makumbe, 2005). Such calls have been characterized by different forms of protests. African citizens have had, for example, to resist the very "liberation movements" that undermined colonial rule but then held onto power at all costs (Duncan, 2016; Bratton and van de Walle, 1992). As mentioned above, while social movements and protest cultures are not new in Africa, the growth in digital cultures has led to new protest cultures which are now being studied and theorized, an attempt we also advance in this present work (Msimanga, 2022; Matsilele, 2019; Matsilele and Ruhanya, 2021; Mpofu and Mare, 2020). Most of the theories that have been used to study protest cultures are from the North with fewer or little theoretical underpinnings that help in understanding the nature of protests in non-Western communities, often referred to as the Global South. This volume gives a deeper understanding of the dynamics, nuances, and the state of social movements and protest cultures in Africa. Key to this book is how chapters have moved away from the central role mass media plays in facilitating protests to becoming an organic mechanism that informs protests. These include socio-cultural norms, values, and discourses that are appropriated in various platforms to "rebel" against the status quo. These are not limited to *ubuntu*, griots, and satire that embody various forms of protest.

These new protest cultures alter the way we understand public deliberations and the public sphere. They also alter the way we have imagined identities and throw into sharp focus the role of globalization and transnationalism. Digital media have been used by these social movements as subaltern public spheres in the Spivakean sense, where the organization of protests takes place and transnational global alliances are forged. Recent developments, inspired by the growth of the internet as a cheaper and unbounded transnational medium of communication, have seen a rise in social movements organized around different interests (Penny and Dada, 2014). As such, Africa has witnessed various forms of protests as different communities seek to assert their state of belonging and have their voices heard (David, 2018). However, the same digital media are infiltrated by the state and the economic elite, creating a convoluted space that presents itself as both an unsafe and safe space for organization, fundraising, and contesting power (Goldstone, 2000; Nam et al., 2021, Sullivan, 2020). The duality that comes with digital media means they can be potent weapons both for oppressive hegemonies and oppressed groups of subaltern social actors. It is this bifurcation that informs both the hopes of the ordinary citizenry and the panicked response by the elite, which moves to regulate the cybersphere. Writing on this issue just over a decade ago, Mamdani (2011) intimated that the memory of Tahrir Square (the center of mobilization for the Arab Spring uprisings that toppled several dictators in North Africa) feeds opposition hopes and fuels government fears in many African political jurisdictions.

MAKING A CASE FOR AFRICA

Statistics by the African Development Bank (ADB) estimate that between 2011 and 2014, there were "five times as many protests per annum in Africa as there had been in 2000." While some of the protests were meant to overthrow military or tyrannical governments, as the chapter will show, some protests were mainly meant to call for government attention to poor service delivery. Notable examples include protests over hiking bus fares in Mozambique in 2012 and the removal of fuel subsidies in Nigeria in the same year. Against this background, Ellis and van Kessel (2009, p. 56–57) observe that "distributional issues are still central in Africa . . . [and] need to be an explicit component of the theory-building agenda of social movement scholars." Given the pervasiveness and increased levels of poverty on the continent, worsened by the COVID-19 pandemic which had devastating effects on all economies, the region is predicted to continue experiencing after-effects which will likely lead to more protests. Political forecasts argue that future protests will focus on economic decay and poor service delivery. Given that Africa has the largest youth population in the world and a youth bulge, the biggest commercial dividend when it comes to the adoption and wide use of digital and social media affordances, a study that looks at these "digital native" protests in Africa would offer interesting insights into the extent to which such appropriations are having an impact on democratization and participatory politics. Such a study will also inform policymakers to price in the cost of protests. Secondly, the image of Africa has for many years been that of a dark, retrogressive continent (Tshuma et al., 2023; Ncube, 2019). However, such a perception and representation has been challenged by scholars who have argued that the portrayal is inaccurate, as most of the problems facing Africa are not unique (Mkandawire, 2010). Thus, without perpetuating such stereotypes, this book notes that protest cultures are a global phenomenon. However, we seek to tease out contextual aspects that are unique to the African continent, especially the sub-Saharan African region.

The continued use of repressive means by governments in Africa to clamp down on voices of dissent has also had an impact on the state of social movements. With citizens failing to have their views expressed through voting and parliamentary processes in dominant party regimes, protest becomes an alternative avenue of expressing discontent (de Waal and Ibreck, 2013). It is thus timely to trace the trajectory of social movements on the continent. Also, given that liberation struggles that ushered in independence in Africa are a product of various forms of protests, the evolution of such protests in contemporary society needs scholarly attention, a trajectory this book delves into. Insights on digital protests can also be developed into the nuances of African politics, the state, and the maturity of democracies on the continent. These are measured not only by protests but also through the response by governments. While various studies have argued that the digital divide is a common feature of communicative life in Africa, protest movements taking place on social media are now common, some of which have forced African governments to react. In their study on transnational hashtag movements in Africa, Matsilele et al. (2021, p. 1) found that the movements associated with hashtags like #EswatiniLivesMatter, #EndSARS, and #Zimbabwean-LivesMatter hashtags, achieved a "modicum of 'success' by forcing some of Africa's enduring dictatorships to make piecemeal concessions of varying degrees."

MEDIA, SOCIAL MOVEMENTS, AND PROTEST IN AFRICA

Protests in Africa are mainly seen as having taken place in three waves: the first wave was aimed at ending colonization and fighting for independence, the second wave, arguably, started in 2000 and advocated for multiparty democracy while the third wave was characterized by public demonstrations conducted both offline and online (Mueller, 2013; Bond and Mottiar, 2013). The use of social media, we argue, has changed the way social movements are theorized. One such reason is that social movements under the first and second waves were elitist and took a top-down approach (Branch and Mampilly, 2013). Moreover, after the Arab Spring, online social movements have become more pronounced. Prior to that, in Africa, the most common protest strategies included the use of graffiti, songs, and street theater (Jolaosho, 2019). Social media has, however, become the dominant platform used by protest movements. Social activist movements such as #BringBackOurGirls have in previous years been used to campaign against the abduction of Nigerian schoolgirls (Endong, 2019). Similarly, the #FeesMustFall and #RhodesMustFall movements gained attention as they symbolized the fall of colonial systems in South Africa (see Mpofu, 2017). Such protests further changed the face of South African student politics in relation to the state when students protested for free and decolonized education (Bosch and Mutsvairo, 2017).

The above-mentioned hashtag movements further show the new trajectory taken by protest movements. The first wave of social movements was ideologically driven with the intention of changing governments (Ellis and Van Kessel, 2009; Posner, 2005). Contemporary social movements fall under what is called "valence protest" which are protests in pursuit of/fighting for material goods or call for better service delivery as opposed to overthrowing governments or regimes (Harris, 2015). Drawing examples from South Africa, Harris (2015, p. 3) supports the above position by noting that protestors took to the streets "in order to change *what is done* by those in power rather than changing *who* is in power" (emphasis in original). However, this is despite the presence of some revolutionary social protests that sought to change who is in power, like the #MugabeMustGo and #ZimbabweanLivesMatter movements, which wanted to remove the then Zimbabwean president, Robert Mugabe, for his political abuse of citizens, and challenge the way in which liberation movements were abusing the people they claimed to have liberated (Tshuma, 2023; Matsilele et al., 2021; Mpofu et al., 2021). Before this, the Arab Spring-associated movements, which led to the overthrow of political leaders in Tunisia and Egypt, have remained one of the most popular social movements. The Arab Spring has been met with mixed reactions from scholars, with some arguing that the uprising was a failure (Khalifa, 2015). The argued success of the Arab Spring is based on the view that it managed to see the fall of the arguably powerful presidents in Tunisia and Egypt. While the protests spread to other countries like Morocco, Libya, Yemen, and Syria, the impact was very minimal or small. The protests were arguably a failure because the "events could be seen as a maintained reverse wave where the situation went from non-democratic governance in the form of autocracy to a non-democratic system with limited democratic measures accompanied by a spirit of theocracy" (Khalifa, 2015, p. 2).

Closely related to the above point, scholarly work has cautioned against the hyping of the power of social media in enabling protest movements (Bodunrin and Matsilele, 2023; Matsilele and Mboti, 2022; Msimanga, Ncube and Mkwananzi, 2021). Chitanana and Mutsvairo (2019, p. 80) contend that while social media platforms such as X, formerly Twitter, have enabled citizens to deliberate on a range of issues in Zimbabwe, they are "yet to create a strong enough counter-hegemonic force to effectively challenge entrenched and competing authoritarian regimes." The medium can indeed be used by authoritarian regimes as a powerful tool for political repression and the spread of extremist propaganda. Tshuma et al. (2022) note that while digital public spaces have traditionally been associated with oppositional voices, pro-ZANU PF actors are using X, formerly Twitter, to articulate official discourses. Due to its interactivity, X allows both pro-ZANU PF and anti-ZANU PF actors to engage and debate political issues. As such, X has become a site of political struggles between hegemonic and counter-hegemonic forces. This view is shared by Eckert (2017, p. 211) who argued that the theme of "Social Movements" does not—and never did—rank high among those issues that historians of Africa would consider crucial. This edited volume, drawing from different case studies from the continent, looks at the intersection of the media, social movements, and protest cultures. While we concede, as asserted by McCurdy (2012), that "research on how the mainstream media portray social movements across various mass media is perhaps the oldest and most-travelled trail in studying the media/social movement dynamic," we argue that with developments necessitated by the advent of communicative ICTs at the turn of the century, for example, the hashtag protest mentioned above, there is a need for an African-focused study looking at how the terrain has changed.

STRUCTURE OF THE BOOK

This volume attempts to highlight and build new theoretical insights in understanding the intersection between media, social movements, and protest cultures in Africa. It seeks to make theoretical contributions toward the creativity of social movements and their resistance by governments or political and economic elites. The book is organized into three sections. Part I of the book focuses on social media and social movements. The first five chapters look at how citizens troll state actors, exposing the excesses of power through the appropriation of digital technologies. Looking at the question of leveraging social media by citizens, Shepherd Mpofu's chapter assesses the intersection of online and offline protests and how social media have played a central role, questioning how various *violences* that occur during protests help to decolonize the human, that is, the citizens. In the same chapter, the author explores the use of violence in various mediated protests as both a dehumanizing, decolonizing, and humanizing agent. Building on the same theme of leveraging social media by sovereigns, Blessing Makwambeni's chapter, using Gramsci's conceptualization of hegemony and counter-hegemony as a framework, analyzes the online-mediated #ThisFlag movement's discourses. His findings reflect the utility of harnessing "captured" national symbols as a resource for mounting resistance against oppressive regimes online. The third chapter from Raheemat Adeniran and Kunle Adebajo examines public reactions to the Nigerian Army's tweets tagging media reports of its involvement as "fake news." Their findings suggest the Nigerian Army's action created a backlash as most Twitter (X) users who responded to the tweets expressed widespread anger and were not convinced by the official narrative. The next chapter (chapter 4) from Trust Matsilele and Blessing Makwambeni examines how the X (Twitter) hashtag, #VoetsekANC, is employed by citizens for cyber trolling activities against South Africa's governing party, the African National Congress (ANC). The section closes with Temitope Opeyemi Falade and Lungile Tshuma's chapter exploring the role social media influencers played in raising awareness of police brutality through the #EndSARS campaign. The chapter argues that influencers are the "new" opinion leaders in the digital spaces that ignite and popularize social movements.

Part II of the book focuses on online protest strategies, especially leveraging creative industries such as civil society, musicians, and satirists as part of the broader protest movement refracted through digital spaces. Thus, the section is largely focused on the creativity by citizens to critique the ruling elite. Tawanda Mukurunge and Lorenzo Dalvit set the tone of the section by exploring strategies being employed by online protesters (X, which is formerly known as Twitter, Facebook, and YouTube) and the counter-strategies used by Mugabe and subsequently the Mnangagwa governments in attempting to contain anti-government protest action in Zimbabwe. The chapter comes against the background of internet shutdowns that the government had imposed to contain online protests. Tânia Machonisse's chapter follows with an examination of the role of civil society in protest movements in Mozambique. Along the theme of media, social movements, and protest cultures, Tânia maps how civil society organizations are using various communication strategies like slogans to provide information (since it is an economic issue) in an accessible fashion about the impact of the "hidden debt" to the Mozambican State and its citizens. In her findings, Tânia demonstrates that social media became a public space where citizens used to protest the Mozambican government. Machonisse argues that protests were decolonial in nature because protestors used various forms of culture and tradition to register their displeasure and call for the government to address their demands. However, data also show that more people with access to the Internet feel more comfortable addressing their opinions and actions informally through social media platforms. Closely related to the chapter from Machonisse looking at how civic organizations use digital affordances for information sharing is the chapter from Karachi Benson Oji's which explores discourses around the #EndSARS protest movement. In this chapter, Ruth sets out to interrogate the protest culture in Nigeria through the use of protest music occasioned by the #EndSARS protest. She argues that music, in African culture, has arguably been one of the effective ways to convey one's thoughts and act as a source of resistance. Ruth's focus is on protest music that was produced at the height of the #EndSARS protest. Her findings demonstrate that both the government—because of supporting the police and not calling them to order—and the police are negatively represented as killers, brutes, thieves, and untrustworthy persons. The section on how creatives are leveraging digital media for protest purposes concludes with Mbongeni Msimanga's chapter tackling the growing phenomenon of satire and humor in Zimbabwe. Msimanga's study concludes that case studies, Bus Stop TV and Magamba TV, tackled human rights and injustice issues in Zimbabwe that dealt with elections, abductions, and violence by the state apparatus.

The last section of the book focuses on the use of various media texts for protest purposes. The section starts off with Solomon Kebede and Abit Hoxha's chapter that discusses the role of diasporic media in mediating the Ethiopian political crises. The chapter concludes that the media act as "protest actors" within authoritarian regimes. To protect the identity of interviewees some of whom are wanted by the state over flimsy charges, the paper kept their identities anonymous. Mphathisi Ndlovu's chapter follows and discusses the *Gukurahundi* genocide, exploring the way in which victims are using guerrilla tactics to protest the silence around the traumatic past. Overall, the chapter demonstrates the key role of popular cultural artifacts (graffiti, music, film, social media, paintings, and theater) that constitute texts to express the traumatic experiences of disempowered communities. The following chapter by Nyasha Zimuto analyzes protest graffiti as a media form in Zimbabwe. The analysis covers various forms of graffiti, including but not limited to those found on dura walls, building walls, and toilet walls. Zimuto also interviewed language experts to throw more light on the graffiti being used to counter the ruling party's power. Given the nature of Zimbabwe's authoritarian regime, interviewees were anonymized. Job Mwaura documents the evolution of protest cultures in Kenya, tracing the contribution of various forms of alternative media and authors from pre-independence to post-independence Kenya and their contribution to various forms of movements. The chapter is important as it provides an understanding of the culture of resistance in Kenya that started in the pre-independence period and has continued to the current era. Concluding this section, and the book, Lungile Tshuma examines the use of photographs in social movements and protests. His work focuses on the relationship between memory and photography in communicating protests. The findings show that photographs are used as agents of protest, as they "bear witness" to the suffering of the people and make sense of the present. Lungile argues that social movements gain more currency due to the use of photographs of the past.

REFERENCES

Bodunrin, I. A. and Matsilele, T. (2023). Social Media and Protest Politics in Nigeria's #EndSARS Campaign. *Handbook of Social Media in Education, Consumer Behavior and Politics: 1*, 111(114), 109.

Bosch, T. and Mutsvairo, B. (2017). Pictures, Protests and Politics: Mapping Twitter Images during South Africa's Fees Must Fall Campaign. *African Journalism Studies,* 4(8), 71–89.

Branch, A. and Mampilly, Z. C. (2015). *Africa Rising: Popular Protest and Political Change*. London, UK: Zed Books.

Clayton, D. M. (2018). Black Lives Matter and the Civil Rights Movement: A Comparative Analysis of Two Social Movements in the United States. *Journal of Black Studies,* 49(5), 448–480.

Crummey, D. (1986). *Banditry, Rebellion and Social Protest in Africa*. London: Currey.

de Waal, A. and Ibreck, R. (2013). Hybrid Social Movements in Africa. *Journal of Contemporary African Studies,* 3(2), 303–324.

Eckert, A. (2017). Social Movements in Africa. In Berger, S and Nehring, H (Eds.), *The History of Social Movements in Global Perspective* (pp. 211–224). London: Palgrave Macmillan.

Ellis, S. and van Kessel, I. (2009). *Movers and Shakers: Social Movements in Africa*. Leiden, Netherlands: Brill.

Goldstone, J. A. (2004). More Social Movements or Fewer? Beyond Political Opportunity Structures to Relational Fields. Theory and Society: *Special Issue: Current Routes to the Study of Contentious Politics and Social Change,* 33(¾), 333–365.

Harris, A. (2015). Voting and Protesting: The ANC Paradox and Democratic Participation in South Africa. Presented at the Annual Meeting of the Midwest Political Science Association, Chicago, IL, April 16–19.

Herbst, J. (1997). Responding to State Failure in Africa'. *International Security,* 21(3), 120–144.

Khalifa, A. A. (2016). *The Failure of the Arab Spring*. New Castle: Cambridge Scholars Publishing.

Makumbe, J. (2005). Electoral Crisis in Zimbabwe: Authoritarian vs the People. *CODESRIA,* 31(3), 45–61.

Mamdani, M. (2011). Short Cuts. *London Review of Books, 33*(12), 24–27.

Matsilele, T. (2019). *Social Media Dissidence in Zimbabwe*. Doctoral Dissertation. University of Johannesburg (South Africa).

Matsilele, T. and Ruhanya, P. (2021). Social Media Dissidence and Activist Resistance in Zimbabwe. *Media, Culture & Society,* 43(2), 381–394.

Matsilele, T. and Mboti, N. (2022). Kusvereredza in Zimbabwe's Social Media Sphere. In Gola, E, Volterrani, A, Meloni, F. (Eds.), *Communication, Digital Media and Future: New Scenarios and Future Changes* (pp. 41–53). Cagliari: UNICA Press.

Matsilele, T., Mpofu, S., Msimanga, M. and Tshuma, L. (2021). Transnational Hashtag Protest Movements and Emancipatory Politics in Africa: A Three Country Study. *Global Media Journal – German Edition,* 11(2), https://doi.org/10.22032/dbt.51029.

Mkandawire, T. (2010). On Tax Efforts and Colonial Heritage in Africa. *Journal of Development Studies,* 46(10), 1647–1669.

Murphy, M. (2019). Introduction to "#MeToo Movement". *Journal of Feminist Family Therapy*, 31(2–3), 63–65. https://doi.org/10.1080/08952833.2019.1637088.

Mpofu, S. (2017). Disruption as a Communicative Strategy: The Case of #FeesMustFall and #RhodesMustFall Students' Protests. *Journal of African Media Studies*, 15(1), 351–373.

Mpofu, S. and Mare, A. (2020). #ThisFlag: Social Media and Cyber-Protests in Zimbabwe. In Martin Ndlela (Ed.), *Social Media and Elections in Africa* Vol 2 (pp. 153–172). Palgrave Macmillan.

Mpofu, S. and Nenjerama, T. (2018). Imaginations and Narrations of the Nation: The Music of Raymond Majongwe and Brian Muteki in the Identity Construction of Post-2000 Zimbabwe. *Muziki*, 15(2), 1–20.

Mpofu, S., Ndlovu, M. and Tshuma, L. (2021). The Artist and Filmmaker as Activists, Archivists and the Work of Memory: A Case of the Zimbabwean Genocide. *African Journal of Rhetoric*, 13(1), 46–76.

Msimanga, M. J. (2022). *Satire and the Discursive Construction of National Identity in Zimbabwe: The Case of Magamba and Bustop TV*. Unpublished Doctoral Dissertation. University of Johannesburg.

Msimanga, M. J., Ncube, G., and Mkwananzi, P. (2021). Political Satire and the Mediation of the Zimbabwean Crisis in the Era of the "New Dispensation": The Case of MAGAMBA TV. In Mpofu, S. (Ed.), *The Politics of Laughter in the Social Media Age: Perspectives from the Global South* (pp. 43–56). New York: Palgrave MacMillan.

Nyerere, J. K. (1968). Education for Self-Reliance. In Julius K. Nyerere (Ed.), *Ujamaa: Essays on Socialism* (pp. 27–35). New York: Oxford University Press.

Penney, J. and Dadas, C. (2014). (Re)tweeting in the Service of Protest: Digital Composition and Circulation in the Occupy Wall Street Movement. *New Media & Society*, 16(1), 74–90.

Posner, D. (2005). *Institutions and Ethnic Politics in Africa*. New York, NY: Cambridge University Press.

Sanches, E. R. (2022). *Popular Protest, Political Opportunities, and Change in Africa*. New York: Routledge.

Sithole, N. (1968). *African Nationalism*, 2nd Edition. New York: Oxford University Press.

Tshuma, L. A. (2023). Heir to the Throne: Photography and the Rise to Presidency by Politicians in Zimbabwe and South Africa. *Visual Studies*, 1–10.

Tshuma, L., Ndlovu, M. and Mpofu, S. (2023). Mass Atrocities and Memory Struggles in Africa and the Global South. In Tshuma, L., Ndlovu, M., and Mpofu, S. (Eds.), *Remembering Mass Atrocities: Perspectives on Memory Struggles and Cultural Representations in Africa* (pp. 1–14). Cham: Springer International Publishing.

Tshuma, B. B, Tshuma, L. A. and Ndlovu, M. (2022). Twitter and Political Discourses: How Supporters of Zimbabwe's ruling ZANU PF party use Twitter for Political Engagement. *Journal of Eastern African Studies*. https://doi.org/10.1080/17531055.2022.2076385.

van de Walle, N. (2002). Africa's Range of Regimes. *Journal of Democracy*, 13(2), 66–80.

Part I
SOCIAL MEDIA AND SOCIAL MOVEMENTS

Chapter 1

Violence as a Decolonizing and (De)humanizing Force, and Social Media(ted) Protests in Africa

Shepherd Mpofu

In this conceptual chapter, I link social media, protests, decolonization, and violence. Violence is the common denominator in all these elements. Whenever there are protests, whether by ephemeral social movements—that is, they appear and disappear depending on whether people need them or not—or by social movement organizations, there are most likely to be reports of violence. This violence could be between the protesters and authorities, protesters and their opponents, and some protesters against others within a particular protest movement. In recent times, there have been protests that have attracted global scrutiny, ranging from the Black Lives Matter protests that engulfed the world when George Floyd was killed by a police officer, to Zimbabwean Lives Matter, Eswatini Lives Matter, and EndSARS in Zimbabwe, Eswatini and Nigeria, respectively. In the #BlackLivesMatter, #ZimbabweanLivesMatter, #ESwatiniLivesMatter, and #EndSARS protests, we saw the collective power of citizens coming together to protest around a clearly defined societal problem. Tausch et al. (2011, p.129) using a model of collective action, posit that "anger in response to injustice motivates action and an efficacy pathway, where the belief that issues can be solved collectively increases the likelihood that group members take action." Drury and Reicher further argue that "to account for both social determination and social change in collective behavior, it is necessary to analyze crowd events as developing interactions between groups" (2000, p. 579) which, in the case of the power available to protesters and police, are asymmetrical, and the treatments the two entities give each other are based on subjective social position understandings. That is, in most cases, the protesters have their placards and other forms of communication and self-understanding while the police, who the protesters see as out-groups, have weapons of violence, rendering the engagement unequal and the former vulnerable, as the police can use violence to control and curtail protesters when they deem it fit to do so.

Depending on the context, in some cases, collective action includes online or offline protests and the signing of petitions handed over to authorities. The belief in solutions might rely on the power of reason or simply on the deployment of *violence*. I italicize the word "violence" here for various reasons, the most important of which is that, as Judith Butler says, violence and nonviolence have no settled boundaries and can mean anything to anyone depending on their vantage point. In the case of protests, damaging property and throwing stones at police could be viewed as violence by authorities but not so by protesters who may argue that disruption and stone-throwing are forms of protest and communication which the authorities will react to. These contested terms, expounds Butler, have seen.

> Some people call wounding acts of speech "violence" whereas others claim that language, except in the case of explicit threats, cannot properly be called "violent". Yet others hold restrictive views of violence, understanding the "blow" as it's defining physical moment; others insist that economic and legal structures are "violent," that they act upon bodies, even if they do not always take the form of physical violence. (2020, p.1–2)

What Butler brings to the fore is that violence cannot be simply defined and must be understood within a broader matrix of power, and broader political and social struggles for justice, equity, equality, and other associated freedoms that human beings need to flourish. In some instances, violence by protestors has yielded change, such as the #FeesMustFall protests led by students in South Africa. Students protested for free education and a decolonized curriculum, and the former was later granted by former president Jacob Zuma. Most formerly colonized societies, especially in Africa, gained flag independence through violent protests and waging wars of liberation, such as Algeria, Angola, Zimbabwe, Mozambique, Namibia, and many others. Elsewhere, there have been examples of violent protests, such as in Kazakhstan, where the government resigned after citizens protested the rising prices of fuel by attacking government buildings in Almaty, Shymkent, and Taraz "with 95 police officers wounded in the clashes" (Walker, 2022).

Others have advocated for non-confrontational and nonviolent protests as these are likely to bear results (Habib, 2020; Doane, 2015; Thomas and Louis, 2014). Gandhi, while in agreement with the non-violent approach, once contended "that non-violent acts exert pressure far more effective than violent acts, for the pressure comes from goodwill and gentleness'' (Thomas and Louis, 2014, p.263). There are examples of peaceful protests such as the one led by Gandhi in India against British colonial laws forbidding Indians from selling salt. Another could be the Alice Paul-led 1913 suffrage parade when more than 5,000 women protested for political equality and participation in Washington DC. In the 1960s, César Chávez "advocated for peaceful boycotts, protest, and a grueling yet nonviolent 25-day hunger strike which led to legislative changes to end exploitative abuse of America's farm workers in the late 1960s" (Werft and Ngalle, 2016). Rosa Parks remains iconic in the United States of America. Her refusal to give up her seat in the bus for a white man in the famous Montgomery Bus Boycott sparked some seminal changes and led to the Supreme Court ruling that segregating blacks in the buses was against the law of the land.

Some researchers have argued that nonviolence is more effective than violent protests. For instance, Chenoweth and Stephan suggest that "historically, nonviolent resistance campaigns have been more effective in achieving their goals than violent resistance campaigns" (2013, p.220). Further, Ackerman and DuVall (2000) estimate that between 1966 and 1999 nonviolent forms of civil disobedience were influential in 50 out of 67 protests against authoritarianism in terms of leading. Violent resistance and protest worked especially in places under colonial occupation where men and women were called to defend their land through military means and, in some instances using subversive techniques as happened in South Africa during apartheid, where anti-apartheid activists destroyed infrastructure such as bridges and other installations (SA History Online, n.d.).

The intention in this chapter is to explore the use of violence in some selected sub-Saharan African protests as a dehumanizing, decolonizing, and humanizing agent in Africa. Mpofu and Steyn (2021, p.1) argue that that being human is contested and "not self-evident or assured . . . can be wilded; and taken away." Further they argue that "threat of its withdrawal from, or permanent denial to, weaker peoples in peripheralised spaces continues to define life within a climate of fear that makes being human a fragile condition and an uncertain reality" (2021, p.1). Male Europeans, as Christians and "paradigmatic human" have been instrumental in defining who is human and who is not, and "employed different approaches in disciplining the bodies of the conquered through violence, arresting the appetites and desires of the natives . . . " (2021, p.1–2). The violence in protests dehumanizes people in that for them to free themselves from what they see as an oppressive and undesirable situation, they must suspend reason and negotiation and resort to violence, thereby performing what one may argue are "antihuman behaviours." It's possible that in the performance of violent acts, human beings see themselves as less than human (Bruneau, 2017). Engagement with the oppressor through violence is a decolonial attempt to achieve humanity. Before explaining how violence decolonizes, it is instructive to explain how it humanizes. Violence in protests humanizes the protestors in that through the act of violently resisting that which they deem oppressive, marginalizing, and a threat to their existence, they bring dignity to themselves. This, as Bruneau and Kteily (2017) also argue, leads to the oppressed dehumanizing—that is, seeing the oppressive powerful out-groups as inhuman. When humanized, the oppressed achieve full humanity and cannot be seen as colonial subjects without agency, intelligence, and the ability to self-define. Social media has been critical as a platform for organizing, carrying out, archiving, and reporting on protests online and offline. The argument is premised on the idea that in most African countries where protests occur, citizens' dignity is undermined by the ruling class, which mirrors the colonial class that was defeated in the 1960s–1980s. Thus, in most protests, when we use the decolonial lens—a departure from how coloniality and modernity have labeled the mostly oppressed people of color in the Global South as subhuman, lacking agency and so forth, the argument arises that the human is still to be decolonized, and the use of violence is a delivery process toward the humanizing and decolonizing agenda. The chapter also addresses tactics of resistance that most ruling elites adopt to maintain the status quo to demonstrate the effects of colonialism and coloniality. This resistance, the chapter argues, is informed by the failure to see citizens as agential and creative beings capable of self-determination. Violence in this research takes physical, emotional, and psychological forms that are adopted by protesters and the leaders or political systems, such as destroying infrastructure, flaming online, internet shutdowns, and imprisonment of protesters. The objective in this chapter is to theorize how online and offline protests and how social media have played a central role in protests. It further sheds light on questions of how the violences that occur during protests help to decolonize, humanize, and dehumanize humans, that is, the citizens. Just like Mpofu and Steyn (2021), I argue that coloniality and Western modernity have "conquered" the Global South and defined who the real humans are and who the non-humans are and "participated in the appropriation of natural resources, exploitation of labour, legal control of 'undesirables', imposition of the interests and world view inherent in a capitalist economy, and denial of the full humanity of the disempowered and the impoverished" (2021, p.2). Resisting Western modernity and coloniality is a form of humanization, and in some cases, this process has been violent. Protests may not be against modernity and coloniality per se but against the enduring structures they have created that deny human wholeness and equality to the oppressed peoples.

PROTESTS AND SOCIAL MEDIA: SELECTED CASES

In this section, I wish to focus on some sub-Saharan African protests and social movements or organizations. The choice of the sub-region and cases is illustrative and seeks to expand research on protests and social movements in Africa. Hitherto

> scholars of social movements and global protest have long neglected social movements in Africa, ostensibly because African societies are too rural, too tradition-or ethnicity-bound, or lacking advanced class formations. Those who have broached the topic tend to focus on South Africa's labour movement and anti-apartheid struggle. (Aidi, 2018)

It must be noted, however, that there is a growing scholarship looking at social movements and organizations outside South Africa (Matsilele et al., 2021; Bodunrin and Matsilele, 2023; Mpofu and Mare, 2020; Mutsvairo, 2016). These protests take different forms in their disruptive or violent nature; in some cases they disrupt the operations of society and business, and, in some instances the protesters destroy government and other private property or confront security services. In this chapter, I will consider the Zimbabwean, Eswatini, Nigerian, and South African social movements and how they were covered in the media, and how violence is deployed in these protests, either by the authorities or by the protesters themselves. Recently, Zimbabwe has seen a rise in the number of social movements, found under the hashtags #TheFlag, #Tajamuka, and #ZimbabweanLivesMatter. These protests shared similarities in that they were led by citizens and the target of protest was the government and its excesses in terms of corruption and human rights abuses. These protests are discussed in the following paragraphs. Zimbabwe has not experienced a period of calm and democracy in practice since independence in 1980, as the state has been used as a site of eating and enrichment for the ruling Zimbabwe African National Congress Patriotic Front ruling elite, members, and their connections. Violence has been the language of organizing society where electoral choices of ordinary citizens are undermined (Moyo, 2019). These movements were largely organized on social media even though they gained offline momentum later.

#ThisFlag was started by a pastor, Evan Mawarire, who argued that what the ruling Zanu-PF was doing in Zimbabwe was against the spirit of the heroes who liberated the country from colonialism. He decried corruption, the death of democracy, and the low quality of living standards because of mismanagement of the economy by the ruling Zanu-PF. Later, the movement fizzled out, but the impact was that despite being non-violent, it managed to galvanize Zimbabweans into undermining Zanu-PF. Offline, people protested through public prayers and by carrying the flag around. The protests not only showed Zimbabwean citizens' displeasure at human rights abuses at the hands of the government but also managed to spotlight the state abuse of human rights to the global community. The state responded, as it does in all protests, by arresting activists such as Mawarire and banning the carrying of the national flag. This, by and large, was a violent display and deployment of force. The #ZimbabweanLivesMatter movement was born out of frustration brought about by economic mismanagement, and this was further compounded by the global COVID-19 pandemic. This movement was modeled around the American #BlackLivesMatter protest movement. Independent media journalists uncovered and reported the corruption by government ministers, officials, and their families that happened during the pandemic, especially in relation to medication and personal protective clothing, leading to their arrest. Civil society, opposition parties, and other members of society protested the corruption, leading to abductions, arrests, and beatings by state security agents. This movement attracted global attention as most celebrities and other global figures such as Ice Cube, Zakes Bantwini, Thandie Newton, and others joined the call #ZimbabweanLivesMatter on Twitter (Matsilele et al., 2021).

Like #ZimbabweanLivesMatter, #EswatiniLivesMatter came about after Eswatini citizens protested the lack of democracy in their country. The protests were sparked by the death of a local university student who was allegedly killed by the police. This led to protests across the country, which saw "dissident lawmakers standing with the demonstrators and calling for the nation to move to a system with an elective prime minister" (Eligon, 2021). King Mswati led the last Southern African country as the last absolute monarch, a system that divides opinion among citizens as some hold their traditions dearly. Mswati ruled with an iron fist, and the hallmarks of his regime were repression, corruption, greed, and violence (Matsilele et al., 2021). Since the 1960s, dissent and protests were not legally protected in Eswatini, and in 2021 protest organizers managed to use social media and protest songs to plan, organize, and execute their protests. The protesters planned night protests called "Kungahlwa Kwenile" (when the night falls), and they targeted properties and business interests of the king and the government (Matsilele et al., 2021). A protester told a newspaper about the campaign:

> As we launch the "Kungahlwa Kwenile" campaign we want the whole country to be on fire starting from Tuesday. People must target King Mswati's properties and businesses like Montigny forests, Game Reserves, properties of MPs who don't have corporate and Government properties among others. All roads must be blocked across the country on Tuesday night. If you are next to Montigny Forest or any forest that benefits the King and his Government burn it, this is just a warning that will run for at least two weeks. (Dlamini, 2021)

Before the killing of the university student, there had been discontent over the lack of democracy in Eswatini, characterized by the banning of opposition parties. Dissent and protests have been outlawed in the country since independence in the late 1960s, leading dissenting movements to creatively find ways of undermining the monarchy through alternative media such as songs, dance, and other art forms (Delby, 2014). When protests erupted again in 2021, the prime minister, Themba Masuku, issued a decree stipulating that all protests are banned by the king. According to Amnesty International (2021), Eswatini is broken as the human rights situation has deteriorated—[as] the Eswatini government continues to ignore the constitutional provisions on human rights and use law enforcement and legal instruments to crush calls for justice and democratic reform. The death of the student prompted calls for an end to police heavy-handedness and brutality, which later morphed into full-blown dissent, including calls for the respect and upholding of the Constitution, human rights, and political rights reforms. King Mswati ruled Eswatini with a tight fist, characterized by corruption and violence (Masuku and Limb, 2016) and "naked greed" (Delby, 2014, p.284) for power, where "opposition parties have been repressed and citizens denied an opportunity to select their own political leader in a multi-party and democratic parliamentary political system" (Matsilele et al., 2021). The authorities reacted disproportionately, killing tens of protesters and injuring or arresting many others. Soldiers were deployed to manage the strike and used live ammunition to kill protesters. The violence by the state was condemned by countries such as South Africa.

#EndSARS is a Nigerian protest movement, and "an archetypical example of contemporary protest that begins online with mass participation of social media users (including celebrities) and later morphs into a large on-the-ground countrywide protest" (Matsilele et al., 2021). #EndSARS was a protest against police brutality. On October 4, 2020, a video surfaced and later went viral showing two officers who belonged to SARS (Special Anti-Robbery Squad), a covertly operating police unit in Nigeria formed in 1992 to deal with violent crime such as armed robberies and kidnappings in metropolitan areas such as Ibadan, Lagos, and Abuja. The video showed the officers dragging two men from a hotel and later shooting one of them outside. As part of their operations, the unit members wore civilian clothing, operated covertly, carried guns, and drove unmarked vehicles. The unit became a law unto itself as it overstepped its mandate and there were many cases, videos, and pictures showing unit members abusing their power through raping, torturing, beating, robbing, extorting, hanging, punching, and kicking, and waterboarding their victims (Ogbette et al., 2018). The Nigerian police force is not favorably ranked; the World Internal Security and Police Index (WISPI) placed the country's police services at the bottom of a 127-country list. WISPI measures the ability of a country's police forces to effectively provide security services. It also measures public confidence in the police force and their abilities to deliver on these services. The brutality of the Nigerian police services dates back to the colonial era where national formal policing started. The colonial-era police served the interests of the whites and were trained to be brutal toward the black majority. According to Falola (2009), the colonial state considered itself above the law and had a monopoly on the use of deadly force, which was used to eliminate and crush dissent and opponents. The October 2020 #EndSARS, which highlighted police violence through images and videos captured by citizens on their mobile phones, led to global condemnation of the violence and calls for SARS to be disbanded. Ordinary Nigerians, celebrities, and international icons joined the call to disband SARS, code-named #EndSARS online and offline. The slogan #EndSARS started in 2017 but was revitalized in 2020 when police violence became excessive. The online outrage expressed via the #EndSARS hashtag was accompanied by offline protests in major Nigerian cities (Bodunrin and Matsilele, 2024). The online and offline protests led to the disbanding of SARS by the government. Just like other protests in Zimbabwe, Eswatini, and South Africa, the #EndSARS protests used social media, offline protests, and to a certain extent, violence to force the government to rethink the existence of the SARS outfit. In addition, these protests created transnational audiences and solidarity.

The South African #FeesMustFall was led by university students who were protesting for free quality education at the tertiary level. This meant that university education must be free and that the curriculum be decolonized and reflect scholarship by Global South and African academics. As the Fallists put it in their book—a collection of activists' diaries—*Rioting and Writing* the #FeesMustFall "movement is/was an attempt from below to disrupt this unequal, racialized social and economic order. It rekindled and questioned the idea about the university in a postcolonial society" (Chinguno et al., 2017, p.16). The #FeesMustFall campaign was intimately related to #RhodesMustFall, a University of Cape Town protest against the statue of John Rhodes, a man who plundered and looted Southern African mineral resources. Both movements were characterized as disruptive rage (Mpofu, 2017). The #FeesMustFall campaign was because of "inconclusive attempts at trying to negotiate a non-fee increment of 10.5 percent for the 2016 academic year in October 2015 at Wits" (Mpofu, 2017, p.356). The protests spread to Union Buildings, the administrative offices of the then president, Jacob Zuma. Students and their sympathizers also disrupted parliamentary proceedings in Cape Town. Later, Zuma announced a "zero percent fee increase." To deal with protests, universities such as the University of Johannesburg and Wits deployed armed security personnel in the form of private security companies and members of the anti-riot arm of the South African Police Services. They were involved in running battles with students, where some were shot, and one man was killed (Sidimba, 2021). To capture the violence by the state and universities, Fasiha Hassan, one of the #FeesMustFall leaders, said,

> Students are being brutalized in broad daylight on their knees and with their hands up. I cannot and will not be silent in the face of such injustices. We will

continue to fight until there is fundamental change and we realize free, quality, and decolonized education. #FeesMustFall. (Sidimba, 2021)

Social media could be said to be the common denominator in all these protests described above. Social media platforms such as Facebook, WhatsApp, and Twitter are regularly used by protest movements to organize protests, archive their activities, report on their activities, and campaign for material and alliance support across national or class boundaries. During colonial periods and after independence, those who protested the establishment were at the mercy of mainstream media, which was part of the elite and establishment-controlled public sphere. This meant that these protests were not covered positively. Thus, social media platforms such as Twitter offer counter or alternative digital public spheres (Fraser, 1992) which are not controlled by professional communicators or journalists and are relatively safe in some cases for protesters, who can use pseudonyms to spread their messages. When Fraser formulated the counter-public sphere concept, she had in mind parallel public spheres where the marginalized congregated and foregrounded their needs and aspirations. As Mpofu states, "Social media platforms are communicative spaces where ordinary people interact without any inhibitions or editorializing as is the case with mainstream media, enhancing freedoms of expression in the process. These platforms become alternative sites of unbounded communication" (Mpofu, 2021, p.22). Editorializing means media professionals choose what gets into the public domain as news or opinion, and this might lead to certain opinions being truncated as they might not be deemed appropriate or due to editorial biases. Eliminating professional journalists allows for unfettered expression and conversations, especially during times of conflict. These counterspaces have amplified political participation and protest action by ordinary people. Digital activism and social movements have been "inextricably entangled with growing media technology and widespread with growing media technology and widespread nature of Internet connections and online engagements" (Hussen, 2018, p.16). Besides, these platforms are better placed as arenas of parallel discussions (Ndlovu, 2021), for circulation of contrarian views, since pamphlets and pavement radio (Ellis, 1989) in terms of efficiency and cost-effectiveness for protesters to organize, communicate, and carry out their protests.

We should not over-celebrate digital media despite their contributions in amplifying the voices of suppressed people on the margins. While digital technologies are linked to human engagement and action, "human agency should take precedence over the novelty and convenience of automation and instant communication that it offers in its post digital form" (Benecke and Verwey, 2020, p. 138). While social media affords citizens agonistic ways of engagement that are critical for radical democracy and giving many contending voices a chance to be heard, it should be noted that oppressive systems can equally use social media to disrupt citizens' activism and counter their protests. Social media has a dark side "such as enabling slacktivism, mass surveillance of activists and fragmentation of a group of people" (Mpofu and Mare, 2020, p.158 see also Morozov, 2011). However, cyber-optimists maintain that social media enable "digital repertoires of action" (Earl and Kimport, 2011) or "connective action" (Bennett and Segerberg, 2012) at national and international levels. However, it should be borne in mind that social media, in and of themselves, are not neutral and can be used to advance or disrupt a cause. Thus, human and activist agency is important in shaping the trajectories of movements. For example, social media could be used to recruit new participants, raise funds, boost protest turnout, and so on (Mundt, Ross, and Burnett, 2018) provided there is thorough human organization and activism behind all these targets.

In most African protests, governments, security agents, and institutions have either infiltrated and collapsed the movements or responded with violence and intimidation (e.g., Zimbabwe, Eswatini, Nigeria, South Africa). While it could be argued that violence is part and parcel of human existence and interactions, it is important to also note the meanings of violence when committed by protesters versus when committed by institutions and governments. Mpofu argues that

> Violence could be both physical and emotional. Violence could also mean failure to carry out certain duties expected, for example. Thus, government failure to deal with issues of decolonization in the postcolony could be read as violence against the poor. . . . Official silence on things that matter to ordinary people is violence. (2017, p.359)

This also includes failed decolonization projects which could be violent against the masses as they fail to harvest the fruits of independence and still live under tyranny whose brute force reminds them as if it could only come from a colonist. The new colonial masters in most African countries are those who fought against colonialism and apartheid, only to mimic the suppressive regimes later.

DECOLONIZATION AND VIOLENCE

When we speak of decoloniality or decolonizing, we need to be clear in terms of definitions. Coloniality, decoloniality, decolonization, and colonialism are sometimes misunderstood. For the purposes of this chapter, colonization happened in the past when the oppressive and largely racist systems of subjugation took over other people's countries and established their own rule, largely defined by dispossession, subjugation, undermining the autonomy, humanity, self-determination, and dignity of the owners of the land, largely black people of Africa and other non-whites elsewhere. Decolonization involved the use of force and other forms of military violence to free these colonized countries. Colonization and decolonization are, in a way, past realities "that have been superseded by other kind of socio-political and economical regimes" (Maldonado-Torres, 2016). Maldonado-Torres further differentiates the former with coloniality and decoloniality thus: "coloniality and decoloniality refer to the logic, metaphysics, ontology, and matrix of power created by the massive process of colonization and decolonization ... tied to what is called western civilization and Western modernity."

He later wrote comprehensively:

> Coloniality is different from colonialism. Colonialism denotes a political and economic relation in which the sovereignty of a nation or a people rests on the power of another nation, which makes such a nation an empire. Coloniality, instead, refers to long-standing patterns of power that emerged as a result of colonialism, but that define culture, labour, intersubjectivity relations, and knowledge production well beyond the strict limits of colonial administrations. Thus, coloniality survives colonialism. It is maintained alive in books, in the criteria for academic performance, in cultural patterns, in common sense, in the self-image of peoples, in aspirations of self, and so many other aspects of our modern experience. In a way, as modern subjects we breathe coloniality all the time and every day. (2007, p.243)

Thus, most previously colonized societies remain very much shaped by the colonial past, with the lessons, influences, and behaviors learned from the colonialists intact. As Mpofu and Steyn (2021, p.14) rightly put it, "The formal end of slavery, colonialism, and apartheid in South Africa ... did not evaporate coloniality: its oppressions and exploitations remain stubbornly durable and haunting to its victims." Many spaces inherited from the colonial system are proficient in this. Universities, churches, schools, and so on, are hegemonic institutions that dehumanize subjects and need decolonization. In some cases, those who hold positions of power and influence previously a preserve of the colonists such as presidents, managers, and leaders of government departments, schools, universities, and departments within universities, exhibit characteristics of what Ngũgĩ Wa Thiong'o called the "good African" in his book *Decolonising the Mind*. But one may argue that the good African theory only applies to those who worked for and under the colonialists and that most leaders in Africa fought against colonialism. Granted, but when they fought against colonialism, they did not fight for the liberation of their race, but rather fought out of coveting the position of the white man and wanting to occupy it. Thus, through this occupation, they become effective students of the system and, therefore, loyal disciples. They replicate the colonists' behaviors and dehumanization tactics, worship at the altar of hierarchies where their humanity and worth are informed by the subjugation and undermining of those serving under them in terms of rank. As Maldonado-Torres (2016) argues under his Fourth Thesis on coloniality and decoloniality, the effects of coloniality and modernity are "naturalization of extermination, expropriation, domination, exploitation, early death and conditions that are worse than death, such as torture or rape." And this happens in most unstable democracies in Africa and in those leading democracies such as America, where black people are far removed from the category and family of humanity.

While the decolonization project that fought against colonialism was violent and called for the deployment of violence as a last resort, coloniality has also called for various forms of violence against the postcolonial leadership that still pushes those of the lower classes into zones of non-being human. This metaphysical catastrophe, as Maldonado-Torres (2016) calls it, allocates humans into zones of being and non-being, and this has different meanings for those who are in the zone of non-being and the zone of being. He elucidates:

> Living in the zone of being human means finding oneself, others, and the institutions of one's society affirming one's status as a full human being with a broad range of potentials and possibilities even in precarious conditions of poverty. Living in the zone of sub-humanity means, not only that one is not meant to have easy access to basic means of existence, but also that it is normal for everything and everyone, including oneself, to questions one's humanity. One can refer to this as a fundamentally misanthropic skeptical attitude. Misanthropic skepticism is a characteristic questioning attitude of modernity/coloniality, whereby the humanity of large part of humanity is questioned. Misanthropic skepticism is the quintessential attitude of modernity/coloniality and one that not only justifies but calls for the elimination of populations, slavery, and permanent war. (Maldonado-Torres, 2007)

Thus, to be fully human is to be in the zone of being where humans function optimally and, according to decolonial studies, coloniality and Western modernity extend this humanity mainly the whites in the Global North who have the power, through coloniality, to categorize and define humanity. Modernity and coloniality have therefore removed people of color from the realm of humanity, and to reclaim this, the latter should be creative and fight for the decolonization of world systems. But again, for systems to be decolonized—that is, cleansed from coloniality—there is a need to decolonize the human at both zones of being and non-being. This means teaching those that think they are fully human to appreciate and concede equality to those considered sub-human. The decoloniality project involves violence in both zones. Violence is the use of force, and this happens whenever force is carried out in such a way that someone is "thereby interrupted or disturbed or interfered with rudely or roughly or desecrated, dishonoured or defiled" (Chasi, 2015, p.288). For, as Fanon (1967) suggests, when systems fail to serve people, they should be broken down and reconstructed, and this involves some forms of violence. Violence could be both physical and emotional. Violence could also mean failure to carry out certain duties expected. For example, Mpofu further adds:

> Thus, government failure to deal with issues of decolonization in the postcolony could be read as violence against the poor. Maintaining colonial . . . symbols in public spaces . . . could also be argued to be violence against those who have to relieve the traumatic experiences of the evil system every time they consciously engage with these symbols and artefacts. Official silence on things that matter to ordinary people is violence. . . . Thus disruption as a communicative form commits violence, as argued by the pro-status quo voices, to the hitherto silence that characterizes the atmosphere which itself is violence against the protestors. (2017, p.359)

It is violent to ask someone to let go of something that is in their comfort zone, as the loss of privilege delivers the subject into realms considered lower, and they might not find this empowering or even dignified since this has given them power and full humanity (even though false) in addition to excesses that accrue, especially in Africa where many worship at the altar of big man syndrome. Equally, it is also violence to subject those who clearly feel that their dreams remain deferred even after the departure of the colonial systems, and now they must fight against coloniality, that is, the practices that resemble those practiced during colonial times. As Mpofu suggests, the marginalized must fight through "disrupting the world as we know it in order to address their (poor's) grievances [and this] is part and parcel of strategic and effective communication" (2017, p.352).

Mpofu (2017) argues that the poor disrupt society as we know it to have their grievances addressed. The cases I use in this chapter are drawn from African contexts where political leaders have behaved in a similar fashion to the former colonialists and have paid less regard to the welfare of their citizens, leading to the latter resorting to disruption and violence as forms of negotiation. Social media planning, activism, and offline protests—some of which could be termed *violent* because of confrontations with the police or destruction of infrastructure belonging to the government or political leaders alert us to the desperation of the marginalized and suppressed majority. The violence they direct at the state, through stoning and burning buildings, police cars or police officers, could be read as self-defense, where their lives have been put in harm's way by the elite, and the only way they can regain their humanity is through protest and fighting in self-defense. Nonviolent means, in some cases, have been futile in the eyes of the poor. For instance, the #ThisFlag Movement in Zimbabwe and #ZimbabweanLivesMatter protests were largely peaceful and did not yield any positive results besides international solidarity. However, when they disrupt and become violent, they have, in some cases, seen results, such as in the case of #FeesMustFall in South Africa. To maintain the status quo, the elite use various forms of violence to silence or eliminate the protesters. This includes human rights violations such as internet shutdowns, which have routinely happened in Burundi, Cameroon, Chad, Democratic Republic of Congo, Guinea, Ethiopia, Sudan, Togo, and Zimbabwe among others in the last few years, where ordinary people's voices have been silenced through internet blackouts. Also, police are set on protesting citizens and, in worst-case scenarios like Nigeria, Zimbabwe, and Eswatini, the world has noticed soldiers being deployed to quash protests through arrests or even by beating them. Violence by the state, which is seen as a legitimate form of coercion (Butler, 2020), should ideally practice restraint given that the instruments of violence under its command can have far-reaching consequences if carelessly deployed. However, the excessive use of force and violence—where people are killed, raped, maimed, and hurt by state machinery—leads us into arguing that this is so because some black leaders do not see their citizens as equal human beings but as sub-human subjects who can be disposed of anytime. How then can decoloniality be key to humanizing both the oppressor and the oppressed? The following section tackles the need to decolonize humans, both as the oppressor and the oppressed.

TOWARD MAKING THE HUMAN

That some people are in power in the post-colony, as Albert Memmi suggests, does not make them adults in the community, and the rest of the mass's children must depend on this "adult." But because the "adult" only gains humanity through degrading, undermining, oppressing, and suppressing those on the margins, there is need for a mental shift and decolonization of this adult, to have him or her realize their equal humanity with the rest of the population for human relations to function optimally. This is a huge call to make since, just like the colonizer whose power and status rely on the oppression of the colonized, the current oppressors depend upon the oppressed and those they continually push into the zone of non-being to maintain their power and sustain their position in the zone of being (Butler, 2020; Maldonado-Torres, 2016). Melissa Steyn and William Mpofu, in arguing for the decolonization of the human, concur that we live in a world "where the powerful and the economically privileged have 'being', and the powerless and oppressed have 'nothingness' and emptiness" (2021, p.14). There are those who get oppressed to an extent of assimilating to oppressor consciousness and act as accessories of oppression where, in their psyche, the oppressive hierarchies and regimes become normalized, and the possibilities of being unshackled become a nightmare they would rather not confront (Freire, 1993). This third group needs to be decolonized too, to realize their potential for full humanity and prospects of enjoying the life of a person belonging to a zone of being.

The oppressive class can only be decolonized through *Ubuntu*. Ubuntu is an African philosophical concept that is communal rather than individual-centered as promoted by Western modernity. Nkoma (2020) outlines Ubuntu thus,

> The principle of caring for each other's well-being will be promoted, and a spirit of mutual support fostered. Everyone's humanity is ideally expressed through his or her relationship with others and theirs in turn through a recognition of the individual's humanity. Ubuntu means that people are people through other people. It also acknowledges both the rights and the responsibilities of every citizen in promoting individual and societal well-being.

There is a possibility that by practicing Ubuntu, some of the oppressive people who see themselves as occupying the zone of being will gradually learn affection and come to see the rest of society, especially the ruled, powerless, and marginalized, as equally and fully human. It is interesting that politicians and other oppressive leaders can deploy Ubuntu for selfish ends. If used as an equalizing philosophy, Ubuntu, together with decoloniality, will empower both the oppressors and the oppressed with ways of seeing each other as equal and human. Mpofu, in a chapter on COVID-19 humor in South Africa and Zimbabwe, demonstrates this point. When ordinary people celebrated the deaths of politicians during the pandemic, politicians came out to chastise the people and reminded them of the tenets of Ubuntu. Mpofu (2021, p. 323) asserts "the brand of ubuntu that politicians demand be extended to them if they die or when people share rumours of their death in celebration and mockery should be equal to the one, they afford their *subjects*" (italics in original). When Ubuntu is effectively extended to those on the margins by those on the center and the latter are transformed by the realization of the humanity of the former and the need to cater to the former, then there is a possibility of the ostracized feeling part of the community and worthy. There are many ways to humanize the former. Give them dignified public amenities. Provide services such as water, sanitation, roads, and schools. Whenever there are misunderstandings, round table discussions, listening, and dignified ways of engagement, which include finding solutions, are essential. In most cases people in Nigeria, Eswatini, and Zimbabwe demand accountability and transparency from political systems regarding the people's problems. Protests arise because of a lack of transparency and shallow democracy characterized by weak institutions, corrupt politicians, and disrespect for human rights. In the three countries that I use to illustrate my argument, the flashpoint between citizens and the political leaders and systems is a disrespect for citizens' human rights.

The coalition of the oppressed and their sympathizers in protests is significant, as shown through the #EswatiniLivesMatter, #FeesMustFall, #EndSARS, and #ZimbabweLivesMatter protests where the affected members of society organized and protested around themes of concern and, in most cases also elicited sympathy outside their immediate communities. This shows the agency in striving for humanity and dignity on the part of the protestors, and the solidarity by coalition and other partners across the divide affirms that humanity. Social media has been critical in casting light on the importance of these solidarities. In some cases, when leaders of movements are arrested, these transnational alliances and solidarity raise funds for legal and other fees, clearly demonstrating the importance of decolonizing humanity in postcolonial Africa. At one time, the Congress of South African Trade Unions (COSATU) refused to offload arms meant for Zimbabwe at a Durban port in 2008. The workers had "concerns Zimbabwean President Robert Mugabe's government might use them against opponents in the post-election stalemate" (Mangwiro, 2008). Zimbabwe was preparing for an election run-off after an inconclusive election where Mugabe nearly lost power. Commentators argued that he lost. The rerun was preceded by violence leading to the opposition leader, Morgan Tsvangirai, pulling out. Global alliances (mostly with the black diaspora) with the Africans protesting their governments suggest that black people's experiences globally need change for the better as they mostly exist in zones of non-being, abused by police and political systems (Abott, 2022; Kendi, 2019).

CONCLUSION

In this chapter, I have engaged with the argument that there is a need for the rebirth of both the oppressor and the oppressed. This metamorphosis, as Mamdani argued when writing about the colonizer and the colonized, will lead into "a single citizenship . . . [when the two] are politically reborn as equal members of a single political community" (2001, p.67). Violence continues to be the language of engagement between the ruling elite and the oppressed, and for there to be harmony, there is need to dismantle coloniality and all modes of power and arrogance that come with it especially for those who deem themselves to be within the zones of being. Violence can be variously understood depending on which zone one stands in. In the African context, as shown in this chapter, the state's failure to accord citizens the dignity they deserve by virtue of being human beings and citizens is seen as violent toward and degrading their humanity. The response by the citizens in reclaiming their dignity is in some cases viewed as violent, especially where property and government infrastructure or physical altercations between the protesters and the police occur. Violence, in protest, is seen as a form of communication that governments understand (Mpofu, 2017). Those who enjoy the status quo use the power of labeling and words to divide society by labeling the protests of the marginalized and suppressed as violent. These labels make it then possible and justifiable for political and institutional leaders to use police and other militarized forms of engagement not only to control protests but to dismantle them and the whole conversation they seek. They further arrest, maim, kill, rape, and torture protesters. All this happens because they are deemed punishable and disposable, and their issues are not important. The cases highlighted in this chapter leave us with a lingering question once asked by Anle, Adejare, and Fasuyi (2021) in a chapter about culture, politics, law, and sexuality in Nigeria: "to what extent are we all humans?". Social media has been critical spaces for the dehumanized. These are platforms where they have tried to get their voices back. Without a voice, one ceases to exist. Also, various social media platforms have enabled protest movements and organizations to organize, archive, and campaign for sponsorship or create solidarities or forge alliances across borders. This has spotlighted the plight of those on the margins and, in some cases, scored some successes. What remains, however, is the need to decolonize humans, and violence plays a central part in this. As previously argued, coloniality, especially in neocolonial Africa, does not rule via consensus, but through violence. Ordinary people must negotiate their lives at every turn with violence, unfulfilled dreams, dehumanization, and tyranny. Their only option out of this, in the absence of rational dialogue, is violence, in self-defense.

REFERENCES

Abott, D. (2022). Police strip-searched a 15-year-old black girl at school. When will these abuses end? https://www.theguardian.com/commentisfree/2022/mar/16/police-strip-search-black-girl-school-east-london-racism-misogyny?utm_term=623217a77d6e684d347b6eb4fe96f222&utm_campaign=BestOfGuardianOpinionUK&utm_source=esp&utm_medium=Email&CMP=opinionuk_email.

Ackerman, P. and Jack, D. (2000). *A force more powerful.* London: Palgrave Macmillan.

Aidi, H. (2018). *Africa's new social movements: A continental approach. Policy Brief PB*-18/36. https://www.policycenter.ma/sites/default/files/2021-01/OCPPC-PB1836.pdf.

Akanle, O., Adejare, G.S. and Fasuyi, J. (2021). To what extent are we all humans? Of culture, politics, law and LGBT rights in Nigeria. In Melissa Steyn and William Mpofu (Eds), *Decolonising the human: Reflections from Africa on difference and oppression* (pp. 47–64). Johannesburg: Wits University Press.

Amnesty International. (2022). *Eswatini the system is broken.* https://www.amnesty.org/en/latest/campaigns/2021/11/eswatini-the-system-is-broken/.

Becker, J.C. and Tausch, N. (2015). A dynamic model of engagement in normative and non-normative collective action: Psychological antecedents, consequences, and barriers. *European Review of Social Psychology,* 26(1): 43–92.

Benecke, D.R. and Verwey, S. (2020). Post digital dialogue and activism in the public sphere. In Martin N Ndlela and Winston Mano (Eds), *Social media and elections in Africa, Volume 2: Challenges and opportunities* (pp. 135–152). Cham: Palgrave Macmillan.

Bennett, W.L. and Segerberg, A. (2012). The logic of connective action. *Information, Communication & Society,* 15(5): 739–768.

Bodunrin, I.A. and Matsilele, T. (2023). Social media and protest politics in Nigeria's #EndSARS campaign. *Handbook of Social Media in Education, Consumer Behavior and Politics: Volume 1,* 111(114): 109.

Bruneau E. and Kteily N. (2017). The enemy as animal: Symmetric dehumanization during asymmetric warfare. *PLoS One,* 12(7): e0181422. https://doi.org/10.1371/journal.pone.0181422. PMID: 28746412; PMCID: PMC5528981.

Butler, J. (2020). *The force of nonviolence: An ethico-political bind.* London: Verso.

Chasi, C. (2014). Violent communication is not alien to ubuntu: Nothing human is alien to Africans. *Communicatio,* 40(4): 287–304.11.

Delby, T. (2014). Culture and resistance in Swaziland. *Journal of Contemporary African Studies,* 32(3): 284–301.

Dlamini, M.Z. (2021, June 27). *KUNGAHLWA KWENILE: Burning of King Mswati, Government's properties starts on Tuesday night as protests manifest into chaos.* Swaziland News. http://www.swazilandnews.co.za/fundza.php?nguyiphi=1300.

Drury, J. and Reicher, S. (2000). Collective action and psychological change: The emergence of new social identities. *British Journal of Social Psychology,* 39(4): 579–604.

Doane, D. (2015). *The protest movement is failing: It's fighting the same old battles with the same poor results.* https://www.theguardian.com/sustainable-business/2015/aug/24/protest-movement-failings-i-dont-believe-in-it-anymore.

Earl, J. and Kimport, K. (2011). *Digitally enabled social change: Activism in the internet age.* Cambridge, MA: MIT Press.

Eligon, J. (2021). *Africa's last absolute monarchy convulsed by mass protest.* The New York Times. https://www.nytimes.com/2021/07/02/us/africa-monarchy-eswatini-protestsswaziland.html.

Ellis, S. (1989). Tuning in to pavement radio. *African Affairs,* 88(352): 321–330.

Fanon, F. (1967). *Toward the African revolution: Political essays.* New York: Grove Press.
Falola, T. (2009). *Violence in Nigeria: The crisis of religious politics and secular ideologies.* New York: University of Rochester Press.
Fraser, N. (1992). Rethinking the public sphere: A contribution to the critique of actually existing democracy. In C. Calhoun (Ed), *Habermas and the public sphere* (pp. 109–142). Cambridge: MIT Press.
Freire, P. (1993). *Pedagogy of the oppressed.* New York: Continuum.
Habib, A. (2020). *Understanding violent protest in South Africa and the difficult choice facing leaders.* https://theconversation.com/understanding-violent-protest-in-south-africa-and-the-difficult-choice-facing-leaders-148751.
Hussen, T.S. (2018). Social media and feminist activism #RapeMustFall, #NakedProtest and #RUReferenceList Movements in South Africa. In Tamara Shefer, Jeff Hearn, Kopano Ratele and Floretta Boonzaier (Eds), *Engaging youth in activism, research, and pedagogical praxis transnational and intersectional perspectives on gender, sex, and race* (pp. 199–214). New York: Routledge.
Kendi, I.X. (2019). *Stamped from the beginning: The definitive history of racist ideas in America.* New York: Bold Type Books.
Koma, S. (2020). Ubuntu and solidarity in the COVID-19 era. https://www.nihss.ac.za/sites/default/files/Covid%20Articles/ubuntu_and_solidarity_in_the_covid-19_era_-_covid-19_0.pdf.
Maldonado-Torres, N. (2016). *Outline of ten theses on coloniality and decoloniality. Franz foundation online.* Available at http://fondation-frantzfanon.com/wp-content/uploads/2018/10/maldonado-torres_outline_of_ten_theses-10.23.16.pdf.
Maldonado-Torres, N. (2007). On coloniality of being: Contributions to the development of a concept. *Cultural Studies,* 21/(2–3): 240–270.
Mamdani, M. (2001). When does a settler become a native? Citizenship and identity in a settler society. *Pretext: Literacy and Cultural Studies,* 10(1): 63–73.
Mangwiro. C. (2008). Zimbabwe arms ship heads for Angola, Mozambique says. https://www.reuters.com/article/topNews/idUSL1862930420080419.
Masuku, B. and Limb, P. (2016). Swaziland: The struggle for political freedom and democracy. *Review of African Political Economy,* 43(149): 518–527.
Matsilele, T., Mpofu, S., Msimanga, M. and Tshuma, L. (2021). Transnational hashtag protest movements and emancipatory politics in Africa: A three country study. *Global Media Journal – German Edition,* 11(2). https://doi.org/10.22032/dbt.51029.
Memmi, A. (1974). *The colonizer and the colonized. Trans Howard Greenfield.* New York: Routledge.
Mpofu, W. and Steyn, M. (2021). The trouble with the human. In Melissa Steyn and William Mpofu (Eds), *Decolonising the human: Reflections from Africa on difference and oppression* (pp. 1–24). Johannesburg: Wits University Press.
Mpofu, S. (2017). Disruption as a communicative strategy: The case of #FeesMustFall and #RhodesMustFall students' protests in South Africa. *Journal of African Media Studies,* 9(2): 355–372.

Mpofu, S. (2021). Dark humour, ubuntu and the COVID-19 pandemic: A case of subaltern humouring of political elite deaths on social media. In S. Mpofu (Ed), *Digital Humour in the Covid-19 Pandemic* (pp. 319–346). Cham: Palgrave MacMillan.

Mpofu, S. (2021). Social media memes, commentary, and health disasters: Listerosis and Covid-19 in South Africa and Zimbabwe. In Shepherd Mpofu (ed), *Digital humour in the COVID-19 pandemic: Perspectives from the Global South* (pp. 19–45). Palgrave Macmillan.

Mpofu, S. and Mare, A. (2020). #ThisFlag: Social media and cyber-protests in Zimbabwe. In Martin N Ndlela and Winston Mano (Eds), *Social media and elections in Africa, Volume 2: Challenges and opportunities* (pp. 153–174). Cham: Palgrave Macmillan.

Moyo, J.N. (2019). *Excelgate: How Zimbabwe's 2018 presidential election was stolen*. Harare: SAPES Books.

Mozorov, E. (2011). *The net delusion: The dark side of internet freedom*. New York: Public Affairs.

Mundt, M., Ross, K. and Burnett, C.M. (2018). Scaling social movements through social media: The case of Black Lives Matter. *Social Media+Society*, 1–14. https://doi.org/10.1177/2056305118807911.

Mutsvairo, B. (Ed). (2016). *Digital activism in the social media era: Critical reflections on emerging trends in Sub-Saharan Africa*. Cham: Palgrave Macmillan.

Ndlovu, M. (2021). Humour in the time of COVID-19 Pandemic: A critical analysis of the subversive meanings of WhatsApp memes in Zimbabwe. In Shepherd Mpofu (Ed), *Digital humour in the COVID-19 pandemic: Perspectives from the Global South* (pp. 259–277). Palgrave Macmillan.

Ogbette, A.S., Idam, M.O. and Kareem, A.O. (2018). An overview of the impact of Special AntiRobbery Squad (SARS) in Nigeria. *International Journal of Human Resource Studies*, 8(4): 180–187.

Sidimba, L. (2021). *Former #FeesMustFall activist now MPL calls Wits protest death 'our worst nightmare'*. https://www.iol.co.za/news/politics/former-feesmustfall-activist-now-mpl-calls-wits-protest-death-our-worst-nightmare-b4650dae-4fc1-4dfe-948f-199761f3cf31.

SA History Online. (n.d.) Umkhonto weSizwe (MK). Available at https://www.sahistory.org.za/article/umkhonto-wesizwe-mk.

Steinert-Threlkeld, Z.C., Mocanu, D., Vespignani, A. and Fowler, J. (2015). Online social networks and offline protest. *EPJ Data Science*, 4, 19. https://doi.org/10.1140/epjds/s13688-015-0056-y

Tausch, N., Becker, J.C., Spears, R., Christ, O., Saab, R., Singh, P. and Siddiqui, R.N. (2011). Explaining radical group behavior: Developing emotion and efficacy routes to normative and nonnormative collective action. *Journal of Personality and Social Psychology*, 101(1): 129–148.

Thomas, E.F. and Louis, W. (2014). When will collective action be effective? Violent and non-violent protests differentially influence perceptions of legitimacy and efficacy among sympathizers. *Personality and Social Psychology Bulletin*, 40(2): 263–276.

Walker, S. (2022). *Kazakhstan protests: Government resigns amid rare outbreak of unrest.* Available at: https://www.theguardian.com/world/2022/jan/04/kazakhstan-president-declares-state-of-emergency-in-protest-hit-areas.

Werft, M. and Ngalle, J. (2016). *5 peaceful protests that led to social and political changes.* https://www.globalcitizen.org/en/content/peace-protests-dallas-response/.

Chapter 2

Disrupting Patriotic Discourse in Zimbabwe

Reading Evan Mawarire's #ThisFlag as Counter-Hegemony

Blessing Makwambeni

In the past decade, digital communication technologies have empowered Zimbabwean citizens to challenge the legitimacy of the ruling ZANU-PF government as well as to champion a wide variety of social and political causes (Chitanana, 2020). Engulfed in a protracted multi-dimensional crisis that has been invariably attributed to the chaotic land reform program in 2000, the contested presidential elections of 2000, the controversial presidential election of 2008, misgovernance, and Western-imposed sanctions (Makwambeni and Adebayo, 2021), Zimbabwean citizens have found themselves reeling from a poorly performing economy, decaying infrastructure, moribund health and service delivery, as well as widespread human rights violations largely perpetrated by the ruling ZANU-PF government. In response to the multi-faceted crisis and growing repression from the ZANU-PF regime, Zimbabwean citizens have embraced digital technologies as a tool for mobilizing social movements and reclaiming their political voices and spaces (Gukurume, 2017; Msimanga, 2022). Social media has become a key tool for disgruntled citizens to organize and strategize across temporal and spatial locations.

Social media and other digital platforms have therefore opened new alternative spaces for civic engagement that are de-institutionalized, de-professionalized, and liberating in Zimbabwe (Mhiripiri and Mutsvairo, 2014). They allow previously disenfranchised citizens who had no access to mainstream media and elite public spheres to articulate their voices. As a result, the last decade has witnessed a glut of hashtag movements that contest the legitimacy and hegemony of the ruling ZANU-PF government taking root in Zimbabwe.

Chitanana (2020) identifies Kubatana, Sokwanele, Magamba, Baba Jukwa, Occupy Africa Unity Square, and #ThisFlag as some of the most notable digital activism groupings that have flourished in Zimbabwe in the period between the early 2000s and the period immediately after the stepping down of the country's founding and long-serving president, Robert Mugabe, in 2017. However, although several hashtag movements have emerged in Zimbabwe over the past decade, only a few of these movements have managed to translate their online traction into offline protest like Evan Mawarire's #ThisFlag (Gukurume, 2017).

More recently, a significant corpus of research has emerged on digital media technologies and public protests in Zimbabwe (Bodunrin and Matsilele, 2023; Mpofu, 2015; Gukurume, 2017; Mpofu and Matsilele, 2020; Mpofu and Mare, 2020; Musarurwa, 2020; Matsilele et al., 2021; Matsilele and Ruhanya, 2021). A review of extant studies on Zimbabwe shows that they either examine the role that social media plays as a mobilizing tool for social movements or have sought to understand how subaltern citizens creatively appropriated digital technologies to recuperate voice and space. For example, Gukurume's (2017) study uses #ThisFlag and #ThisGown movements as lenses to understand how Zimbabwean citizens use social media to mobilize protests. Mpofu and Mare (2020) have gone on to examine the creative use of the national flag by citizens to mount a protest against the ruling ZANU-PF government. In a much broader study, Mpofu and Matsilele (2020) have focused their analysis on the different forms of citizen-led protests that have been witnessed in Zimbabwe since 2000. Most studies that have examined the use and appropriation of social media for protests in Zimbabwe have included the #ThisFlag movement in their analysis.

Thus, although there is significant scholarly work that has focused on the #ThisFlag movement, limited research has been developed to understand the specific counter-hegemonic discourses and subject positions that Mawarire's #ThisFlag monologue, which laid the foundation of the #ThisFlag movement, mobilized to challenge the ruling ZANU-PF government's patriotic discourse, and galvanize Zimbabweans to protest the ruling ZANU-PF government. It is against this background that this study employs Gramsci's conceptualization of hegemony and counter-hegemony and Norman Fairclough's approach to Critical Discourse Analysis (CDA) to analyze the counter-hegemonic discourses and subject positions that underpin Mawarire's #ThisFlag monologue.

#THISFLAG MOVEMENT: A BRIEF OVERVIEW AND CONTEXTUAL BACKGROUND

The origin of the #ThisFlag movement can be traced back to April 2016 when a young Baptist cleric called Evan Mawarire posted a spoken word video recording of himself on social media questioning the meanings attached to the Zimbabwean national flag (Gukurume, 2017; Matsilele, 2022). The video was posted during Zimbabwe's 36th Independence celebrations. Mawarire's monologue video went viral on Facebook and other social media platforms, garnering more than 100,000 views and shares within a week of being posted. The monologue gained traction and morphed into both a transnational movement and a symbol of protest against the ruling ZANU-PF government's failure to address the protracted multi-dimensional crisis that has saddled Zimbabweans for over two decades. #ThisFlag movement ignited a successful stayaway dubbed #ShutDownZimbabwe in 2016, as well as anti-government protests that paralyzed cities around the country. The movement galvanized Zimbabweans at home and abroad to demand that the ruling ZANU-PF government act to address the country's multi-faceted challenges (Musarurwa, 2016). #ThisFlag further awakened the voices of ordinary Zimbabweans that had been muzzled under the Robert Mugabe regime (Gukurume, 2017).

The year 2016, when the #ThisFlag spoken video was recorded and posted, was characterized by unprecedented events in Zimbabwe that prompted citizens to brazenly speak out against the government. Some of the events that triggered the backlash from citizens included the promulgation of Statutory Instrument 148, which reduced the duty rebate for travelers from US$ 300 to US$ 200, and the complete scrapping of the rebate for travelers using small cross-border transport (Musarurwa, 2016); the shocking revelation by Robert Mugabe during his 91st birthday that Zimbabwe had lost a huge US$15 billion in revenue from diamond mining; the imposition of a mandatory National Pledge by the government; the announcement by the government of a plan to ease cash shortages by introducing a bond note; and the gazetting of Statutory Instrument 64, which banned the importation of goods without a license.

SITUATING #THISFLAG IN THE BROADER CONTEXT OF THE ZIMBABWEAN CRISIS

Around the 1990s, the first signs of the independent state's failure to deliver on the developmental and economic promises made during the protracted liberation struggle and at independence in 1980 began to emerge (Ndhlovu-Gatsheni and Willems, 2009). The Economic Structural Adjustment Programme (ESAP) prescribed by Bretton Woods Institutions had even more disastrous economic and social consequences. These consequences included high food prices and the retrenchment of public-sector workers because of reduced public expenditure. The structural reforms brought by ESAP created hostilities between the ZANU-PF government and college and university students, war veterans, and trade unions. A significant number of Zimbabweans began to blame nationalism for the failure to deliver a developmental state and began to advocate for a more liberal political and economic dispensation (Ndhlovu-Gatsheni and Willems, 2009).

By 2000, Zimbabwe had deteriorated into a full-blown crisis characterized by economic stasis, decay in infrastructure, moribund health and service delivery system, and political repression, which left a significant number of citizens disillusioned (Hodzi, 2014; Makwambeni, 2017). The unfolding crisis further polarized Zimbabweans, with some citizens attributing the crisis to the pitfalls of nationalism and misgovernance by the ruling party (ZANU-PF) government, while other citizens saw the crisis as issuing from the neo-colonial machinations of the former colonial power, the United Kingdom, and its "appendages," the newly formed Movement for Democratic Change (MDC) and most of civil society. With its developmental nationalism having failed, its legitimacy and hegemony under scrutiny, and facing both local and international challenges after 2000, the ruling ZANU-PF party had to renew its hegemony using both coercion and consent. The government became increasingly authoritarian and introduced a raft of measures to protect communicative space from alternative discourses that challenged the "patriotic" narrative it had employed (Ndlela, 2010; Tendi, 2008).

As observed by Ndlovu-Gatsheni and Willems (2009) and Tendi (2008), when governments fail to meet citizens' material expectations and economic resources dwindle, they tend to resort to both culture and (patriotic) history to renew their hegemony. Post the year 2000, when the ZANU-PF government's legitimacy became increasingly contested by the opposition, civil society organizations, the former colonial power, the United Kingdom, and its allies, it had to draw from the nationalist struggle to re-justify its rule (Ndlovu-Gatsheni and Willems, 2009; Tendi, 2008). Cultural nationalism, premised on patriotic history, became an important national project and a tool for renewing its hegemony and countering what the government perceived as a "regime change" agenda, promoted by the MDC and its allies.

CULTURAL NATIONALISM AND THE RISE OF PATRIOTIC DISCOURSE IN ZIMBABWE

The ruling ZANU-PF government had to engage in a cultural nationalistic struggle post-2000 for two main reasons. First, the struggle was waged to compensate for the shortcomings of developmental nationalism that had failed to usher in meaningful economic development as promised during the liberation struggle, and second as a response and a foil to hegemonic global ideologies of human rights, democracy, and neo-liberalism and their attendant ideals of pluralism and cosmopolitanism (Ndlovu-Gatsheni and Willems, 2009). Contrary to the liberation ideals that were premised on pluralism and a civil conception of the nation, the patriotic discourse that the ZANU-PF government peddled post-2000 sought to project democracy and human rights as alien values that were inimical to national sovereignty. Cultural nationalism became a project of hegemonic renewal running concurrently with coercion to foster a narrow patriotic history that drew from ZANU-PF's role in the liberation struggle (Tendi, 2008). Patriotic discourse was based on issues such as land and sovereignty, with anyone opposed to the "hegemonic discourse" being invariably described as "puppets," sellouts, "un-African," and/or "pro-colonial" (Tendi, 2008).

ZANU-PF's state-sponsored cultural nationalism slowly morphed into Afro-radicalism and a nativist interpretation of the nation (Ndlovu-Gatsheni and Willems, 2009). To cement its hegemony, the ruling ZANU-PF government had to revive anti-colonial discourse and articulate the issue of land to issues of cultural heritage. Land became not only a metonym of the economy and sovereignty but also deeply intertwined with the cultural and symbolic politics of the Third Chimurenga (Mate, 2012). Post-2000 cultural nationalism in Zimbabwe found expression through state-sponsored activities such as music galas and commemorations, where the image of the country constituted a conflation of state, nation, the ruling party ZANU-PF, and the person of Robert Mugabe (Ndlovu-Gatsheni and Willems, 2009). Central to the performance of the nation as an expression of national sovereignty was the assimilation of the national anthem, the national flag, and national colors by both the state and the ruling ZANU-PF party. The capture of national symbols and colors constituted an important part of both the ruling ZANU-PF government's hegemonic project, as well as the mediation of patriotic history that sought to promote a narrow and self-serving version of national identity.

ELITE CAPTURE OF NATIONAL SYMBOLS AND THE STRUGGLE FOR HEGEMONY

Post-2000, the ruling ZANU-PF government set in motion a sustained cultural nationalist project that ran under the "Third Chimurenga" (Ndlovu-Gatsheni and Willems, 2009). While the First and Second Chimurenga were two phases of the war of liberation against white settler rule, the "The Third Chimurenga" was described as an economic war that sought to redress economic imbalances created by colonialism. A wide range of cultural activities and events were rolled out by the Ministry of Information and Publicity, intent on legitimizing ZANU-PF's continued rule in the face of counter-hegemonic groups such as the MDC and civil society organizations. These events and activities syncretized elite memorialization of the liberation struggle. In the process, national symbols were captured and deployed in the celebration and performance of the new nation. As observed by Turino (2004), re-imagining a nation involves cultural and artistic domains where cultural symbols are particularly useful in developing national sentiment for political purposes. This form of cultural nationalism celebrated cultural uniqueness while also rejecting "foreign" practices. It is a form of cultural nationalism that resembles that of the Chinese government. From the 1980s, the Chinese government has been actively using cultural nationalism programs to promote patriotism among its citizens because of counter-perceived domestic and external threats (Rose, 2000).

The elite capture of national symbols by the ZANU-PF government post-2000 should be read as part of its efforts to renew its hegemony. According to Gramsci (1971), culture and national symbols are vital in the reproduction of power as hegemony cannot simply be produced through coercion but should be balanced with consent. Thus, the elite capture of national symbols such as the national flag by the ruling ZANU-PF government was meant to provide citizens with a new way of imagining the nation (Cohen, 1996). National symbols represent the nation and, after repeated use, can be perceived as the nation by association (Eriksen, 2007). In the Third Chimurenga, a form of banal nationalism emerged where national symbols and colors became important primary means for reminding Zimbabweans of their nationhood and patriotic history in their everyday life. According to Billig (1995), intense displays of nationalist flag-waving, as witnessed in Zimbabwe, are usually provoked by internal or external threats. In the case of Zimbabwe, flag-waving was also prompted by intense nationalism resulting from the ruling ZANU-PF government's vulnerability to attack from its political opposition, civil society, and the United Kingdom and its allies. Arguably, the architects of the cultural nationalist struggle thought that the hyper-identification resulting from the perceived national threats would generate a strong undercurrent of hostility toward those individuals, groups, and countries perceived as the source of threat (Butz, 2009).

NATIONAL SYMBOLS AND COUNTER-HEGEMONY

Although scholars have observed that national symbols such as national flags can play a central role in re-imagining a nation, fostering cultural nationalism and hegemony in countries facing internal and external threats (Butz, 2009), studies have also shown that they hold potential for divisive responses, associations, and reactions (Butz, 2009). Butz (2009) contends that in some nations where there is a strong push to increase people's exposure to national symbols, these efforts are often met with opposition (Butz, 2009). Thus, national symbols such as national flags should be viewed more as complex symbols of ideological concepts, memories, and beliefs that can vary substantially across individuals and groups within the same country. Besides playing a critical role in nation-building and re-imagining a nation (Anderson, 1991), national symbols may sometimes function as symbols of dissent and counter-hegemony.

Firth's (1973) study aptly shows that national symbols are often appropriated by counter-hegemonic groups that seek to establish their legitimacy for causes and to protest the legitimacy of the nation's ideology. Like the #ThisFlag movement, which was initiated by Ivan Mawarire in Zimbabwe, the 1980s solidarity movement against communism in Poland appropriated key national symbols such as the national anthem and national colors as their primary strategy. Thus, while national symbols are useful particularly at the inception of the nation-state and have been used by political leaders to direct public attention, integrate citizens, and motivate public action, they are often contested by various ethnic and political groups (see Kolsto, 2006). Although there is significant literature on social media and protest movements in Zimbabwe as well as work that engages with nationalism and cultural production, most of this material has not attended to the actual ways in which national symbols have been appropriated by counter-hegemonic groups to contest the dominant discourses of the ruling ZANU-PF government, as is the case with #ThisFlag.

CONCEPTUALIZING HEGEMONY AND COUNTER HEGEMONY

The chapter makes use of Antonio Gramsci's concepts of hegemony and counter-hegemony as a lens for understanding the discourses that Evan Mawarire's #ThisFlag protest speech mobilized to disrupt the ruling ZANU-PF government's "patriotic history" and its attendant discourses in Zimbabwe. Gramsci's concepts of hegemony and counter-hegemony are useful in understanding how elite power in Zimbabwe has been maintained, and how protest movements such as #ThisFlag can build a counter-hegemonic project. The concepts provide insight into how the ruling elite in society produce hegemony and how subaltern groups in society contest this hegemony by drawing from ideologies or discourses (Karriem, 2009).

Gramsci contends that the ruling or dominant elite in society gains hegemony through complex processes of both consent and coercion (1971). These processes consist of a series of cultural, political, and ideological practices (Hargreaves and McDonald, 2000). Thus, the ruling class in society does not only use force to establish its hegemony, but it also draws on consent to attain some form of intellectual and ideological leadership. In this light, the ruling elite achieves consent by incorporating some of the interests of subordinate classes and forging alliances with them (Gramsci, 1971). For hegemony to be established, it is critical for the subaltern class to accept the dominant ideas of the hegemonic class as commonsensical. According to Gramsci, common sense, conceptualized as the unconscious and uncritical ways in which individuals make sense of and perceive the world around them, is a critical arena where the hegemony of the ruling class is not only exercised but should also be challenged by counter-hegemonic groups (1971). This chapter contends that Mawarire's #ThisFlag constitutes a form of counter-hegemonic discourse that disrupts the "common sensical" ideas of "patriotic history or discourse" that, post-2000, the ruling ZANU-PF government had entrenched in public discourse.

Gamsci's notions of hegemony and counter-hegemony (1971) make a significant contribution toward understanding how hegemony is both established and contested. He contends that hegemony is never absolute and is continuously contested by subaltern groups and oppositional forces in society who critically engage with the dominant ideas of the hegemonic group. As a result, hegemony should be viewed not as static but dynamic. It continuously needs to be renewed to absorb both internal and external pressures (Gramsci, 1971). Notably, hegemonic groups' exercise of power or their ability to maintain their privileged position in society is always subject to change and resistance (Karriem, 2009). On the other hand, for counter-hegemonic forces to be successful in contesting hegemonic groups in society, they need to engage in political and ideological struggle that critiques hegemonic ideas that have become "common sensical" in society (Karriem, 2009). This critique needs to resonate with broader national popular demands in society.

METHOD

This chapter purposively selected Evan Mawarire's #ThisFlag speech that was posted on Facebook as its unit of analysis (see Mawarire, 2016). The speech was analyzed using Norman Fairclough's approach to CDA to reveal its counter-hegemonic discourses. CDA was applied in this study to reveal the relationship between the linguistic features of #ThisFlag, and the social context in which the speech was created and still circulates (see Makwambeni, 2017; Chikuni, Makwambeni, and Chigona, 2021). The study used three inter-related processes of analysis. Mawarire's #ThisFlag was treated as a text. The words used in the speech such as "I don't see any crops in my country," "Hatichada" (We are fed up), were analyzed closely to reveal their underlying ideological beliefs, interests, and aspirations. This approach was used on the understanding that the speech did not come about through chance but is a product of intent on the part of the speaker (see Makwambeni, 2017).

The second stage of the analysis focused on the discourses in the spoken word (nationalism, citizenship, cosmopolitanism) which were gleaned by analyzing the text in relation to The Evan Mawarire's interviews and subsequent Facebook posts which were posted on the internet as part of the #ThisFlag movement. The third and final stage of the analysis was aimed at explaining the relationship between the text, discursive practice, and social context. In this light, the researcher related the text and discursive practice to the broader social, economic, and political context in Zimbabwe where #ThisFlag was produced. As reflected in CDA, #ThisFlag is a form of social practice that relates to other forms of social media protests in Zimbabwe such as #ThisGown and #Tajamuka.

On reflection, the CDA process followed in the study is like that used in mainstream CDA studies (see Makwambeni, 2017; Chikuni, Makwambeni, and Chigona, 2021). The line between data collection and analysis was often blurred during the analysis. Consequently, the data collection stage was nonlinear. Rather, following the initial data collection phase, the analysis consisted of finding indicators and themes in the speech, expanding these themes into similar categories, and then relating them to the social-historical context. For the purposes of this chapter, Norman Fairclough's three-dimensional approach to CDA proved to be richer and more nuanced than textual analysis. Its strength was in the ability to unpack the relationship between #ThisFlag as a text, as discursive practice, and the sociopolitical and economic context in which #ThisFlag was produced and consumed.

FINDINGS AND DISCUSSION

The study's findings show that Evans Mawarire harnessed the national flag, which has long been captured as a key tool for furthering the ruling ZANU-PF government's patriotic discourse and cultural nationalism program, to mount a counter-hegemonic discourse that resonated with the quotidian interests and experiences of Zimbabweans post-2000. Mawarire's monologue managed to disarticulate and disentangle the national flag from state-sponsored and ZANU-PF-driven patriotic discourse by contesting normative knowledge and memory production premised on narrow nationalism, patriotism, sovereignty, and a re-configured and polarizing discourse of the nation (Mawere, 2020). Mawarire's monologue mobilized counter-hegemonic discourses drawn from both the liberation struggle and post-Cold War global discourses of human rights, democracy, and other attendant ideals of pluralism and cosmopolitanism. Phrases such as "I don't feel like a part of it" in reference to post-Independence Zimbabwe and "I don't know who they sold it to and how much they got for" referring to the plunder of minerals show how #ThisFlag contests patriotic discourse. Mawarire's #ThisFlag monologue shows while national symbols and colors can be subject to elite capture in authoritarian states, they can also serve as tools for counter-hegemony.

#THISFLAG: CONTESTING PATRIOTIC DISCOURSES NOTIONS OF NATIONALISM AND CITIZENSHIP

The role that Mawarire's #ThisFlag monologue plays as a form of counter-discourse can be understood within the post-2000 context in Zimbabwe when the ruling ZANU-PF government intensified its cultural nationalism program to mask its failures as well as to thwart local and international criticism. Premised on patriotic discourse, the state-driven cultural nationalism project sought to link the national flag to nationalism and citizenship with the aim of bringing diverse Zimbabweans together to serve narrow ZANU-PF interests. As argued by Kriger (2003), ZANU-PF's conception of the nation, unity, and nation-building is founded on a conflation of the party and the nation and the party and the state to ensconce itself as the legitimate and permanent custodian of the nation and the state. Consequently, the national flag's colors and features have been usurped to popularize patriotic history and its attendant discourses, which legitimizes and give the ruling ZANU-PF Party the authority to govern in Zimbabwe (Mawere, 2020). This hegemonic conception of the nation and the state views citizens as either patriots or sell-outs, with anyone who disagrees with patriotic discourse and its conceptions of the nation and citizenship branded as "western sponsored/ a puppet/ a sell-out."

#ThisFlag monologue manages to disarticulate the national flag, a symbol of patriotic discourse and a tool used to legitimize ZANU-PF's hegemony post-2000, from elite capture and repurpose it to forge a counter and subversive discourse of nationalism and citizenship (Mawere, 2020). Using the national flag as a rallying point, Mawarire's #ThisFlag monologue mobilizes the discourses of plurality and cosmopolitanism that underpin both the liberation struggle and neo-liberal conceptions of citizenship to advance new imaginations of the nation that subvert hegemonic patriotic discourses of nationalism and citizenship. Mawarire's #ThisFlag disrupts patriotic discourse and its idea of the nation that is based on a conflation of the party and the nation by advancing an alternative discourse of the nation that contends that nationhood should cohere with a practical feel of nationhood among citizens and also resonate with the interests and aspirations of citizens. It is a discourse of nationhood that does not alienate the citizens as indicated in the monologue below. Mawarire, through his handle @PastorEvanLive, posted:

> Sometimes when I look at the flag it is not a reminder of my pride and aspiration, it seems as if I want to belong to another country. This flag. So, I must look at it again with courage and try to remind myself that it is my country.

Mawarire's #ThisFlag monologue contests patriotic discourse's hegemonic conception of the nation and citizenship that bifurcates Zimbabwean citizens into either patriots or sell-outs. He does so by averring that "*I don't feel like I am a part of it*" referring to his feeling of alienation from the nation as symbolized by the state. Conversely, Mawarire uses the #ThisFlag monologue to advance a conception of the nation and citizenship that promotes inclusivity and citizen participation. The discourse of the nation and citizenship that he advances to contest patriotic discourse challenges and questions ZANU-PF's ownership of the national flag and, by implication, the nation and its aspirations. Mawarire's use of the national flag to disrupt patriotic discourse shows the fluidity of symbols and symbolic meaning (Mawere, 2020). The study's findings further attest to the possibilities of channeling cultural tools to challenge the ruling elite's hold on national knowledge and power.

CONTESTING PATRIOTIC DISCOURSES OF CITIZENSHIP AND PATRIOTISM

Prior to 2000, the ruling ZANU-PF government had not fully deployed national symbols to entrench its hegemony. However, after 2000, with the introduction of the cultural nationalism project, possession of the national flag became associated with patriotism, loyalty, and the sanctioning of land occupation (Mawere, 2020). Patriotic discourse began to equate patriotism with the performance of a narrow form of citizenship that was against any form of critique of both ZANU-PF and the government. In this light, patriotism and citizenship amounted to either acquiescence or gratuitous acts of defending ZANU-PF's hegemony. In this context, grand discourses on Zimbabwean citizenship and patriotism took an insider or outsider dichotomy that necessitated the vilification and insidious surveillance of people and their actions.

The study's findings show that Mawarire's monologue contests the discourse of citizenship and patriotism that informs patriotic discourse. Drawing from the discourses of citizenship and patriotism that underpin neo-liberalism, Mawarire forges a counter-discourse that equates citizenship and patriotism to civic engagement and critique as opposed to acquiescence. Mawarire, through his handle @PastorEvanLive, posted:

> This flag, every day that it flies, it's begging for you to get involved, begging for you to say something, it is begging for you to cry out and to say why must we be in the situation we are in.

Mawarire's discourse of patriotism is the antithesis of patriotic discourse that views any form of critique against ZANU-PF and the government as acts of sabotage. It is a discourse that evokes the discourse of change that is associated with "regime change" and unpatriotic behavior in Zimbabwe post-2000. Thus, Mawarire's #ThisFlag monologue constitutes a counter-hegemonic discourse against notions of citizenship and patriotism that have been used by the ZANU-PF government to prevent citizens from speaking about its failure to meet the promises of the liberation struggle and developmental nationalism. The phrase below derived from this #ThisFlag monologue constitutes a subversive act meant to rescue the national flag and, by proxy, the nation from elite capture. Mawarire, through his handle @PastorEvanLive, posted:

> This flag, it's your flag. It is my flag. This flag.

By insisting that the Zimbabwean flag is "my flag," Mawarire is disrupting patriotic discourse that uses the national flag to "other" Zimbabweans who differ with its narrow nationalist ideology. He therefore recasts the national flag as an inclusive national symbol, as envisaged in the early post-independence Zimbabwean state. Consequently, the #ThisFlag monologue frees the national flag from the narrow *"Chinhu Chedu"* (Our thing) capture by patriotic discourse and its adherents.

In this light, the #ThisFlag monologue re-imagines a new form of active and empowered citizenship and patriotism that resonates with the aspirations of the liberation struggle and neo-liberalism notions of citizenship. It promotes a form of citizenship and patriotism that foregrounds the discourses of rights and freedom of expression that cohere with post-colonial aspirations and post-Cold War global ideologies of democracy and neo-liberalism. This version of citizenship and patriotism is captured in the quotation below. Mawarire, through his handle @PastorEvanLive, posted:

> I will fight for it. I will live for it and will stand for it. This is the time that a change must happen

Thus, the above quote shows that, unlike patriotic discourse that valorizes acquiescence to power as a reflection of one's patriotism and citizenship, #ThisFlag associates' patriotism and citizenship with holding leaders to account and speaking and fighting against the status quo as permissible forms and acts of citizenship and patriotism.

DISRUPTING PATRIOTIC DISCOURSE: RE-IMAGINING A POST-INDEPENDENT ZIMBABWE

A CDA of #ThisFlag shows that the monologue contests patriotic discourse and its claim that the Land is the Alpha Omega of post-independence Zimbabwe (see Tendi, 2002). The monologue mobilizes alternative imaginations of post-independent Zimbabwe that resonate with notions of economic prosperity that inspired both the war of liberation and developmental nationalism of the 1980s and 1990s (Ndhlovu-Gatsheni and Willems, 2009). By doing so, the monologue represents the continuation and intensification of the earlier imaginings of Zimbabwe and rejects patriotic discourse that depicts the land as the economy and land occupation as a success. Thus, Mawarire's monologue disrupts the myth of the success of the land reform program that saw a massive reduction in agricultural production in the country. Mawarire, through his handle @PastorEvanLive, posted:

> They tell me that green, the green is for vegetation and for the crops. I don't see any crops in my country.

#ThisFlag disrupts patriotic discourse by re-connecting new imaginings of the post-independence Zimbabwean nation to the promises of the liberation struggle that sought to transform the skewed economic system developed by settler colonialism with a view to eradicating poverty among workers and peasants and to initiate sustainable economic development. At a symbolic level, the failure of the land reform program represents the failure of the post-colonial Zimbabwean state to nourish the material needs of its citizens. The discourses that underpin #ThisFlag resonate with youths' aspirations and needs in Zimbabwe that are constructed outside the ambit of the land and the ruling party's patriotic discourse (Makwambeni, 2017).

Evan Mawarire's #ThisFlag monologue provides a profound critique of notions of freedom and independence that underpin patriotic discourse (Mawere, 2020). The monologue manages to disrupt patriotic discourse using the national flag, one of the most potent symbols that have been monopolized by the ruling ZANU-PF government to exert its hegemony in Zimbabwe post-2000. This use of the national flag resonates with previous studies that have shown that flags and other national symbols can be turned into vehicles for achieving subversive acts (Allison, 2016). In this case, the national flag became a tool for contesting the notion of "majority rule" that was hyped by patriotic discourse after independence. Mawarire makes use of the color black, which represents the black majority in Zimbabwe, to denote the emptiness of independence. Mawarire, through his handle @PastorEvanLive, posted:

And yet for some reason I don't feel like I am a part of it.

The above quote shows how Mawarire finds himself in the zone of the non-citizen in post-Independence Zimbabwe. #ThisFlag mounts a counter-hegemonic discourse against the discourses of "freedom" that are articulated by the ruling ZANU-PF government using patriotic discourse. The monologue positions itself within discourses of democracy and cosmopolitanism that informed the liberation struggle. These discourses promote a wide range of freedoms, including one's freedom to express oneself without fear, the freedom to belong to a political party of one's choice, as well as freedom of association. Using the national flag as a symbol, Mawarire contends that the victory attained at independence was pyrrhic as it is being negated by the current regime that has usurped the freedoms fought for. Mawarire, through his handle @PastorEvanLive, posted:

> The red, the red, the red they say is the blood, the blood that was shed to secure freedom for me and I am so thankful for that. I just don't know if that they were here, if they were here that shed their blood and saw the way this country is that they would demand their blood be brought back. This flag.

The role of #ThisFlag as counter-hegemony should be understood within the broader political context in Zimbabwe, where most citizens have been denied political and economic freedoms post-2000. Read in this context, Mawarire's #ThisFlag performs a paradoxical function of re-articulating the national flag and the nation to its founding values that include correcting socio-political-economic ills and restoring democracy (Mawere, 2020).

MOBILIZING DISCOURSES OF DEMOCRACY, TRANSPARENCY, ACCOUNTABILITY, AND GOOD GOVERNANCE

The findings of the study show that Mawarire's #ThisFlag monologue harnessed discourses such as transparency, accountability, and good governance to contest patriotic discourse. It is significant to note that post-2000, the ruling ZANU-PF government began to promote a narrow patriotic discourse that deviated from the core values of the liberation struggle by patently disparaging democracy and its attendant values, such as human rights, good governance, and accountability as alien values that undermined national sovereignty and worked in the interests of former colonizers. #ThisFlag monologue became a counter-discourse to patriotic discourse and its propensity to associate democracy and good governance with regime change and neo-imperialism (see Makwambeni, 2017). Using the national flag as a key symbol of resistance, Mawarire's monologue appropriated yellow, which represents mineral resources on the Zimbabwean flag, to foreground the discourse of accountability, transparency, and good governance in post-independence Zimbabwe. Mawarire, through his handle @PastorEvanLive, posted:

> Hanzi, the yellow, the yellow is for all the minerals, goridhe (Gold), diamonds, platinum, chrome. I don't know how much of it is left. I don't know who they sold it to and how much they got for it.

In this light, the #ThisFlag contests and challenges the hegemonic patriotic discourse that is promoted by the ruling ZANU-PF government, which projects Britain and its Western allies as the sole architects of Zimbabwe's multi-dimensional crisis (see Tendi, 2008; Musarurwa, 2016). #ThisFlag as a counter-discourse contends that rather than being externally driven, Zimbabwe's travails, including economic stasis, decay in infrastructure, moribund health and service delivery systems, and political repression, which left a significant number of citizens disillusioned, are largely a product of internal problems (see Hodzi, 2014; Makwambeni, 2017). They are inextricably linked to corruption that has fundamentally alienated most citizens from their country's resources. Mawarire's counter-hegemony resonates with the liberation discourse of "Gutsa Ruzhinji" which spoke about the need of the objective of democratic nationalism to spread the national cake to the majority as well as to foster transparency and accountability in post-independence Zimbabwe.

CONCLUSION

This study made use of Fairclough's three-dimensional approach to CDA to understand the specific discourses that Mawarire's #ThisFlag monologue mobilized to galvanize Zimbabweans to protest the ruling ZANU-PF government in 2016. The findings of the study show that Mawarire's #ThisFlag monologue harnessed the national flag, a national symbol that had been captured by the state and ZANU-PF, as a counter-hegemonic symbol for disarticulating and disentangling the national flag from state-sponsored and ZANU-PF-driven patriotic discourse. The monologue uses the national flag and its colors to contest normative knowledge and memory production in Zimbabwe that had become premised on narrow nationalism, patriotism, sovereignty, and a re-configured and polarizing discourse of the nation post-2000 (see Mawere, 2020). The findings of the CDA reflect that Mawarire's monologue foregrounded discourses derived from both the war of liberation against white settler colonialism in Zimbabwe and neo-liberalism to contest patriotic discourse.

The specific discourses that inform the monologue include human rights, democracy, good governance, and their attendant ideals such as pluralism and cosmopolitanism. The findings of the study contribute toward emerging literature on the role that social media and national symbols play in fostering resistance in authoritarian states such as Zimbabwe, where national symbols and mainstream public spheres are usually monopolized by hegemonic groups. The study's findings resonate with previous studies that attest to the utility of harnessing national symbols and social media as resources for mounting resistance and counter-hegemony in oppressive regimes. Mawarire's #ThisFlag monologue shows clearly that although national symbols and colors can be subject to elite capture, they can also serve as key resources for advancing counter-hegemony (see Firth, 1973; Billig, 1995; Gukurume, 2017). The findings further resonate with Gamsci's (1971) position that hegemony is never absolute and is continuously contested by subaltern groups and oppositional forces in society who critically engage with the dominant ideas of the hegemonic group.

REFERENCES

Anderson, B. (1991). *Imagined Communities. "Reflections on the Origin and Spread of Nationalism."* London: New York.

Bechhofer, F. and McCrone, D. (2013). Imagining the nation: Symbols of national culture in England and Scotland. *Ethnicities*, 13(5): 544–564.

Billig, M. (1995). *Banal Nationalism.* London: Sage.

Bodunrin, I.A. and Matsilele, T. 2023. Social media and protest politics in Nigeria's #EndSARS campaign. *Handbook of Social Media in Education, Consumer Behavior and Politics: Volume 1*, 111(114): 109.

Butz, D. (2009). National symbols as agents of psychological and social change. *Political Psychology*, 30(5): 779–804.

Chikuni, P., Makwambeni, B. and Chigona, W. (2021). Dominant discourses on institutional e-learning policies in Higher Education Institutions in South Africa. *International Journal of Education and Development using Information and Communication Technology*, (IJEDICT), 17(4): 5-21.

Chitanana, T. (2020). From Kubatana to #ThisFlag: Trajectories of digital activism in Zimbabwe. *Journal of Information Technology & Politics*, 17(2): 130–145.

Cohen, A.P. (1996). Personal nationalism: A Scottish view of some rites, rights, and wrongs. *American Ethnologist,* 23(4): 802–815.

Eriksen, T.H. (2007). Some questions about flags in Europe and America. In Eriksen, Thomas Hylland and Richard Jenkins (Eds), *Flag, Nation and Symbolism in Europe and America* (pp. 1–13). London: Routledge.

Firth, R. (1973). *Symbols: Public and Private*. Ithaca: Cornel University Press.
Gramsci, A. (1971). *Selections from the prison notebooks*. New York: International Publishers.
Gukurume, S. (2017). # ThisFlag and# ThisGown cyber protests in Zimbabwe: Reclaiming political space. *African Journalism Studies, 38*(2): 49–70.
Hargreaves, J. and McDonald, I. (2000). Cultural studies and the sociology of sport. In J. Coakley and E. Dunning (Eds), *Handbook of sports studies* (pp. 48–60). London: Sage.
Hodzi, O. (2014). The youth factor in Zimbabwe's 2013 harmonised elections. *Journal of African Elections, 13*(2): 48–70.
Jarvie, G. and Maguire, J. (1994). *Sport and leisure in social thought*. London: Routledge.
Karriem, A. (2009). The rise and transformation of the Brazilian landless movement into a counter-hegemonic political actor: A Gramscial analysis. *Geoforum*, 40: 316–325.
KolstØ, P. (2006). National symbols as signs of unity and division. *Ethnic and Racial Studies*, 29(4): 676–701.
Kriger, N. (2003). War veterans: Continuities between the past and the present. *African Studies Quarterly, 7*(2–3):139–152.
Makwambeni, B. (2017). Zimbabwe dancehall music as a site of resistance. In Onyebadi, U.T. (Ed.),*Music as a platform for political communication* (pp. 238–256). IGI Global.
Makwambeni, B. and Adebayo, J.O. (2021). 'Humour and the politics of resistance': Audience readings of popular amateur videos in Zimbabwe. In Mpofu, S. (Ed.), *The Politics of Laughter in the Social Media Age* (pp. 155–173). Cham: Palgrave Macmillan.
Mate, R. (2012). Youth lyrics, street language and the politics of age: Contextualising the youth question in the Third Chimurenga in Zimbabwe. *Journal of Southern African Studies, 38*(1):107–127.
Matsilele, T. (2022). *Social media and digital dissidence in Zimbabwe*. London: Palgrave Macmillan.
Matsilele, T., Mpofu, S., Msimanga, M. and Tshuma, L. (2021). Transnational hashtag protest movements and emancipatory politics in Africa: A three country study. *Global Media Journal: German Edition, 11*(12): 1–28.
Matsilele, T. and Ruhanya, P. (2021). Social media dissidence and activist resistance in Zimbabwe. *Media, Culture & Society*, 43(2): 381–394.
Mawarire, E. (2016). This Flag-A Lament of Zimbabwe-Evans Mawarire [SpokenWord]-Day 1. *YouTube*. Accessed 10 October 2020. https://www.youtube.com/watch?v=LubMilbHiPg.
Mawere, T. (2020). The politics and symbolism of the #ThisFlag in Zimbabwe. *Strategic Review for Southern Africa*, 42(1): 165–188.
Mhiripiri, N.A. and Mutsvairo, B. (2014). Social media, new ICTs and the challenges facing the Zimbabwe democratic process. In Information Resource Management Association, *Crisis Management: Concepts, Methodologies, Tools, and Applications* (pp. 1281–1301). IGI Global.

Mpofu, M. (2015). ICTs in the struggle for democracy: Civil society, democratisation and organisational forms in the Zimbabwean crisis, 2000–2013. *Unpublished Doctor of Philosophy thesis. University of Oslo.*

Mpofu, S. and Mare, A. (2020). # ThisFlag: Social media and cyber-protests in Zimbabwe. In Ndlela, M.N. and Mano, W. (Eds), *Social Media and Elections in Africa, Volume 2* (pp. 153–173). Cham: Palgrave Macmillan.

Mpofu, S. and Matsilele, T. (2020). Social media and the concept of dissidence in Zimbabwean politics. In *The History and Political Transition of Zimbabwe* (pp. 221–243). Cham: Palgrave Macmillan.

Msimanga, M.J. (2022). *Satire and the Discursive Construction of National Identity in Zimbabwe: The Case of Magamba and Bustop TV*. Unpublished Doctoral Dissertation. University of Johannesburg.

Musarurwa, H. (2016). The rise of youth activism and non-violent action in addressing Zimbabwe's crisis. *Conflict Trends*, 3: 50–56.

Ndlovu-Gatsheni, S.J. and Willems, W. (2009). Making sense of cultural nationalism and the politics of commemoration under the Third Chimurenga in Zimbabwe. *Journal of Southern African Studies*, 35(4): 945–965.

Ndlela, N.M. (2010). Alternative media and the public sphere in Zimbabwe. In Howley, K. (Ed,). *Understanding Community Media* (pp: 87–95). Los Angeles: Sage.

Rose, C. (2000). 'Patriotism is not taboo': Nationalism in China and Japan and implications for Sino–Japanese relations. *Japan Forum*, 12(2): 169–181.

Tendi, B.M. (2008). Patriotic history and public intellectuals critical of power. *Journal of Southern African Studies, 34*(2): 379–396.

Chapter 3

Testing the Illusory Truth Effect

An Analysis of Comments to Nigerian Army's "Fake News" Tweets on Lekki #EndSARS Shootings

Raheemat Adeniran and Kunle Adebajo

Mass protests rarely occur in contemporary Nigeria, with frequent accusations of citizens of being too complacent in the face of bad governance and poor management of the country's resources (Adeniyi, 2017). But occasionally, citizens rise to challenge the status quo. One of these occasions was the 2020 nationwide protest police brutality tagged #EndSARS. The protesters called for the disbandment of the notorious Special Anti-Robbery Squad (SARS), a special unit of the Nigerian Police Force created in 1992 "to combat armed robbery and other serious crimes," then a growing cause for concern (Malumfashi, 2020; Matsilele et al., 2021). Over the years, the unit has been widely criticized for its widespread harassment, extortion, and abuse of innocent young Nigerians under the pretext, among others, of seeking out suspected cybercriminals. For over two weeks in October 2020, Nigerian youths protested in major cities across the country. They "spoke loudly," calling for the scrapping, besides other police reforms, of the SARS unit over its extrajudicial excesses.

There had been repeated calls for the demobilization of SARS which remained unheeded by the government until the October 2020 upheaval when "thousands of young Nigerians mostly under 30" trooped to the streets across several Nigerian cities with a renewed call for the government to disband the notorious unit (Busari et al., 2020). The clamor was sparked by the alleged killing of a young man in Delta State, in the oil-rich Niger-Delta region of the country (Malumfashi, 2020). In the wake of the lingering protests, the government announced the dissolution of the unit, but protesters remained adamant voicing their lack of trust in the pronouncement based on previously promised reforms that had never materialized (Malumfashi, 2020). The protests continued for days afterward with expanded demands that went beyond police brutality to other grievances (Bodunrin and Matsilele, 2023; Busari et al., 2020). The protest later became chaotic with wanton destruction of property and deaths in parts of the country (Adediran, 2020).

Lagos, the commercial nerve center of the country was not spared (Adediran, 2020). Following the destruction of public property and the loss of lives in several parts of the state, the governor, Babajide Sanwo-Olu, abruptly imposed a 24-hour curfew on October 20, 2020, effective from 4 p.m. that day. When the authorities realized that it was impractical to announce a curfew with such short notice, the start time was shifted to 9 p.m.. Despite the deadline, however, protesters appeared set for a showdown.

That night, pictures and videos of alleged shootings by soldiers and other security officials flooded the Nigerian online space drawing widespread anger and criticism. The scene was the Lekki tollgate, the epicenter of the protest. The viral videos showed men in military uniforms apparently shooting at a crowd of protesters at the tollgate, located in a highbrow suburb of Lagos. Numerous viral images of the men appearing to shoot directly at the protesters evoked strong emotions among many and drew widespread criticism across the country and beyond. The Lekki shooting was the climax of the protest and was dogged by controversies, as different groups blamed each other for the occurrences of that fateful night (BBC News, 2020).

In the wake of the crisis, the Nigerian Army, the security agency responsible for the country's national security, took to its Twitter page (now X), @HQNigerianArmy, tagging all media reports linking the army to the shootings at the tollgate as "fake news." Between October 20 and October 21, 2020, the army posted six tweets attempting to debunk a total of 15 news headlines and one individual's tweet that alleged the military's involvement in the Lekki shootings as "Fake news." These tweets attracted massive reactions at a time when tensions were high with varied pictures on social media purportedly relating to the shootings. As of November 30, 2020, the reactions on each of the tweets ranged from over 14,000 to less than a thousand comments. Most of the responses were sent within hours of the army's tweets. Few comments were added weeks later, as confirmed reports of the army's involvement emerged. The army which had initially denied deploying soldiers to the tollgate later confirmed their presence, on the invitation of the state government to restore "normalcy" to the state "because the police had been overrun" (BBC News, 2020). The army had insisted it had merely shot blank bullets into the air, but it later confirmed the soldiers also had access to live ammunition (Adediran and News Agency of Nigeria {NAN} 2020; Busari et al., 2020).

The army's attempt to deny its involvement in the Lekki shootings ran contrary to corroborating evidence, but what does this portends for the renewed efforts in combating misinformation and promoting public trust in the media in Nigeria's information ecosystem? In this piece, we present a qualitative analysis of public replies to the Nigerian Army's attempt to deny its involvement in the shootings. The wider context of this approach is to evaluate public perception of a "fake news" claim within media reportage of a national crisis. In the following sections, we provide context for the analysis by conceptualizing "fake news" and exploring the Nigerian Army's recent employment of the term. We examine the implications of this situation for the country's information ecosystem.

CONCEPTUALIZING FAKE NEWS

The term "fake news" is often contested and is used for varied meanings depending on the perspective of the author. The term was originally used "to describe formats of political satire" but has "since 2016 come to characterize a variety of phenomena related to questions of truth and factuality in journalism and political communication" (Egelhofer et al., 2020, p.1323). There is a growing debate as to the appropriateness or otherwise of continuing to use the phrase. Some have argued that we need to use more specific terms to describe the nature of information to which we are referring (Funke, 2018; USAID, 2021) while others contend that avoiding the term in scholarly discourse will not automatically resolve its problematic use, nor stop its continued appearance in public discourse (Meyer, 2018).

Egelhofer, et al., (2020, p.1324–6), reviewed existing literature operationalizing fake news and identified three common uses of the term in research inquiries. These include:

1. A genre: Fake news as a genre of disinformation online; explained as fabricated contents intentionally produced and presented as credible news stories, mimicking news media contents, but without undergoing real news verification process (Lazer, et al., 2018).
2. A Label: Weaponization of the term by critical political actors as a label to delegitimize news media and discredit disliked claims, even if the claim were true; and
3. A buzzword: "fake news" as an empty buzzword, simply used to describe something as false, debatable, or bad; and increasingly used to describe a wide spectrum of ideas.

This chapter follows the conceptualization of fake news as a label, focusing on the weaponization of the term by a government agency, the Nigerian Army, to discredit media outlets amid a public outcry over its involvement in shooting at youthful protesters who had called for far-reaching police reforms. Unfortunately for the army, the factuality of the reports on its involvement in the October 20, 2020, shootings of protesters at the Lekki tollgate were later confirmed by a commission of inquiry into the incident.

The weaponization of fake news is a cause for concern. It undermines democratic institutions and has the potential to erode public trust in the media. It is increasingly being used by authoritarian regimes to justify their restriction of press freedom, by "claiming news sources are faulty or corrupt" (USAID, 2021, p.5). Even in institutionalized democracies, the term is increasingly being used to attack legacy news media, with former U.S. president, Donald Trump, leading the trail (Egelhofer, et al., 2020; Egelhofer and Lecheler, 2019). Egelhofer and Lecheler (2019, p.105) capture the consequences of fake news labelling thus:

> such weaponization of the term fake news has become a part of political instrumentalization strategies with the goal of undermining public trust in institutional news media as central parts of democratic political systems. As a political instrument, the fake news label thus portrays news media as institutions that purposely spread disinformation with the intention to deceive.

It is important to understand the consequences of fake news labeling by government institutions and other political actors. This study's examination of the fake news label as a political weapon by the Nigerian Army, contributes therefore to filling the gap in research inquiries into the fake news phenomenon and its consequences as suggested by Egelhofer and Lecheler (2019). First, we examine the Nigerian Army's use of the term over time.

THE NIGERIAN ARMY AND ITS "FAKE NEWS" LABEL

The Nigerian Army has claimed it is fighting false information, through broadcast and online media, and does so in collaboration with local religious and political leaders (Adegoke and BBC Africa Eye, 2018). In recent times, The Nigerian Army, in its attempt to step up its "war" against misinformation, regularly tag misleading media reports and public comments on its activities or personnel as "fake news." The army usually tags such identified publicly shared "false" information with a large "FAKE NEWS" stamp inscribed across identified media reports and other public information. The tagged reports are then shared widely on the agency's various social media handles. Its sincerity of purpose is however doubtful as the army has several times attempted to debunk supposed false information published in the media which was later proven to be true (Adebajo, 2020).

For greater insight on this, we conducted an analysis of over 5,400 tweets on the verified handle of the Nigerian Army posted since April 2013, using Twitter's analytical tool, Tweetbeaver. The result shows that Nigerian Army mentioned "fake news" at least 67 times. In 56 of those tweets, mostly from 2020, the security agency was calling out various media publications or other reports. The first time such a tweet was issued was in September 2017, in reaction to a publication by *PM News Nigeria* but it has since been deleted. In the second instance the following month, the army reacted to a report in *Vanguard* newspaper (Iheamnachor, 2017) which said people panicked in Port Harcourt, Rivers State, over forced vaccination against monkeypox by soldiers. After these initial tweets, other related posts were more detailed, sometimes involving the use of press statements to refute misinformation (Nigerian Army, 2019a). For example, in a series of tweets on September 19, 2019, the army took time to explain why rumors about planned terrorist attacks should be disregarded (Nigerian Army, 2019b).

However, starting from July 11, 2020, a change in approach was noticed. On this day, the army uploaded screenshots of reports by *Global Sentinel* (Iroegbu, 2020) and *Premium Times* (Adebayo, 2020) about the voluntary retirement of hundreds of soldiers and stamped them, in bold red fonts, as "FAKE NEWS." It still provided justification here, arguing that the disengagement was a normal routine and that the force was not in short supply of willing recruits. In most of the 32 "fake news alerts" shared between August and November 2020, no further explanations were provided. The notices only had screenshots from the online reports, with the boldly inscribed "FAKE NEWS" stamp, and a caption that said either "fake news" or "be aware," often accompanied by three exclamation marks.

Some of the reports so tagged as Fake News have since been found to be true. More instances came to light during the #EndSARS campaign in October 2020. In one tweet, the army first described a hooded official who called on his colleagues not to kill demonstrators in a viral video as a "fake soldier" (Nigerian Army, 2020a). Two days later, it announced that it had identified and arrested the officer for cybercrimes (Nigerian Army, 2020b). Similarly, the army went from claiming none of its men were at the Lekki tollgate and that no shot was fired, to explaining that it intervened after it was invited by the state government; that its men only fired blank shots (Abba, 2020) but later confirming they had live bullets (Adediran and NAN, 2020).

Unlike conventional debunking providing verifiable facts to support evidence of falsehood in claims, the army's approach makes it difficult for people to understand why a news report should be considered untrue. The approach however enables the army to tag public reports relating to its activities as false without providing any evidence to support its claims. This blanket dismissal of media reports can be described as an attack, without justification, on media integrity (Egelhofer and Lecheler, 2019). No doubt, such an approach promotes public distrust of the media. Unfortunately for the army, the discrediting of unfavorable media reports on its activities (despite overwhelming evidence in the public space supporting these criticisms) also has the potential to erode the army's integrity and damage citizens' regard for the institution. This can have far-reaching effects beyond the army as the accuracy of accounts by other government institutions may increasingly be questioned by the citizenry, thus eroding public trust in the government of the day.

Regrettably, the inclination to describe unfavorable reports as false by relevant authorities in the country is not limited to the Nigerian Army. For example, in November 2020, Nigeria's Information and Culture Minister, Lai Mohammed, dismissed a CNN investigation about the extrajudicial killing of protesters in Lekki as "fake news" and "misinformation," without specifically explaining why (Mangut et al., 2020). The information minister has become infamous for making false or unsubstantiated claims in his defense of the Buhari administration, even when official facts and narratives prove the contrary. This has not gone unnoticed. Many of his utterances might have undermined public trust in the Buhari administration with one writer noting, "his first name doesn't just share an uncanny phonemic kinship with 'lie'; he embodies lies in the most audaciously disreputable way imaginable" (Kperogi, 2017). Even his political party's Deputy National Publicity Secretary, Yekini Nabena, dismissed him as "the biggest problem of Buhari government" who has "failed woefully" as "whatever he says is considered as a lie" (Nwachukwu, 2021).

As evident in the official data from the World Economic Forum Global Competitiveness Index 2017–2018, public trust in the Nigerian government has declined over the years (The World Bank n.d.). With failed electoral promises, and pressing economic and infrastructural challenges, many Nigerians are disgruntled with the Buhari's administration. Therefore, unsubstantiated dismissal of media reports may not only harm public trust in the media but may inadvertently dampen government trust ratings. People may increasingly query government sources with the perceived notion that official sources often distort facts to their advantage. The government and its agencies, thus need to be mindful of its official communication to avoid unintended consequences.

THE ILLUSORY TRUTH EFFECT

The illusory truth effect is a cognitive research paradigm that seeks to explain people's tendency, after repeated exposure to a lie, to believe false information to be true. It suggests that when "you say something enough times . . . people start to believe it" (Shepherd, 2020, para 2). Shepherd reported its basic characteristics thus:

- "If repeated enough times, the information may be perceived to be true even if sources are not credible.
- The illusory truth effect is very evident on subject matter people perceive themselves to know about; and
- the effect can happen even if someone had previous knowledge that the information was false."

The illusory truth effect reportedly originated from Hasher, Goldstein, and Toppino's 1977 study (Hassan and Barber, 2021). Participants were asked to rate the accuracy of 60 diverse plausible statements in three repeated sessions. Some statements were repeated across the sessions. Participants reportedly gave significantly higher truth ratings to the repeated statements than they did in previous sessions, with no change in the validity judgments for the non-repeated statements (Hasher et al., 1977). The notion has been tested over the years with similar outcomes often reported. Hassan and Barber's (2021) meta-analysis of studies testing the illusory truth effect on a wide array of issues suggests overwhelming evidence of the robustness of its postulations. The notion is well understood by diverse stakeholders—professionals, politicians, cult leaders, and so on—and is often used by to push their agenda (Shepherd, 2020). Hence, the best way to guard against the illusory truth effect is being alert to repetitive statements that appear without substantive evidence; and then actively considering what objective facts corroborate each promoted idea (Bird, 2017).

Former United States president, Donald Trump, has come to epitomize the illusory truth effect. He has been credited with popularizing the phrase, "fake news." During his 2016 election campaign and thereafter, Trump used the phrase loosely and frequently to describe news about himself which he considered unsavory. Justifying his action in a media interview, he reportedly said, "You know why I do it? I do it to discredit you all and demean you all so that when you write negative stories about me no one will believe you" (Mangan, 2018). And it might have worked, with the number of people having confidence in the U.S. press plummeting over the years (Hetherington and Ladd, 2020). The Nigerian Army thus seems to have adopted Trump's approach with the press, increasingly labeling unfavorable reports as "fake news."

In this study, we therefore tested the perceived effect of such labeling on a controversial issue in Nigeria. To what extent did the army's fake news labeling achieve the illusionary truth effect among the citizenry? What are the potential consequences of such labeling for the Nigerian Army and the country in general? We sought answers to these questions in the following sections.

METHOD

We analyzed public responses to Nigerian Army's tweets falsely debunking its involvement in the Lekki shootings, using the thematic analysis approach. We identified six tweets by the Nigerian Army shared on its official Twitter handle, @HQNigerianArmy within hours of the October 20, 2020 Lekki shootings. The six tweets tried to undermine a total of 15 media reports and public comments alleging its involvement in the incident. We purposively sampled two of such tweets and analyzed all tweeted replies to them. The two selected tweets have the highest number of replies among the six tweets issued. The first tweet (Nigerian Army, 2020c) selected for this analysis has over 14,000 comments. It "debunked" two media reports. The first accuses the army of shooting at protesters at the tollgate and the other notes that the army seized the corpses of those killed. The second tweet (Nigerian Army, 2020d) selected for analysis, has almost 8,000 comments. It "debunked" a tweet by Reno Omokri, a former special assistant to former president Goodluck Jonathan. Omokri had tweeted a post calling for criminal charges against the army leadership, with international sanctions on Nigeria. We read through the comments on the two selected tweets and analyzed them qualitatively for recurring themes.

FINDINGS

Findings from the analysis of public comments on Nigeria army labeling of media reports as fake news show that the label failed to achieve its intended purpose as members of the public appeared convinced of the army's involvement in the shootings despite the repeated tweets. The following themes emerged from the analysis of the tweeted comments.

Debunking Misinformation Goes beyond "Fake News" Tagging

A major finding from our analysis is the public's expectation that there should be a clear presentation of facts that can dispel the alleged misinformation.

Many of the comments queried the army's simple dismissal of the reports requesting evidence to support the army's claim. One user asked, "*Oga*, how is it fake? Explain to us ooooooo." Another queried, "What is now the original news?" A number of users were quick to counter the army's submission with supposed "evidence" of videos and images circulating online, some of which were later fact-checked to be false (Philip, 2020). To the average person, those videos and images were clear evidence of what transpired that night at the tollgate, and that narrative could not simply be wished away with a blanket dismissal of media reports on the events.

Providing evidence to substantiate the claims might have helped in swaying people's opinions if the army was indeed truthful in its description of the reports as fake news. Unfortunately, the tweets might have increased people's disbelief in official narratives. Many of the comments confirmed they had lost confidence in the factuality of information provided by the army. To some commentators, the army's "fake news" tagging is a clear indication that many of the posts often tagged as fake news were more likely to be true. This was based on their belief that, if the army could try to discredit such an openly witnessed incident as the Lekki shootings, then attempts by the military to cast doubt on other events that the public might not be privy to, were also likely to be unfounded and false.

Many also dismissed the army's blanket dismissal of the reports wondering why they failed to stop the shootings or take legal action against the media organizations or individuals making the claims, if indeed those doing the shooting were not soldiers. Unfortunately for the army, its admittance weeks later, at the Judicial Panel of Inquiry, of the presence of soldiers with live bullets at the Lekki tollgate that night further discredited their earlier claims (Adediran and NAN, 2020; Busari et al., 2020). Twitter users readily returned to the earlier tweets for further engagements. One user wrote: "So now they've said the truth and shamed the devil that they were there, when should we expect your apology to the public or you remain in your stand that 'No soldiers were there???'".

Curses Galore

The comments on the tweets were dominated by curses directed at the army personnel involved in the shootings. These curses were extended to President Muhammadu Buhari, the state governor, Babajide Sanwo-Olu, and then chief of army staff, General Tukur Buratai. Many believed these key officials were instrumental in authorizing the attack on protesters. This assertion was not based on any evidence but on people's perception of the likelihood of guilt. The curses were often directed at the families of the soldiers involved. There was a continuous reference to an army officer, Ifo Omata, who purportedly led the soldiers to the Lekki tollgate. Other Twitter users who "liked" the army's tweets were not spared the verbal attacks either. Many of the profanities in the comments we analyzed are too gory to be reproduced here.

Myths of Resistance: Waving the Nigerian Flag

There were repeated references to the fact that the army shot at protesters while the victims were waving the Nigerian flag and singing the national anthem, suggesting that many believed the now debunked viral message which suggested that the army will not shoot at protesters holding the national flag (Kevin-Alerechi, 2020). Even though this claim was debunked in several fact-checks published after the shootings, evidence from public comments supports widespread belief in the claim. It is unclear if people might have changed that misconception purportedly prohibiting the army from shooting at anyone waving the flag and/or singing the national anthem after being exposed to the fact-checks debunking the notion. This is because many of the comments analyzed in this study were posted within hours of the incident before the fact-checks were published.

The Army's Betrayal of Public Trust and Sympathy

Many of the commentators were displeased with the soldiers, considering their actions as a betrayal of public trust and collective efforts toward achieving a better Nigeria. Many believed the army could have stood with the people rather than allowed themselves to be used by politicians. One user wrote:

> Most of you, the soldiers, have 6–10 children living in a dirty environment in the barracks, attending some of the worst schools. Instead of supporting the youths to build a better future for your kids, you've chosen to obey Buhari that will leave office soon. Shame!

The army's action also appeared to have resulted in the loss of public sympathy in its fight against Boko Haram, with many mocking them for their inability to decisively tackle the insurgents. Many decried their inability to confront the Boko Haram insurgents while being trigger-happy with harmless protesters, with one post regretting the fact that [he/she?] used to feel "sad when I read a soldier was killed by Boko Haram."

Discontent with the Nigerian State, Government, and the Army

Many comments suggest a lack of confidence in the Nigerian state and its leaders. Respondents expressly criticized the shootings with many showing discontent with the Nigerian state and their citizenship. The president, Muhammadu Buahri, and the Army chief, General Tukur Buratai, were repeatedly vilified for the shootings, with some carelessly calling for the country's dissolution. One comment read, "This is the highest shame of Buhari and Buratai military govt: shooting at unarmed protesters who are asking accountability to their leaders. Buhari is quite dead in conscience and a jihadist. Nigeria is finished." Another notes, " . . . and you guys are still denying Nigeria is on fire and it was lighted by Nigerian government, Nigerian soldiers, and Nigerian police." The Lagos State Governor, Babajide Sanwo-Olu, was not spared as he was repeatedly labeled a "MURDERER" in several posts.

Raised Emotions, Little Caution

Despite repeated campaigns and media literacy articles to educate the public on fact-checking, verification, and information consumption, many of the comments show little evidence of critical evaluation of the facts by members of the public, as many failed to query the authenticity of the viral videos following the shootings. Many "dismissed" the army's claim by postings misleading videos which have since been debunked by fact-checkers. The most common of these was the video of a soldier "allegedly firing at unarmed protesters at the Lekki toll gate with a high-calibre mounted machine gun" which has since been debunked in published fact-checks on the Lekki shootings (Philip, 2020; AFP Nigeria, 2020). There were very few critical voices querying the authenticity of the reports and viral videos and images. These commentators were however bullied and vilified for doubting the videos or images falsely attributed to the Lekki shootings.

Members of the public who reacted to Nigerian Army's fake news tweets on the Lekki shootings called for specific action against the Nigerian Army and the government. One user, called on Twitter to sanction the army's Twitter handle noting, "They spread fake news to cover their evil deeds." He ended with #EndSARS, #EndBadGovernanceInNigeria, and #EndPoliceBrutalityNow. Many also called out the International Criminal Court (ICC) to prosecute those involved in the shootings. Some commentators were defiant expressing their determination to continue the protest despite the shootings and imposition of curfew, with calls for good governance.

One comment read, "I rather die here than go home. I'm fighting for my generation. If I die in the process, so be it. #EndBadGovernanceInNigeria." One of the comments sums the agitation thus,

> We fight for a better Nigeria, A Nigeria where nepotism isn't our future, where the money isn't just for the people in power alone. No food, no job, no light, no road, nothing works. We are tired of suffering. They send their kids abroad to have better life cus (because) they know life here is sh*t.

CONCLUSION

Despite the seeming determination of the #EndSARS protesters, the government eventually quelled the agitations and unrest, restoring normalcy days after the shootings. The Panel of Inquiry set up to investigate the incident and other infractions against members of the public by law enforcement officers submitted its report to the state government in November 2021 (Premium Times, 2021). The report was however rejected by the Federal and Lagos State Government sighting lapses in the Panel's findings, particularly discrepancies in the number of casualties recorded (Adediran, 2021). It remains unclear how future events will turn out. However, despite later developments substantiating the accuracy of the media reports, the Nigerian Army failed to delete any of the relevant tweets. This reinforces the assumptions that it may have a goal greater than just "fighting fake news" and may be banking on the illusory truth effect to promote distrust in the mainstream media. Unfortunately, this resulted in harming public trust in the Nigerian Army as evident in our findings. Rather than achieving the illusionary truth effect, the public remained convinced of the army's involvement in the October 20, 2020 incident.

In the absence of credible information in the early days of the shootings, misinformation thrived, and with plummeting public trust ratings of government, subsequent government communication on the incident was greeted with widespread cynicism. Such actions by government institutions hinders the fight against information disorder in society. It is likely to affect public perception of the army's future attempt to debunk false information. Even when verifiably false information is debunked, people may continue to believe such to be true, enabling misinformation to thrive further.

The current government has repeatedly placed winning the fight against insurgency and other forms of insecurity as a top priority. It is unclear from our findings if the army's fake news labeling of media reports might have promoted media distrust, but it has undoubtedly harmed the army's reputation. This poses a threat to Nigeria's lingering fight against Boko Haram insurgents, and the army's purported "psychological operations" being used in their counter-insurgency campaigns to influence public's behavior and views on issues related to national security objectives (Abubakar, 2017, p.155). Security agencies, especially the Nigerian Army, must be committed to sincerity and transparency, so long as this does not compromise the security of the country. The army needs to engage appropriately in "strategic communication" in its true sense to achieve its purpose. As noted by Williams (2017, cited in Abubakar, 2017, p.142) "strategic communications are an honest attempt—always honest—to frame the way people around the world understand what is at stake."

The army thus failed in its responsibility to provide an honest frame of its involvement in the Lekki shootings, while also discrediting the mass media which should be its key partner in its strategic engagement of the public. Resorting to propagandistic tendencies may therefore result in unintended consequences as evidenced in this study. Labeling media reports on its involvement in the Lekki Shootings as fake news provides insight into possible consequences of false official narratives amid public distrust in governance. The onus thus lies on public institutions to ensure that they provide the public with accurate and timely information which they can convincingly substantiate irrespective of contrasting views making rounds in the public space. Ensuring the accurate and timely release of its public communication might enhance the army's credibility ratings over time; reducing the tendency for related misinformation to spread among the populace. The army however needs to see journalists and other opinion-shapers as partners in progress and not enemies who must be crushed. It has more to gain from partnering with the media than discrediting media operations.

REFERENCES

Abba, A. (2020). "Lekki shootings, Shitte killings and other lies peddled by Nigerian Army since 2015." *International Centre for Investigative Reporting*, November 12, 2020. https://www.icirnigeria.org/lekki-shootings-shitte-killings-and-other-lies-peddled-by-nigerian-army-since-2015/.

Abubakar, T. A. (2017). "Strategic communications, Boko Haram and counter-insurgency." *Defence Strategic Communications*, 3(Autumn): 139–170. https://openaccess.city.ac.uk/id/eprint/18576/.

Adebajo, K. (2020). "How Nigerian army is weaponising 'Fake News' to discredit journalists." *HumAngle*, July 18, 2020. https://humangle.ng/how-nigerian-army-is-weaponising-fake-news-to-discredit-journalists/.

Adebayo, T-H. (2020). "Nigerian Army faces morale crisis as 356 soldiers exit over "loss of interest." *Premium Times,* July 11, 2020. https://www.premiumtimesng

.com/news/headlines/402343-nigerian-army-faces-morale-crisis-as-356-soldiers-exit-over-loss-of-interest.html.

Adediran, I. (2020). "How hoodlums took advantage of #EndSARS, wreaked havoc in Lagos." *Premium Times*, October 25, 2020. https://www.premiumtimesng.com/news/headlines/422983-how-hoodlums-took-advantage-of-endsars-wreaked-havoc-in-lagos.html?tztc=1.

Adediran, I. (2021). "#EndSARS white paper: Lagos govt says no massacre at Lekki tollgate." *Premium Times*, December 1, 2021. https://www.premiumtimesng.com/news/headlines/498239-endsars-white-paper-lagos-govt-says-no-massacre-at-lekki-tollgate.html.

Adediran, I. and NAN. (2020). "Lekki shooting: Nigerian Army changes position again, says troops had 'blank and live ammunition'." *Premium Times*, November 21, 2020. https://www.premiumtimesng.com/news/headlines/427302-lekki-shooting-nigerian-army-changes-position-again-says-troops-had-blank-and-live-ammunition.html.

Adegoke, Y. and BBC Africa Eye. (2018). "Like. Share. Kill: Nigerian police say false information on facebook is killing people." *BBC*, November 13, 2018. https://www.bbc.co.uk/news/resources/idt-sh/nigeria_fake_news.

Adeniyi, T. (2017, January 03). "Culture of silence." *The Guardian (Online Version)*. Retrieved December 12, 2018 from https://guardian.ng/opinion/culture-of-silence/.

AFP Nigeria. (2020). "The footage predates Nigeria's protests against police brutality." *AFP Fact Check*, October 23, 2020. https://factcheck.afp.com/footage-predates-nigerias-current-protests-against-police-brutality.

BBC News. (2020). "Nigeria's Lekki shooting: What has happened so far at Lagos judicial panel." *BBC News*, November 27, 2020. https://www.bbc.com/news/world-africa-55099016.

Bird, M. (2017). "What workplace investigators can learn from psychics and ghost hunters: Overcoming cognitive bias in the search for the truth." September 18. Accessed November 27, 2020. https://rubinthomlinson.com/workplace-investigators-can-learn-psychics-ghost-hunters-overcoming-cognitive-bias-search-truth/#:~:text=The%20Illusory%20Truth%20effect,a%20%E2%80%9Cflip%2Dflopper%E2%80%9D.

Bodunrin, I. A. and Matsilele, T. (2023). "Social media and protest politics in Nigeria's# EndSARS campaign." *Handbook of Social Media in Education, Consumer Behavior and Politics: Volume 1*, 111(114): 109.

Busari. S., Nima. E., Gianluca. M., and Katie, P. (2020). "How a bloody night of bullets and brutality quashed a young protest movement." *CNN World*, November 19, 2020. https://edition.cnn.com/2020/11/18/africa/lagos-nigeria-lekki-toll-gate-feature-intl/index.html.

Egelhofer, J. L. and Lecheler, S. (2019). "Fake news as a two dimensional phenomenon: A framework and research agenda." *Annals of the International Communication Association,* 43(2): 97–116. https://doi.org/10.1080/23808985.2019.1602782.

Egelhofer, J. L., Loes, A., Jakob-Moritz, E., Sebastian, G., and Sophie, L. (2020). "From novelty to normalization? How journalists use the term "Fake News" in their reporting." *Journalism Studies*, 21(10): 1323–1461745343. https://doi.org/10.1080/1670X.2020.1667.

Funke, D. (2018). "Reporters: Stop calling everything 'fake news'." *Poynter*, August 28, 2018. https://www.poynter.org/fact-checking/2018/reporters-stop-calling-everything-fake-news/.

Hasher, L., David, G., and Thomas, T. (1977). "Frequency and the conference of referential validity." *Journal of Verbal Learning and Verbal Behavior,* 16(1): 107–112. https://doi.org/10.1016/S0022-5371(77)80012-1.

Hassan, A. and Barber, Sarah, J. (2021). "The effects of repetition frequency on the illusory truth effect." *Cognitive. Research,* 6(38). https://doi.org/10.1186/s41235-021-00301-5.

Hetherington, M. and Ladd, J. M. (2020). "Destroying trust in the media, science, and government has left America vulnerable to disaster." *Brookings*, May 1, 2020. https://www.brookings.edu/blog/fixgov/2020/05/01/destroying-trust-in-the-media-science-and-government-has-left-america-vulnerable-to-disaster/.

Iheamnachor, D. (2017). "Pupils on the run as immunization officials arrive Rivers schools for vaccination." *Vanguard*, October 17, 2017. https://www.vanguardngr.com/2017/10/pupils-run-immunization-officials-arrive-rivers-schools-vaccination/.

Iroegbu, S. (2020). "Shock as 386 soldiers fighting boko haram terrorists voluntarily disengage from Nigerian Army." *Global Sentinel*, July 10, 2020. https://globalsentinelng.com/2020/07/10/shock-as-386-soldiers-fighting-boko-haram-terrorists-voluntarily-disengage-from-nigerian-army/.

Kevin-Alerechi, E. (2020). "How true is claim that holding Nigerian flag would prevent soldiers from shooting protesters?" *Dubawa,* October 23, 2020. https://dubawa.org/how-true-is-claim-that-holding-nigerian-flag-would-prevent-soldiers-from-shooting-protesters/.

Kperogi, F. A. (2017). "Large Lies of Lying Lai Mohammed." (Blogpost). Accessed September, 20, 2021. https://www.farooqkperogi.com/2017/06/large-lies-of-lying-lai-mohammed.html.

Lazer, David M. J., Matthew Baum, Yochai Benkler, Adam J. Berinsky, Kelly M. Greenhill, Filippo Menczer, Miriam J. Metzger, Brendan Nyhan, Gordon Pennycook, David Rothschild, Michael Schudson, Steven A. Sloman, Cass R. Sunstein, Emily A. Thorson, Duncan J. Watts, and Jonathan L. Zittrain. (2018). "The science of fake news." *Science,* 359(6380 March): 1094–1096. http://science.sciencemag.org/content/359/6380/1094.

Malumfashi, S. (2020). "Nigeria's SARS: A brief history of the Special Anti-Robbery Squad." *Aljazeera English*, October 22, 2020. https://www.aljazeera.com/features/2020/10/22/sars-a-brief-history-of-a-rogue-unit.

Mangan, D. (2018). "President Trump told Lesley Stahl he bashes press 'to demean you and discredit you so ... no one will believe' negative stories about him." *CNBC,* May 22, 2018. https://www.cnbc.com/2018/05/22/trump-told-lesley-stahl-he-bashes-press-to-discredit-negative-stories.html.

Mangut, A., Angela, D., and Nada, B. (2020). "Nigeria threatens CNN with sanctions but provides no evidence Lekki toll gate investigation is inaccurate." *CNN*, November 19, 2020. https://edition.cnn.com/2020/11/19/africa/nigeria-shooting-lekki-toll-gate-investigation-response-intl/index.html.

Matsilele, T., Mpofu, S., Msimanga, M., and Tshuma, L., (2021). "Transnational hashtag protest movements and emancipatory politics in Africa: A three country study." *Global Media Journal: German Edition,* 11(2): 2–23.

Meyer, R. (2018). "Why it's okay to call it 'fake news'." *The Atlantic,* March 9, 2018. https://www.theatlantic.com/technology/archive/2018/03/why-its-okay-to-say-fake-news/555215/.

Nigerian Army (@HQNigerianArmy). (2019a). "Press release: Fake news statement credited to Brigadier General Sani Kukasheka Usman (Rtd) - 'I will not be part of . . . .'" *Tweet.* February 20. https://twitter.com/HQNigerianArmy/status/1098316932200177664.

Nigerian Army (@HQNigerianArmy). (2019b). "Information circulating on social media revealed that some mischievous elements are insinuating and peddling rumours of 'terrorists' plan to execute deadly attacks . . ." *Thread.* September 2019. https://twitter.com/HQNigerianArmy/status/1174574331055263745.

Nigerian Army (@HQNigerianArmy). (2020a). "Fake soldier." *Tweet.* October 19. https://twitter.com/HQNigerianArmy/status/1318276524227911681.

Nigerian Army (@HQNigerianArmy). (2020b). "The hooded soldier has been apprehended." *Tweet.* October 21. https://twitter.com/HQNigerianArmy/status/1318804121739251712.

Nigerian Army (@HQNigerianArmy). (2020c). "Fake News!!!" *Tweet.* October 20. https://twitter.com/HQNigerianArmy/status/1318684952146419713.

Nigerian Army (@HQNigerianArmy). (2020d). "Fake News!!!" *Tweet.* October 20. https://twitter.com/HQNigerianArmy/status/1318646006855192579.

Nwachukwu, J. O. (2021). "Lai Mohammed the biggest problem of Buhari govt – Nabena." *Daily Post,* February 17, 2021. https://dailypost.ng/2021/02/17/lai-mohammed-the-biggest-problem-of-buhari-govt-nabena/.

Philip, I. (2020). "Fact-checking social media claims on lekki shooting, others." *Aledeh News,* October 23, 2020. https://aledeh.com/2020/10/fact-checking-social-media-claims-on-lekki-shooting-others/.

Premium Times. (2021). "EndSARS: Lagos Govt releases online version of Judicial Panel of Inquiry reports." *Premium Times,* December 5, 2021. https://www.premiumtimesng.com/news/top-news/499256-endsars-lagos-govt-releases-online-version-of-judicial-panel-of-inquiry-reports.html?tztc=1.

Shepherd, M. (2020). "Repeating misinformation doesn't make it true, but does make it more likely to be believed." *Forbes.* August 17, 2020. https://www.forbes.com/sites/marshallshepherd/2020/08/17/why-repeating-false-science-information-doesnt-make-it-true/?sh=28ef3f01ffd5.

The World Bank. (n.d.). "GovData360: Public trust in politicians. World Economic Forum Global Competitiveness Index, 2017-2018." Accessed October 10, 2021. https://govdata360.worldbank.org/indicators/h5c4a5dee?country=BRA&indicator=665&viz=line_chart&years=2007,2017.

USAID. (2021). "Centre of excellence on democracy, human rights, and governance: Disinformation primer." https://pdf.usaid.gov/pdf_docs/PA00XFKF.pdf.

Chapter 4

#VoetsekANC

(Un)Civil Disobedience as Protest Action in South Africa's Twittersphere

Trust Matsilele and Blessing Makwambeni

South Africa remains a dual economy with one of the highest persistent inequality rates in the world, with a consumption expenditure Gini coefficient of 0.63 (The World Bank, 2021). The Gini coefficient measures the deviation of the distribution of income (or consumption) among individuals or households within a country from a perfectly equal distribution from a value of 0 representing absolute equality, to a value of 100 absolute representing inequality. A study by Oxfam, pointing to endemic inequalities, observed that on average, a (white, male) CEO in South Africa takes home as much in salary as 461 black women who reside in the bottom 10% of earners. In recent history, these inequalities were worsened by the global pandemic. The World Bank estimates that the South African economy contracted by 7% in 2020, as the pandemic weighed heavily on both external demand and domestic activity, and the government implemented containment measures. This severe contraction is estimated to have increased poverty by 2 million people.

Other than poverty and inequality, the southern African nation also faces challenges of unemployment. South Africa is facing an increasing trend of high unemployment, especially among the youth demographic group, which spans the age range 15–34 years and numbers over 20.6 million (34.3% of the total population). South Africa's Statistics South Africa entity measures the fluctuations on unemployment with the youth demography measuring ages 15 to 34. As of 2021, the Youth Unemployment Rate in South Africa remained unchanged, at a staggering 66.50%, from the third to the fourth quarter of 2021 (Trading Economics, 2021). A recent survey by the Statistics South Africa reported in its Quarterly Labour Force Survey (QLFS) that, for the first quarter of 2021 the number of employed persons was 15 million, which was a decrease of some 28,000. The same report saw the number of unemployed persons at 7.2 million, an increase of 8,000 compared to the fourth quarter of 2020. The number of discouraged work-seekers increased by 201,000 (6.9%). Discouraged workers are eligible and able but not actively seeking work. These figures paint a damning picture for the country and the governing party which has become subject of cyber-attacks by citizens.

The Labour Quarterly Survey also revealed the worrying trend that, in the fourth quarter of 2021, there were some 10.2 million young people aged 15–24 years, of which 32.8% was not in employment, education, or training (NEET). This was three whole percentage points higher than in the fourth quarter of 2020. In this age group, the NEET rate for males and females increased by 3.1 percentage points and 2.9 percentage points, respectively. It is no wonder then, that the youth demographic group is increasingly being disenchanted by national politics, disengaging in electoral processes, and turning to social media to express anger and outrage. This view is given weight in Bosch's (2017, 223) study, which intimates that "South African youth demonstrate low levels of civic and political participation, a lack of public interest in civic and political affairs and a lack of trust in and respect for democratic processes." The frustration with formal politics is what led political-economist Moeletsi Mbeki to predict in 2015 that the nation faced a "ticking time bomb" ready to explode (Thesnaar, 2018).

According to the Independent Electoral Commission, as of 2013, only 10% of 18- to 19-year-olds in the country are currently registered as voters. The highest percentage of 15% is in the Eastern Cape and the lowest of 4% in the Western Cape. These figures have not improved over the years. For example, in 2021 Local Government Elections, of the nearly 1.8 million 18- to 19-year-olds who were eligible to vote in that last plebiscite, 90% did not register. Similarly, less than 20% of the population aged 20 to 35 registered to vote, in contrast with over 90% of the population aged 40 (Bekker and Runciman, 2022). The decline in the turnout rate of registered voters (from 73% in 2014 to 66% in 2019) was the sharpest since the 2004 elections. It meant that, for the first time since the founding democratic elections in 1994, less than half (49%) of all eligible South Africans cast a vote in 2019 (Schulz-Herzenberg, 2020).

Poverty, unemployment, and inequality have been termed "the triple challenges" facing South Africa. However, corruption has now become the fourth. Admitting to this, the government's anti-corruption unit conceded that corruption was one of the greatest impediments to the country's growth and development. The state corruption agency noted that the Special Investigative Unit (SIU) had finalized investigations into 164 COVID-19 related contracts with a total value of R3.5 billion. Between April 2020 and June 2021 total COVID expenditure by government departments exceeded R138 billion. Of this R14.8 billion, over 10% of the money was being referred for investigation by the SIU. Commenting on corruption in the country, Justice and Correctional Services Minister Ronald Lamola noted that some of the cases that have been concluded include the R10.1 million tender that was irregularly and corruptly awarded by the Eastern Cape Department of Health to Fabkomp Pty Ltd to deliver 100 scooter ambulances. This tender has since been declared unlawful and invalid. Other successfully concluded cases include the irregular awarding of five contracts for masks worth R18.6 million (over US$ 900,000) by the Mpumalanga Department of Health and R300 million contract for the construction of 1,800 temporary shelters by the Eastern Cape Human Settlement.

This chapter argues that this macro-environment ventilated above has contributed to the increasing rage, especially in the social media sphere, against the governing African National Congress (ANC) party. Besides mismanaging unemployment among youths, which is driving the young citizens away from the polls, the same environment has further been worsened by the overt corruption taking place at the behest of the party. Research conducted by the Afrobarometer found that state institutions were widely seen as corrupt with high percentages of citizens saying that "most" or "all" officials are involved in corruption. For the police this stood at 56% of respondents, for the president's office it reached 53%, for local government councils 51% thought the officials were corrupt, while those in Parliament came in at 50% (BusinessTech, 2021). Non-governmental organizations, traditional leaders, and religious leaders are less commonly seen as corrupt.

It is this backdrop that informs social media trolling targeted at the government. As Duncombe (2019, p.409) intimates, "social media pervades our everyday life. From how we communicate with each other, to acting as key sources of news and information, social media is at the center of the very structures of our daily interactions." According to the Social Media Landscape 2021, there has been a 59% increase in respondents saying that social media is an effective public relations channel and 123% increase in respondents saying that it lowers the cost of communication. Like many countries following the lockdown, South Africa saw a growth in internet use registering 64% among South African adults, amounting to 38.19 million users representing a 1.7 million increase over the previous year.

SOCIAL MEDIA AND PROTEST CULTURES IN AFRICA

The use of social media during the Arab Spring uprisings is a key marker of the rise and early victory of social media affordances when it comes to organizing offline protests in Africa. As observed by Mare (2014), social media and other new media technologies played a key role in coordinating action by protesters as well as in the general reporting of events surrounding the historic events. In the aftermath of the Arab Spring uprisings, several studies have examined the role of social media in protests on the continent pointing to varying degrees of success and failure.

With most African countries still facing the specter of authoritarianism and shrinking space for democratic deliberation, citizens are increasingly utilizing social media for civic engagement and protest (Makwambeni and Adebayo, 2021). According to Mhiripiri and Mutsvairo (2014), a key liberating attribute of social media is its ability to forge a space that is de-institutionalized, de-professionalized. As a result, social media allows previously disenfranchised citizens with no access to mainstream public spheres to articulate their voices often in protest. In the last decade, African countries have witnessed a steep rise in hashtag movements that protest the ruling elite. Several African scholars have studied the use of social media in promoting protest cultures in Africa (Mpofu and Mare, 2020; Matsilele and Mutsvairo, 2021; Msimanga, 2022; Matsilele, 2019; Bosch, 2017; Bosch et al., 2018).

Scholars such as Matsilele et al. (2021) and Mpofu (2017) have devoted their attention to studying transnational hashtag movements in Africa. These movements include #EswatiniLivesMatter; #EndSARS; #ThisFlag; #MugabeMustGo and #ZimbabweanLivesMatter. The studies contend that the hashtags movements achieved some success by compelling some of Africa's enduring dictatorships to make piecemeal concessions of varying degrees. However, these studies call for further examination of the success of hashtag movements on the continent which is often assumed. In the South African context, Bosch and Mutsvairo (2017) have examined how the #FeesMustFall and #RhodesMustFall hashtag movements and protests gained attention as symbols of the fall of colonial systems. Both the #FeesMustFall and its corollary, the #RhodesMustFall protests changed the face of South African student politics in relation to the state when students protested for free and decolonized education. Before this, the Arab Spring associated movements, which led to the overthrow of political leaders in Tunisia and Egypt have remained one of the most popular and, arguably, successful social movements.

A significant corpus of research on social media and protest cultures has emerged from Zimbabwe where several scholars (Mpofu, 2015; Gukurume, 2017; Mpofu and Matsilele, 2020; Musarurwa, 2020; Matsilele and Ruhanya, 2021) have examined how subaltern groups have employed social media as a mobilizing tool for protest movements. These studies note #ThisFlag; #ThisGown; and #Sokwanele movements and digital groupings such as Kubatana, Sokwanele, Magamba, Baba Jukwa, and Occupy Africa Unity Square as some of the most notable digital activism groupings that have flourished in Zimbabwe in the period between the early 2000s and the period immediately after the stepping down of the country's founding and long-serving president, Robert Mugabe, in 2017. Notably, although several hashtag movements have emerged in Zimbabwe over the past decade, only a few of these movements like #ThisFlag have been able to translate their online momentum to offline protest. However, Matsilele and Ruhanya (2021), studying social media activism in Zimbabwe, note that social media has facilitated the spreading of news across the country and even beyond borders. It has also afforded citizens with the capacity to build networks and collaborate to resist authoritarian regimes.

While several studies on social media and protest cultures in Africa have been largely techno optimistic in nature and orientation, some scholars, (Matsilele and Mboti, 2022; Chitanana and Mutsvairo, 2019; Bodunrin and Matsilele, 2023) caution that while social media platforms have enabled citizens to deliberate, engage and protest on a range of issues, they have not really mounted sustained counter-hegemony to effectively challenge authoritarian regimes in Africa. Instead, recent studies are showing that authoritarian regimes in Africa have also begun harnessing social media as tools for political repression and spreading propaganda. Tshuma et al. (2022) observe that while counter-hegemonic groupings were the first to appropriate social media and other digital platforms for protest purposes and to disrupt hegemonic discourses, authoritarian regimes in countries such as Zimbabwe are now using social media to also articulate their hegemonic discourses. Consequently, social media has become a site of struggle where hegemonic and counter-hegemonic forces engage in constant struggle.

Considering this, social media poses as a double-edged sword that has been harnessed by authoritarian regimes for the purpose of surveillance (Markham, 2014) and practices of sousveillance by citizens (Newell, 2020). Mann et al. (2003, p.332) described sousveillance as "an inverted form of 'veillance' (or watching) by resituating surveillance technologies of control on individuals, offering panoptic technologies to help them observe those in authority." This bifurcated picture demonstrates that context matters when study social media inspired protests as one success in one geography cannot be easily transferable to other geographies. As Markham (2014, p.90) rightly noted:

> There is little point in denying the role that social media has played in the Arab spring and other recent protest movements such as that in Iran after the 2009 elections. On an organizational level there is ample evidence of its effectiveness showing for instance that Twitter social media users were more likely to have attended the first day of mass protests in Egypt in January 2011 than non-users.

This view, however, should be juxtaposed with other compelling views that were advanced by Malcolm Gladwell in his seminal paper on cyber protests, "Small Change," arguing that social media activism on platforms like Facebook and Twitter "succeeds not by motivating people to make a real sacrifice but by motivating them to do the things that people do when they are not motivated enough to make a real sacrifice" (2010, p.44). One of the leading skeptics when it comes to the effects of social media use in protest movements is Morozov, a researcher and intellectual from Belarus who studies the political and social implications of technology. Arguing on the effects of social media, especially on the Iranian Twitter revolution, he notes:

> By its very design, Twitter only adds to the noise: it's simply impossible to pack much context into its 140 characters (now 280). All other biases are present as well: in a country like Iran, it's mostly pro-Western, technology-friendly, and iPod-carrying young people who are the natural and most frequent users of Twitter. They are a tiny and most important, extremely untypical segment of the Iranian population (the number of Twitter users in Iran—a country of more than seventy million people—was estimated at less than twenty thousand before the protests). Whatever they do with Twitter may have little relevance to the rest of the country, including the masses marching in the streets. (Morozov, 2009, p.12)

Thus, Africa has witnessed various forms of protests as different communities seek to assert their state of belonging and have their voices heard. However, the same digital media are infiltrated by the state and the economic elite, creating a convoluted space that presents itself as both an unsafe and safe space for organization, fundraising, and contesting power (Sullivan, 2020). The duality that comes with digital media means they can be potent weapons both for oppressive hegemonies and oppressed groups of subaltern social actors. It is this bifurcation that informs both the hopes of the ordinary citizenry and the panicked response of the elite, which moves to regulate the cybersphere. Writing on this issue just over a decade ago, Mamdani (2011) intimated that the memory of Tahrir Square feeds opposition hopes and fuels government fears in many African polities.

SOCIAL MEDIA AND THE TROLLING OF POWER

Social media has become a place for discussion and debate on controversial topics and thus provides an opportunity to influence public opinion (Paavola et al., 2016; Sharra and Matsilele, 2021; Msimanga et al., 2021). Social media also offers a place where millions of young people perform and explore their identities in public. Writing on the social media platform, TikTok Herman (2020, np) argues that:

> Social media has become a prominent venue for ideological formation, political activism, and trolling . . . it has homegrown pundits, and despite its parent

company's reluctance to being involved with politics—the service does not allow political ads—it has attracted interest from campaigns. It is also a space where people can be gathered and pressed into action quickly.

As Herrick (2016, p.102) writing on the United States, and this chapter argues elsewhere, note, "domestically and internationally, social media and networked systems are being deployed to organise anti-government dissent, spread disaster information, enhance political campaigning." This possibility has given rise to a specific behavior known as trolling, which can be found in almost every discussion that includes emotionally appealing topics. Trolling has existed since the early days of the internet and was already common by 1996 (Saka, 2018). Writing on trolling, De Seta (2017, p.391) argues that

> trolling, along with a shifting constellation of related or overlapping terms (flaming, spamming, cyber-bullying, online harassment, social media abuse, and so forth), belongs to the wider domain of social media practices that resulted from the popularization of Internet access and participatory digital media platforms.

As this chapter will argue, South Africa's netizens use social media to troll the government for its failure to deliver on basic social services such as water, electricity, and employment. It is this trolling culture that birthed the #VoetsekANC hashtag.

Trolling is defined as "the activity of posting messages via a communications network that are intended to be provocative, offensive or menacing" (de la Vega and Ng, 2018, p.3701). Saka (2018, p.163) has weighed in arguing that "in internet slang, a troll 'is a person who sows discord on the internet by starting arguments or upsetting people by posting inflammatory comments.'" People who post such comments are known as trolls (Matsilele, 2019). According to Hardaker (2010), a troll's "real intention(s) is/are to cause disruption and/or trigger or exacerbate conflict for the purpose of their own amusement." For this study, we deploy de la Vega and Ng (2018) definition that confines trolling to online posting of messages that are meant to be provocative.

METHODOLOGICAL CONSIDERATION

This qualitative study employs content analysis design to understand the nature, typology, and language of cyber protest targeted at the governing ANC. Qualitative research "uses a naturalistic approach that seeks to understand a phenomenon in context-specific settings, such as real-world setting [where] the researcher does not attempt to manipulate the phenomenon of interest" (Patton, 2002, p.39). Content analysis is defined as a family of systematic, rule-guided techniques used to analyze the informational contents of textual data (Mayring, 2000). Weighing in this, (Cole, 1988) asserted that content analysis is a method of analysing written, verbal, or visual communication messages. As Elo and Kyngäs (2008, p.108–109) note, this method was first used for analysing hymns, newspaper and magazine articles, advertisements, and political speeches in the nineteenth century. In qualitative content analysis, as Forman and Damschroder (2007, p.40) argue, "data are categorized using categories that are generated, at least in part, inductively (i.e., derived from the data), and in most cases applied to the data through close reading." As Weber (1990) observed, the specific type of content analysis approach chosen by a researcher varies with the theoretical and substantive interests of the researcher and the problem being studied. For this study, the researchers' main interest was understanding the nature, typology, and character of cyber protest from South Africa's netizens that is directed at the governing ANC. The researchers conducted a manual search for tweets using #VoetsekANC as keyword. The term *voetsek* in Southern Africa is an offensive, informal expression, referring to outright dismissal or rejection. As the Collins Dictionary (2022) explains, etymologically the term is Afrikaans, developed from the earlier Dutch *voort se ek*, meaning "forward." It is commonly directed at animals, especially domesticated dogs. Joubert and Wasserman (2020, p.11) note that "voetsek," means "get lost!" or "scram!". The use of the term is therefore an expression of outrage and is only reserved for extreme situations. This hashtag campaign sees much activity in the virtual sphere on Fridays, weekends, and public holidays as netizens will have more time to engage in political developments.

DIGITAL PUBLIC SPHERE AND THE CARNIVAL

The study makes use of the digital public sphere and Bakhtin's concept of the Carnivalesque to understand the nature, typology, and language of cyber protest targeted at the governing ANC in South Africa. The digital public sphere draws from Habermas's seminal work on the public sphere. As Schäfer (2015, p.323) notes,

> most studies have envisioned the digital public sphere along the lines of deliberative theory, that is as the heir to the Greek ideal of the Agora, to New England-style colonial-era town hall meetings, Parisian café culture or Viennese salon discussions of previous centuries.

In this view, the public sphere is seen as a communicative space in which matters of common relevance are discussed by those affected and interested in a way that fulfills the imaginations of a rational space accommodating statements supported by an appropriate reasoning whose validity can then be checked by others. Building on Mpofu (2013), this study endeavors to adapt Habermasian public sphere theory to internet studies and show how new media is used to subvert elite public spheres in South Africa. According to Ndlela (2010) and Makwambeni and Adebayo (2021), new digital technologies have ushered in an alternate digital public sphere or a counter public sphere that creates new spaces characterized by interactivity where the subaltern can forge counter hegemonic discourses in society.

The study supplements the digital public sphere with Bakhtin's (1941) concept of the carnivalesque. The concept is derived from notions of the medieval carnival as a place in which people are not distinguished as either performers or viewers, but rather as active and equal participants. The carnival allows participants to openly show their true selves without restriction or bias. Rules, inhibitions, and regulations that determine the course of everyday life are suspended. It is important to note that just like on social media, the use of language in the carnival is playful, imaginative, and filled with mockery. Speech patterns and discourses that are largely excluded from official intercourse can freely accumulate in the carnival. Díaz-Cintas argues (2018) that the carnivalesque is structured around three main aspects: participants/collective, individual freedom, and breakdown of hegemony. Makwambeni (2017) has used Bakhtin's concept of the carnival to understand how Zimbabwean youths utilize vulgarity laced dancehall music as a tool of protest, opposition, and resistance. We argue in this chapter that like the carnival, on social media, "Kings" are dethroned and the morality that is dictated by the ruling power bloc in society is subverted (Bakhtin, 1984). Thus, unlike in mainstream public spheres where it is shunned, vulgarity is normalized in the carnival and on social media. We argue in this study that just like in the carnival, social media is a lobotomy that offers the subaltern temporary respite from normal relations of domination and inequality in South Africa.

DISCUSSION

Patterns of Youth and Social Media Appropriation in South Africa

Our findings confirm that South Africa has been seeing a steady rise on social media uptake. The biggest demographic group that has been appropriating social media for communicative purposes is the youth dividend. Social media uptake among youths in South Africa is in line with other findings globally. For example, the findings of a study conducted by Harvard's Berkman Klein Center for Internet and Society showed that youths felt obligated to use Facebook and other emerging social media platforms (Shava and Chinyamurindi, 2018). In South Africa, youths between the ages of 13–35 constitute almost 65% of the total number of social media users. It is this group, this chapter contends, that has largely appropriated social media for protest purposes. This is the same group experiencing high levels of unemployed as already illustrated earlier in this chapter. Writing on youths, social media, and political participation in South Africa, Bosch (2013, p.121) intimated that

> while the youth are not overtly politically active in the mainstream sense of participation in political organizations; nor do we see a pattern of participation in traditional forms of citizenship through Facebook and social media interaction, in South Africa we see youth engagement and disengagement occurring simultaneously.

This engagement and disengagement, in part, confirms the lack of trust in political processes that some academics argue is contributing to voter apathy (Chauke, 2020; Oyedemi and Mahlatji, 2016; Potgieter and Lutz, 2014).

The usage is determined by the geographical location of the youth. As Shava and Chinyamurindi (2018, p.2) observe, "rural South African youth may be utilising social media platforms mainly for socialising purposes, leading to some becoming addicted and others feeling obligated to participate in Facebook activities." While this study does not make attempts to understand the profiles of social media users among youths, the researcher argues that a close reading of the tweets and publicly accessible user profile anecdotally points to a youth demographic group that is increasingly turning to social media to protest the worsening conditions in the country. We argue in this study, that youths' engagement through the hashtag #VoetsekANC in South Africa, manifests key characteristics of both a digital public sphere and a carnivalesque. The findings of the study show that young people in South Africa are appropriating social media to contest hegemonic narratives on key national questions such as corruption, immigration, and the lockdown. Consonant with the carnival, young people are subverting morality as dictated by the ruling power bloc by normalizing vulgar language to vent their disquiet (see Bakhtin, 1984).

Rethinking the Role of Insults and Trolling in the Cybersphere

Few studies have examined the role of insults and trolling in the cybersphere and their contribution to democratic discourse. Matsilele's (2019) doctoral study, tries to understand the role insults and trolling place in the cybersphere, especially in relation to power. Matsilele (2019, 98), and here cited extensively, argues that for countries like Zimbabwe (we argue South Africa falls within this categorization):

> There is a place for extreme trolling located in the tradition of *zvituko* and *kunemera* where children and adults insult each other inside and outside the bounds of decency. Most *zvituko* focus on the anatomy, while other degrade the person's kin, clothes, home, and belongings. Every (extremely) angry Zimbabwean knows and resorts to certain types of these insults. This extreme trolling functions to provoke *extremely*, sometimes to fisticuffs or even blood feuds. A loose analogy can be drawn with the "Yo mama" insults. Those with a weak constitution often wilt in the face of such attacks. Others fight and insult back.

Similarly, Makwambeni's (2017) study on Zimdancehall music as a site of resistance contends that the vulgarity and immorality that permeates the emergent music genre should not detract scholars from eliciting youths' aspirations and concerns in Zimbabwe. This chapter argues that the same way Zimbabweans would use extreme expletives to protest domination (see Matsilele, 2019; Makwambeni, 2017) is the same way the term "voetsek" and other attendant expletives should be understood within the South African context. In this light, the use of expletives and vulgarity on social media in South Africa is consistent with Baktin's notion of the carnivalesque as a space where language is used imaginatively by the subaltern to protest and contest different forms of domination.

Contesting Corruption through the Twittersphere

Our findings show that social media like Bakhtin's carnival (1984) is being appropriated by citizens to protest the excesses of the ruling ANC government in South Africa. The ANC has been accused of corruption since the turn of the country from apartheid to the democratic dispensation. However, the corrupt activities allegedly intensified during the period of former president Jacob Zuma's rule. Following the COVID-19 pandemic, several high-ranking ANC and government officials were implicated in corruption related to personal protection equipment (PPE). The reported corruption gained a lot of attention in the mainstream and social media sphere forcing the governing ANC to operationalize the "step-aside" rule for party officials' implication and charged for corrupt activities and other serious crimes. In one tweet, a user posts an image of hyenas hunting for prey to illustrate the extractionist approach of the governing party when it comes to state coffers. The image demonstrates the backlash the ANC has faced for moral collapse as the party is accused of having used the crises for personal gain. The use of hyena is meant to project the ANC as a heartless party and inherently corrupt. Such characterization is consistent with the carnivalesque where kings were momentarily "dethroned" and criticized by ordinary citizens. This form of protest can only happen on social media, which like the carnival provided a sacred space where immorality and character assassination would take place without reprisals. Social media allows users to manufacture, edit, and delete identities (Matsilele et al., 2021) unlike in the offline world.

PROTESTING MANAGEMENT OF COVID-19 FUNDS AND THE LOCKDOWN

Besides depicting the tenets of the carnival, South Africans engagement through the hashtag "Voetsek ANC," reflects the role that Twitter plays as an alternative public sphere where citizens can interact and engage in counter-hegemony (see Ndlela, 2010; Makwambeni and Adebayo, 2021). In the context of COVID-19, some of the major challenges South Africa faced include corruption by political elites linked to the ANC; growing unemployment; low economic growth and failure of the government to mitigate against the pandemic that has led many to express outrage. Social media as an alternative public sphere provides citizens with space to engage with these issues. However, just like in Bakhtin's carnival (1984), social media as an alternative public sphere does not mirror the morality and ethics that characterize mainstream public spheres. Conversely, it allows for expression that would normally be excluded or considered as prosecutable in the offline world. The image above is a case in point, a netizen is using two images juxtaposed to each other to register discontentment with COVID-19-related mitigation actions but also using the "kick" to illustrate deserving punishment the ANC should be meted with for failing to protect lives and livelihoods.

Notably, some of the accounts that tweet and retweet #VoetsekANC look like parodies and do not demonstrate much activity rendering them as suspicious ghost accounts. For example, the Twitter account, @CaptainPeeKay, has 210 followers and 204 accounts. A close reading of tweets this account generates demonstrates affinity toward outrage, for example, insinuation of support for the al-Qaeda network's attacks on the United States in 2001. The account also promotes anti-mask mandate during the COVID-19 lockdown levels, campaigned against looting of COVID-19 funds and mocked the Black Lives Movement of the United States. In the tweet above, the account seems to be using Chris Hani to shame South African politicians who have turned into corrupt political elites at the expense of the masses. It is plausible to argue that one form of trolling tries to draw parallels between the pre-1994 ANC to the post-1994 ANC which are complete opposites. The post-1994 ANC is regarded as a vehicle for primitive accumulation by political elites who have departed from values advanced by deified liberation heroes in the mold of Chris Hani. In the main, what these findings show is that South African citizens are appropriating social media as an alternative space to contest counter-hegemonic discourses that are treated as "commonsensical" by mainstream media (see Makwambeni, 2017). For example, narratives that question the wearing of masks and show partiality for al-Quaeda would not ordinarily find coverage in mainstream media.

Questioning Illegal Immigration in South Africa

Twitter as a digital public sphere allows South Africans to engage on key challenges in the country. An analysis of the #VoetsekANC hashtag campaign shows that the twittersphere is a communicative space in which matters of common relevance are discussed by those affected (see Ndhlela, 2010). One of the challenges deliberated on through the #VoetsekANC hashtag is the influx of illegal immigrants. With increasing unemployment levels in South Africa, now at 35%, there has been growing anti-foreigners' sentiments that saw the rise of movements such as Operation Dudula and #PutSouthAfricaFirst. An analysis of these two movements demonstrates a close overlap as they share interests—ensuring that South Africa deals with the issue of illegal immigrants. While it is not clear how the illegals are identified, isolated, and punished for being illegal, the creation of foreigners as bogeymen is gaining traction among poor communities. The tweet above tries to show that foreigners have who have "invaded" South Africa are a present danger and should be dealt with. This language is not isolated from official forms of communication. For example, speaking on illegal immigrants, the Home Affairs Minister, Aron Motsoaledi, recently described illegal immigrants as the 'rascals' who ran away from their countries (AmaShabalala, 2022). The above tweet seems to be addressing immigrants from the Apostolic sect who gather to pray in the open. The undertones of the tweet are that these congregants may be attacked. The tweet above read in conjunction with the one below shows the "present danger" presented by illegal immigrants: if they are not invading the country and filling up spaces, they are committing cable theft among other crimes. It is the ANC's policies on immigration that netizens have led to the influx of illegal immigrants. Notably, while these findings illustrate the public spherical role of twitter, they also indicate the need to embrace this role with caution due to the rampant disinformation, illustrated above, that characterize the platform.

PROTESTING SERVICE DELIVERY ON TWITTER

The data analyzed in the study confirms previous studies (Mpofu and Mare, 2020; Matsilele and Mutsvairo, 2021; Matsilele, 2019; Bosch, 2017;

Makwambeni and Adebayo, 2021; Bodunrin and Matsilele, 2023) that have shown that new media is providing citizens with alternative space to engage as well as protest the power bloc in society. The hashtag #VoetsekANC provides space for concerned South Africans to protest the governing ANC party that has been struggling to provide basic services. The country has been facing incessant challenges of reliable electricity supply. For example, South Africa's precarious electricity supply, for which Eskom is almost entirely responsible, presents a national crisis (Kenny et al., 2015). As the tweet below illustrates, Eskom's load-shedding challenges has seen the netizens expressing outrage at the governing party. For example, the tweet below is expressing outrage that Eskom could not keep the lights on during the Easter weekend. Notably, our findings show that social media, like Bakhtin's carnivalesque (1984), now allows South African citizens to directly mock and protest the power block on a wide range of issues that affect them. Paavola et al., (2016) as well as Sharra and Matsilele (2021) posit that this engagement and rage on social media fundamentally influences public opinion thereby deepening democracy.

CONCLUSION

This study sought to understand the nature, tone, language, and character of cyber trolling targeted South Africa's governing party, the ANC through the lenses of the hashtag campaign #VoetsekANC. A theoretical framework consisting of the digital public sphere and Bhakhtin's Canivarlesque was used as a lens to understand how the Twittersphere contributes to democracy. Building on the work of Mpofu and Matsilele (2020), the study focusing on South Africa found that hashtag trends such as #VoetsekANC provide citizens with an alternative public sphere to protest and reflect on perceived failures of the governing party. The findings show that South African citizens use Twitter as a space to protest issues such as immigration, management of COVID-19, corruption, and service delivery. Citizens engagement on twitter simulates Bhakhtin's conceptualization of the carnival where morality and hierarchy are overthrown. Our findings show that citizens employ a wide range of language tropes that include mockery, vulgarity, and a tone of rage to communicate their deep feelings of betrayal by the governing ANC party. Besides confirming the findings of previous studies that contend that social media is an alternative public sphere that provides citizens with space to protest, the study also shows the value of the Carnivalesque in conceptualizing the role that rage and vulgarity on social media play in expanding democracy and democratic discourse.

REFERENCES

AmaShabalala. M. (2022). *I will resign once all foreign 'rascals' are locked up and keys thrown away: Aaron Motsoaledi.* Accessed 22 April 2022. https://www.timeslive.co.za/politics/2022-04-19-i-will-resign-once-all-foreign-rascals-are-locked-up-and-keys-thrown-away-aaron-motsoaledi/.

Ansong, E. D., Takyi, T., Damoah, D., Ampomah, E. A. and Larkotey, W. (2013). Internet trolling in Ghana. *International Journal of Emerging Science and Engineering*, 2(1): 42–43.

Bekker, M. and Runciman, C. (2022). *The youth vote in the 2021 Local Government Elections within five metropolitan municipalities.* Konrad Adenauer Stiftung. Accessed 17 April 2022. https://www.kas.de/en/web/suedafrika/single-title/-/content/the-youth-vote-in-the-2021-local-government-elections-within-five-metropolitan-municipalities-1.

Bakhtin, M. (1941). *Rabelais and his world.* Translated by Héléne Iswolsky (1984).

Bakhtin, M. M. and Bakhtin, M. (1984). *Rabelais and his world (Vol. 341).* Indiana University Press.

Bodunrin, I. A. and Matsilele, T. (2023). Social media and protest politics in Nigeria's# EndSARS campaign. *Handbook of Social Media in Education, Consumer Behavior and Politics: Volume 1*, 111(114), 109.

Bosch, T. (2013). Youth, facebook and politics in South Africa. *Journal of African Media Studies*, 5(2), 119–130.

Bosch, T. (2017). Twitter activism and youth in South Africa: The case of# RhodesMustFall. *Information, Communication & Society*, 20(2), 221–232.

Bosch, T., Wasserman, H. and Chuma, W. (2018). South African activists' use of nanomedia and digital media in democratization conflicts. *International Journal of Communication,* 12, 18.

BusinessTech. (2021). South Africans think corruption is getting worse under Ramaphosa. Accessed 17 April 2022. https://businesstech.co.za/news/trending/521918/south-africans-think-corruption-is-getting-worse-under-ramaphosa/.

Chauke, T. A. (2020). Youth apathy in an electoral democracy: A critical discourse on civil participation in South Africa. *African Journal of Gender, Society & Development*, 9(3), 35.

Cole, F. L. (1988). Content analysis: Process and application. *Clinical Nurse Specialist*, 2(1), 53–57.

Collins Dictionary. (2022). Voetsek. Accessed 22 April 2022. https://www.collinsdictionary.com/dictionary/english/voetsek.

de la Vega, L. G. M. and Ng, V. (2018). Modeling trolling in social media conversations. In *Proceedings of the Eleventh International Conference on Language Resources and Evaluation (LREC 2018).*

De Seta, G. (2017). Trolling, and other problematic social media practices. *The SAGE handbook of social media. Thousand Oaks, CA: SAGE*, 390–411.

Díaz-Cintas, J. (2018). 'Subtitling's a carnival': New practices in cyberspace. *Jostrans: The Journal of Specialised Translation*, (30), 127–149.

Duncombe, C. (2019). The politics of Twitter: Emotions and the power of social media. *International Political Sociology*, 13(4), 409–429.

Elo, S. and Kyngäs, H. (2008). The qualitative content analysis process. *Journal of Advanced Nursing*, 62(1), 107–115.

Forman, J. and Damschroder, L. (2007). Qualitative content analysis. In Jacoby, L. and Simminof, L. (Eds.), *Empirical methods for bioethics: A primer*. Emerald Group Publishing Limited.

Gladwell, M. (2010). Small change. *The New Yorker*, 4(2010), 42–49.

Hardaker, C. (2010). Trolling in asynchronous computermediated communication: From user discussions to academic definitions. *Journal of Politeness Research*, 6(2), 215–242.

Herrman, J. (2020). TikTok is shaping politics. But how. *New York Times*. Accessed 22 April 2022. https://www.nytimes.com/2020/06/28/style/tiktok-teen-politics-gen-z.html.

Herrick, D. (2016, May). The social side of 'cyber power'? Social media and cyber operations. In *2016 8th International Conference on Cyber Conflict (CyCon)* (pp. 99–111). IEEE.

Joubert, M. and Wasserman, H. (2020). Spikey blobs with evil grins: Understanding portrayals of the coronavirus in South African newspaper cartoons in relation to the public communication of science. *Journal of Science Communication*, 19(7), A08.

Kenny, A., Cronje, F., Jeffery, A., Moloi, L., Dimant, T., Kane-Berman, J., and Zwane, S. (2015). The rise and fall of Eskom—and how to fix it now. *Policy Bulletin*, 2(18), 1–22.

Kidd, D. and McIntosh, K. (2016). Social media and social movements. *Sociology Compass*, 10(9), 785–794.

Lamola, R. (2021). Special investigations unit annual report 2020/2021. Accessed 17 April 2022. https://www.siu.org.za/wp-content/uploads/2021/11/SIU_Annual_Report_2020-2021.pdf.

Mare, A. (2014). Social media: The new protest drums in Southern Africa? In *Social Media in Politics* (pp. 315–335). Springer, Cham.

Markham, T. (2014). Social media, protest cultures and political subjectivities of the Arab spring. *Media, Culture & Society*, 36(1), 89–104.

Matsilele, T. (2019). *Social media dissidence in Zimbabwe*. University of Johannesburg (South Africa).

Matsilele, T. and Mutsvairo, B. (2021). Social media as a sphere of political disruption. In *Decolonising Political Communication in Africa* (pp. 179–190). Routledge.

Matsilele, T. and Ruhanya, P. (2021). Social media dissidence and activist resistance in Zimbabwe. *Media, Culture & Society*, 43(2), 381–394.

Mayring, P. (2000). Qualitative content analysis in forum qualitative research. In *Sozialforschung Forum Qualitative (Vol. 1, No. 2)*. https://doi.org/10.17169/fqs-1.2.1089

Morozov, E. (2009). Iran: Downside to the" Twitter revolution". *Dissent*, 56(4), 10–14.

Mpofu, S. (2013). Social media and the politics of ethnicity in Zimbabwe. *Ecquid Novi: African Journalism Studies*, 34(1), 115–122.

Mpofu, S. (2013). The power of citizen journalism in Zimbabwe. *International Migration*, 38(5), 41–57.

Mpofu, S. and Mare, A. (2020). # ThisFlag: Social media and cyber-protests in Zimbabwe. In *Social Media and Elections in Africa, Volume 2* (pp. 153–173). Palgrave Macmillan, Cham.

Mpofu, S. and Matsilele, T. (2020). Social media and the concept of dissidence in Zimbabwean politics. In Ndlovu-Gatsheni, S. and Ruhanya, P. (Eds.), *The History and Political Transition of Zimbabwe: From Mugabe to Mnangagwa*, (pp. 221–243). London: Palgrave.

Msimanga, M. J., Ncube, G., and Mkwananzi, P. (2021). Political satire and the mediation of the Zimbabwean crisis in the Era of the "New dispensation": The case of MAGAMBA TV. In Mpofu, S (Ed.), The politics of laughter in the social media age: Perspectives from the Global South (pp. 43–56). Palgrave MacMillan: New York.

Msimanga, M. J. (2022). Satire and the discursive construction of national identity in Zimbabwe: The case of Magamba and Bustop TV. Unpublished Doctoral Dissertation. University of Johannesburg.

Ndlela, N. M. (2010). Alternative media and the public sphere in Zimbabwe. In Howley, I.K. (Ed.), *Understanding Community Media*, (pp. 87–95). Thousand Oaks, CA: Sage Publications.

Ndlovu, M., Tshuma, L., and Mpofu, S (Eds). (2023). *Remembering mass atrocities: Perspectives on memory struggles and cultural representations in Africa*. Springer International Publishing.

Newell, B. (2020). Introduction: the state of sousveillance. *Surveillance & Society*, 18(2), 257–261.

Oyedemi, T. and Mahlatji, D. (2016). The 'born-free' non-voting youth: A study of voter apathy among a selected cohort of South African youth. *Politikon*, 43(3), 311–323.

Paavola, J., H, T., Jalonen, H., Sartonen, M., and Huhtinen, A. M. (2016). Understanding the trolling phenomenon: The automated detection of bots and cyborgs in the social media. *Journal of Information Warfare*, 15(4), 100–111.

Pew Research Center. (2012). Teens, social media and privacy. Accessed 22 April 2022, from http://www.pewinternet.org/files/2013/05/PIP_TeensSocialMediaand Privacy PDF.pdf.

Potgieter, E. and Lutz, B. F. (2014). South African youth: Political-LY Apathetic?. *Election Update: South Africa*, 2014, 262–273.

Saka, E. (2018). Social media in Turkey as a space for political battles: AKTrolls and other politically motivated trolling. *Middle East Critique*, 27(2), 161–177.

SA SOCIAL MEDIA LANDSCAPE. (2021). Social Migration. Accessed 17 April 2022. https://website.ornico.co.za/wp-content/uploads/2021/06/The-SA-Social-Media-Landscape-Report-2021.pdf.

Schäfer, M. S. (2015). Digital public sphere. *The International Encyclopedia of Political Communication*, 15, 1–7.

Shava, H. and Chinyamurindi, W. T. (2018). Determinants of social media usage among a sample of rural South African youth. *South African Journal of Information Management*, 20(1), 1–8.

Schulz-Herzenberg, C. (2020). The South African non-voter: An analysis. *Konrad Adenauer Stiftung*. Accessed 17 April 2022. https://www.kas.de/documents/261596/10543300/The+South+African+non-voter+-+An+analysis.pdf/acc19fbd-bd6d-9190-f026-8d311078b670?version=1.0&t=1608.

Sharra, A. and Matsilele, T. (2021). This is a laughing matter: Social media as a sphere of trolling power in Malawi and Zimbabwe. In *The politics of laughter in the social media age* (pp. 113–134). Palgrave Macmillan, Cham.

Statista.com. (2021). Distribution of social media users in South Africa as of January 2021, by age group and gender. Accessed 18 April 2022. https://www.statista.com/statistics/1100988/age-distribution-of-social-media-users-south-africa/#:~:text=As%20of%20January%202021%2C%20it,media%20audiences%20in%20South%20Africa.

Statista.com. (2021). Most used social media platforms in South Africa as of the 3rd quarter of 2021. Accessed 18 April 2022. https://www.statista.com/statistics/1189958/penetration-rate-of-social-media-in-soutafrica/#:~:text=Penetration%20rate%20of%20social%20media%20in%20South%20Africa%202021&text=As%20of%20the%20third%20quarter,percent%20and%2073%20percent%2C%20respectively.

Statistics South Africa. (2022). Quarterly labour force survey. *Quarter,* 4, 2021. Accessed 17 April 2022. http://www.statssa.gov.za/publications/P0211/P02114thQuarter2021.pdf.

Thesnaar, C. (2018). Alternative and innovative approaches to reconciliation: A South African perspective. In *Alternative approaches in conflict resolution* (pp. 125–136). Palgrave Macmillan, Cham.

The World Bank report. (2021). South Africa economic update: South Africa's labor market can benefit from young entrepreneurs, self-Employment. Accessed 22 April 2022. https://www.worldbank.org/en/country/southafrica/publication/south-africa-economic-update-south-africa-s-labor-market-can-benefit-from-young-entrepreneurs-self-employment.

Tshuma, L. A. (2023). Heir to the throne: Photography and the rise to presidency by politicians in Zimbabwe and South Africa. *Visual Studies*, 1–10.

Tshuma, B. B., Tshuma, L. A., and Ndlovu, N. (2021). Humour, politics and Mnangagwa's presidency: An analysis of readers' comments in online news websites. In Mpofu, S. (Ed), *The politics of laughter in the social media age: Perspectives from the Global South*, (pp. 93–111). Springer International Publishing, Cham.

Weber, R. P. (1990). *Basic content analysis (No. 49)*. Sage.

Chapter 5

#EndSARS

The Role of Social Media Influencers in Raising Awareness of Police Brutality in Nigeria

Temitope Opeyemi Falade and Lungile Tshuma

In Nigeria, social media is an essential tool for propagating various forms of national discourse. The medium provides the society with an avenue for exercising their right to freedom of speech and association (Olaniyan and Akpojivi, 2020). This can also be linked to the impact of viral content shared on social media, which not only attracts the attention of ordinary users, but also makes an impact on national and global leaders (Bebić and Volarevic, 2018). #EndSARS is a social media movement that began in 2017 to address problems associated with police brutality in Nigeria (Bodunrin and Matsilele, 2023). The use of the hashtag peaked during the nationwide lockdown caused by the COVID-19 pandemic in the year 2020. The brutal treatment of young people by members of SARS during the COVID-19 lockdown ensured that people reported their experiences via social media, but also that they tagged influential people, including celebrities and government officials: in this way, their posts received greater attention. Therefore, #EndSARS social media movement was a tool used by young Nigerians for raising awareness of the problem of police brutality and the behavior of a special division of the Nigerian Police force called the Special Anti-Robbery Squad (popularly known as SARS). The protest went viral and the Inspector General of police responded by announcing reforms to the unit and with advice on how citizens could relate to members of the force (Okakwu, 2017). Despite these measures announced by the Inspector General, cases of police brutality against innocent citizens did not end. The #EndSARS movement circulated the belief that members of the SARS profiled young males in Nigeria as Internet fraudsters (Yahoo boys), simply based on their appearance, especially if they engaged in any of the following; wearing dreadlocks, driving flashy cars, and even owning a laptop or a high-end phone (Mordi, 2020). Although the #EndSARS social media protest began in the year 2017 (Malefakis, 2021), its impact did not achieve significance until the pandemic year 2020, when the hashtag gained a lot of traction leading to mass protests in different parts of Nigeria. This helped secure the attention of influential people in Nigerian society, including thought leaders, policymakers, and celebrities. In one such instance, a viral video was shared on Twitter that showed a young man who had been shot by members of the Nigerian Police being left for dead, while a police officer drove his car to an unknown destination in Enugu State. The video sparked a lot of reactions from social media influencers and celebrities. In a bid to show solidarity to affected persons on social media, some Nigerian celebrities clamored to take the campaign offline and encouraged Nigerian youths to join the protest in specified locations in different cities across the country. The involvement of social media influencers changed the attitude of the government and the Nigerian Police. This chapter will focus on how social media influencers contributed to raising awareness of police brutality using the #EndSARS hashtag. Earlier studies have shown that through consistency in the messages posted by social media influencers on issues raised by victims of police brutality, and through the direct engagement of social media influencers with relevant authorities, the level of awareness of police brutality rose significantly. The aim of this chapter is to analyze the role played by social media influencers in mediating the protests during the #EndSARS movement.

A REVIEW OF SOCIAL MEDIA AND PROTEST CULTURES

In recent times, social media has become a very powerful tool globally. It has been useful for raising awareness on social issues and promoting accountability from public office holders. The movements that take place in different parts of the world also lead to protests on social media platforms (Tshuma et al., 2022; Poell and Dijck, 2018). Likewise, social movements initiated on social media platforms, also lead to protests that take place in the real world. Movements such as the Arab Spring (Smidi and Shahin, 2017) and Occupy movements relied heavily on social media for their propagation (Kavada, 2015). The effects of globalization have seen to the replication of social media movements and social change in many nations of the world. For instance, the Umbrella Movement in Hong Kong showed that despite the use of conventional media, alongside social media, and alternative media, social media and alternative media platforms, like online forums and citizen journalism, played more crucial roles in influencing public opinion and organizing demonstrators than the use of traditional media (Lin, 2016). This is also buttressed by the findings of (Jurgenson, 2012), which presents an argument that the widespread use of cellphones and social media changed how we view the world and has blurred the boundaries seen between virtual and real worlds. A similar study by (Eltantawy and Wiest, 2011) showed how social media impacted the Arab Spring, especially the Egyptian Revolution. The authors contend that social media significantly contributed to the mobilization of demonstrators and the development of a feeling of collective identity and purpose. They do, however, also opine that the standard theory of resource mobilization would not fully account for the dynamics of the Arab Spring, given that social media enabled novel types of decentralized and networked mobilization outside of conventional organizational structures. It is therefore imperative to put into consideration the distinctive traits of social media and how social media influencers raise awareness of social causes.

In Africa, the Arab Spring is one of the popular and, arguably, successful protest movements in the continent. However, debates have emerged on the nature of these movements in Africa as they have sometimes not been successful and have led to authoritarian regimes becoming aggressive and more oppressive (see Ndlovu et al., 2023; Tshuma et al., 2022; Matsilele et al., 2022). Scholars agree that social media has revolutionized political communication with social media playing a crucial role in exposing and exerting pressure on regimes, especially on abuse of human rights (Moyo, 2011; Mutsvairo, 2016; Wasserman, 2011). In Zimbabwe, during the late Robert Mugabe's reign, social and political movement groups #ThisFlag and #Tajamuka mobilized online dissidents particularly on Facebook to protest the brutality that they were facing at the hands of Mugabe (Mpofu, 2017). In South Africa, #FeesMustFall, students used social media to call for free action, and for the decolonization of the education system (Endong, 2019). Thus, the #FeesMustFall and #RhodesMustFall were useful as they symbolized the falling of colonial systems (see Mpofu, 2017, p.353). Of important to note and related to this study is what Davis (2013) and others have referred to as "hashtag politics," where networked communities of strangers come together to form issue publics, defined as groups of people who have a heightened interest in a particular issue. More so, Highfield and Leaver (2015, p.9) noted that the "use of the hash (or sometimes called the pound or number sign) character before certain terms indicated a desire to group tweets socially." As was the case with Nigeria, contemporary protest that begins online with mass participation of social media users (including celebrities) and later morphs into a large on-the-ground countrywide protest (Abiodun et al., 2020). In this chapter we thus look at the use of social media by different influencers to champion and rally people, both locally, and internally to support the fight against abuse of human rights. In their seminal study on hashtag movement, Matsilele et al. (2020) indicated hashtags, due to the nature of social media, are transnational, and result in different players, especially, influencers joining in solidarity with users whom some are their followers in other countries.

COVID-19 LOCKDOWN AND #ENDSARS SOCIAL MEDIA MOVEMENT

The use of the #EndSARS hashtag for raising awareness of police brutality peaked during the 2020 nationwide lockdown caused by the COVID-19 Pandemic. The harsh treatment of young people by members of SARS during this period prompted the victims to report their experiences via social media and also tag influential people, including celebrities and government officials. In one such instance, a viral video was shared on Twitter which alleged that a young man was shot dead by a police officer in Ughelli, Delta State (Iwuoha and Aniche, 2021). The video sparked many reactions from social media influencers and celebrities and the #EndSARS hashtag immediately topped the global trends on Twitter (Al Jazeera and News Agencies, 2020)

In a bid to show solidarity to affected persons on social media, some Nigerian celebrities clamored to take the movement offline and encouraged youths to join the protest in specified locations in different cities across the country such as Lagos, Abuja, Port Harcourt, Warri, Asaba, Benin City, Ibadan, Akure, Abeokuta, Osogbo, Jos, Kano, and Kaduna. The involvement of social media influencers changed the reaction of the government and the Nigerian Police force to the protest. Aina et.al. (2019) have shown that through social media, influencers contribute significantly to the raising of awareness of social issues. Flavián and Barta (2022), in their study on social media influencer typology, recognized categories of users based on their number of followers and the type of contact influencers have with their followers. However, issues of factors influencing persuasiveness were not fully developed. This study seeks to determine how different categories of social media influencers contribute to persuaviness and inpact social movement. Through content analysis, this study identifies four typologies of social media influencers that were active when the usage of the #EndSARS hashtag peaked. These typologies are based on the number of followers and level of authority of the influencers. Level of authority was determined based on the number of followers, rate of retweets, number of accounts followed, social authority score of followers, age of the account, and social engagement (Bray, 2013).

SOCIAL MEDIA INFLUENCERS AND POLITICAL PROTESTS

Research has proven that social media play an important role in promoting social movements. It is in fact the most popular means for propagating online activism (DigiActive, 2009). Social media promotes online activism which in turn leads to offline activism through the active promotion of messages that will trigger action on the part of the target audience (Harlow, 2011). New forms of activism have also been promoted through social media. In Nigeria, terrorist organizations use social media to communicate their actions and encourage followership (Adekalu et al., 2015). Civil society groups have used social media for positive causes that have brought about the needed societal changes in Nigeria (Hari, 2014). Countries such as Guatemala have also benefited from social media movements which moved offline in protest for the murder of prominent lawyer Rodrigo Rosenberg. Facebook played an important role in the "Justice for Sepur Zarco" movement, which aimed to hold military leaders responsible for abuses of human rights during the nation's civil war (Harlow, 2011). This also draws attention to the social media's drawbacks in the context of the Guatemalan justice movement. They point out that activity and offline organizing were essential for sustaining the campaign because social media alone was insufficient. They also talk about the difficulties and dangers of utilizing social media.

The focus of this study is on social media influencers. Given the nature of this chapter's subject, politics, and human rights violations, social influencers may temporarily switch to become political influencers. Riedl et al. (2023, p.2) define political influencers as "content creators that endorse a political position, social cause, or candidate through media that they produce and/or share on a given social media platform." In this study, most of the political influencers were celebrities who took part or joined the social activism for a social cause. Thus, influencers rally their audience to be part of the social cause (Wellman, 2022). Political influencers can be distinguished from influencers in other content domains "in their willingness to associate their online influence with political and social causes" (Goodwin et al., 2023, p.1616). Therefore, the term "political influencer" encompasses both those wholly focus on political issues on their social media accounts. Therefore, some of these Nigerian influencers while they were not into politics, during the #EndSARS campaign, they assumed the political influencer tag. Thus, being a political influencer is contextual based on issue being propagated at that particular time.

THEORETICAL PERSPECTIVE

This chapter theorizes social media influencers as digital opinion leaders. In this social network context, a new group of communicators has emerged, the so-called SMIs (Hudders et al., 2020). The range is somewhere between ordinary users and celebrities, which earned them the nickname "microcelebrities" (Senft, 2008). SMI wield a lot of influence as through their following, they can direct toward a point of direction. When it comes to social movements, SMI are capable of influencing followers to behave in a certain way. However, this does not mean that their respective followers are passive and lack their agency. Instead, social media platforms have created virtual communities where people with similar interest converge (Tshuma et al., 2023). According to Durau (2022, 2012), SMIs act as change agents "who have the ability to shape and change their follower's behaviors with their content." Their work in social movements enable them to opinion leaders as they influence and popularize the movements. Their voice becomes the voice of the voiceless, and as the case with opinion leaders, their voices are the voices of authority. In this regard, SMIs can be conceptualized as what Lazarsfeld et al. (1944) called "opinion leaders," mainly due to the facet they have key characteristics that are important for opinion leaders to influence certain decisions. these are: charisma and communicative competence.

METHODOLOGY

This study is focused on the #EndSARS Protest of October 2020. This is the period where the networking effect of social media peaked in raising awareness of police brutality in Nigeria, it also marks the period when key actions were taken by citizens and the government alike. Data used in this study have been obtained from Twitter, which is the social media platform that played a pivotal role of the protest, as the campaign originated on Twitter (Malefakis, 2021) before going viral on other social media platforms. The tweets analyzed were generated on October 12, 2020, the day that protesters gathered at the Lekki tollgate for the first time, which was marked as the epicenter for the protests. It was also the day when the Nigerian president, Muhammadu Buhari, made a televised speech on the disbandment of SARS for the first time (Ukpe, 2020). Primary data used within this study is from September 12, 2020 to October 12, 2020. The data consists of 15,000 mentions and was obtained by using an online monitoring tool called brand 24 (Brand24, 2020). Purposive sampling was adopted to determine the most relevant accounts that tweeted or retweeted a post on October 12, 2020, after the announcement of the president. 100 tweets were analyzed, based on available resources.

This study used thematic analysis to analyze the data. According to Braun and Clark (2009, p.2), thematic analysis is "a method of identifying, anaylsing and reporting patterns and themes within data." Thematic analysis can be can semantic and latent. The former involves detecting themes at "the surface or semantic appearance" and the researcher will not be looking for anything beyond what is captured by the text (Boyatzis, 1998; Bryman, 2001). The latter requires going from description to a deeper meaning of what the data is all about, and it is through this form that a theory can be developed based on patterns that might have emerged (Braun and Clarke, 2006). Braun and Clark (2009, p.13) further note that this method, "tends to provide less a rich description of the data overall, and more a detailed analysis of some aspect of the data."

In doing thematic analysis, we followed six key stages. We had to first familiarize ourselves with data, that is, going through the tweets. Javadi and Zarea (2016, p.33) adds that "in order to find out the content depth, the immersion of the researcher in the data is necessary." As such, we had to repeatedly go through the tweets so that we become more familiar with information. We moved on to develop codes to help come up with key characteristic of the data. The next stage was to closely look at codes with the aim of identifying patterns that were emerging. After that, we had to review the themes. At this stage, we looked at the themes that were coming out of the data and they included amplification and social media influencers as political activists. The last stage involved writing up the information. Braun and Clark (2009) notes that this stage involves extracting powerful quotes or examples that speaks to chosen themes.

DATA ANALYSIS

In this section, we discuss the study findings. Our discussion is based the objectives of the study. The discussion mainly looks at the role or the place of influencers in political communication within this case being their participation in social movements. We identified two major themes fundamental to the role of social media influencers in the #EndSARS movement. These themes are:

- Spreading the word: influencers and amplification the message.
- Social media influencers as political activists.

SPREADING THE WORD: INFLUENCERS AND THE AMPLIFICATION OF THE MESSAGE

Social media influencers were instrumental to the amplification of the voices of the victims of police brutality due to the large number of their followers.

Their tweets were far reaching and had a snowball effect which made more people join the online protest. Under this role, influencers were implying the key message that was being pushed by protesters or fellow Nigerians. One influencer posted: "*It is not about introducing a new unit, SWAT.*" The message was in reference to protests that continued despite the disbandment of SARS. The influencer, Flavour of Africa, through his handle @2niteFlavour shared a poster of the demands of the protesters, and some of the demands were: "Immediate release of all the protesters. Justice for all the victims of police brutality and appropriate compensation for their families. Setting an independent commission to oversee the investigation and prosecution of all reports of police misconduct."[1]

Knowing the power of algorithms, sharing and the hashtag movement ensures that the message trend and attract international attention (Matsilele, 2022; Duffy and Meisner, 2022). In this case, the amplification attracted the attention of global media channels such as Al Jazeera, CNN, and BBC. Similarly, Nigerians in diaspora contributed to further raising awareness by having physical gatherings for protesting in solidarity with fellow Nigerian citizens in their home countries. The outcome of this amplifications helped to get a response from stakeholders in government. The attention piled pressure on government to act or respond to people´s demands. In response, the then Nigerian president Muhammadu Buhari responded through his twitter handle, @MBuhari by saying:

> The disbanding of SARS is only the first step in our commitment to extensive police reforms in order to ensure that the primary duty of the police and other law enforcement agencies remains the protection of lives and livelihood of our people.[2]

The disbandment of SARS by the president spurred different reactions on Twitter. The protesters were not reassured that police brutality would end, as many of the protesters were experiencing further torture by policemen even after the disbandment of the squad was announced. Hence, the protesters did not back out as they needed the government to end all forms of abuse of power by the police and other armed forces.

The outcomes of the #EndSARS campaign includes strong interconnectedness between social media influencers and their followers helped to foster loyalty and a sense of purpose which enabled the protests to gain ground. The protest moved from the cry of the oppressed to become a national movement against police brutality. This aligns with the study by (Zhang et al., 2023), which opined that there is a very high tendency for information to cascade down in a networked environment and amplification occurs when elites champion conversations on social media. Similarly, the theory on the six degrees of separation (Zhang and Tu, 2009) focused on the ease of information flow among users in a networked environment. Twitter provided users the opportunity for every member of government who had a significant role to play in ending police brutality were readily available. It also provided a platform for transnational solidarity, with influencers from different nations also advocating for the disbandment of SARS (Matsilele et al., 2021).

SOCIAL MEDIA INFLUENCERS AS ACTIVISTS

Due to the growth of social media, and the creating of "virtual communities," societal issues are widely deliberated online. In this case, the #EndSARS campaign gathered momentum leading to influencers taking part or shaping discourses. The findings show that social media influencers became activists. One activist, Aisha Yesufu, @AishaYesufuhese,[3] posted:

> These protests are not like any other protests this govt has seen. This one is leaderless. The day some want to stop is the day others want to march. Eat the humble pie and come and meet their needs. Listen to their demands. You have everything to lose. They don´t #SARSMUSTEND.

The other influencers, Japheth Omojuwa took government officials to task for their attempt to ban or censor protest in the country. Through his handle, @Omojuwa,[4] he posted:

> You can't ban protests sir. The constitution that empowers you as governor empowers citizens to protest. Your power as governor doesn't supersede the rights of citizens to protest. You guys need to acquaint yourselves with the constitution beyond your privileges! #EndSARS.

The above sentiment from influencers shows that the #EndSARS protest has proven to the world that social media influencers are critical to political discourse in the digital space. Influencers not only have the capacity to attract the attention of youths and citizens, but they also have the capacity to influence leaders in making policies in favor of the oppressed. The boldness of influencers during the protest ensured that the rights of citizens were upheld, despite the position of political office holders. Interesting to note is that social media influencers, some who focus on entertainment and entrepreneurship, took up the "arms" and delved into politics by acting as activists. This confirms earlier perspective that while social media influencers don't focus on politics, during social movements, they do engage in political issues (Tshuma et al., 2023; Byrne et al., 2017; Chwialkowska, 2019).

To add more, Nigerian influencers were relentless in ensuring that protesters did not cower in the presence of oppression. Hence, they leveraged their networks to ensure their safety and well-being. More so, influencers utilized social media platforms to promote political or social causes. Their success is tethered to understanding how algorithms may support or suppress one's own content (Duffy and Meisner, 2022). In this, their popularity ensured that they become the voice of the voiceless and went further to lead from the front through offering donations, and medical expenses for victims of police brutality. For example, @fkabudu[5] posted a message having hired a lawyer to assist some of the victims. The message reads:

> Instruction has been given for them to be released, but they haven't been released yet. Our lawyers and one of their mums and others are waiting outside. Desmond Elliot is on his way there to make sure they get out as instructed (that's his constituency). They must leave tonight.

The above views show that influencers went beyond being activist online but to assist victims. The campaign is one of the few or notable social media campaigns that became successful online leading to further physical protests (see Matsilele et al., 2022). Social media influencers went beyond raising awareness on social media. They took part in the physical protests that were held in different parts of the country. In this, we thus argue that social media influencers became what Lazarsfeld et al. (1944) called "opinion leaders," because they showed key characterizes of opinion leaders and these are charisma and communicative competence. With influencers characterized as be able to use their outreach, followership, command, and respect to inform their followers about specific topics and allow them to peek into their everyday life (Freberg et al., 2011), in this study, we argue that influencers used their influence to leads in giving direction, and addressing people's needs while calling the government to implement suggested policies. In this case, the key message was to ban the notorious police unit.

CONCLUSION

This study observed that although conversations on the hashtag, #EndSARS have been reoccurring since 2017, there was no mention of the hashtag from September 12, 2020 to October 2, 2020. However, by October 3, 2020, the hashtag became active again and its usage continued to peak. This was the point where many influencers on social media joined the conversation.

The resulting typology from this study indicates that social authority and the number of followers play an important role in determining the ability of an influencer to raise awareness on important societal issues, such as police brutality, which is the focus of this study. The role of influencers in social activism in the African setup remains scant. This study developed into this untapped field and examined the rile and influence by social media influencers in Nigeria during protests. In this study, we conclude that influence of influencers in Nigeria played a crucial role in activism and amplifying the message around protests, due to their international support, and the power of algorithmic work, the message spread like veldfire leading to more international support.

Due to their popularity and huge online audiences, influencers are often considered as digital opinion leaders (Bause, 2021), and for this reason, their opinion matters especially in political activism. Influencers on social media can be effective spokespersons for causes of social justice. Influencers can contribute to increasing public awareness of social issues. The findings show that influencers played a crucial in mobilizing and challenging the government to climb down from their high horse and address the demands being made by the masses. According to Casero-Ripollé (2020, p.171), note that the growth on digital technologies have further expanded the classical concept of opinion leadership as they allow a more diverse set of actors to exert social influence. This study recommends that government agencies leverage the authority of influencers to promote actions that can help drive social change. In addition, the study recommends that influencers at different stages can be engaged by think tanks for the implementation of policies and advocacy for addressing social issues. Also, it is recommended that using the typology derived from this study, further studies should apply the typology for evaluating the role of influencers in raising awareness of social issues that go viral on social media platforms. Although the primary use of social media is networking, other factors such as social authority and the number of followers is key considerations for effective networking. Effective networking will eventually lead to developing social authority and an increase in the number of followers. Influence on social media is determined largely by social authority (Followerwonk, 2022). A high social authority score indicates the ability of an account to engage its users with maximum impact. User accounts with high social authority scores and a high number of followers make more impact with their posts on social media and they have receptive followers who will act based on their posts. Although influencers on social media may not have direct roles in making policy changes, they play an important role in raising awareness on important national issues that require the attention of political office holders. Finally, this study recognizes the importance of social authority and the need for more studies to be focused on influencers and social authority. New theories need to be developed for understanding different forms of social authority.

NOTES

1. Okoli, C. (2020, 16 October). Available: https://twitter.com/2niteflavour/status/1317141755721109504. Accessed on 17 April 2024.
2. Buhari, M. (2020, 12 October). Available at: https://twitter.com/MBuhari/status/1315631722604748804. Accessed on 17 April 2024.
3. Yasefu, A. (2020, 12 October). Available at: https://twitter.com/AishaYesufu/status/1315632596802514949. Accessed on 17 April 2024.
4. Omojuwa, J. J. (2020, 13 October). Available: https://twitter.com/Omojuwa/status/1315787260802072576 . Accessed on 17 April 2024.
5. Kabudu, F. (2020, 12 October). Available at: https://twitter.com/fkabudu/status/1315727027769675778 . Accessed on 17 April 2024.

REFERENCES

Adekalu, S. O., Cephas, O. R., Suandi, T., & Samah, I. H. (2015). Bring back our girls, social mobilization: Implications for cross-cultural research. *Journal of Education and Practice*, 6(6), 64–75.

Adetayo, A. O., & Sidiq, B. O. (2018). Economic recession and the way-out: Nigeria as case study. *Global Journal of Human-Social Science: E-Economics*, 18(1), 181–192.

Adiele, P. O. (2017). *The popes, the catholic church and the transatlantic enslavement of black Africans 1418–1839*. Zurich: Georg Olms Verlag.

Aina, T. A., Atela, M., Ojebode, A., Dayil, P., & Aremu, A. (2019). Beyond tweets and screams: Action for empowerment and accountability in Nigeria – The case of the #BBOG movement. *IDS Working Paper*.

Al Jazeera and News Agencies. (2020, October 22). *Timeline: #EndSARS protests in Nigeria*. Retrieved from Aljazeera: https://www.aljazeera.com/news/2020/10/22/timeline-on-nigeria-unrest.

Alfandika, L., & (2020). The airwaves belong to the people: A critical analysis of radio broadcasting and licensing in Zimbabwe. *Communicatio*.

Aljazeera. (October 22, 2020). *Nigeria's SARS: A brief history of the Special Anti-Robbery Squad | Protests | Al Jazeera*. Retrieved from https://www.aljazeera.com/features/2020/10/22/sars-a-brief-history-of-a-rogue-unit.

Amnesty International. (2016). *'YOU HAVE SIGNED YOUR DEATH WARRANT'*. London: Amnesty International.

Amusa,, L. B., & Yahya, W. B. (2016). Data mining of nigerians' sentiments on the administration of the federal government of nigeria. *Annals. Computer Science Series*, 14(2), 69–75.

Baxter, P. (2012). *Selous Scouts: Rhodesian counter-Insurgency specialists*. Warwick: Helion & Company Ltd.

Bebić, D., & Volarevic, M. (2018). Do not mess with a meme: The use of viral content in communicating politics. *Communication & Society*, 43–56.

Bhagat, S., Moira Burke, M., Diuk, C., Onur Filiz, I., & Edunov, S. (February 4, 2016). *Three and a half degrees of separation*. Facebook Research.

Bhebhe, N. (1999). *The ZAPU and ZANU guerrilla warfare and the Evangelical Lutheran Church in Zimbabwe*. Gweru: Mambo Press.

Birth of the Nigerian Colony. (January, 2014). Retrieved from Google Arts & Culture: https://artsandculture.google.com/exhibit/birth-of-the-nigerian-colony-pan-atlantic-university/ARi_MKdz?hl=en.

Bodunrin, I. A., & Matsilele, T. (2023). Social media and protest politics in Nigeria's #EndSARS campaign. *Handbook of Social Media in Education, Consumer Behavior and Politics: Volume 1*, 111(114), 109.

Bonello, J. (2010). The Development of early settler identity in Southern Rhodesia: 1890–1914. *International Journal of Africa Historical Studies*, 43(2), 341–367.

Brand24. (October 12, 2020). *#Endsars*. Retrieved from Brand24. https://brand24.com/.

Bray, P. (February 13, 2013). *Social authority: Our measure of Twitter influence*. Retrieved from Moz: https://moz.com/blog/social-authority.

Chaffey, D. (February 8, 2018). *Global social media research summary 2018*. Retrieved from Smart Insights: https://www.smartinsights.com/social-media-marketing/social-media-strategy/new-global-social-media-research/.

Chari, T. J. (2017). Electoral violence and its instrumental logic: Mapping press discourse on electoral violence during parliamentary and presidential elections in Zimbabwe. *Journal of African Elections*, 16(1), 72–87.

Chibuwe, A. (2020). Social media and elections in Zimbabwe: Twitter war between Pro-ZANU-PF and Pro-MDC-A Netizens. *Communinicatio South African Journal for Communication Theory and Research*, 46(4), 7–30

Chitanana, T. (2019). *Disinformation and digital disparities in fledgling democracies. A case study of postMugabe Zimbabwe*. Harvard: Berkman Klein Center.

Chung, F. (2006). *Re-living the Second Chimurenga: Memories from the liberation struggle in Zimbabwe*. Harare: Weaver Press.

Coltart, D. (2016). *The struggle continues: 50 years of tyrrany in Zimbabwe*. Johannesburg: Jacana Media (Pty) Ltd.

Costelloe, D. (2016). Treaty succession in annexed territory. *International and Comparative Law Quarterly*, 65, 343–378.

Crunchbase. (n.d.). *Followerwonk*. Retrieved June 17, 2022, from https://www.crunchbase.com/organization/followerwonk.

Dallywater, L. S. (2019). *Southern African liberation movements and the global Cold War 'East'*. Boston: De Gruyter.

Dzimiri, P. R. (2014). Naming, identity, politics and violence in Zimbabwe. *Studies of Tribes and Tribals*, 12(2), 227–238.

Eltantawy, N., & Wiest, J. B. (2011). The Arab Spring| social media in the Egyptian revolution: Reconsidering resource mobilization theory. *International Journal of Communication*, 1207–1224.

Feldstein, S. (2019). *The global expansion of AI surveillance*. Massachusetts: Carnegie Endowment for International Peace.

Feldstein, S. (2020). *Testimony before the U.S.-China Economic and Security Review Commission Hearing on China's Strategic Aims in Africa*. Massachusetts: Carnegie Endowment for International Peace.

Flavián, C., & Barta, S. (2022). *Encyclopedia of Tourism Management and Marketing*, 14(4), 159–161.

Floyd, B. N. (1962). Land Apportionment in Southern Africa. *Geographical Review*, 52(4), 566–582.

Followerwonk. (June 16, 2022). *What can followerwonk do for you?* Retrieved from Followerwonk: https://followerwonk.com/social-authority.

Glenn, E. N. (2015). Settler colonialism as structure: A framework for comparative studies of U.S. race and gender formation. *Current (and Future) Theoretical Debates in Sociology of Race and Ethnicity. American Sociological Association*, 1(1), 54–74.

Gomba, C. (2020). Post-colonial theory in Zimbabwe's education system: Headmasters' view. *International Journal of Research Studies in Education*, 7(7), 77–88.

Grondin, J. (2015). The hermeneutical circle. In N. Keane, & C. Lawn (Eds), *A companion to hermeneutics*, (pp. 299–305). Chichester: Wiley-Blackwell

Gu, M. (2020). What is 'decoloniality'? Apostcolonial critique. *Post Colonial Studies*, 23(4), 596–600.

Gukurume, S. (2017). #ThisFlag and #ThisGown Cyber Protests in Zimbabwe: Reclaiming political space. *African Journalism Studies*, 38(2) 49–70.

Gukurume, S. (2019). Surveillance, spying and disciplining the university: Deployment of state security agents on campus in Zimbabwe. *Journal of Asian and African Studies,* 54(5), 763–779.

Hari, S. I. (2014). The evolution of social protest in Nigeria: The role of Social Media in the "#OccupyNigeria" protest. *International Journal of Humanities and Social Science Invention,* 3(9), 33–39.

Harlow, S. (2011). Social media and social Facebook and an online Guatemalan justice movement that moved offline. *New Media & Society*, 1–19.

Harms Smith, L. (2020). *Epistemic decoloniality as pedagogical movement in social work education: Ā turn of theory to anti-colonial theorists such as Fanon, Biko and Freire*. London: Routledge.

Helps, A. (1856). *The Spanish conquest in America, and its relation to the history of slavery and to the government of colonies Volume 1*. New York: Harper & Brothers.

Huey, L. (2015). This is not your mother's terrorism: Social media, online radicalization and the practice of political jamming. *Journal of Terrorism Research*, 1–16.

Iwuoha, V. C., & Aniche, E. T. (2021). Protests and blood on the streets: Repressive state, police brutality and #EndSARS protest in Nigeria. *Security Journal* 35(4),1102–1124.

Jurgenson, N. (2012). When atoms meet bits: Social media, the mobile web and augmented revolution. *Future Internet*, 83–91.

Kavada, A. (2015). Creating the collective: Social media, the Occupy Movement and its constitution as a collective actor. *Information, Communication & Society*, 872–886.

Klandermans, B. (1984). Mobilization and participation: Social-psychological expansions of resource mobilization theory. *American Sociological Review*, 49(5), 583–600.

Kriger, N. J. (1991). *Zimbabwe's guerrilla war: Peasant Voices*. Cambridge: Cambridge University Press.

Kriger, N. J. (2003). *Guerrila Veterans in Post-war Zimbabwe: Symbolic and violent politics, 1980–1987*. Cambridge: Cambridge University Press.

Lin, Z. (2016). Traditional media, social media, and alternative media in Hong Kong's umbrella movement. *Asian Politics & Policy*, 365–372.

Logan, R. K. (2016). McLuhan's philosophy of media ecology: An introduction. *MDPI*, 133–140.

Craven, M. (2015). Between law and history: The Berlin Conference of 1884–1885 and the logic of free trade. *London Review of International Law*, 3(1), 31–59.

Makubuya, A. N. (2018). *Protection, patronage, or plunder? British Machinations and (B)uganda's struggle for Independence*. Cambridge: Cambridge Scholars Publishing.

Maldonado- Torres, N. (2007). On the coloniality of being. *Cultural Studies*, 21(2), 240–270.

Maldonado-Torres, N. (2007). On the Coloniality of being. In *Cultural Studies* (pp. 240–270). Routledge.

Malefakis, M. A. (January 29, 2021). *Using social media and #ENDSARS to dismantle Nigeria's Hierarchical Gerontocracy*. Retrieved from Toda Peace Institute: https://toda.org/global-outlook/using-social-media-and-endsars-to-dismantle-nigerias-hierarchical-gerontocracy.html.

Marowa, I. (2009). Construction of the 'Sellout' identity during Zimbabwe's war of liberation: A case of the Dandawa Community of Hurungwe district c1975-1980. *Identity, Culture & Politics: An Afro-Asian Dialogue*, 10(1), 121–131.

Masiya, T., & Maringira, G. (2018). The use of heroism in the Zimbabwe African National Union Patriotic Front (ZANU-PF) Intra-party factional dynamics. *Strategic Review*, 39(2), 1–24.

Matsilele, T. (2022). *Social media and digital dissidence in Zimbabwe*. London: Palgrave Macmillan.

Matsilele, T., Mpofu, S., Msimanga, M., & Tshuma, L. A. (2021). Transnational hashtag protest movements and emancipatory politics in Africa: A three country study. *Global Media Journal- German Edition*, 11(2), 1–23.

Mazango, E. M. (2005). Media games and shifting of spaces for political communication in Zimbabwe. *Westminster Papers in Communication and Culture*.

Mcleod, S. (February 16, 2023). *Albert Bandura's social learning theory*. Retrieved from Simply Psychology: https://simplypsychology.org/bandura.html.

McLuhan, M. (1964). *Understanding media*. Canada: McGraw-Hill.

Mgbejume, O. (1991). Constraints on Mass Media Policies in Nigeria. *Africa Media Review*, 47–57.

Mordi, K. (2020). *How Nigerian Prince stereotypes led to a police brutality crisis*. Retrieved from Wired: https://www.wired.co.uk/article/nigeria-end-sars-protests-police.

Moyo, L. (2009). Repression, propaganda, and digital resistance: New media and democracy in Zimbabwe. In W. J. Okoth Fred Mudhai (Ed.), *African media and the digital public sphere* (pp. 57–71). New York: Palgrave Macmillan.

Mukhtar, A. (2012). Nigeria's security challenges and the crisis of development: Towards a new framework for analysis. *International Journal of Developing Societies*, 107–116.

Ndlovu, M. (2018). Coloniality of knowledge and the challenge of creating African Futures. *Ufahamu: A Journal of African Studies*, 40(2), 95–112.

Ndlovu-Gatsheni, S. J. (2010). Reinvoking the past in the present: Changing identities and appropriations of Joshua Nkomo in post-colonial Zimbabwe. *African Identies*, 8(3), 191–208.

Ndoma, S. (2017). Majority of Zimbabweans want government out of private communications, religious speech. *Afrobarometer*, 165.

Ndlovu, M., Tshuma, L., & Mpofu, S. (Eds). (2023). *Remembering mass atrocities: Perspectives on memory struggles and cultural representations in Africa*. Cham: Springer International Publishing.

Okakwu, E. (December 4, 2017). *#ENDSARS: Police orders immediate re-organisation of SARS*. Retrieved 2017, from https://www.premiumtimesng.com/news/headlines/251351-just-endsars-police-orders-immediate-re-organisation-sars.html.

Okunade , K. J., & Esiri, M. J. (2014). Nigeria's communication policy and news determination. *Journal of Law, Policy and Globalization*, 8–17.

Olaniyan, A., & Akpojivi, U. (2020). Transforming communication, social media, counter-hegemony and the struggle for the soul of Nigeria. *Information, Communication & Society*, 422–437 .

Owen, O. (2014). *The Nigeria police force: Predicaments and possibilities*. Oxford: UK's Economic and Social Research Council.

Pike, J. (May 24, 1998). *Nigeria Police Force (NPF)* . Retrieved from https://irp.fas.org/world/nigeria/npf.htm.

Poell, T., & Dijck, J. V. (2018). Social media and new protest movements . In J. Burgess, A. Marwick, & T. Poell (Eds.), *The SAGE handbook of social media* (pp. 546–561). London: Sage.

Reed, W. C. (1993). International politics and national Liberation: ZANU and the politics of contested sovereignty. *African Studies Review*, 36(2), 31–59.

Smidi , A., & Shahin, S. (2017). Social media and social mobilisation in the Middle East: A survey of research on the Arab Spring. *India Quarterly: A Journal of International Affairs*, 196–209.

Smith, A., Silver, L., Johnson, C., Kyle, T., & Jiang, J. (May 13, 2019). *Publics in emerging economies worry social media sow division, even as they offer new chances for political engagement*. Retrieved from Pew Research Centre: https://www.pewinternet.org/2019/05/13/publics-in-emerging-economies-worry

-social-media-sow-division-even-as-they-offer-new-chances-for-political-engagement/?utm_source=Pew+Research+Center&utm_campaign=1768dd5c96-EMAIL_CAMPAIGN_2019_05_16_06_56&utm_medium.

Southall, R. (2020). *Fight and fortitude: The decline of the middle class in Zimbabwe.* Cambridge: Cambridge University Press.

Statista. (2021). *Most famous social network sites worldwide as of April 2019, ranked by number of active users (in millions).* Retrieved December 18, 2021, from Statista: https://www.statista.com/statistics/272014/global-social-networks-ranked-by-number-of-users/.

Stigger, P. (1971). Volunteers and the profit motive in the Anglo-Ndebele war: 1893. *Rhodesian History*, 2, 11–23.

Tawse, J. (1935). Native administration in Southern Rhodesia. *Journal of the Royal Society of Arts*, 83(4319), 973.

Tirivangasi, H. M. (2021). Revisiting electoral violence in Zimbabwe: Problems and prospects. *International Journal of Criminology and Sociology*, 10(1), 1066–1074.

Tshuma, B. B., Tshuma, L. A., & Ndlovu, M. (2022). Twitter and political discourses: How supporters of Zimbabwe's ruling ZANU PF party use Twitter for political engagement. *Journal of Eastern African Studies*, 16(2), 269–288.

Tshuma, L., Ndlovu, M., & Mpofu, S. (2023). Mass atrocities and memory struggles in Africa and the Global South. In Ndlovu, M., Tshuma, L., & Mpofu, S (Eds.), *Remembering mass atrocities: Perspectives on memory struggles and cultural representations in Africa* (pp. 1–14). Cham: Springer International Publishing.

Ukpe, W. (October 25, 2020). *#EndSARS: A day by day timeline of the protest that has brought Nigeria to its knees.* Retrieved from https://nairametrics.com/2020/10/25/endsars-protest-a-timeline-of-all-the-major-events-from-october-3rd/.

Varrella, S. (March 23, 2021). *Total number of active social media users in Nigeria from 2017 to 2021.* Retrieved from Statista: https://www.statista.com/statistics/1176096/number-of-social-media-users-nigeria/.

World Population Review. (n.d.). *Nigeria population 2021 (Demographics, Maps, Graphs).* Retrieved from https://worldpopulationreview.com/countries/nigeria-population.

Zhang, L., & Tu, W. (2009). *Six degrees of separation in online society.* Retrieved from ResearchGate: https://www.researchgate.net/publication/255614427_Six_Degrees_of_Separation_in_Online_Society.

Zhang, Y., Chen, F., & Lukito, J. (2023). Network amplification of politicized information and misinformation about COVID-19 by conservative media and partisan influencers on Twitter. *Political Communication*, 24–47.

Part II

ONLINE PROTEST STRATEGIES

Chapter 6

Online Protests and Government Countermeasures in Zimbabwe

A Decolonial Perspective

Tawanda Mukurunge and Lorenzo Dalvit

Zimbabwe has long been in a crisis, which intensified after the year 2000. Lewanika (2013) attributes the deepening of the crisis to the nature of an authoritarian regime that used or misused the apparatus of the state to prolong its stay in power. Moyo (2009) is of the view that the crisis was caused and exacerbated by the breakdown in the rule of law and disregard for human rights by the state which resulted in overwhelming pressure from civil society, opposition parties, and the local and international liberal news media fraternity to make the government embrace democratic reforms. In the state-controlled mainstream media, civil society is demonized for, allegedly, committing the cardinal sin of appropriating people's voices, as if the people cannot speak out for themselves (Lewanika, 2013). People getting back their voices is attributed to the emergence of the Internet and the social media platforms that come along with it (Moyo, 2009), despite relatively high data costs and low Internet penetration (Moyo-Nyende and Ndoma, 2020). Matsilele and Ruhanya (2020) note that resistance to the Zimbabwe National Union-Patriotic Front (ZANU-PF)[1] rule in Zimbabwe has always been there since the party got into power, but social media resistance came to prominence in 2016 with Evan Mawarire's Twitter-based #ThisFlag as well as #Tajamuka/sesijikile. Prior to that, resistance to the ZANU-PF government was predominantly in the form of stay-away action organized by the Zimbabwe Congress of Trade Unions (ZCTU), tertiary student organizations under the Zimbabwe National Students Union (ZINASU), and after the year 2000, by the opposition Movement for Democratic Change (MDC). Political consciousness and social movements in Zimbabwe date back to the pre-independence era, long before the manifestation of social movements on the

Internet that resulted in the fall of long-standing dictatorships in the Middle East and North Africa (MENA) region. In the MENA region, social media played an important role in citizens' participation in communication discourse and mobilization in an intense manner mainly because of the authorities' failing rationales against protestors (Shirazi, 2013). South African tertiary students successfully tapped into the online mobilization of protests: the #RhodesMustFall and #FeesMustFall (Manderson, 2016) before the impactful Zimbabwean #ThisFlag, #ThisGown, and #Tajamuka/sesijikile (Gukurume, 2017; Msimanga, 2022). For the latter, the protests built momentum till Mugabe's eventual fall in November 2017. The state was on high alert against online mobilized protests as early as 2011 at the height of the MENA region Arab Spring revolution as a gathering by civil society and all other opposition forces was disrupted and participants at the meeting were arrested (Aidi, 2018). The study of protest movements in Zimbabwe is somewhat complicated by the government presenting itself as anti-colonial and by it still being regarded as a liberation force by some sections of Zimbabwean society. However, the state's heavy-handedness against the #ZimbabweLivesMatter movement led to the government of South Africa sending a delegation on a fact-finding mission on the allegations that the government of Zimbabwe was violating the rights of its own citizens (Mutlokwa, 2020). In this chapter, we discuss strategies employed by Zimbabwean online protesters as well as governmental counterstrategies through a decolonial theoretical lens to uncover the links between the present and the past.

UNDERSTANDING DECOLONIALITY

Decoloniality entails the demystification of Eurocentric impositions of Western knowledge systems, cultural sensibilities, traditions, and their racial imbeddednes (Smith, 2020). To believe that all things emanating from Europe are superior to those from the Global South is the banality that decolonial research seeks to demystify. Decoloniality can best be understood by looking back at the phenomenon of colonialism which stratified the global population in terms of superiority and inferiority because of the color of one's skin and location of one's origin. Europeans, in the quest for resources to service their rapidly developing industries, went out to conquer and plunder countries in the Global South (Makubuya, 2018). In 1890, Cecil John Rhodes's company, the British South Africa Company (BSAC) invaded the Zimbabwean plateau in the hope of discovering rich gold fields like those the company monopolized in the Gauteng area of the Transvaal in South Africa (Bonello, 2010). This was after European government representatives had met in Berlin from 1884 to 1885 to distribute African territories among themselves (Craven,

2015). No African leader was invited to represent African interests (Nilsson, 2013). Africa had its own imbalances before colonialism such as black upon black enslavement. However, this was at a smaller scale and of a different nature compared to the European institutionalized system (Adiele, 2017). Europeans carved out whole empires out of Global South territories to dominate socially, politically, and most importantly economically (Maldonado-Torres, 2007).

Against this background, Gu (2020) states that the concept of decoloniality refers to a critique and subsequent liberation from coloniality, that is unmasking and addressing the consequences of historical colonialism in the present. Gu explains that colonialism impacted all, that is, those on the receiving end and those in positions of power. Similar considerations apply to the relationship between oppressors and subalterns within former colonies such as Zimbabwe. Ndlovu-Gatsheni (2015) emphasizes the aspect of the way of thinking that must do away with the coldness and self-centeredness brought about by coloniality that decoloniality should deal with. The formerly colonized mindset must be informed about the benefits of focusing on matters that will develop and benefit our people in our own way. For Zimbabwe, development can go a notch higher with the elimination of, especially violence in politics which is a colonial legacy based on the dehumanization, humiliation, and violation of the weak by the politically powerful as they seek to prolong their stay in power in order to plunder the resources of the nation for personal benefit.

Europe empowered itself to determine global law through the mere extension of European law to the global stage. In the conquest and annexation of foreign territories, the European powers used legislation to impose their will on the colonized people (Costelloe, 2016). Quijano (2000) writes about Spanish law being applied to the conquered territories of South America by the Spanish conquistadors. The law was in favor of the Spanish colonial masters based on their perceived racial superiority (Helps, 1856). Writing on the confusion and destruction caused by colonialism on the colonized, Quijano (2000) identifies three dimensions of coloniality as that of emasculation (coloniality of power), eradication of the colonized's way of life to replace it with European mores, ethics and values (coloniality of being) as well as their thought production patterns (coloniality of knowledge). In post-colonial Zimbabwe, the construct of race was replaced by other dimensions of inequality such as socioeconomic status and political affiliation while asymmetric access to resources persists. The white middle class that was put in place by the colonial government was replaced by a black middle class affiliated to the ruling party (Southall, 2020). The elite send their children to the United Kingdom, Australia, and the United States of America because they think that is where their children will get the best education and because they can afford it. In the education system, curriculum from primary school up to tertiary level is still predominantly a residue of the colonial era, that is, a curriculum designed to produce an efficient civil servant who can effectively follow instructions (Gomba, 2020). Coloniality of knowledge is a result of colonialism bringing sudden and violent shifts in ways of generating knowledge to the extent that the West still dominates the Global South's knowing, seeing, creating, and imagining. Ndlovu (2018) says that the continued presence of the colonial system in the education sector has contributed immensely to the emptying of African mindsets of their traditional knowledge and memories to replace them with foreign ways of knowing and remembering. As part and parcel of the decoloniality paradigm shift, African minds will therefore have to learn to transcend colonial domination in the sphere of knowledge production, including media representations of reality. Coloniality of being shines the spotlight on the effects and negative impact of coloniality in a colonized people's lived experience. As a glaring example, the criminalization of entire racial groups or of political opponents can be interpreted as a continuation of colonial attitudes (Glenn, 2015). In this chapter, colonialities of power, knowledge, and being are operationalized by discussing state violence, media counternarratives, and citizens' surveillance and monitoring, respectively.

VIOLENCE AND THE LEGACY OF COLONIALISM

Colonialism was executed with merciless and ruthless violence against the peoples of the Global South and that legacy is still persistent in some parts of the formerly colonized world. For the black people of Zimbabwe, violence was an integral part of the colonial system from dispossession of land, forced labor on the white settler-owned farms, mines and factories in urban areas. The Anglo-Ndebele war of 1893 (Stigger, 1971) waged by the settler regime to dispossess Africans of their land and livestock, led to the nationwide uprising by blacks popularly known as the first Chimurenga. Failure of the uprising led to systematic disenfranchisement and the establishment of reserves or communal homelands for Africans which served as labor reservoirs for white interests. The settler government further dispossessed Africans of land through legislation such as the Land Apportionment Act (1930), Land Husbandry Act (1951), and Land Tenure Act (1960) (Tawse, 1935; Floyd, 1962; Anderson and Green, 2015). As resistance was met with ruthless force and attempts at peaceful mediation failed, African political nationalists eventually resorted to armed struggle in order to overthrow the settler regime which had unilaterally declared its independence from Britain in 1965. Levels of violence escalated after November 1965 till a United Nations supervised ceasefire in 1979 (Chung, 2006; Helliker Bhatasara and Chiweshe, 2021). The armed struggle during this period saw unprecedented violence being visited especially upon rural communities at the hands of both the settler regime, for supporting the guerrillas and at the hands of the guerrillas themselves for collaborating with the colonial settler regime, for example, by working as civil servants, police officers, or security service personnel (Kriger, 1991; Kriger, 2003; Maxey, 1975). Even within the Black Nationalist movement questing for liberation, violence was the order of the day, for example, to remove the oppressive Rhodesian regime, to discipline wayward guerrillas, to educate the masses who did not readily accept that the nationalist guerrillas were their liberators and who displayed any form of resistance, to prosecute perceived and real sellouts (Marowa, 2009) who informed on guerrilla activities. Violence was also used against other nationalist movements despite them fighting for the same course (Muwati et al., 2010).

Violence against opposition voices and activists in Zimbabwe is therefore engrained in the psyche of the political elite since the colonial era when state-sanctioned humiliation and brutalizing of the weak ruled through beatings, rape, arrests, torture, and murder (Dzimiri et al., 2014). Such a violent legacy was inherited together with political power in 1980, making the country a nation still wallowing in the deadly grip of colonialism (Masiya and Maringira, 2018). Those who became leaders of the nation overnight straight from a guerrilla war needed to be reintroduced to civilian life. Many of them were child soldiers who grew up in the war, killing and witnessing their colleagues dying in combat (Dallywater et al., 2019). Violence is found in the language of ZANU-PF as evidenced by the choice of words such as labeling opposition parties sellouts (*vatengesi*) and the slogan of down with (*pasi*) whose significance is to kill the person being denigrated (Marowa, 2009). Those who oppose ZANU-PF and vie for power even through democratic means of contesting elections are regarded as enemies rather than political opponents (Tirivangasa et al., 2021). The talk against opponents often translates into action through the violence of torching opposition supporters' houses, destroying their property, and killing critics. Such a move reflects a tradition emanating from the days of colonialism (Chari, 2017). The nation, the ruling elite, and the rural electorate still live immersed in the suffering and violence of the colonial era (Ndlovu-Gatsheni, 2012). They need to be liberated before liberal democratic cultures can take root.

Violence in post-colonial Zimbabwe is sponsored by the hardliners in ZANU-PF, writes Coltart (2016), who perceive the solution to any opposition to the party's grip on power lying in violence as the resolution. Coltart details how the state apparatus; the military, the police, and the intelligence sector supported by veterans of the liberation struggle and youth militias are employed in the systematic elimination of opposition to ZANU-PF.[2] This started with the campaign against Joshua Nkomo's PF-ZAPU who were labeled dissidents before being subjected to physical persecution (Ndlovu and Tshuma, 2022). The result was *Gukurahundi* genocide, the systematic killing of the Ndebele-speaking people in Matabeleland and Midlands provinces from 1983 to 1987, resulted in the callous murders of PF-ZAPU supporters, women, and children. Joshua Nkomo was hounded into exile with the former ZPRA leadership being incarcerated. After having absorbed PF-ZAPU into ZANU-PF, the wrath of ZANU-PF turned against the Movement for Democratic Change and its supporters from the year 2000 onward. Sachikonye (2011) details how the state reacted to the threat of its pseudo one-party state status through the strategy of state-sponsored violence against civil society, opposition activists, ordinary rural and farm community supporters of the opposition in the 2002 pre-election campaign and toward the presidential election rerun of 2008. Violence also characterized the land redistribution exercise of 2000 against white farmers and their employees. Violence was at its peak toward the presidential runoff to the extent that Morgan Tsvangirai of the MDC had to withdraw from the contest expressing disgust at the continuous murder of his supporters.

COUNTERNARRATIVES

The Zimbabwean government's practice of deliberately employing misinformation against opponents has its roots in the liberation struggle from 1966 to 1979. At the time, both the Rhodesian settler regime and the liberation movements deliberately misinformed the population and the international community (Masiya and Maringira, 2018). Through radio broadcasts and fliers dropped into villages from airplanes, the settler regime labeled African nationalists as communist-sponsored terrorists. On the other hand, through radio stations broadcasting from exile and through night-long education meetings (pungwes) led by political commissars, nationalists exaggerated their capacity and the exploits of the guerrillas in battle (Chitanana, 2019). The former guerrilla fighters operating Voice of the People (VOP) through Radio Mozambique, a ZANU radio broadcasting into Zimbabwe during the war, were given the mandate of managing ZBC radio stations and television after independence and they carried on with the culture of ZANU propaganda (Mosia et al., 1994). Particularly among rural constituencies, radio and television have been regarded as the only authentic news outlets since the colonial era and the ZANU-PF government perpetuated such belief after 1980 (Alfandika and Gwindingwe, 2020). In mainstream media, the coloniality of knowledge is perpetuated through the the government's hold on Zimbabwe Newspapers Limited (Zimpapers), a print media company whose majority shares are owned by the state. Zimpapers interests, since 2010, have expanded beyond print to include radio and television for the sole purpose of the government's perpetual control of the narrative (Mazango, 2005). Until the early 2000s, media infrastructure, content generation, dissemination, and management had not changed much from the colonial era (Melber, 2004).

Having realized that monopoly of broadcast media and mainstream print was no longer effective as the Internet had opened opportunities for long-suppressed voices to find outlets online, the government became aggressively involved on social media platforms (Hove and Chenzi, 2020). During the build-up to the 2013 general elections, the Baba Jukwa Facebook page acted as government's counterstrategy to online opposition voices, causing confusion with the ZANU-PF machinery failing to control the faceless character that was providing a political narrative (Matsilele and Ruhanya, 2020; Msimanga et al., 2021). Gukurume (2017) gives the example of the Mugabe-era Minister of Information concocting a pro-government hashtag movement running the #OurFlag to counter the popular #ThisFlag online protest movement that spurred demonstrations against the Mugabe government in 2016. In the Mnangagwa era, the government has deployed its own team of cyber activists going by the name Varakashi (the beaters) to fight online opposition. The narrative gravitated toward the generation of fake news/misinformation campaigns/disinformation as mudslinging and image tarnishing escalated between the Varakashi and the pro-MDC/Chamisa cyber activists popularly known as Nerrorists (Chibuwe, 2020). Of the Varakashi ZANU-PF online cadres, Tshuma et al. (2022) argue that there are a number of accounts engaging in sanitizing the Mnangagwa regime after the 2017 coup as well as to try and legitimize the post-2018 election government which was grappling with legitimacy issues. The Varakashi phenomenon exemplifies social media as a space for the emergence of computer-generated ghosts or robots and the counterattack by trolling (Chibuwe, 2020). The liberating potential of social media is thus limited to the low levels of irrational exchanges, mudslinging, insults, and outright lies (Tshuma et al., 2022; Chibuwe, 2020; Matsilele, 2022).[3] As another counterstrategy, ZANU-PF supporters challenge online opposition figures like journalist Hopewell Chin'ono to open debates online. Chin'ono responded that if ZANU-PF wanted debate, it would have to be on Zimbabwe Television (ZTV), the single government-controlled television in the country, accessed by most of the population and monopolized as a government mouthpiece since independence. Opposition parties have been demonized on ZTV from the days of Joshua Nkomo's Patriotic Front-Zimbabwe African People's Union (PF-ZAPU) to the present day where opposition voices are often lambasted without being given the opportunity to give their own side of the story on ZTV (Ndlovu-Gatsheni and Willems, 2010).

SURVEILLANCE AND MONITORING

The current government inherited a system experienced in surveillance, monitoring, and tracking of political opponents from the Rhodesian government which had a dedicated Special Branch of the security forces in that domain (Coltart, 2016). The Zimbabwe African Liberation Army (ZANLA) and the Zimbabwe People's Revolutionary Army (ZPRA), the armed wings of ZANU-PF and PF-ZAPU, respectively, had their cadres receive training in intelligence by the communist bloc countries; China for ZANLA and the United Soviet Socialist Republic (USSR) for ZPRA (Bhebhe, 1999). The Rhodesian government infiltrated the ZANLA and ZIPRA ranks and operational zones through the Selous Scouts (Baxter, 2012). The Selous Scouts were a Rhodesian brigade trained for counterinsurgency, of which espionage was an important aspect (Rosenau, 2007). Following this tradition, the post-independence government has long tried to contain every form of opposition to its hold on power by exercising surveillance, monitoring, and tracking of targeted perceived opponents. These targets are personnel from political opposition parties, civil society organizations, and tertiary students and their lecturers (Gukurume, 2019). Ngwenya (2014) says that since 1980, the government of Zimbabwe has passed legislation meant to control and restrict free and active citizenry.

Laws such as the Access to Information and Protection of Privacy Act (AIPPA) of 2002, Public Order and Security Act (POSA) of 2002 (ensured continuation of the Rhodesian Law and Order Maintenance Act of 1960). The Official Secrets Act (also directly inherited from colonial Rhodesia) and Criminal Law (Codification and Reform Act) of 2006 bear testimony to the government's desire to maintain a stranglehold on the communications system in the country. The Interception of Communications Act of 2007 grants law enforcement officers the power to intercept communications, including calls, emails, and other messages. Officers can apply for interception warrants if they know the identities of individuals whose calls and messages they want to intercept. Such legislation, meant to combat crime, is employed to pursue political aims and stifle dissent. Ngwenya (2014) states that the law served to confirm the suspicion that the government conducted communications surveillance of its opponents and human rights activists. In fact, many citizens are conscious that the government deploys state apparatus to spy on them. For instance, Ndoma (2017) writes that 69% of the Zimbabwean population says that the government should respect citizens' privacy and stop monitoring their private communications.

The state responded to online protests such as #ThisFlag, #ThisGown, and, more recently, #ZimbabweanLivesMatter with a combination of old and new repressive tools, suitable to the digital age. The government entrenched existing surveillance law through Statutory Instruments (SI) 142 on Postal and Telecommunications (Subscriber Registration) Regulations. Before his forced resignation in November 2017, Mugabe set up a Ministry of Cyber Security, Threat Detection and Mitigation to catch "mischievous rats" that "abused" social media (MISA-Zimbabwe, 2019). As a case in point, in July 2020, two well-known online activists were arrested for allegedly planning an anti-government protest and were only released on condition that they surrendered their passports, agreed not to use social media to promote public violence, and reported regularly to a police station. One of the activists was rearrested in November for the infringement of such draconian conditions. In a separate instance, on May 30, 2020, the editor of the online news site Mail and Review reported more than 2,000 malicious login attempts, which led to the temporary shutdown of his website. Building on a long-standing relationship forged during the struggle and under the auspices of tapping into the trade benefits associated with the Brick and Road Initiative (BRI), the Zimbabwean government acquired and deployed surveillance technology from China. Feldstein (2020) cites Zimbabwe as one of the rogue states that are using the technology from the Chinese initiative to entrench repression of its polity. Feldstein elaborates this point by noting that in return for access to surveillance technology and the opportunity to copy China's digitally enabled authoritarian system, the Zimbabwean government facilitates sending biometric data on millions of its citizens to help China develop facial recognition algorithms that work with different ethnicities. Beyond digital surveillance and intimidation, Zimbabwean authorities can resort to Internet shutdowns, for instance, in July 2016 and in January 2019 as an extreme repressive measure to counter civil unrest.

Critiquing how surveillance is causing harm to the media fraternity in Zimbabwe, Munoriyarwa and Chiumbu (2020) say that trust between journalism and their sources is now characterized by distrust and fear. They say the state finds legitimacy in snooping into citizens' communications in the Interception of Communications Act and the result is that journalists and their sources exercise caution based on distrust and fear of exposure. Tshuma et al. (2022) substantiate Munoriyarwa and Chiumbu's (2020) position on state surveillance of journalists critiquing that these actions by the state is a violation of the privacy of the journalists, civil society, and ordinary citizens who are labeled enemies of the state.

CONCLUSION

The ZANU-PF government appears to perpetuate the settler colonial regime in countering online activism using violence, counternarratives, and surveillance or monitoring. The violent anti-protest stance which characterized the Mugabe government persists under the new political dispensation despite the Mnangagwa government's sustained efforts to sell the country as a liberal democracy that is open for business. Violence is expressed in terms of the words used to describe political opponents as enemies to be destroyed as well as in the violent actions reminiscent of settler and colonial intimidatory practices. The government is also active online to push its own agenda and to drown out opposition voices. While television remains the most widely accessed and reputable media for most Zimbabweans, online countermeasures range from employing an army of pro-government cyber activists to promote alternative hashtags and openly challenge opponents. Cyber surveillance and monitoring, a necessary component of crime prevention in any country, have been bent to serve political aims. Leveraging long-standing relationships with authoritarian regimes, surveillance technology has been put to use to sabotage dissenting voices and intimidate or silence activists. In extreme cases, the Internet itself is temporarily shut down to restrict independent avenues of communication and mass mobilization.

NOTES

1. Patriotic Front Zimbabwe African People's Union (PF-ZAPU) was a nationalist movement formed on December 17, 1961, under the leadership of Joshua Nkomo. ZANU-PF broke away from ZAPU in 1963, but they fought side by side against the colonial settler regime till the 1979 ceasefire. PF-ZAPU was the first main opposition party to the ZANU-PF government in independent Zimbabwe. Mugabe wanted Zimbabwe to be a one-party state and PF-ZAPU stood in his way. He therefore set out to eliminate PF-ZAPU and its liberation war armed wing Zimbabwe African People's Revolutionary Army (ZIPRA). A special brigade of the Zimbabwe National Army; 5 Brigade was established to eliminate the PF-ZAPU/ZIPRA threat. The North Korean-trained brigade was deployed to the Matabeleland and Midlands provinces and carried out an operation called *Gukurahundi*, which is translated to mean cleanse the land of chaff after winnowing grain. The result was the death of an estimated 20,000 civilians of the Matabeleland and Midlands provinces.

2. The government of Zimbabwe sought to establish a one-party state in the 1980s and almost succeeded when the main opposition Patriotic Front Zimbabwe African People's Union (PF-ZAPU) was absorbed into ZANU-PF in December 1987. Civil society, the opposition political parties, and international media organizations exposed Mugabe and ZANU-PF dictatorship and fought for the democratization of the Zimbabwe political space formally and informally. Organizations such as World Alliance for Citizen Participation, the European Union, and International Media Support have been helping with the democratization processes in Zimbabwe. However, the conservative nature of traditional Zimbabwean politics of distrust of the West due to the colonial history and respect for the ZANU-PF government because of its liberation struggle credentials make it difficult for the pro-liberal democratic forces to establish roots and operate freely in Zimbabwe.

3. The Twitter interventions were alternative forms of communication to mobilize against the Mugabe dictatorship which had closed the democratic communication space by putting in place laws that limited participation of opposition voices in

mainstream media political communication. Laws such as the Access to Information and Protection of Privacy Act (AIPPA), Official Secrets Act (OSA), Public Order and Security Act (POSA), for instance, made media owners and journalists to exercise self-censorship because contravening these laws could easily lead to the deregistration of both journalists and media organizations. The online space such as Twitter was therefore the most convenient platforms for those voices constricted by regulation of the mainstream media space.

REFERENCES

Adiele, P. O. (2017). *The popes, the Catholic Church and the transatlantic enslavement of Black Africans 1418–1839.* Zurich: Georg Olms Verlag.
Aidi, H. (2018). *Africa's new social movements: A continental approach. Policy Brief.* Rabat: OCP Policy Center.
Alfandika, L., and Gwindingwe, G. (2021). The airwaves belong to the people: A critical analysis of radio broadcasting and licensing in Zimbabwe. *Communicatio: South African Journal of Communication Theory and Research*, 47(2): 44–60.
Baxter, P. (2012). *Selous scouts: Rhodesian counter-Insurgency specialists.* London: Helion & Company Ltd.
Bhebhe, N. (1999). *The ZAPU and ZANU guerrilla warfare and the Evangelical Lutheran Church in Zimbabwe.* Gweru: Mambo Press.
Bonello, J. (2010). The Development of early settler identity in Southern Rhodesia: 1890–1914. *International Journal of Africa Historical Studies,* 43(2): 123–141.
Chari, T. J. (2017). Electoral violence and its instrumental logic: mapping press discourse on electoral violence during parliamentary and presidential elections in Zimbabwe. *JAE,* 16(1): 72–96.
Chibuwe, A. (2020). Social media and elections in Zimbabwe: Twitter War between Pro-ZANU-PF and Pro-MDC-A Netizens. *Communication South African Journal for Communication Theory and Research,* 46(4): 123–144.
Chitanana, T. (2019). *Disinformation and digital disparities in fledgling democracies. A case study of post Mugabe Zimbabwe.* Cambridge: Harvard, Berkman Klein Center.
Chung, F. (2006). *Re-living the second Chimurenga: Memories from the liberation struggle in Zimbabwe.* Uppsala: The Nordic Africa Institute. Weaver Press.
Coltart, D. (2016). *The struggle continues: 50 years of tyrrany in Zimbabwe.* Johannesburg: Jacana Media (Pty) Ltd.
Costelloe, D. (2016). Treaty succession in annexed territory. *International and Comparative Law Quarterly,* 65: 343–378.
Craven, M. (2015). Between law and history: The Berlin conference of 1884–1885 and the logic of free trade. *London Review of International Law,* 3(1): 31–59.
Saunders, C., Fonseca, H. A., and Dallywater, L. S. G.. (2019). *Southern African liberation movements and the global Cold War 'East'.* Boston:De Gruyter OLDENBOURG.
Dzimiri, P., Runhare. T., Dzimiri. C. T., and Mazorodze, W. (2014). Naming, identity, politics and violence in Zimbabwe. *Studies of Tribes and Tribals,* 12(2): 227–238.

Feldstein, S. (2019). *The global expansion of AI surveillance*. Massachusetts: Carnegie Endowment for International Peace.

Feldstein, S. (2020). *Testimony before the U.S.-China Economic and Security Review Commission Hearing on China's Strategic Aims in Africa*. Massachusetts: Carnegie Endowment for International Peace.

Floyd, B. N. (1962). Land Apportionment in Southern Africa . . . *Geographical Review*, 52(4): 566–582.

Glenn, E. N. (2015). Settler colonialism as structure: Ā framework for comparative studies of U.S. race and gender formation. *Current (and Future) Theoretical Debates in Sociology of Race and Ethnicity. American Sociological Association*, 1(1): 54–74.

Gomba, C. (2020). Post-colonial theory in Zimbabwe's education system: Headmasters' view. *International Journal of Research Studies in Education*, 7(7): 77–88.

Gu, M. D. (2020). What is 'decoloniality'? Apostcolonial critique. *Post Colonial Studies*, 23(4): 596–600.

Gukurume, S. (2017). #ThisFlag and #ThisGown cyber protests in Zimbabwe: Reclaiming political space. *African Journalism Studies*, 38(2): 49–70.

Gukurume, S. (2019). Surveillance, spying and disciplining the university: Deployment of state security agents on campus in Zimbabwe. *Journal of Asian and African Studies*, 54(5): 763–779

Harms Smith, L. (2020). Epistemic decoloniality as pedagogical movement in social work education: A turn of theory to anti-colonial theorists such as Fanon, Biko and Freire. In *Handbook of post-colonial soial work*. London: Routledge.

Helliker, K., Bhatasara, S., and Chiweshe, M. (2021). The second Chimurenga: Guerrillas-Peasants, spirituality and patriarchy. In Helliker, K., Bhatasara, S., and Chiweshe, M. (Eds.), *Fast Track Land occupations in Zimbabwe in the context of zvimurenga*. (pp: 93–124). London: Springer.

Helps, A. (1856). *The Spanish conquest in America, and its relation to the history of slavery and to the government of colonies Volume 1*. New York: Harper & Brothers.

Kriger, N. J. (1991). *Zimbabwe's guerrilla war: Peasant voices*. s.l.: Cambridge University Press.

Kriger, N. J. (2003). *Guerrilla veterans in Post-war Zimbabwe: Symbolic and violent politics, 1980–1987*. Cambridge:Cambridge University Press.

Makubuya, A. N. (2018). *Protection, patronage, or plunder? British Machinations and (B)uganda's struggle for Independence*. Cambridge: Cambridge Scholars Publishing.

Maldonado- Torres, N. (2007). On the coloniality of being. *Cultural Studies*, 21(2): 240–270.

Manderson, L. (2016). South Africa's student protests: Īgnored by the world, a symptom of a global loss of faith that change is possible. *Research Gate*. Available at: file:///C:/Users/Admin/Downloads/SouthAfricasstudentprotests_Manderson_ResearchGate.pdf. Accessed: 02 July 2024.

Marowa, I. (2009). Construction of the 'Sellout' identity during Zimbabwe's war of liberation: A case of the Dandawa Community of Hurungwe district c1975–1980. *Identity, Culture & Politics: An Afro-Asian Dialogue*, 10(1): 121–131.

Masiya, T., and Maringira, G. (2018). The use of heroism in the Zimbabwe African National Union Patriotic Front (ZANU-PF) Intra-party factional dynamics. *Strategic Review*, 39(2).

Matsilele, T. (2022). *Social media and digital dissidence in Zimbabwe*. London: Palgrave Macmillan.

Matsilele, T., and. Ruhanya, P. (2020). Social media dissidence and activist resistance in Zimbabwe. *Media, Culture and Society*, 43(2): 381–394.

Maxey, K. (1975). *The fight for Zimbabwe: The armed conflict in Southern Rhodesia since UDI*. London: Collings.

Mazango, E. M. (2005). Media games and shifting of spaces for political communication in Zimbabwe. *Westminster Papers in Communication and Culture*, 2, 33–55.

Melber, H. (2004). Media, public discourse and political contestation in Zimbabwe. Stockholm: Nordiska Afrikainstitutet, UPPSALA.

Mosia, L., Riddle, C., and Zaffiro, J. (1994). From revolutionary to regime radio: Three decades of nationalist broadcasting in Southern Africa. *Africa Media Review*, 8(1).

Moyo, C. (2019). Social media, civil resistance, the Varakashi factor and the shifting polemics of Zimbabwe's social media "war". *Global Media Journal*, 12(1): 1–36.

Moyo, L. (2009). Repression, propaganda, and digital resistance: New media and democracy in Zimbabwe. In W. J. T. a. F. B. Okoth Fred Mudhai, (Ed). *African media and the digital public sphere* (pp. 57–71). New York: Palgrave Macmillan.

Moyo- Nyede, S., and Ndoma, S. (2020). Limited Internet access in Zimbabwe a major hurdle for remote learning during pandemic. *Afrobarometer Dispatch*, Issue 371. Available at: https://www.afrobarometer.org/publication/ad371-limited-internet-access-zimbabwe-major-hurdle-remote-learning-during-pandemic/. Accessed: 02 July 2024.

Msimanga, M. J., Ncube, G., and Mkwananzi, P. (2021). Political satire and the mediation of the Zimbabwean crisis in the Era of the "New Dispensation": The case of MAGAMBA TV. In Mpofu, S (ed), *The politics of laughter in the social media age: Perspectives from the Global South* (pp. 43–56). New York: Palgrave MacMillan.

Msimanga, M. J. (2022). *Satire and the discursive construction of national identity in Zimbabwe: The case of Magamba and Bustop TV*. Unpublished Doctoral Dissertation. University of Johannesburg.

Munoriyarwa, A. and Chiumbu, S. (2020). Big brother is watching: Surveillance regulation and its effects on Journalistic practice in Zimbabwe (Special issue: Practices, Policies and Regulation in African Journalism). *Equid Novi African Journalism Studies*, 40(3): 26–41.

Mutlokwa, H. (2020). *The impact of social media hashtags on human rights in Zimbabwe*. Available at: https://www.e-ir.info/2020/09/14/the-impact-of-social-media-hashtags-on-human-rights-in-zimbabwe/#google_vignette. Accessed: 02 July 2024.

Muwati, I., Mutasa. D. E., and Bopape, M. L. (2010). The Zimbabwean liberation war: Contesting representations of nation and nationalism in historical fiction. *Literator*, 31(1): 147–173.

Ndlovu-Gatsheni, S. J., and Willems, W. (2010). Reinvoking the past in the present: Changing identities and appropriations of Joshua Nkomo in post-colonial Zimbabwe. *African Identities*, 8(3): 191–208.

Ndlovu-Gatsheni, S. J. (2012). Elections in Zimbabwe: A recipe for tension or a remedy for reconciliation?. Pretoria: Institute for Justice and Reconciliation.

Ndlovu-Gatsheni, S. J. (2015). Decoloniality as the future of Africa. *History Compass,* 13/10: 485–496.

Ndlovu, M. (2018). Coloniality of knowledge and the challenge of creating African Futures. *Ufahamu: A Journal of African Studies,* 40(2): 181–202.

Ndoma, S. (2017). Majority of Zimbabweans want government out of private communications, religious speech. *Afrobarometer,* 165. Available at: https://www.afrobarometer.org/publication/ad165-majority-zimbabweans-want-government-out-private-communications-religious-speech/. Accessed: 02 July 2024.

Ngwenya, N. (2014). *Surveillance under the garb of rule of law.* Global Information Society Watch. Available at: https://www.giswatch.org/en/country-report/communications-surveillance/zimbabwe. Accessed on 03 July 2024.

Nilsson, D. (2013). Sweden-Norway at the Berlin Conference 1884–1885: History, national identity-making and Sweden's relations with Africa. Stockholm: Nordiska Afrikainstitutet, UPPSALA.

Quijano, A. (2000). Coloniality of power, eurocentrism, and Latin America. 15(2): 215–232.

Reed, W. C. (1993). International politics and national liberation: ZANU and the politics of contested sovereignty. *African Studies Review,* 36(2): 31–59.

Rosenau, W. (2007). Subversion and insurgency. California: RAND National Defense Institute.

Sachikonye, L. (2011). *When a state turns on its citizens: 60 years of institutionalised violence in Zimbabwe.* Harare: Weaver Press.

Shirazi, F. (2013). Social media and the social movements in the Middle East and North Africa. *Information Technology & People,* 26(26): 28–49.

Southall, R. (2020). *Fight and fortitude: The decline of the middle class in Zimbabwe.* Cambridge: Cambridge University Press.

Stigger, P. (1971). Volunteers and the profit motive in the Anglo-Ndebele war: 1893. *Rhodesian History,* 2:11–23.

Tawse, J. (1935). Native administration in Southern Rhodesia. *Journal of the Royal Society of Arts,* 83(4319): 973–985.

Tirivangasi, H. M., Nyahunda, L., and Maramura, T. C. (2021). Revisiting electoral violence in Zimbabwe: Problems and prospects. *International Journal of Criminology and Sociology,* 10(1): 1066–1074.

Tshuma L. A. (2023). Space of loud silences: Digital media start-ups and women's experiences of Gukurahundi atrocities. In Khalid, A., Holmes, G., and Parpart, J. L. (Eds), *The politics of silence, voice and the in-between* (pp. 202–212). London: Routledge.

Tshuma, B. B., Tshuma, L. A., and Ndlovu, M. (2022). Twitter and political discourses: How supporters of Zimbabwe's ruling ZANU PF party use Twitter for political engagement. *Journal of Eastern African Studies,* 16(2): 269–288.

Tshuma, L. A., Msimanga, M. J., and Sibanda, M. N. (2022). "Playing" in the eyes of the Ferret team: Examining the use of surveillance strategies by the Zimbabwean journalists. *African Journalism Studies,* 43(1): 53–69.

Chapter 7

I Don't Pay Hidden Debts

An Analysis of Public Integrity Center (CIP) Digital Communication Campaign in Mozambique

Tânia Machonisse

According to the BBC,[1] between 2013 and 2014, three newly established Mozambican companies took $2.2bn of debt, much of it without the knowledge or approval of the country's parliament. Auditors reportedly discovered that $500 million of this money could not be accounted for. The Mozambican government stood as guarantor of the loans. The money was allegedly used to buy a large tuna factory and a maritime security fleet, as well as to finance other deals involving companies in which the state was a leading shareholder. In 2016, the government swapped some of the debt for a conventional bond, issued by the state. Soon afterward, the government admitted to the full scale of the borrowing, which triggered an economic crisis in Mozambique. The country's currency lost a third of its value, inflation surged, and foreign donors pulled out.

After the revelation of the debts, 26 Civil Society Organizations (CSOs) in Mozambique created a coalition to demand accountability from the government and to protest the payment. The coalition argued that the Mozambican State should not pay the debts, which amounted to $1.86 billion. One of the organizations that had provided the loans was the bank Credit Suisse, which collapsed in March 2023. The opposition to the deal began to grow. Paula Monjane from the *Fórum de Monitoria do Orçamento* (Civil Society Budget Monitoring Forum) referred to the need for accountability:

> The officials who broke the law in Mozambique need to be held accountable by the Administrative Court and the Central Office for Combating Corruption. This

includes the lenders and financial institutions which facilitated these loans. In defence of the common good and against the continued impoverishment of the Mozambican people, we do not want, do not accept and will not pay the debts of EMATUM, ProIndicus and MAM.[2]

Since the disclosure of the illegal debts, as well as the economic and political scandal they caused, many initiatives have been organized to exert pressure on the government and former president Armando Guebuza. One of the most visible and impactful initiatives was the media campaign "I don't pay the hidden debts," which produced seven (07) audiovisual contents. These seven audiovisuals were produced and broadcasted on the CIP website, delivering core information about the context of the economic crisis, the negative impacts that these illegal debts were provoking in the economy, as well as the legal steps that had to be taken to demand accountability. This has been accompanied by a slogan led by the Public Integrity Center (CIP – *Centro de Integridade Pública*), a CSO created in 2005 to contribute to promoting transparency, anti-corruption, and integrity in Mozambique.

The profile of the Public Integrity Center (CIP – *Centro de Integridade Pública* in Portuguese) illustrates the stark contrast between *moral* political collectives, dedicated to the public good, and the secretive and corrupt behavior of state and corporate interests. CIP was created in 2005 with the aim of contributing to the promotion of Transparency, Anti-corruption, and Integrity in Mozambique. CIP is a non-profit, non-partisan, independent entity with administrative, financial, and patrimonial autonomy, created as a heterogeneous group of Mozambicans interested in contributing to the deepening of democratic governance in the country. Consisting of investigative journalists, academics, lawyers, and social scientists, CIP was accredited or recognized as Transparency International's Chapter in Mozambique.

This chapter focuses on the character of social movements in Mozambique to increase our understanding of the peculiarities of the Mozambican political, social, and economic contexts. As noted above, the chapter will help in understanding the mobilization strategies embedded in the "I don't pay hidden debts" movement. The chapter further argues that social movements in the African context have contributed to the perpetuation of complaints, reductionism, and regular focus on the lack of attention and contextual approaches that Western studies and theories have given to African social movements. The next section contains a review of social movement literature in Africa and Mozambique, followed by the methodological premise that underpins the study.

SOCIAL MOVEMENTS IN MOZAMBIQUE

The first manifestation of a nationalist movement in Mozambique is the liberation of the country from Portuguese colonial power. According to Arcénio Cuco (2016, p.145), this movement was consolidated by the formation, in 1962, of the Liberation Front of Mozambique (*Frente de Libertacão de Moçambique* – FRELIMO). This new force was the union of three formerly separate liberation movements, namely the National Democratic Union of Mozambique (*União Democrática Nacional de Moçambique* – UDENAMO), the Mozambique African National Union (MANU), and the African Union of Independent Mozambique (*União Africana de Moçambique Independente* – UNAMI). The armed conflict between the group and Portuguese colonial forces lasted from 1964 to 1974, when Portugal's Carnation Revolution took place. This set the scene for Mozambique's independence, achieved on June 25, 1975. Two years later, in 1977, FRELIMO was constituted as a political party, with a socialist orientation. FRELIMO adopted a Marxist-Leninist ideology and established a one-party system in Mozambique.

In a second wave of rebellion, discontent emerged in many sectors of society since FRELIMO's interpretation of socialist policies restricted people's fundamental citizenship rights such as freedom of expression, freedom to protest, or indeed, any manifestation of public dissent (Monjane, 2016, p.147). Moreover, the rural policies implemented by FRELIMO after independence devalued the traditional leaders and practices such as traditional medicine, representing it as obscurantism (Bertelsen, 2016, p.28). Likewise, agricultural policies did not respect or attempt to integrate the prevailing structural organization of the peasants, obliging them to shift to a collective means of production and to live in community villages to exercise closer regime control (Feijó, 2016; Darch, 2018). In the international arena, the world was dealing with two opposite political and economic ideologies, represented by the socialist and capitalist blocs, which affected Mozambique because national liberation movements were pitted against one another. Dissatisfaction with FRELIMO in both rural and urban areas began to grow, providing an opportunity for the formation of the rebel movement, the Mozambican National Resistance (*Resistência Nacional de Moçambique* – RENAMO). This group received support from racist Rhodesia and later from South Africa's apartheid regime (Bertelsen, 2016; Feijó, 2016; Darch, 2018). As a result, a civil war took place in Mozambique from 1977 to 1992.

With the General Peace Agreement (GPA) signed between FRELIMO and RENAMO on 4th October 1992 in Rome, a new democratic and multi-party-political era was initiated in Mozambique. According to Mário. (2011, p.11), in 1990, Mozambique adopted a democratic multi-party Constitution [reviewed in 2004], establishing the principles of the separation of powers and the right to form political parties. Among other measures, it also enshrined freedom of expression and of the press and the independence of the judiciary.

Additionally, in 1991 the approval of the law 8/91 on the formation of associations in Mozambique stimulated the creation of CSOs and many other associations. The pre-and post-independence history of Mozambique established a context in which civil society was unable to function and exercise its rights and duties in defense of citizens. Civil society is still at an embryonic stage (UNDP/ Civicus, 2007). Its emergence coincides with the introduction of democracy in 1990, which was followed by the approval of the Law on Associations in July 1991 (Mário, 2011, p.13). In this context, international and national NGOs, CSOs, and associations of all types and interests began to gain space, and served as a platform to demand accountability and represent the interests of socially excluded groups such as women in the governance process (Casimiro, 2015; Sambo, 2015; Feijó, 2016; Monjane, 2016). The studies on social movements in Mozambique claim that all these third-sector organizations emerged in Mozambique after 1990 due to a loss of trust in the public administration institutions which have been politicized. Taela et al. (2016, p.2) adds:

> Formally, Mozambique is a democratic republic with a multi-party system. In reality, there is the dominance of a single political party (Frelimo – Frente de Libertação de Moçambique, Mozambican Liberation Front), the ascendance of the party over state institutions and of the executive over the judiciary and the legislative, weak democratic institutions, politicisation of electoral and state bodies, weak opposition parties and lack of social accountability.

This scenario, according to Darch (2018), constitutes a fertile terrain to trigger the dissatisfaction of opposition political forces, mainly the REMANO party, which in 2013 began a military incursion into the central area of the country.

> In April 2013, therefore, in the run-up to the 2014 presidential and legislative elections, RENAMO's residual armed forces, never fully demobilised (under the pretence of guarding the leadership), decided to "return to the bush" and begin a drawn-out campaign of terrorist attacks in what was in effect a kind of "armed propaganda." (Darch, 2018, p.8)

Likewise, Taela et al. (2016, p.2) explains that

> In October 2014, Mozambique held its fifth presidential elections amidst a political climate characterised by increased distrust and deterioration of

dialogue between Frelimo (in power for the past 40 years) and Renamo which led to localised military action that is increasingly looking like a civil war.

Furthermore, the growth of the extractive industry in Mozambique in the 2000s, which spoke of improving the lives of the local communities where these mega-projects have been installed, as well as the economic growth of the country, has been constantly frustrated by the rising cost of living and flagrant corruption involving government officials and civil servants. Hossain et al. understand that the natural resources are not providing the necessary economic growth for Mozambique due to high levels of corruption.

> Mozambique has invested billions of dollars in oil and gas investments in recent years, but its high rates of economic growth have generated slow and uneven progress on poverty and human development (World Bank, 2017a). The country is correctly understood as a predatory authoritarian state, in that the domination of power chiefly serves to enrich political elites and their business allies. (Hossain et al. 2018, p.24)

Also, Ouassif and Kitenge describe the corruption problems that prevent the extractive industry from properly contributing to the reduction of poverty in Mozambique. The discovery of a huge ruby deposit and a giant gas field in Cabo Delgado in 2009–2010 raised hopes of better living conditions for Mozambicans in general and the inhabitants of Cabo Delgado in particular. However, these hopes were quickly dashed, raising concerns about corruption and monopoly of resources by a small fraction of the governing elite (Ouassif and Kitenge, 2021, p.9). Moreover, the lack of a culture of accountability on how the dividends of these natural resources that belong to all Mozambicans are being spent has contributed to the emergence of both peaceful and violent social protests across the country (Sambo, 2015). Also, two major events are boosting the general indignation of people: the hidden/illegal debts as noted above (discovered in 2015/2016) and the terrorist attacks that have been taking place in Cabo Delgado province (north of Mozambique) claimed by the Islamic State. These attacks started in 2017, whose motivations are associated with the prospects of oil and natural gas (Ouassif and Kitenge, 2021, p.7). This environment triggered street and online collective actions to demand accountability and peace in Mozambique. Furthermore, street riots, labeled "Food Riots," have taken place in Mozambique mainly in 2008 and 2010 in the capital Maputo, as well as in other provinces, due to high prices of fuel and transportation, as well as bread and other basic products and services such as electricity (de Brito et al., 2014; Bertelsen, 2016; Taela et al., 2016; Hossain et al., 2018).

PROTEST CULTURE AND THE ROLE OF SOCIAL MOVEMENTS IN MOZAMBIQUE

What tends to capture the attention of many scholars in Mozambique is the magnitude of the conflicts generated between the protestors and the government authorities. These conflicts may be physically violent, mainly when involving street riots, or symbolic when involving threats and judicial prosecution from the government to the protesters (media organizations and civil organizations, or even political and academic commentators). In this sense, collective actions that do not intend to generate conflict, or are not instigated by a reactionary attitude from the government and civilians, as well as civil organizations, NGOs, and associations, lack proper space in the scientific agendas of the social movements' scholars in Mozambique.

For instance, the hybrid protests and campaigns in 2013 and 2015 (offline and online) organized by CSOs to demand freedom of expression with regard to the judicial notification issued by the Attorney General's Office of Mozambique against the renowned academic and economist Nuno Castel-Branco, newspapers *Canal de Moçambique* and *mediaFAX* for publishing the open letter in which Nuno Castel-Branco criticizes the governance of the former president of Mozambique, Armando Guebuza (2005–2015) were almost ignored by scholars. The Attorney General's Office argued that the open letter published on Nuno Castel-Branco's Facebook page constituted an insult to the former president of Mozambique, Armando Guebuza. Likewise, the protests and campaigns (online and offline) organized from 2017 to 2021 by CSOs to demand peace in Cabo-Delgado province, as well as calling on the government to provide attention and a public pronouncement about the conflict in that province, have not yet received the substantial scientific attention within the academic community. Even the object of this chapter, the "I don't pay hidden debts" online and offline campaign, does not have a profound scientific discussion. Apart from Food Riots of 2008 and 2010 (de Brito et al., 2014), campaigns against the environmental impacts and marginalization of rural communities due to the extractive industry (Feijó, 2016), women's rights movements (Casimiro, 2015), and peasant campaigns regarding land protection and land rights (Monjane, 2016), which tend to be more offline than online, tend to receive little attention from social movement scholars in Mozambique.

It seems that the weight of a social movement and its categorization as a social movement are directly linked to its potential to generate conflicts or social disturbance. In this perspective, it sounds reasonable to question (1) if the legacy of conflicts to achieve major changes in Mozambique, through colonial liberation struggles, civil war, military incursions from Renamo, and Food Riots from civilians constitute the main rationale to conceptualize social movements and the subsequent construction of protest culture in Mozambique? (2) How, then, can the "pacific" actions developed by civilians and the third sector in Mozambique be conceptualized within the context of social movements, since both reactionary and peaceful (advocacy) collective actions are valid ways to promote human rights and improve democratic standards in the country? For instance, the literature uses the Food Riots that took place in 2008 and 2010 in the capital city of Maputo as case studies to build an understanding of typologies of social movements in Mozambique, comparing the effectiveness and performance of the informal popular protests/strikes (*greves* in Portuguese) to the formal and institutionalized protest campaigns and street manifestations organized by CSOs and NGOs (Hossain et al., 2018). Next, briefly, it is presented in the context of these *greves*. It is important to notice the role that social media, mainly Short Message Services (SMS), played as a core mobilization means to spread and explain the need of the *greves*, which allowed these popular street riots to have no leadership both in 2008 and 2010. As Bjørn Bertelsen explains in his article "Effervescence and Ephemerality: Popular Urban Uprisings in Mozambique" (2018, p.34): "Since protesters sent text messages using 'pay-as-you-go' SIM cards purchased from informal street vendors, it was almost impossible for the government to identify senders or receivers." Until after the 2010 strike, 95% of mobile phone users in Mozambique used such street-bought SIM cards with no obligation to register their details (Archambault, 2011). This situation has now changed, as the Mozambican state has made it compulsory for all users to register their SIM cards (Mabila et al., 2010, p.4).

Additionally, the legacy of colonial liberation movements and the civil war are important frameworks to analyze the typology of collective actions, usually involving violence between the police forces and the protestors. As Macamo (2014) states

> Traditionally, protests have been studied within the framework of the theoretical and conceptual framework established by the notion of social movements. Social movements are generally understood as manifestations of dissidence that translate into collective demands through relevant repertoires of collective action.

CONCEPTUALIZATION OF THE DYNAMICS THAT GUIDE CIVIC ENGAGEMENT IN AFRICA

Some authors agree that it is important to understand that social movements in Africa are hybrid, which means that they are the direct product of local imperatives and global agendas.

Most of the social movements in Africa are hybrid in nature, sometimes utilising and adapting Western ideas, funding and methods of activism. With the support of technology, individuals are now able to self-organise and put in place ad-hoc structures in response to perceived needs of the protests. (Elongué and Vandyck, 2019, p.3)

Criticism about the international donors' financial aid and consequently foreign agendas that they supposedly demand in return must be analyzed in a realist sense and not in a totally negative, passive, and oppositional fashion (Maguchu, 2009; Ellis and Kessel, 2009; Gaynor, 2011; Elongué and Vandyck, 2019). In addition, the authors mentioned above state that many African states are challenged by fragile democratic regimes, which in many cases are corrupt, and do not provide the ideal environment where CSOs, NGOs, media organizations, and citizens may enjoy a safe environment to openly express their ambitions with regard to access to better living conditions and a better distribution of existing resources, through policies that promote accountability and spaces for dialogue between populations and the rulers. In this way, through international stimuli, CSOs and NGOs have emerged to serve as a link between those who have no voice and their respective governments, as well as agents of change and promoters of human rights in the communities where they act and their rulers.

However, in some cases in the African context, CSOs and NGOs are criticized not only for depending exclusively on international funds but also for not being able to directly solve poverty issues, as well as their interventions, which are more likely to change public policies. "However, a disproportionate support to professional NGOs, which are perceived to be excellent at 'accounts-ability' rather than bringing social change, is leading to an unbalanced and unrepresentative civil society monoculture" (Elongué and Vandyck, 2019). In this sense, the article by Hisham Aidi (2018, p.4) defends that spontaneous street protests or no institutionalized or formal organizations, are effective in achieving immediate results and responding to political changes. He adds: "mid-2000s, people in myriad African cities took to the streets demanding change—with no designated leaders, political organization or political programs; the demand was simply for total change."

METHODOLOGY

The study utilizes thematic analysis, which identifies "patterns or themes within qualitative data" (Maguire and Delahunt, 2017, p.3352). Additionally, Vaismoradi and Snelgrove (2019, p.2) state that a "'theme' can be described as the subjective meaning and cultural-contextual message of data." Such themes can be codes embedded in cultural-contextual (Vaismoradi and Snelgrove, 2019, p.2). This study utilized latent analysis, which includes inductive, conceptualized, and deepest underlined ideologies embedded in the data as a method of analysis (Maguire and Delahunt, 2017). In conducting thematic analysis, six steps were considered. First, familiarizing with the data. Specifically, this study presents a transcription of the object of this research, which consists of all seven (07) audiovisual content pieces produced and published on the CIP website, Advocacia – CIP, from 2016 to 2020 to protest against "the hidden debts." Second, coding entails the process of exhaustively reading the data to capture the potential convergence of the information under analysis. Taking note of the initial patterns and main features of the data is the goal of this second step. Applying it to the present study means that by reading the digital protest content, first commonalities in the data were identified and aligned manually. Third, creating themes using the previous groups of codes and the main features detected in the data and organizing them through themes generated by the range of contexts, both theoretical and cultural, that support the conceptualization of the study.

In this study, the immediate themes were related to the repeated words and common symbolic representations of protests, such as accountability, parliament, corruption, the amount of money involved in these debts, illegalities committed, cartoon motions, and symbolic representations of political power. Fourth, reviewing the themes by refining the analysis of the codes and generating meaningful and consistent connections among the codes and previous themes. By reviewing the themes, it was possible to find similarities in the symbolic and contextual ways in which the collective identity and actions tended to be framed. Fifth, labeling the themes by digging into the symbolic meanings embedded in the pre-existing group of themes and naming those according to the similarities and meaningful connections that they seem to have. In this process, three final themes emerged: (1) Slogan as core mobilization resource for accountability; (2) Framing corruption in Mozambique as a symbol of national and international shame; and (3) Resisting state reactionary attitudes through hip-hop and cartoon motions. The next section analyzes the data.

SLOGAN AS CORE MOBILIZATION RESOURCE FOR ACCOUNTABILITY

According to Jamil (2018), diagnostic framing refers to the identification of the good and bad sides of a social issue, the edges that determine and locate the reasons, the actors, and the adversaries of the ideals that are proposed by the SMs. In other words, "problem identification and attribution" (Benford and Snow, 2000, p.615). Davis (2002, p.7) states that prognostic framing "involves the identification of possible remedies and may include the delineation of appropriate tactics and strategies." Moreover, motivational framing "relates to the efforts to invite public to participate and engage in the social movements" (Jamil, 2018, p.176). Finally, moral framing "proposes that individuals' moral systems consist of five key dimensions: care/harm, fairness/cheating, loyalty/betrayal, authority/subversion, and purity/degradation" (Graham et al., 2013 cited by Wang and Liu, 2018, p.353).

The framing process is an important tactic to mobilize allies, including mainstream media and people in general, to act against an unjust social, economic, and political situation. In so doing, building a meaning, a social cause, and a symbolic representation of collective understanding of a given issue implies the use of language, ideology, and illustrations (through arts and imagery) to create a sense of collective identity and action toward that issue (Ndovu et al., 2023; Polletta, 1998; Steinberg, 1998; Benford and Snow, 2000; Eyerman, 2005; Carty and Onyett, 2007; Jamil, 2018; Wang and Liu, 2021). One important element of framing injustice is defining oppositional sides, through which one side did or is doing wrong, and the other side, represented by Social Movements (SMs), identifies the social inequalities and provides actions to change. "When successful, frames foster a sense of injustice, identity, and collective efficacy—cognitions that a situation is wrong, that it is not immutable and that 'we' can battle 'them' in order to change it" (Polletta, 1998, p.421).

In this context, the slogan "I do not pay hidden debts" represents the identification, on the one hand, of the position and the corresponding action that the Public Integrity Center (CIP – *Centro de Integridade Pública*, in Portuguese) is taking and sharing with society. On the other hand, the slogan "I do not pay hidden debts" summarizes, contextualizes, and materializes the struggle and the protest against those institutions and individuals that are responsible for the economic crises in Mozambique, as well as demands that the debts should not be paid by the Mozambican people. By choosing "hidden debts" CIP is exposing the context in which these debts were contracted, without the approval of the Mozambican parliament, as well as the context in which they were revealed by the *Wall Street Journal*, surprising even the new Minister of Economy in Mozambique, Adriano Maleiane (2015–2022), who had no idea that these debts existed. He also received information via international and national media. Also, it is important to mention that CIP was able to translate "the hidden debts" slogan into an official national discourse through which a variety of entities in Mozambique, such as national and international media, academic elites, NGOs, Civil Society, and citizens, used to define and contextualize the current economic crisis in Mozambique. This labeling process of the circumstances through which these debts were contracted is an important achievement of CIP through this protest campaign since it enabled the creation of an immediate comprehensive framing, language, and context of what was going on in Mozambique, immediately after the public revelation of these debts. In conclusion, the slogan produced for this protest campaign constituted a way to ease the comprehension of society so that it could easily understand and comprehend the wrong deeds of the government, by providing a clear diagnosis of the problem (diagnosis framing), to promote a sense of a specific and immediate action. The immediate action was for the people not to accept that the Mozambique State should pay these debts (prognostic framing). In doing so, the move was to stimulate the engagement of people in this protest by making clear what could be done with the amount of money that was illegally loaned (motivational framing), and to shame the government of Mozambique by deploring the morality of the people involved in this scandal (moral framing).

FRAMING CORRUPTION IN MOZAMBIQUE AS A SYMBOL OF NATIONAL AND INTERNATIONAL SHAME

By referring to elements of illegality that drove the contract of this debt, CIP used a frame designed to mobilize shame, denouncing the corrupt acts of the elements of the government involved in this financial scandal. Carty and Onyett (2006, p.235) describe the mobilization of shame as a discursive tactic to expose entities that are involved in illegal acts. "by displaying or publicising norm-breaking behavior to embarrass neglectful political officials to get them to conform to norms—using what is referred to as the 'mobilization of shame.'" For instance, in the video "Mozambicans demand accountability for the illegal contracting of debt" (1:11 min), CIP (2016) explains the story of how the "hidden debts" were contracted using narrative features such as questioning the public if they knew the period in which these debts were illegally contracted, implicitly identifying the government that was responsible for the illegal debts. Part of the message on CIP (2016) reads:

> Are you aware that because of hidden business led by the government of Mozambique between 2013 and 2014 involving $2.2bn, which were not approved by the Mozambican parliament, violating the Constitution of Republic of Mozambique as well as Budget Law, the Mozambican international debt increased much more?

Moreover, CIP illustrates in the 0:45 sec video "Let's put the cards on the table" how the political and justice system was/is constituted so that it is difficult to hold those in power accountable in Mozambique. The narration above demonstrated one of the key roles that civil society plays in society, and this is giving policy direction (Ejeh & Orokpo 2022). In this part, the organization is raising the population's awareness of its right, and interpreting the constitution for all to understand the risk and gravity of the matter. CIP (2016) builds a narrative that contextualizes and denounces the corrupt government, calling it cheaters, since its members may change, but the impunity that prevails not only reveals but stimulates a lack of integrity and transparency. CIP (2016) message read:

> Let's put the cards on the table. In 2009, the government was in the hands of a range of Ministers and Deputies close to a famous winner. Overseeing this government, we had a handful of aces. But, as it can always happen in this game, someone cheated. The country lost out. It was bet on a new deck. In the next game, the trump cards just changed hands. The same cards returned to the table, even those that had played foul play. How can cheaters be held responsible if the cards are always the same?

Concomitantly, the video "I don't owe to anyone" (1:09 min) reinforces the narrative of impunity and lack of sense of justice regarding corruptive acts within the political elites of Mozambique, referring to the need for an intervention by international powers to conduct impartial investigations into the Mozambican political class. The decry from Mozambique mirrors the image of the work of NGOs in Nigeria, who have also taken it upon themselves to address state corruption. Besides exposing the rot, CSOs, as seen by these findings, offer solutions to these problems, especially local legal routes that citizens can take (Gebeyehu, 2011). This video raises important questions related to the weak role that the Mozambican General Attorney's Office had/has been playing to ensure that those involved (institutions and people) are arrested. CIP (2016) message read:

> *With the discovery of the hidden debts, the government of Mozambique pressured by international donors, civil society, and the press, accepted to undertake an independent audit to bring out the truth. . . . In light of the revealed facts, what is the Attorney General's Office waiting for intervention? Why does it protect the interests of a few individuals to the detriment of all citizens? Why do the persons responsible for the largest embezzlement of funds in the history of our country remain unpunished and out of jail? The Mozambican people deserve justice and should not have to pay an illegal and unfair debt. For the sake of transparency and democracy, DEMAND JUSTICE, it is your right.*

In addition, the inertia and the shameful position of the justice system in Mozambique are demonstrated in the video "I don't pay—Manuel Chang"

(1:13 min), through which CIP explains that it was only possible to arrest one of the main responsible persons of the recent economic crisis in Mozambique, the former Minister of Economy, Mr. Manuel Chang, when he was at OR Tambo International Airport in the Republic of South Africa (RSA), where Interpol could intervene and arrest him: *On 12/29/2018 the Former Minister of Finance of the Republic of Ducks, Chopstick, was arrested in the RSA, on his way to Dubai, where he was going to take a vacation with the millions he received in bribes for his participation in the default of $2 billion of hidden debts that bankrupted.* Therefore, this chapter argues that CSOs are also playing the journalistic role of exposing corruption and setting an agenda for the broader society (Ejeh and Orokpo, 2022).

RESISTING REACTIONARY STATE ATTITUDES THROUGH HIP-HOP AND CARTOON MOTIONS

As indicated by Steinberg (1998) and Davis (2002), culture is a crucial element in the process of building meaning since cultural recognition in the framing process enables the integration of storytelling, narratives, symbols, and artistic performances. "As a set of cultural tools, discourse provides the conventions and range of reproducible meanings through which actors find possibilities to make sense of social situation" (Steinberg, 1998, p.853). As Steinberg (1998) asserts, culture contains, among other features, storytelling; stories encompass narratives, and the latter includes a variety of components that serve as strategies to facilitate the interpretation of a given meaning. For this reason, "storytelling thus objectifies its subjects, confers a kind of fixity and stability on them" (Polletta, 1998, p.423). An activist, for example, may be trying more to make sense of what is happening around her than to mobilize participation, but when he or she tells a story of the collective "we," he/she is helping to bring that identity into being. On the other hand, "narrativity is what grips us, what keeps us listening or reading" (Polletta, 1998). Davis (2002) and Eyerman (2005) stress that it is in the "narrativity" that creativity may be explored, and different means to convey meaning are explored. "these features *might* involve narratives—be it vocabularies of meanings, expressive symbols, music, film, rules, rituals, history, sacred places, or so on" (Davis, 2005, p.10). In this context, the concept of frame amplification needs to be addressed since storytelling and narrativity aim to trigger collective identity toward an idea and action. According to Jamil (2018, p.177), frame amplification "is generally characterized by the making of slogans or symbols consisting of several words that can provoke emotions. This is the process of emphasizing an issue from a particular point of view." Likewise, Eyerman (2005) defends that emotional bonds are essential to promote collective identity and moral empathy so that collective action is possible.

In doing so, CIP invested in cartoon motions and a hip-hop song to build the storytelling and narrativity that served as a frame amplification strategy. The role of music and hip hop in political communication in Mozambique is well documented (de Brito et al., 2015; Hossain, 2007; Sitoe, 2018; Sitoe and Guerra, 2019). Therefore, the hip-hop song in this campaign, "I don't pay hidden debt or gas!" is a resistance symbol per se since in Mozambique this cultural movement has been recognized as a counter-hegemonic space against all types of injustices that people from Mozambique face. Additionally, the symbolic protest is addressed in the song when it says, *"You better pay before we clash,"* which constitutes an interesting reflection point about the culture of protest embedded in Mozambique. This study hypothesizes this culture as a legacy of colonial violence and civil war, which today is reflected in the perception that strikes and confrontations with governmental authorities are necessary for change to occur. The arguments that sustain the slogan "hidden debts" are well explored in this hip-hop song. CIP's (2016) message read:

> *Why do I have to pay for something that I don't even know how to explain/ when they contracted the debt they didn't even come to consult us if we would agree with it or not/that's why I don't agree that my taxes sustain your comfort/ because of that, I am facing several problems/You better pay before we clash .... These debts, hidden debts, I don't pay not even with gas. Notify the finance minister or the Head of State. (Chorus)*

The academic literature is also rich in describing the counter-hegemonic and dissident role that humor and cartoons have been playing in African protest movements, as well as in repressive regimes. Moreover, humor is valued as a pacific or non-violent form of protest. It is hyped for being able to build a collective connection and mobilize symbolic political action with the protests since it reinforces cultural bonds and uses cultural symbols to represent, explain, and amplify the main injustices that people are facing (Mpofu, 2021; Hart, 2007; Hart, 2016; Damir-Geilsdorf and Milich, 2020). To add on, cartoons represent freedom of expression from the media organizations and an artistic fashion to represent symbolically the political dilemmas that the African countries face, due mainly to corruption and lack of accountability. Cartoons are a means to promote critical thinking and engage all strata of society to understand social and political problems (Hammett, 2010; Ojo, 2015; Eko, 2017; Rivers, 2018). In this digital protest campaign, there are several examples of humor and cartoons being used to criticize the government of Mozambique, exploring peculiar cultural contexts that involved these debts. For instance, in the video "The story of Croc, the son of *Patolândia* [Duck land]" (1:22 min), Mozambique is described as Duck land or the "Republic of Ducks" by CIP to remind the public of the answer that Armando Guebuza, former president of Mozambique (2005–2015) right after he was elected president in 2005, gave when asked by a journalist how he became so rich. The president's answer was "raising and selling ducks." Moreover, by using the word "Croc" meaning crocodile, which is an animal used in many Mozambican fables to indicate the son of former president Armando Guebuza, CIP intends to represent, by analogy, how ingenious Ndambi Guebuza was to, supposedly, persuade his father to contract these debts. This is captured by CIP (2016)'s message which says: *"Croc, the son of the baron of Duck land, convinced Papa croc to borrow 2 bilion dollars, without the consent of the people, and for 'refreshment'—croc received 50 million chickens ($) from Jean Boustani of Privinvest."* From the discussion above, the chapter notes that CSOs play a fundamental role in fighting corruption. The findings are like the studies in Nigeria where, since the return to democratic rule, civil society has been at the forefront advocating for good governance and offering better policy measures (Pérouse de Montclos, 2005).

CONCLUSION

The creative framing of the context under which the hidden debts were contracted constitutes one of the most outstanding achievements of this campaign. Moreover, by integrating elements of illegality that drove the contract of this debt, CIP engaged in frame mobilization, denouncing the corrupt acts of the elements of the government involved in this financial scandal, as well as providing arguments for collective action through the "I don't pay hidden debts" slogan. Also, CIP was able to translate "the hidden debts" slogan into an official national discourse. Symbols of resistance embedded in the Mozambican protest culture are present in this protest campaign, which supports the hypothesis that "clashes," *greves* or riots are valued as necessary means to demand change in the country, as well as sustains the hypothesis that the protest culture in Mozambique has its foundation and rationale in the armed conflicts that the country faced to achieve structural transformations in its political regimes (colonial and socialist).

NOTES

1. Information published on https://www.bbc.com/news/world-africa-58304737, August 23, 2021

2. Information published on https://debtjustice.org.uk/blog/mozambiques-secret-loans-scandal-started-london, September 9, 2016.

REFERENCES

Benford, R. D., and Snow, D. A. (2000). Framing processes and social movements: An overview and assessment. *Annual Review of Sociology*, 26(1), 611–639.

Bertelsen, B. E. (2016). Effervescence and ephemerality: Popular urban uprisings in Mozambique. *Ethnos*, 81(1), 25–52.

Carty, V., and Onyett, J. (2006). Protest, cyberactivism, and new social movements: The reemergence of the peace movement post 9/11. *Social Movement Studies*, 5(3), 229–249.

Casimiro, I. M. (2015). Movimentos sociais e movimentos de mulheres em Moçambique. In Silva, Teresa and Casimiro, Isabel (eds.), *A Ciência ao Serviço do Desenvolvimento* (pp: 51–66). Dakar: CODESRIA.

Cusco, A. F. (2017). FRELIMO: de um movimento revolucionário a partido político. *Revista NEP-Núcleo de Estudos Paranaenses da UFPR*, 2(2), 137–152.

Damir-Geilsdorf, S., and Milich, S. (2020). Forms and Functions of Political Humor in Arab Societies. In Damir-Geilsdorf, S. and Milich, S. (Eds.), *Creative Resistance* (pp. 9–50), New York: Columbia University Press.

Darch, C. (2018). *The Mozambican conflict and the peace process in historical perspective*. FES: Maputo.

Davis, J. E. (2005). Narrative and social movements the power of stories. In Davis, J (Ed.), *Stories of Change: Narrative and Social Movements*. New York: Suny Press.

de Brito, L., Chaimite, E., Pereira, C., Posse, L., Sambo, M., and Shankland, A. (2014). Hunger revolts and citizen strikes: Popular protests in Mozambique, 2008–2012. Food Riots and Food Rights project report. Brighton/Maputo: Institute of Development Studies/Instituto de Etudos Sociais e Economicos. www.foodriots.org.

Earl, J. et al. (2014). New technologies and social movements. In Della Porta, D., & Diani, M. (Eds.), *The Oxford Handbook of Social Movements*. Oxford University Press.

Eko, L. (2007). It's a political jungle out there: How four African newspaper cartoons dehumanized and deterritorialized' African political leaders in the post-cold war era. *International Communication Gazette*, 69(3), 219–238.

Ejeh, A. W., and Orokpo, O. F. (2022). The civil society and the fight against corruption in Nigeria. *International Journal of Innovative Social Sciences & Humanities Research*, 10(1), 1–10.

El Ouassif, A., and Kitenge, S. Y. (2021). Terrorist insurgency in Northern Mozambique: Context, analysis, and spillover effects on Tanzania. *Policy Centre for the New South*. Available at: https://www.policycenter.ma/index.php/publications/terrorist-insurgency-northern-mozambique-context-analysis-and-spillover-effects?page=1. Accessed 14 July 2024.

Feijó, J. (2016). Investimentos, assimetrias e movimentos de protesto na província de Tete. *Observador Rural*, 44, 1–30.

Gaynor, N. (2011). Globalising resistance: Social movement activism in Malawi. Paper presented at the Social Movements in Africa ECAS 4th European Conference on African Studies, Uppsala, Sweden. June 15th–18th.

Gebeyehu, N. Z. (2011). *The role of African civil society in combatting corruption*. Master Thesis Submitted to the Catholic University of East.

Hammett, D. (2010). Political cartoons, post-colonialism and critical African studies. *Critical African Studies*, 2(4), 1–26.

Hart, M. T. (2007). Humour and social protest: An introduction. *International Review of Social History*, 52(S15), 1–20.

Hossain, N., Aremu, F., Buschmann, A., Chaimite, E., Gukurume, S., Javed, U., and Taela, K. (2018). Energy protests in fragile settings: The unruly politics of provisions in Egypt, Myanmar, Mozambique, Nigeria, Pakistan, and Zimbabwe, 2007–2017. Brighton: Institute of Development Studies.

Jamil, A. (2018). Social movements in framing perspectives: A study on corruption case issues in Indonesia. *JURNAL Komunikasi Indonesia,* 2(7)*,* 174–191.

Macamo, E. (2017). O lugar e o papel da crítica social no "programa de investigação" sobre movimentos sociais. In Brito, L. (Ed), *Agora eles têm medo de nós! Uma colectânea de textos sobre as revoltas populares em Moçambique (2008–2012)* (pp. 195–211). Maputo: Institute of Social and Economic Studies (IESE).

Maguchu, P. (2020). Grassroots social movements: A new narrative on human rights in Africa?. *Revista RDY Republica Derecho*, 5(5), 1–26.

Maguire, M., and Delahunt, B. (2017). Doing a thematic analysis: A practical, step-by-step guide for learning and teaching scholars. *All Ireland Journal of Higher Education*, 9(3), 3351–3514.

Majumdar, A. (2022). Thematic analysis in qualitative research. In Information Resources Management Association *Research anthology on innovative research methodologies and utilization across multiple disciplines* (pp. 604–622). Pennsylvania: IGI Global.

Monjane, B. (2016). Movimentos sociais, sociedade civil e espaço público em Moçambique: uma análise crítica. *Cadernos CERU*, 27(2), 144–155.

Mpofu, S., Ndlovu, M., and Tshuma, L. (2021). The artist and filmmaker as activists, archivists and the work of memory: A case of the Zimbabwean genocide. *African Journal of Rhetoric*, 13(1), 46–76.

Ndlovu, M., Tshuma, L., and Mpofu, S. (Eds). (2023). *Remembering mass atrocities: Perspectives on memory struggles and cultural representations in Africa*. Cham: Springer International Publishing.

Ojo, P. A. (2015). Cartooning contemporary Sub-Saharan African experiences: A new perspective. *Review of Arts and Humanities*, 4(1), 60–71.

Polletta, F. (1998). Contending stories: Narrative in social movements. *Qualitative Sociology,* 4(21), 419–446.

Rivers, D. J. (2018). Political cartoons as creative insurgency: Delegitimization in the culture of convergence. In *Discourses of (De) Legitimization* (pp. 248–268). Routledge.

Sambo, M. G. C. A. (2015). *The youth dimension of the social protests in Maputo–Mozambique (2008 and 2010)*. Unpublished Master Dissertation, International Institute of Social Studies, The Hague.

Sitoe, T. H. (2018). Para Além de uma Escolha: Da música de crítica e protesto social às identidades político-partidárias em Moçambique. *Cadernos de Estudos Africanos*, (35), 135–148.

Sitoe, T., and Guerra, P. (2019). Reinventar o discurso e o palco: o rap, entre saberes locais e saberes globais.

Steinberg, M. W. (1998). 27 *Tilting the frame: Considerations on collective action framing from a discursive turn*. Theory and Society (27), 845–872.

Vaismoradi, M., Jones, J., Turunen, H., and Snelgrove, S. (2016). Theme development in qualitative content analysis and thematic analysis. *Journal of Nursing Education and Practice*, 6(5),100–110.

Wang, R., and Liu, W. 2021. Moral framing and information virality in social movements: A case study of #HongKongPoliceBrutality. *Communication Monographs*, 88(3), 350–370.

Chapter 8

Of Protests and Satire

Representations of #EndSARS Brutality in Selected Nigerian Hip-Hop Music

Ruth Karachi Benson Oji

Music has long been used as a means of protest and to satirize contentious issues in society. This is owing to the popularity of the medium and its capacity to make poignant remarks with which an audience can identify. Given that most of the authoritarian regimes in Africa are unapproachable, carefully constructing lyrics seems to be a prominent way for musicians to communicate their thoughts on issues and protest the negative events taking place in their respective countries. Hence, music can be considered an effective way to convey one's thoughts on a given matter. Consequently, protest music is composed by artists with the intention of inciting positive change and promoting certain ideologies in the society. Hampton (1986 as cited in Lawrance, 2000) notes that protest songs promote cultural contexts that enable sociopolitical movements as well as organizations in their development of political ideologies. This they do by framing the issues in a way that elicits the support of the listeners. That such framing is integral to the goal of the protest is Klandermans' (1997) emphasis when he notes that it enables artistes to denounce injustice—by highlighting the social actors responsible for the problems being experienced in the country. More so, framing helps them construct a *we* versus *them* dichotomy. People can readily connect with the artistes' production and see themselves in the way issues are framed. In addition, some researchers have argued that culture plays a role in this. In other words, when people gather to protest, culturally, they see music as a tool that enables them to push their ideologies across to the opposition. That is Reed's (2005, p.299–300) position when he suggests that members of a movement can through music feel energized and empowered to challenge dominant ideas, values, and tactics of those in power by evoking emotions and meanings within the audience. When popular music therefore serves the purpose of educating the society about the history of their place as well as demand the authorities a solution to a perceived injustice, it does what a protest song does. Stewart et al. (1984) summarize the persuasive functions of protest songs as including the promotion of cohesion and camaraderie among those involved in a movement and the urging of specific actions regarding the cause.

Protest music in Nigeria dates to the era of Fela Anikulapo-Kuti, who challenged the government to correct anomalies in the system (Matsilele and Msimanga, 2022). Osuagwu (2019) notes that Fela was influenced by black American Jazz and politics. She suggests that his music was rife with political consciousness that reflected rebellion against the Nigerian authority. He not only used his music to motivate his people to develop a sense of nationalism but also used it to criticize several military regimes in Nigeria. The likes of Ras Kimono, Peterside Ottong, the Mandators, and Isaac Black through their music at different times also satirized the government and resisted military rule (Nweke, 2020).

In Nigeria, corruption, bad leadership, and oppression remain the focus of some artists to highlight such issues and call for change (Matsilele et al., 2021). A popular artist in Nigeria whose music incorporates lots of protest themes is Eedris Abdulkareem. As a songwriter, singer, hip hop and Afro-beat artist, he uses his music to promote activism and protest inconsistencies that are rife in the society. One of his most popular releases in 2004 is titled *Jaga Jaga*, which is a Yoruba word that may mean "disorientation" or "in a shamble." And he used this song to show what he projected as the debased state of the Nigerian milieu.

Chinagorom Onuoha, popularly known by his record name, African China, is another such artist. Okuyade's (2012) study finds that African China's protest music depicts the sufferings endured by individuals who are highly marginalized in Nigeria. It also critiques and resists the social structures from which such suffering emanates and is glorified, and the music also sends a call to action to the listeners to do something about their situation to improve their lot in life. African China's career started in 1999, and he has since then released about two albums entitled *Crisis* (2004) and *Mr. President* (2006), depicting what he describes as the sorry state of the country. Nineteen years after releasing the latter album, issues Chinagorom protested are still abundant in society, and this has led to further protests by the populace. Arguably, agitations and protests have always been an integral part of the Nigerian system. Adebowale (2020) undertakes a historical perspective of the issue of protests in Nigeria and finds that in about 1900, the masses were disgruntled over a government policy involving a tax levy, and this led to women in the eastern region protesting. Even though many women were said to have been killed during the protest, more women joined, leading to the Aba Women's riot of 1929. In 1947, there was also the case of Madame Olufunmilayo Ransome-Kuti leading a protest over tax laws, with 10,000 women—resulting in some success with having their demands met. More so, there were the June 12, 1993 protests the military regime of Major General Sanni Abacha—and this led to the deaths of many, including students. Adebowale (2020) suggests that protests continue so that posterity would not hold those now alive accountable for leaving a bad world for them. And this may suggest why many artistes continue to use music as a platform for protesting the anomalies in society. Several other Nigerian musicians have protested and satirized the unbalanced state of affairs in the country—the killing of innocent citizens and lack of jobs for the youth, owing to no god-fatherism or connections; corruption; and bribery, as experienced in many quarters of the government. Such artists include Dremo Drizzy, Falz Falana, Burna Boy, Kvng Kila, and Ajebo Hustlers.

As has been shown, the discourse of protest is not new in Nigeria. Studies have engaged these protests from several lens (Labinjoh, 1982; Mason, 1973; Osuagwu, 2019; Onanuga and Akingbe, 2020). However, the #EndSARS protest is unique in Nigeria because that was the first time Nigerian youth moved out in their numbers to protest police brutality. Studies from the academic mainstream have investigated the #EndSARS protest from musicological discourse perspective (Iliya, 2022), social media perspectives (Bodunrin and Matsilele, 2023; Iwuoha et al., 2021; Dambo et al., 2021; Akerele-Popoola et al., 2022; Uwalaka et al., 2022), negotiation management perspective (Etim et al., 2022), femininst perspectives (Nwabunnia, 2021), and a right to protest perspective (Ekeke, 2023). These studies are revealing and insightful about the protests. However, studies on hip-hop music have not sufficiently engaged the #EndSARS protest.

The motivation for engaging the discourse from the hip-hop lens is that even after the #EndSARS protest, the realities of the protest continue to resonate in several Nigerian music. The musical genre that has anchored this prominently is the hip-hop. Even though studies have engaged the hip-hop discourse (Benvenga, 2022; Akingbe et al., 2020; Crosley, 2005; Alridge et al., 2005; Riesch, 2005; Shevy, 2008; Kistler et al., 2009), the discourse of #EndSARS has not enjoyed much scholarly interrogation in hip-hop music in Nigeria. The only two prominent hip-hop artistes that have commendably articulated the #EndSARS protest in their music are Aboriomoh Femi Raymond, known by his stage name Dremo Drizzy, and Damini Ebunoluwa Ogulu, known as Burna Boy. Dremo Drizzy hails from Edo State, Nigeria, and focuses on afro-pop and hip-hop genre in his performances. He has actively been singing since 2013 and has about 18 collections to his name. Burna Boy is a songwriter, singer, and record producer and is an indigene of

Port Harcourt, in Rivers State, Nigeria. He does afrobeats, reggae, and pop, among others, and has about 49 collections to his name.

This study is interested in anchoring van Dijk's socio-cognitive model of critical discourse analysis. While extant studies have combined insights from perspectives such as media, musicology, feminism, and negotiation management, there has not been enough engagement of the resourcefulness of van Dijk's socio-cognitive frame in analysing the #EndSARS protest. The motivation for the choice of van Djik's socio-cognitive theory is that it examines how social situations, contexts, and social actors are linked in text interpretations. Besides, existing studies on hip-hop discourse have not engaged how the perception of hip-hop artistes are contextually articulated. This explains why this study investigates how hip-hop artistes perceive social actors in the #EndSARS protest.

The specific objectives of this study are to examine how social actors are constructed in the #EndSARS protest and the implications of such construction for the language of the hip-hop discourse. A study of this nature is significant for several reasons. Apart from showing that the engagement of protest in #EndSARS goes beyond a semiotic reading, it will also show how the perception of the artistes are contextually constructed. This study, therefore, examines the musical lyrics around the #EndSARS protest of two Nigerian artists, namely, Dremo Drizzy and Burna Boy, in order to achieve the stated objectives.

#ENDSARS IN NIGERIA

The #EndSARS protest which occurred in October 2020 encapsulated series of mass protests around the country against uncontrolled police brutality in Nigeria. The protests revolved around the call for disbanding the Special Anti-Robbery Squad (SARS). It seems ironic that a police unit specifically charged with protecting the masses from robbery, abuse, extorting, and murder has adopted the same modus operandi as those it aims to apprehend. The #EndSARS movement started in 2017 on Twitter, but in 2020, given the high volume of complaint on social media, many young people decided to own the protest physically in many locations around the country. According to Adisa (2021), Segun Awosanya, a human rights activist led the campaign online. The hashtag #EndSARS became popular on Twitter, and this led to 10,195 persons filing petitions for the disbandment of SARS by the Nigerian National Assembly. By 2020, the protests had surged online, given the introduction of the phrase "soro soke," meaning "speak loudly," leading to about 10,467 female authors and 20,883 male authors posting comments on the call for #EndSARS. Akinyetun (2021) and Ekoh et al. (2021) both note that the circulation on all social media handles of the evidence of the killing of a young man in Delta State on October 3, 2020, and the killing of another man in Oyo State on October 8, 2020, both by SARS members, further fuelled the protests in 21 states in Nigeria, culminating in the October 20 Lekki tollgate protest in Lagos that led to the death of some of the protesters. This reinforces Harlow's (2011) findings that users' protest-related and motivational comments, in addition to their use of links and other interactive elements of social media handles, help to organize massive protests demanding justice and an end to violence. In addition to protesting the extortions and killings by the police group, the #EndSARS movement was also used to demand good governance on many fronts by Nigerian citizens. However, the October demonstrations led to the killing of about 29 unarmed young protesters at the Lekki tollgate and at other times during the protests by those wearing the uniforms of the Nigerian Police and Army. Iwuoha et al. (2021) claim that these killings took place between October 10 and 21, 2020.

The #EndSARS protest of October 2020 was supported by musicians in a bid to show the world what Nigerian rulers are like, and what they would prefer to see instead. Artists such as Africa China, Eedris Abdulkareem, Timaya, Falz, Asa, Laycon, Dremo, RudeBoy, Ruggedman, Dotman, and Burna Boy called for Nigerian leaders to practice democracy and give the people their rights as citizens. Even though some researchers have suggested that there is a decline in the creation and production of protest music (Nweke, 2021; Ige, 2020), evidence has it that the youth are not relenting in voicing their opinions through music.

LITERATURE REVIEW

Many studies have been carried out to show how protest is done via the medium of music in Africa (Matsilele et al., 2023; Matsilele and Msimanga, 2022; Heilbronner, 2016). Heilbronner (2016) reviews the intersections of political cultures and popular music cultures. He bases his review on the 1960s and attests that the era, from both a political and cultural perspective, was filled with protests during a period when "family values" were also meant to have become prominent. The review brought to light why musical artists view music as an indirect agent of change since it provides some protection against human tragedy. He suggests that protest music is more than the sum of its lyrics, on the basis that it has the power to move people to action. He points to the evidence of such action by highlighting among other things how protest music facilitated angry reactions in people in the United States in 1968 and onward (2016, p.690–691). Related to this, Haycock (2015) explores protest music from a pedagogical point of view.

He examines the relationship between this form of expression and social change—in other words, he reviews how protest music is a learning point for the consumers. He considers protest music as a mass cultural practice exchanged as a form of commodified product, made available to the public through digital platforms. Using the example of adult education, he links two concepts, namely "hegemony" and "conscientization," since public pedagogy adds an epistemological lens that enables an interrogation of protest music as it is produced and exchanged. The major concern of his article is with:

> the inherent knowledge and cultural production and exchange processes of protest music as a form of mass/popular music; how musicians as performers and producers of popular/protest music texts might be understood as public pedagogues; and how audiences, consumers or users of protest music texts might be considered adult learners. (Haycock, 2015, p.426–427)

The above assertion takes presupposes that the audience, while listening to protest music, are saddled with the responsibility of learning and inferring from the message or "teaching" documented by the artistes. If the musician is a teacher, the listener is a learner. Thus, change can be attained if people deeply engage with the "education" conveyed by such music. When this is done, there are high chances that the purpose of the protest music can be actualized. Undertaking a comparative analysis of two protest songs from 2018—"This is America" by Gambino, and "This is Nigeria" by Falz (2020)—Akingbe and Onanuga (2020) show that the exasperation of the musicians parallels the frustrations of youths in both cultures. Their analysis unveils how the two music videos are protests used by both artists as:

> instrument of resistance to draw attention to perceived social, economic and political problematics as they affect the cross-cultural American and Nigerian societies, and to proffer solutions that could lessen their impact on the aforementioned societies, or possibly eliminate them to the benefit of all. (Akingebe and Onanuga, 2020, p.2)

This study is similar to Akingbe and Onanuga's (2020) in that it shows how Nigerian artists use their music to protest against bad governance, corruption, and other ills dominant in the society. However, a major departure from theirs for this study is that the focus is on how the social actors perceived to be responsible for the anomalies in the society are constructed and the implications this has for the language of hip-hop discourse. Some studies have interrogated the issue of protest music from a much wider perspective. Lewis et al. (2020, p.2) have the following as the major aim in their article:

to unpack a new issue for development research along five related lines of initial enquiry: the tradition of Western 'protest' music; musical resistance in the Global South; music-based development interventions; commodification and appropriation; and, finally, music as a global development vernacular.

To unravel these, their research investigated music and development from the lens of Global North and Global South and their representations of states in their music—issues of marginalization and soliciting for funds. They hoped to attract the attention of key stakeholders to such developmental issues as documented in their research. Oftentimes, that seems to be the purpose of such documentation—to show how things are. The authors have a laudable initiative. However, their focus has nothing to do with hip-hop music, which is the primary lens of this study, given how it is being used in the Nigerian context. In addition, it is pertinent to explicate how language is used to contextualize the social actors referred to in the music, and that is what this study does. Other studies, Mondak (2008) and Damodaran (2016), aver that protest music is a tool for political persuasion and argues that if such music did not elicit a positive response from the listeners, it would be fruitless for social critics to include them in their campaigns when speaking against the incumbent government and a change is sought. The argument is further that both history and social context play a huge role in protest music's representational and functional aspects— which is why there are different kinds of protest music for the purpose of engaging issues of politics. This stance supports the position taken in this chapter that protest music is used by artistes to not only advance their ideological propositions but those of the wider society who also feel the need for a change. What is more, the way artistes contextually construct societal issues portends a lot for how the audience interprets them and act on them.

PROTEST AND SATIRE IN AFRICAN SONGS

Many African artists are also generally interested in protest music, which also serves as a satirical tool to expose the political corruption of their respective governments. This possibility of protesting negative occurrences in society, occasioned using music, is an activity that permeates the global space. Interrogating the use of music by Majiavana (an artist from a minority tribe in Zimbabwe), Dube and Ncube (2019) show how authority can be questioned and challenged. Examining Majiavana's music, they explore how the artist enables his tribe to "fight back" against repression and own their political identities. According to Dube and Ncube (2019), the government was perceived as local colonialists who tried to prevent the tribe from voicing their concerns, and this resulted in the people turning to music to both protest and satirize this phenomenon. Several themes permeate the songs, such as economic hardship, forced migration, social exclusion and nostalgia, and they thus "provided a public space for the voiceless" (Dube and Ncube, 2019, p.162). This study correlates with that of Haycock (2015) who posits that artistes are like public pedagogues who provide their listeners with knowledge required to act. Heilbronner's (2016) perspective is also simulated here. Through Majiavana's music, his tribe acts, and this is one goal of protest songs.

From a completely different perspective, Chitando (2007) explores how the gospel music genre in Zimbabwe serves as an opportunity for artists to protest. While reference is made in his article to several genre of songs that served to get the people thinking about and appreciating their freedom, especially on Independence Days, the author examines how the government's failure to keep up with their promises to make life easier for the masses served as a boost to get the people to protest again and again through their songs. However, many of such post-colonial songs came from the religious background with a view to "conceal the sting" of the protest and make them appear like "a plea to either God or the ancestors" (Chitando, 2007, p.340). Chitando, (2007, p.341) further argues that there is a "convergence between popular protest songs and the subterranean protest in gospel music." The use of gospel music to protest the inefficiencies of the government is a creative way for the artists to focus less attention on themselves while highlighting the anomalies in the society. This clandestine approach seems to work because hardly are gospel artistes called out for their representations of slavery and emancipation. While the current study zooms in on protest songs, its focus is, not on gospel songs but on hip-hop music that protests the #EndSARS movement in Nigeria.

In Nigeria, several scholars have attempted exploring musical pieces and their underlying meanings. Osuagwu (2019) explores protest music and the Nigerian situation. In her work, she undertakes a survey approach to highlight the perception of the youth on protest music in Nigeria, and she finds that rather than the assertion that connection to the music may not be made by individuals who listen to it, the youth not only understand the message behind the lyrics but are also motivated by them, and this finding supports Heilbronner's (2016) stance regarding the effect of protest music on people who listen to it.

From a linguistics perspective, some scholars have interrogated pragmatic and related acts performed through music in Nigeria. For example, Sunday (2021a, p.1) examines how a Nigerian artist's (Olamide) music embedded a lot of ideological constructs and pragmatic acts in order to project a rejoinder to people's views about him. He finds that the artist

> engaged the use of hedonistic and supremacist ideologies; deployed the practs of asserting, informing, mocking, warning and threatening; attacked his

unnamed detractors pungently while asserting his own invincibility; tactically used similes, metaphors, allusion and code alternation; deployed traditional and modern imagery to cater for old and young listeners; used mainly call-and-response in presenting the song; and deployed the members' resources of the Yoruba artistically to ward off attack and instil fear in his enemies.

This analysis confirms the stance that Nigerian musicians through their music respond to the happenings in society. Such strategies that Sunday (2021a) finds are indicative of the artiste's recourse to both satire and protest in his songs resonate with some studies done in Africa assessing the power of satire (Msimanga et al., 2022; Msimanga et al., 2021). And while the strategies deployed are bold, rather than subterranean—like was observed in Chitando's analysis of gospel protest music, they highlight how language is used to represent the state of things in society. People use language to assert, inform, mock, warn, threaten, and attack. It is, however, important to synthesize from a socio-cognitive model additional way that language is used by hip-hop artistes to protest anomalies. Sunday (2021b) also shows how COVID-19 was fought through music by his examination of Cobhams Asuquo's (2020) *We Go Win Corona*. He approaches his analysis from a Critical Stylistic perspective in order to show what stylistic devices were used to demystify issues around the virus. Using Halliday's (2014) Systemic Functional Grammar and van Dijk's (2006) approach to Critical Discourse Analysis, he finds that "declaratives, modals and conditional sentences are used to present what needs to be done to win the battle against the virus." His findings show that such music has been used to bolster the "inner strength needed to fight and win the Coronavirus battle."

These studies considered are very insightful, having articulated the need for an in-depth examination of protest songs, and they are relevant to the current study in that the subject of protest songs and how they move people to action is a recurring theme. However, this study argues that the engagement of protest in #EndSARS goes beyond a semiotic reading. This study also investigates how the perception of participants are contextually constructed. Also, while these reviewed studies are insightful, none of them deploys van Dijk's socio-cognitive model to investigate the construction of social actors from a contextual frame. In other words, these studies have not sufficiently interrogated how participants in the #EndSARS protest songs are contextually constructed. This explains why this study deploys this theory to interrogate this.

THEORETICAL BASE

Downing (2001) explains that radical media can refer to media that is generally small-scale and in many different forms, that express an alternative vision to hegemonic policies, priorities, and perspectives. Downing (2001, p.ix) further states that radical media "represent radically negative as well as constructive forces" depending on the vantage point of the observer. Downing (2001, p.8) further states that radical media "focuses attention on the matrix of radical alternative media, relatively free from the agenda of the powers that be and sometimes in opposition to one or more elements in that agenda." Radical media shine light on abuses of power and agitate for social justice and political change (Vatikiotis, 2005; Downing, 2001; Msimanga, 2022). This often leads to clashes with authorities. While radical and alternative media has traditionally been associated with the press (cf. Atton, 2002), it has increasingly incorporated satire, graffiti, music, and theatre, among others.

Teun van Dijk's (2008) socio-cognitive approach to discourse analysis serves as the theoretical framework for this study. Emphasis is placed on how the context contributes to shared background information and the relationship between discourse and social inequality (van Dijk, 2006, 2014, 2015). This is applied by analyzing the lyrics of the texts, describing the language used by the artists to identify the social actors, and exploring the lexical choices used to convey the artists' representations of social actors in the #EndSARS protest. Every expression has an ideological base, and it is pertinent to examine such basis so that things are not taken for granted or ideological positions get to be the norm by people. Using the merged approach in this study helps to situate the real position of concepts described in the protest music under analysis. Halliday's approach is predicated on the metafunctions of language—ideational (use of language in conveying understanding and perception of the real world); interpersonal (use of language to express roles and attitudes and convey judgment); and textual (use of language to organize the text [spoken or written] for linguistic purposes) aspects (Morley, 1985; Halliday and Mattthiessen, 2014). van Dijk's approach borders a lot on how mental and context models control and determine discourse, and they depend on the metafunctions of language earlier identified. Emphasis is placed on how the context contributes to shared background information and the discourse in general (van Dijk, 2006, 2014, 2015). In relation to this study, the merged approach helps to show how protest discourses in music are constructed and the ideological underpinnings behind the meanings, considering the metafunctions of language and the contexts of the discourses. This is applied by analyzing the lyrics of the texts, describing the language used by the artists, and exploring the linguistic tools and lexical choices used to convey the artists' representations of #EndSARS protest and the resulting brutality meted out to the protesters.

METHODOLOGY

The data for this study comprises two songs by two Nigerian artists, namely Dremo Drizzy and Burna Boy. The songs were purposively selected because of the proliferation of protest lyrics in them. Only two songs were selected because of their length and content so that they can be fully explicated. Also, they were downloaded from an online site—YouTube. Some parts of the songs are recorded in Pidgin English but are also translated in Standard British English to help international audience to understand. The analysis of data—the lyrics of the songs—were subsequently premised on the theoretical base, which is van Dijk's (2008) socio-cognitive approach to critical discourse analysis. To achieve this, the songs are subjected to a contextual analysis as postulated by van Dijk (2008) where the inherent and underlying representations in the songs are uncovered—lexical choices, clauses, and the ideological implications for them are examined. The context around such image creation is considered because it helps to reveal why issues are represented the way they are by the artists. In other words, linguistic choices are identified and linked to social engagement, social interaction, and social structures, which are foundational tools in van Dijk's socio-cognitive approach to discourse.

PROTEST MUSIC BY DREMO DRIZZY AND BURNA BOY AND REPRESENTATIONS OF #ENDSARS BRUTALITY

This section focuses on the protest songs of Dremo and Burna Boy as representations of the #EndSARS brutality experienced by many of the youth who went out to protest the nefarious activities of the SARS group in all quarters of the country. In analysing the songs, the social background and the context that gave rise to the song are referred to. I begin this section with an analysis of Dremo Drizzy's (2020) "Thieves in Uniform." In the totality of this music, Dremo critically describes the Nigerian Police Force with lexical items that denote the lived experiences of the people. He articulates his description in a way to protest the ill-treatment of the youth by an arm of the government instituted to protect lives and property. The analysis is followed by Burna Boy's (2020) "20-10-20"—a music sung to decry the shooting and killing of Nigerian youth at Lekki tollgate. His lexical choices satirize and protest the activities of the SARS group in Nigeria.

NEGATIVE REPRESENTATION OF NIGERIAN POLICE

The chapter begins this section with an analysis of Dremo Drizzy's (2020) "Thieves in Uniform." The analysis aims to show how the artiste represents the social actors in his music and the language he deploys to achieve this. Dremo starts the discourse on a rhetorical note. Such use of language creates a sense of dissatisfaction with the services of the Nigerian police. This also serves as an instrument for engaging the listeners to identify with the predicament of this artiste. This is so because the question, "When will the ongoing police brutality end?" does not require the listener to respond. Instead, it requires them to identify, sympathize, and empathize with the plight of the artiste, especially as it concerns the activities of the Nigerian police. The choice of words introduces the timelessness of this plight. The social actor portrayed here is the Nigerian police. The choice of the pronominal "we" introduces collectivism of the Nigerian people to wage war against the arbitrary use of power by the Nigerian police. The phrase "dey try" translated as the verb "endeavour" denotes the collective will of Nigerians, which is geared toward making frantic efforts to avoid the Nigerian police as they wield power uncontrollably. "Comot," translated as the phrasal verb "go out," denotes some measure of social engagement with the Nigerian police. Additionally, the artiste introduces the god-factor—"I pray we never run out of luck." The contextual meaning of luck is a literal one. In other words, meeting the Nigerian police spells doom because they are always out to inflict pain and discomfort on the Nigerian youth. In this case, protest music, as argued by (Allen, 2004, p.1) "functions as a trenchant political site in Africa primarily because it is the most widely appreciated art form on the continent." For the Nigerian youth, Dremo asserts, stepping out of their homes is enough to get into the trap of the SARS team—as they must find a means to extort and defraud those who get into their net. Little wonder they are described as "thieves in uniform." Such description in the title is a dysphemistic, offensive way to represent the police. People in uniform are supposedly respectable persons, but for the police to be so described implies that they are an upgraded level of criminals who seem to legitimately wear uniforms. Therefore, music is a key site in which power and politics is negotiated and contested (Askew, 2002; Ogude and Nyario, 2003).

Dremo further highlights other actions that negatively represent the Nigerian police. Through using a conditional sentence structure—the first conditional—to describe what has a real possibility of occurring when contact is made with the Nigerian police. It is almost certain that one would be accosted by the police if they drove a "big car," perhaps a luxury car. More so, to show the discursive essence of the artiste's engagement, he uses the pronoun "you" in a contextual way to represent every other person in the society who could get in trouble with the police. He also uses the third person plural pronoun "they" to refer to the police, thus placing them as the "other." Dremo further uses an active verb structure starting from the contracted "they'll," as in "will be pointing"—a verb phrase in its future continuous tense—to represent the continuity of the actions of the Nigerian police in negatively treating the people. Writing on protest music in Kenya, Mutonya observes that music functions as a site of struggle as it "is one of most important modes through which ordinary Kenyans express their wishes, identities and aspirations" (2004, p.21). The contextual implication of pointing fingers at someone and persistently doing so is seen as one of disrespect for the other person. Social structures demand that people are treated respectfully in a mutual way. However, Dremo's discursive representation shows the opposite for the Nigerian police. Rather than treat people respectfully, they even "talk like they want to fight you." The choice of active verb structures signifies the use of power by the police force. They are portrayed as having the people carry out a set of orders conveyed via imperative statements. They ask people to "stop," "park," "turn on inner lights." They use their authority to get people to do their bidding, the artiste asserts. Dremo's understanding and representation of the police is mirrored in his use of language. Another verb phrase "would snatch" is used to depict what the police do to people's phones. The act of snatching a thing is an activity that is the sole preserve of criminals who take things that do not belong to them. Likening the police to snatchers who are criminals underpins his mental cognition of their action toward the people. The artiste uses the last sentence in the excerpt above to discursively show his disdain for the police's attitude. He leaves his listeners to wonder if the police have the right to engage in the act of snatching things from people. Mano (2007, p.62) argues that music "expresses social reality in its themes and consent . . . sets the agenda for society . . . and generate(s) forms of knowledge in the audience." In the context of interaction, people request things from others, not snatch them.

Focusing on Burna Boy's "20-10-20" we tease out similar negative representation as those of Dremo Drizzy. In his music, Burna Boy reflects on the happenings at the Lekki tollgate where the protest to end SARS was convened. The title of his song vividly reflects the date of the attack on the youth who converged to engage in the protest. It is a day many vowed not to forget. His lexical choices show how he represented the actions of the Nigerian Army and the government in general and their perception of the youth. The social actors identifiable here in Burna Boy's music are the chief of staff, the commander, and the graduates in Nigeria. They all interact together in one way or the other. Burna Boy uses direct address in showcasing his view of the elite in Nigeria. He uses the expression, "the money you stole is enormous in your account." In other words, he negatively represents them as criminals who steal huge sums of money and deposit them in their bank accounts. The negative effect of this on the populace is captured in such clause as "you have turned our graduates to common beggars," apparently because the treasury is being looted constantly and the youth have nothing to their name. They are graduates, but they have no jobs. He also negatively represents the education received in Nigeria, for he says, "their education does not mean a thing." This is an irony because education is seen in most societies as the way to success. The higher forces, however, seem to wield so much power over the masses that the latter have no say. The artiste invokes the godfather element in representing how difficult it is getting a job without having a godfather in Nigeria. Here we see a "you" versus "they" dichotomy by the artiste.

Burna Boy also protests the untrustworthiness of the police force. He does this through some lexical choices in his representation of the police force and their superiors. The social actors here are the chief of staff, the commander, the Nigerian Army, the president of the country, and the governor of Lagos State. By naming them, the artiste implicates them in the crisis that happened. He makes recourse to a social context of an order given from above—"and the army that carried out the order." He must expect his listeners to remember that an order was given to shoot the protesters. And based on this order and its execution, he negatively paints the actors. He does this by his lexical choices, referring to their "atrocities" and "double standards." This description is based on the artiste's memory of what transpired, and now he seeks to transmit such representation to his listeners.

REPRESENTATION OF ARTISTES' IDEOLOGY

Dremo Drizzy also emphasizes the ideology of lack of trust. Ideologies follow from social cognitions, which van Dijk (1990, p.65) argues are largely acquired, used, and changed through texts. And such cognitions relate to beliefs, representations, and mental or memory structures. Van Dijk (2002) notes that social cognition is connected to social memory, which is not just about remembering things but also about the opinions, representations, and ideologies that individuals have and share. Considering Dremo's social cognition, observable from his ideological representation of the Nigerian police through his use of language, we connect with his experience. He supplies a lot of context that makes his position inarguable.

First, there are three social actors the artiste depicts here: the police, the Nigerian government, and the rest of the people, whom he represents using the third-person plural pronouns, "we" and "us". He therefore includes himself as being among those who experience police brutality. Thus, speaking from "memory" or his ideological construct of his perception of the police, he highlights the theme of distrust. He appeals to shared cultural context and reminds his listeners that they all would never trust a thief with a gun. He reinforces and invokes not just his but also the societal ideology of lack of trust in the police force by mentioning that "the difference is not really much"; that is, between a thief with gun and armed police. He further uses invective language to represent his ideology of the police force. He abuses them by calling them "armed robbers in uniform." Such recourse to abuse is likely for the purpose of shaming the police and probably getting them to change their attitude, but that does not seem to be the case because the artiste goes on to show how the "ingroup—us" are affected by the actions of the "outgroup— they" in their doings. Van Dijk (2012) notes that speakers adjust their selection of words to the knowledge of the receiver so that their intention is understandable. This supports the artiste's stance in selecting words that depict the societal ideology regarding the police—"they only try to extort us." Including the rest of his listeners using the collective pronoun "us" signals that everyone ought to be on the same page with the artiste. The government is not spared from this negative ideology, since they do not feel perturbed by the happenings unless one of their own is involved.

Another ideological representation of the police is that they are killers. The activities of the SARS team were constantly reported on social media by those who fell victim to them. For some, they did not live to tell the story of what transpired but their relatives took to social media to relate the happenings. Quite several negative meanings are ideologically linked to the Nigerian police. The negative representation of their actions is noted by van Dijk (2009) to be deducible from the lexical choice and meaning attached to the expressions from a contextual point of view. In the excerpt above, the artiste links the police to those who "cut short" the lives of others. His lexical choice in depicting this is, "so many dreams are cut short because of one gunshot." Even though he does not categorically mention the police in this line, the artiste builds on the social context that allows his listeners know whom he is referring to. In fact, in the following line, he prescribes an action through his lexical choice. He uses an imperative statement in conveying what should be done to end the negative acts of killing of the police. He suggests, "let's end SARS so that all this nonsense will stop." He also suggests, "we have to fight back to win this combat." Using the inclusive pronouns "we" and "us" is a strategy deployed by the artiste to make his listeners act on his suggestions. This conforms with Heilborner's (2016) finding that protest music serves the purpose of getting the audience moved to action when they listen to the lyrics of the song. The artiste also names the conflict "this combat." It is so described because it is known to his listeners. Moreover, a combat is supposed to be a fight between armed forces. Could the artiste be suggesting that he and his audience also equip themselves for a battle against the police? This might be if as he suggests, the police are a killer, and an enemy.

Burna Boy also depicts the Armed Forces as killers, especially given their contribution to the death of innocent youths on October 20, 2020. The protest which was carried out at the Lekki tollgate turned out to be bloody, as many of the youth were killed. On the social media pages of individuals who were streaming the event live, and much later national television, it was shown how humans, the youth, were being sporadically shot at. This left many in anguish, not knowing the way out. The social actors here are the president of Nigeria—represented by the second-person singular pronoun "you"; the artiste himself—represented by the first-person singular pronoun "I"; the inclusive "we"—both the artiste and his listeners (thereby creating a common ground with them); and the fallen youths—"they" who were killed at the tollgate. Burna Boy the subject-verb(-object) structure to highlight the negative actions taken by the military who obeyed the order to kill the protesters—"You took the army to kill . . . ", "They failed my people," "They killed my people." They were the ones that took all the negative actions of killing. He, however, positively projected himself and the dead youth by highlighting their own actions—"I could not control my tears . . . ", "We gave them many chances," "We cried for justice," "Their lives are on you," "We will never forget . . . " This positive ingroup and negative outgroup representation shows clearly the ideological underpinning of the artiste.

CONCLUSION

This chapter has examined protest culture as projected in selected Nigerian music. Nigerian artists have consistently protested the negative trends observed in the country, especially as perpetrated by those in government. They have also used music as a medium to satirize such happenings and most importantly call for a change in society. Through a socio-cognitive critical discourse analysis of two selected songs—"Thieves in Uniform" and "20-10-20" performed by Dremo Drizzy and Burna Boy—it has been shown how lexical choices by the two artists reveal how they perceive the social actors involved in the #EndSARs protest. Both artists negatively represented the happenings by presenting the leaders and members of the armed forces of Nigeria in an extremely negative light while projecting the youth in a positive light as those who want to bring about a change in the society. Through an examination of their language and the context of use, it is apparent that the negative representations of men of the armed forces and the government in general is a theme that resonates in the selected songs. This study has shown that both the government—because of supporting the police and not calling them to order—and the police are negatively represented as killers and criminals and the underlying ideology is that they are untrustworthy persons. This reveals the state of affairs in Nigeria and shows a need for positive change as clamored for in the songs. Additionally, this analysis reveals that the language of hip-hop discourse as shown in the songs is not only for entertainment but also for the engagement and articulation of social issues.

REFERENCES

Adebowale, O. (2020). *History of Protests in Nigeria: Reactions and Conversations.* Available at: https://guardian.ng/life/history-of-protesrs-in-nigeria-reactions-and-consequences-2/(Accessed: 5 May, 2023).

Adisa, H. (2021). *Protests in Nigeria: The Influence of Social Media. Global History Dialogues.* Available at: https://globalhistorydialogues.org/projects/protests-in-nigeria-the-influence-of-social-media/ (Accessed: 15 May, 2023).

Akerele-Popoola, Azeez, A, L., and Adeniyi, A. (2022). Twitter, Civil Activisms and EndSARS Protest in Nigeria as a Developing Democracy. *Cogent Social Sciences,* 8(1): 1–16.

Akingbe, N., and Onanuga, P, A. (2020). Voicing Protest: Performing Cross-cultural Revolt in Gambino's 'This is America' and Falz's 'This is Nigeria'. *Contemporary Music Review*, 39(1): 6–3.

Akinyetun, T. S. (2021). Reign of Terror: A Review of Police Brutality on Nigerian Youth by the Special Anti-Robbery Squad. *African Security Review,* 30(3): 368–385.

Alridge, D, P., Bois, W. E. B. Du., Garvey. M., and Wells-Barnett. (2005). From Civil Rights to Hip Hop: Toward a Nexus of Ideas. *The Journal of African American History*, 90(3): 226–252.

Benvenga, L. (2022). Hip-hop, Identity, and Conflict: Practices and Transformations of a Metropolitan Culture. *Frontiers in Sociology,* 1–11. https://doi.org/10.3389/fsoc.2022.993574.

Bodunrin, I. A., and Matsilele, T. (2023). Social Media and Protest Politics in Nigeria's# EndSARS campaign. *Handbook of Social Media in Education, Consumer Behavior and Politics: Volume 1*, 111(114): 109.

Burna Boy. (2020). *The Elements*: Lagos.

Chitando, E. (2007). 'Come Down, O Lord!' Music, Protest and Religion in Zimbabwe. *Scriptura,* 96: 334–347.

Crosley, S. (2005). *Can't Stop Won't Stop: A History of the Hip Hop Generation.* London: Ebury Press.

Dambo, T., H., Ersoy, M., Auwal, A. M., and Olorunsola, V. O. (2020). Nigeria's #EndSARS Movement and Its Implication on Online Protests in Africa's Most Populous Country. *Journal of Public Affairs*, 22(3): 1–11.

Damodaran, S. (2016, August 05). *Protest and Music. Oxford Research Encyclopedia of Politics.* Available at: https://oxfordre.com/politics/view/10.1093/acrefore/9780190228637.001.0001/acrefore-9780190228637-e-81 (Assessed 13 Mar. 2024).

Dremo Drizzy. (2020). *Thieves in Uniform.* Styno: Lagos.

Dube, V., and Ncube, B. (2019). Majaivana and Protest Music in Zimbabwe: A Challenge to Political Hegemony and Marginalization. In Uche Onyebadi (Ed.), *Music and Messaging in the African Political Arena*, 149–165. IGI Global: USA.

Ekeke, A., C. (2023). Right to Peaceful Protest in Nigeria and the Recurrent Syndrome of Brutalization: The #EndSARS Protest Debacle. *Journal of African Law*, First View: 1–11.

Ekoh, P., and George, E. (2021). The Role of Digital Technology in the EndSARS protest in Nigeria during Covid-19 Pandemic. *Journal of Human Rights and Social Work*, 6: 161–162.

Etim, E., Duke, O., Fatile, J., and Akah, A. U. (2022). Protest Policing Strategy and Human Rights: A Study of End SARS Protests in Nigeria. *African Security Review*, 31(2): 226–239.

Halliday, Michael A. K., and Matthiessen, Christian I. M. M. (2014). *Halliday's Introduction to Functional Grammar*. London and New York: Routledge.

Harlow, S. (2011). Social Media and Social Movements: Facebook and an Online Guatemalan Justice Movement that Moved Offline. *New Media & Society,* 14(2): 225–243.

Haycock, J. (2015). Protest Music as Adult Education and Learning for Social Change: A Theorisation of a Public Pedagogy of Protest Music. *Australian Journal of Adult Learning,* 55(3): 423–442.

Heilbronner, O. (2016). Music and Protest: The Case of the 1960s and its Long Shadow. *Journal of Contemporary History*, 51(3): 688–700.

Ige, Tofarati. (2020). *I'm Not Afraid of Speaking Truth to Power.* Available at: www.punchng.com/im-not-afraid-of-speaking-truth-to-power-ade-bantu/. (Accessed on 23 May 2024).

Iliya, Davou, B. (2022). A Musicological Discourse on Selected Popular Songs Used During the 2020 #EndSARS Protest in Lagos, Nigeria. *Journal of the Association of Nigerian Musicologists*, 16(1): 48–62.

Iwuoha, Victor, C., and Aniche, E., T. (2022). Protests and Blood in the Streets: Repressive State, Police Brutality and #EndSARS Protest in Nigeria. Springer Nature. *PMC National Library of Medicine,* 35(4): 1102–1124.

Kistler, Michelle., and Lee, Moon. (2010). Does Exposure to Sexual Hip-Hop Music Videos Influence the Sexual Attitudes of College Students? *Mass Communication and Society*, 13(1): 67–86.

Klandermans, B. (1997). *The Social Psychology of Protest*. Oxford: Blackwell Publishers.

Labinjoh, J. (1982). Fela Anikulapo-Kuti: Protest Music and Social Processes in Nigeria. *Journal of Black Studies*, 13(1): 119–134.

Mason, Michael. (1993). The History of Mr. Johnson: Progress and Protest in Northern Nigeria, 1900-1921. *Canadian Journal of African Studies,* 27(2): 196–217.

Matsilele, T., Mpofu, S., Msimanga, M., and Tshuma, L. A. (2021). Transnational Hashtag Protest Movements and Emancipatory Politics in Africa: A Three Country Study. *Global Media Journal,* 11(2): 2–23.

Matsilele, T., Msimanga, M. J., and Tshuma, L. A. Popular Music and Political Contestations in Zimbabwe: An Analysis of Winky D's and Jah Prayzah's Music. *Journal of African Media Studies,* 15(3): 291–308.

Mondak, J. J. (2008). Protest Music as Political Persuasion. *Popular Music and Society*, 12(3): 25–38.

Msimanga, M. J., Ncube, G., and Mkwananzi, P. (2021). Political Satire and the Mediation of the Zimbabwean Crisis in the Era of the "New Dispensation": The Case of MAGAMBA TV. In Mpofu, S (Ed), *The Politics of Laughter in the Social Media Age: Perspectives from the Global South,* 43–56. Palgrave MacMillan: New York.

Msimanga, M. J., Tshuma, L. A., and Matsilele, T. (2022). The Why of Humour during a Crisis: An Exploration of COVID-19 memes in South Africa and Zimbabwe. *Journal of African Media Studies,* 14(2): 189–207.

Nwabunnia, O. A. (2021). #EndSARS Movement in Nigeria: Tensions and Solidarities Amongst Protesters. *Gender & Development,* 29(2–3): 351–367.

Nweke, F. (2021). Why has Protest Music Dried Up? *The Conversation.* Available at: Retrieved 21st June, 2021 from www.theconversation.com/why-has-protest-music-dried-up-in-nigeria-147929.

Okuyade, O. (2012). African China, Nigerian Popular Music, National Development and the Search for Musical Idiom. *Muziki*, 8(2): 50–59.

Osuagwu, T., R. (2019). *Music and Messaging in the African Political Arena*. Pennsylvania: IG Global

Reed, T. V. (2005). *The Art of Protest: Culture and Activism from the Civil Rights Movement to the Streets of Seattle*. Minneapolis: University of Minnesota Press.

Riesch, R. J. (2005). *Hip Hop Culture: History and Trajectory*. Research Papers. Paper 32. https://opensiuc.lib.siu.edu/gs_rp/32.

Shevy, M. (2008). Music Genre as Cognitive Schema: Extramusical Associations with Country and Hip-hop Music. *Psychology of Music,* 36(4): 477–498.

Stewart, C. J., Smit, C. A., and Denton, R. E., Jr. (1984). *Persuasion and Social Movements*. Rospect Heights, IL: Waveland Press.

Sunday, A. B. (2021a). "Throw the Money in the Air": Ideological Rejoinder in Olamide's Omo Abule Sowo. *Muziki,* 1–18.

Sunday, A., B. (2021b). 'Fighting COVID-19 through Music: A Critical Stylistic Analysis of Cobhams Asuquo's We Go Win (Corona)'. *UNIUYO Journal of Humanities (UUJH),* 25(1): 66–84.

Uwalaka, T, Nwala, B., and Chinedu, C. (2021). Social Media, Fake News and COVID-19 Cures in Nigeria. *Journal of African Media Studies*, 13: 435–449.

van Dijk, Teun, A. (2002). Political Discourse and Political Cognition. In Chilton, P., and Schaffner (Eds.), *Politics as Text and Talk: Analytic Approaches to Political Discourse*, 203–237. Amsterdam: John Benjamins Publishing

van Dijk, T. A. (2008). *Discourse and Context. A Sociocognitive Approach*. Cambridge: Cambridge University Press.

van Dijk, Teun, A. (2012). *Ideology and Discourse. A Multidisciplinay Introduction*. Barcelona: Pompeu Fabra University.

van Dijk, Teun. (2006). Discourse and Manipulation. *Discourse & Society*, 17(3): 359–383.

van Dijk, Teun. (2009). Critical Discourse Studies: A Sociocognitive Approach. In Wodak, R. and Meyer, M. (Eds.), *Methods of Critical Discourse Analysis* (2nd ed.), 62–86. London: SAGE.

van Dijk, Teun. (2014). Discourse-Cognition-Society: Current State and Prospects of the Socio-cognitive Approach to Discourse. In Christopher Hart and Poitr Cap (Eds.), *Contemporary Studies in Critical Discourse Analysis*, 121–146. London: Bloomsbury.

van Dijk, Teun. (2015). Critical Discourse Analysis. In Deborah Tannen, Heidi E. Hamilton, and Deborah Schriffrin (Eds.), *The Handbook of Discourse Analysis* (2nd ed.), 466–485. Chichester: Wiley Blackwell.

Chapter 9

Ironic Activism and Social Justice

A Case Study of Political Satire and Social Media in Zimbabwe

Mbongeni Msimanga

Zimbabwe has since the turn of the millennium continued to face a multi-faceted crisis (Mhiripiri and Ureke, 2019; Chiumbu and Musemwa, 2012) spanning from the Mugabe era to the Mnangagwa regime, known as the "New Dispensation." The "New Dispensation," under Emmerson Mnangagwa succeeded Robert Mugabe's government through a military coup in 2017 (Munoriyarwa and Chambwera, 2020). This was after two main factions, the Lacoste faction led by then vice president and now president Emmerson Mnangagwa and the G40 faction fronted by the then minister of higher education Jonathan Moyo, fought a nail-biting contest over the succession of long-time ruler Mugabe as his reign entered the twilight (Mpofu et al., 2022). However, Zimbabwe's multi-dimensional crisis is a result of a plethora of causes that range from political authoritarianism, international isolation, famine, and violence (Zamponi, 2005). Scholars such as Ndlovu-Gatsheni (2015) have blamed on the erstwhile leader, Robert Mugabe, in contributing to the economic, political, and social meltdown. The seeming continuity of authoritarian rule, between the old regime and the current government, has prompted scholars to question the "newness" of the "New Dispensation" and to argue that "the Mnangagwa regime is a direct child of Mugabeism" (Ndlovu-Gatsheni and Ruhanya, 2020, p.4). Thus, within the constellation and continuation of "Mugabeism" there continues to be a renewed abuse of human rights, corruption, and a clampdown on, and censoring of journalists. This has been evident as the "New Dispensation" has previously dispersed soldiers on ordinary citizens in 2019 over fuel protests, arrests and intimidation of journalists such as Hopewell Chingono, Mduduzi Mathuthu, and political activists such as Jacob Ngarivume and Fadzai Mahere. Satirists such as Samantha Kureya and Sharon Chideu have also been abducted, harassed, and intimidated by the police and Central Intelligence Organisation (CIO). As Rwodzi (2019, p.196) further explains, the "New Dispensation" era "appears to be increasingly focusing its energies towards consolidating power through any means necessary as opposed to constructing effective representative institutions that make economic development and improved standards of living in the country possible." Tagwirei (2021) has called the "New Dispensation" era the "Patriotic present" (Tagwirei, 2021). He further explains that Mnangagwa's government "carries traces of the old, including the motivation to monopolise narratives about Zimbabwe and entrench ZANU PF dominance" (Tagwirei, 2021, p.19). It is within this context that I approach this study considering how both regimes under the leadership of Robert Mugabe, and Emmerson Mnangagwa, have not only perpetuated the Zimbabwean crisis but also contributed to serious forms of social and human injustice.

The central question here is how, amid this crisis, social media platforms (with a reference to YouTube) have been appropriated to reflect on and critique Zimbabwe's multi-dimensional calamity, while commenting on human rights abuses. The two case studies that this chapter draws upon, Magamba and Bustop TV are virtual spaces that speak truth to those in power (Msimanga et al., 2021). Considering the above issues, the study pursues two major objectives: (1) to understand the dominant social justice and human rights issues that concern Zimbabwe social media users, and (2) to identify the motives of the individuals leading the fight for social justice. The chapter considers these platforms under study as forms of protest and dissidence, that not only challenge the status quo but also the discourses emanating from the state-controlled media environment, which stifle alternative voices (Msimanga et al., 2021; Matsilele and Ruhanya, 2020; Mpofu et al., 2022). The next section gives a brief background to these case studies.

MAGAMBA AND BUSTOP TV: A BRIEF BACKGROUND

The name "Magamba" is a Shona word that means "liberation war Heroes" and the television station uses youth activism to open democratic space in Zimbabwe (Msimanga et al., 2021). Magamba was founded in 2007 by Samm Farai Monro, who is known as Cde (Comrade) Fatso, and Tongai Makawa, known as "Outspoken." This was at the height of the Zimbabwean Crisis, when the country was going through hyperinflation, and political violence. Cde Fatso, who presents the show *The Week*, uses the historical moniker "Comrade" as it denotes a common struggle against a common enemy, dating back to the liberation struggle. In the context of Magamba TV, Comrade is a connotation of common struggles of nationalism, patriotism and liberation ideology, that run as a critical parallel to the values expressed by the ZANU-PF government. Magamba TV produces skits that are shared on social media platforms Facebook, YouTube, and Instagram. The television station is part of Magamba Network that runs digital activism, activism, and innovation programs in particular Shoko Festival (a festival of urban culture in Zimbabwe and hosts standup comedy, poetry, film, and hip-hop acts), Open Parly (an initiative that empowers young people in Zimbabwe to be citizen journalists and report live from parliament) and Moto Republik. However, Moto Republik is a creative hub that hosts bloggers, artists, designers, creative entrepreneurs, and activists. It also hosts vulnerable groups in society such as the LGBTQ community. All these programs are youth-led initiatives and spaces for political commentary and activism. Ureke (2021, p.219) classifies Magamba as a form of artivism. Artivism, he explains is "activism through art videos, revealing the factors that influence their content and how these factors reflect their broad radical agenda of 'speaking truth to power.'" He further classifies Magamba TV skits as "comic news or newmour (newsy humour)" (Ureke, 2021, p.232–233).

The television station mostly comments about the Zimbabwean Crisis and inspires young people to be part of the "freedom fighters of today" and reclaim the narrative from ZANU-PF, by reconceptualizing the definition of "heroes" that, post-independence, has been defined through "a Zanu-PF lens" (Msimanga et al., 2021, p.46). Mpofu states that the established trope of Zimbabwean heroes has been "politically motivated" rather than "rational in nature" and has been defined along "political, sexual orientation or ethnic grounds" (Mpofu, 2016, p.68). Magamba TV seeks to contribute to a meta discourse, re-situating often neglected youth, as active participants in sociopolitical and socioeconomic spaces (Majoni, 2020). Broadly, I define the skits produced by Magamba TV as constitutive of radical media (Downing, 2001) and forms dissident media or media dissidence (Mpofu and Matsilele, 2020). Radical media and dissident media use technological media to shine light on abuses of power and agitate for social justice and political change (Vatikiotis, 2005; Downing, 2001; Matsilele, 2019). In most cases, often leads to clashes with authorities. While radical and alternative media has traditionally been associated with the press (Atton, 2002), it has increasingly incorporated satire, graffiti, music, and theater, among others. This is a common trait in Magamba TV skits that speak against Zimbabwe's political culture under the ZANU-PF government. However, Magamba TV skits mostly range between five to ten minutes and focus on various themes that are topical every week in Zimbabwe's sociopolitical or socioeconomic sphere.

Bustop TV, formerly PO Box TV, is a popular Zimbabwean social media channel that produces news, skits, and documentaries that speak about socioeconomic and sociopolitical issues affecting citizens (cf. Nyaungwa, 2021). PO Box TV was established by Lucky Aaroni, Rolland Lunga, and Admire

Kuzhangaira in 2014 (Aaroni, 2020), but in 2015 these individuals fell out over contractual and financial disagreements linked to corporate sponsorship (Zimoyo, 2016). Aaroni then partnered with the Mufakose Film Society and Totally Second Animation Studio, rebranding the channel as Bustop TV (Ureke, 2021). Compared to Magamba TV, Bustop TV is younger but much more popular, drawing its name from the concept of a bus stop where people on their way to different destinations meet one another. In Zimbabwe, transport woes mean that people stay at bus stops for longer than they need to and vent their frustrations freely while waiting for late, delayed, inadequate, or price-gouged transport. The bus stop is framed not only as a strategic meeting place for citizens but as a democratic site and space for the discussion of pertinent sociopolitical and socioeconomic issues that are affecting communities and the country (Aaroni, 2020). This is also clear from the description accompanying the 2016 premiere of the original jingle for the skits, produced by popular Zimbabwean Afro-fusion musician, Jah Prayzah. In this chapter, I interpret the bus stop as an iteration of the Habermasian coffee shop. The bus stop becomes a form of public sphere that opens itself to dialogue and self-expression among Zimbabweans. As a space for ad hoc discussion, there is no fear of being targeted for censorship since there is no prior intention to meet and no specific agenda set in advance. The themes addressed by Bustop TV are drawn from the daily struggles that Zimbabweans encounter (Aaroni, 2020), and the material is dominated by three actors: Maggie (Sharon Chideu), Gonyeti (Samantha Kureya), and Dereck Nzwiyakwi (DRC), although they occasionally invite guest performers. Unlike Magamba TV, Bustop TV skits are short, TikTok-like skits addressing one theme. Both Magamba and Bustop TV use the suffix "TV," which seems to indicate a yearning for the opening of public space to more creative or alternative broadcasters, that is, that are not affiliated to the ZANU-PF government (Ureke, 2021).

SOCIAL MEDIA ACTIVISM, DISSIDENCE, AND HUMOR IN ZIMBABWE

There is a burgeoning field of social media activism and dissidence because of the compressed media landscape that is tightly controlled by the ZANU-PF government. The use of social media platforms in Zimbabwe as forms of activism, dissidence, and democratization has been widely discussed by scholars in Zimbabwe (Matsilele, 2022; Mutsvairo and Ronning, 2020). These studies have assessed the impact of social media activism and its effectiveness in attempting to bring about change in Zimbabwe's political, economic, and social terrain. The year 2012 witnessed a vibrant and active growth of social media activism in Zimbabwe (Chitanana and Mutsvairo,

2019). This growth could be attributed to 2013 elections that were fraught with disputes that range from electoral rigging and violence by ZANU-PF (Chitanana and Mutsvairo, 2019). However, Twitter and Facebook activism saw an emergence of a plethora of platforms: #ShutdownZimbabwe, Pachedu, Baba Jukwa, Zimbabwe Yadzoka, Her Zimbabwe, Magamba Network, and Bus-Stop TV among others. These platforms played a pivotal role in their attempt to democratize communication, expose ZANU-PF misdeeds, appeal to the active participation of women in mainstream politics and, ultimately, to protest against ZANU-PF's political culture in its entirety (Chitanana, 2020; Karekwaivanane, 2019; Mpofu, 2016).

For purposes of this study, it is important to show how the available literature on social media is used for activism and political protests purposes such as the Baba Jukwa Facebook page (Karekwaivanane, 2019). Baba Jukwa is a Shona word meaning "Jukwa's father." It is a self-given nickname for a Zimbabwean political online blogger, who mostly shared his information on Facebook in the run-up to the 2013 elections. He is believed to be part of the Vapanduki crew (a Shona word, translated as "rebels" or "defectors") a group which includes disgruntled ZANU-PF insiders, service chiefs, and other civil servants in Zimbabwe. The Baba Jukwa Facebook page enhanced a certain level of online participation, political debate, and helped to democratize media systems in Zimbabwe (Mutsvairo and Sirks, 2015; Mujere and Mwatwara, 2016). Commenting on Baba Jukwa Facebook page, Mujere and Mwatwara (2016, p.216) further show how "Zimbabweans . . . reacted to the narrowing of the democratic space by resorting to subterranean methods." Thus, the rise of citizen journalism and social media activism can be traced to the *shrinking* media space in Zimbabwe (Mujere and Mwatwara, 2016). Karekwaivanane (2019, p.68) also uses Baba Jukwa to further argue a different dimension and show how netizens used "reasoned argument, diatribe, the expression of religious sentiment, as well as a carnivalesque mode of expression" in expressing activism on social media platforms. Symbolically laden pseudonyms with political connotations were used by citizens on cyber space to confront those in power, particularly, Robert Mugabe and the then ZANU-PF government.

Since the use of Baba Jukwa, there has been a growth of social media activism movements in Zimbabwe such as #ThisFlag, #Tajumuka Sesijikile, #ThisGown, @ProfJMMoyo and #BeatThePot, and Her Zimbabwe (Matsilele, 2022). These platforms contest government policies, inequalities in society, social injustices, and human rights such as electoral rigging, the use of the police and army to disperse protesters and the torture of civil society and opposition leaders. Gukurume (2017) also explores how #ThisFlag and #ThisGown have been used to mobilize people both online and offline. In his study, Gukurume (2017) is of the view that ordinary citizens, especially the youth, the majority of which is unemployed, freely express the quandary of economic and political struggles they continue to face in post-independent Zimbabwe. Young people, who are excluded from economic and political fora use these platforms to advocate for their rights, generational renewal within the ZANU-PF government, and inclusion in mainstream politics and employment in key parastatals in Zimbabwe (Gukumere, 2017). Mpofu (2016) tackles how the blog Her Zimbabwe addresses issues pertaining to women that are ignored by mainstream media. Some of the issues discussed include women exclusion from political discourses and participation, gender-based violence against women and reproductive rights.

However, in Zimbabwe, the normative role of satire appears always to have been to caricature the elite class who wield economic and political power (Msimanga et al., 2021). Scholars in Zimbabwe have generally agreed that satire is a means of speaking back to power (Siziba and Ncube, 2015; Makombe and Agbede, 2016), with humor considered as a particularly effective tactic (Msimanga et al., 2021). One can point examples of the Comic Pastor, Magamba TV, and Simuka Comedy club. Willems (2011) also characterizes satire, during the Robert Mugabe era, as one of the everyday forms of resistance, arguing that satire acts as a form of political resistance, and creates alternative spaces for divergent views. Recent scholarship on satire shows how it mediates politics in the "New Dispensation," and is employed to understand complex economic policies, and oppose establishment narratives on the political configuration of cyberspace (Tshuma et al., 2021; Msimanga et al., 2021). However, although this corpus of literature exists, this chapter seeks to show how performative activism in the form of humor challenges the status quo in the current era of the "New Dispensation." In the next section, I discuss the conceptual framework adopted by the study.

CONCEPTUAL FRAMEWORK: SATIRE AND DISSENT/DISSIDENCE

The study utilizes Amber Day's conceptualization of satire as form of Dissent. The conceptual framework guides in answering the following questions: How do citizens speak to power when there is dearth of spaces to do any such speaking? In places where speaking against those in power is criminalized, how do the disenfranchised express their displeasure with the prevailing realities? What tools or weapons are at the disposal of such defenceless citizens? What role can alternative media play in materializing and offering different views on prevailing realities? Can media offer views that contrast those that are propagated by the state through its control of mainstream media?

Amber Day's (2011) seminal study of satire and dissent considers the contemporary turn within the satiric register of genres such as parodic news shows (for instance, *The Daily Show* and *The Colbert Report* in the United States, and *This Hour Has 22 Minutes* and *The Rick Mercer Report* in Canada), satiric documentary (for instance, the films of Michael Moore and Morgan Spurlock) and ironic activism (for instance, *Billionaires for Bush*, *The Yes Men*, and *Reverend Billy*). These genres incorporate:

> deconstructions of real news events, improvisational pranks (which) share a uniquely performative form of parody and satire that injects the satirist's body into the traditional political world, as he or she physically engages, interrogates, and interacts with the real. (Day, 2011, p.2)

Day's re-examination of the contemporary relationship between satire and dissent is threaded through readings of spectacle, irony, authenticity ("ironic authenticity"), truth ("truthiness"), and activism, among other themes. For Day, parodic news shows, ironic activism, and satiric documentary facilitate a form of viable circumvention of inauthentic (even stage-managed, scripted, and choreographed) political discourse and, in so doing, provide audiences with a sense of community. Day also notes that digital technologies are at the heart of contemporary digital dissidence because they are used to mediate the everyday. It is no surprise, then, that political communication has followed social media. For Day (2011, p.25) new forms of technology have enabled:

> ironic juxtapositions, the crafting of mashups that meld familiar snippets of popular culture with one another to generate unexpected moments of resonance, the creation of sophisticated parodies, and the shaming of public figures through collections of contradictory or duplicitous statements.

Day emphasizes that "it is in the everyday iterations of popular culture where the battle over hegemony is continuously waged" (Day, 2011, p.21). Finally, Day regards the space of contemporary satiric register as, if not exactly counter-hegemonic, then certainly operating on the margins of organized politics. These margins are sources of a more productive, dialogic, and authentic political praxis compared to the sterile, scripted fare of mainstream discourse. Aside from the fact that Bustop TV and Magamba TV appear to fit squarely into what Day calls "oppositional counter publics," the Zimbabwean digital platforms also incorporate several "satiric devices" that Day has compellingly identified as central in the satiric register. In the same way that the generative aspect of satiric dissidence in concepts such as *kusvereredza* (trolling power) (Matsilele, 2019), Day observes that part of the salience of satire comes from its brazenness. One "brazen" element of satiric dissent that is of critical interest to this study of contemporary digital satire in Zimbabwe is what Day (2011) calls "identity nabbing," a practice where:

> participants pretend to be people they are not, appear in public as exaggerated caricatures of their opponents, or ambiguously co-opt some of their power. Members draw on irony to rhetorically head opponents off at the pass, performing their own version of the other side. (Day 2011, p. 146–7)

Many of the skits analyzed in this chapter are examples of "identity nabbing," where the ridicule becomes highly marked because of the satirists brazenly mimicking and pretending to be government officials or politicians. The satirists "borrow" power from government officials, while, in the process, making fun and critiquing their inadequacies, misdeeds, and wrongs. A further "satiric device" within the register identified by Day (2011) is what she calls "culture jamming," a term popularized by Mark Dery (1993) in his work titled *Culture Jamming*." Dery (1993) conceptualizes culture jamming as the manipulation of advertisements and messages to subvert meaning from established routines, while Day describes it as "the repurposing, deconstructing, or hijacking of mass culture, using the media as a means to critique the media" and "a catchall term for . . . ironic activism" (Day, 2011, p.149) that involves a "creative, easily replicable, mediagenic style designed to capture attention." This, along with "identity nabbing" is yet another practice that Bustop TV and Magamba utilize, especially in the case of the latter.

Today's activists, according to Day (2011, p.150), "are often savvy cultural producers as well as consumers. And it is within this larger context that irony has come to the fore as a type of countercultural dominant." Tactics such as irony and parody have become synonymous with younger "ironic" activists (Day, 2011, p.149). Finally, Day (2011) emphasizes the central importance of irony—the "language of dissent"—not only within the satiric register but also in the all-important field of digitality. She argues that:

> There is something synergistic about the relationship between new technologies and the emergent forms of irony, satire, and parody. The way in which contemporary irony has developed is intimately tied to the creation of digital technologies. (Day, 2011, p.24)

Indeed, satiric irony is identified as the core element of satiric dissent. For instance, irony works "to combat indifference, to advocate for change, and to get others riled up" (Day, 2011). In the next section, I give an outline of the methodological premise of the study.

METHODOLOGY

This chapter adopts a multiple case study approach precisely in the sense that it "includes more than one single case" (Baxter and Jack, 2008, p.550), that is Magamba and Bustop TV. The research questions in this study called for this approach that included actual viewing of the skits produced by Magamba and Bustop TV on the YouTube channels. It was not possible to do a study of this nature without repeatedly and closely watching the content to familiarize with the satiric register and barb. Magamba and Bustop TV were purposively sampled from the many satiric platforms that include The Comic Pastor, Simuka Comedy International, Umahlekisa Comedy Club amongst others. The two case studies were selected as they were consistent in posting material on a weekly basis. The data for analysis was purposively sampled from both Magamba and Bustop TV's YouTube channels. I selected YouTube because the material was systematically organized, convenient to sample, and up to date. The skits sampled for analysis from both Magamba and Bustop TV were organized under the heading "playlists" on their YouTube channels and dated back to the time when the social media platforms started posting skits on YouTube in 2015. For Magamba TV, videos that were purposively chosen are *The Week*, *Tsaona*, *Minister of Impending Projects*, and *Zambezi News*. A total of four videos were used and thematically analyzed. The skits selected make use of performative strategies such as identity nabbing, satiric barb, culture jamming, parody and ironic activism, and are drawn from both the Mugabe and Mnangagwa era.

FINDINGS AND DISCUSSION

In the following section, I present and discuss the findings that arise from Magamba TV and Bustop TV skits. The findings demonstrate that activism challenges the ruling elite, calling them to account. The findings and analysis are anchored around the following themes:

- Police and Army Brutality Against Political Activists and Citizens.
- Electoral Violence and Propaganda in Zimbabwe.

Police and Army Brutality Against Political Activists and Citizens

Police brutality toward opposition political parties, civic society organizations, and civilians is one of the central issues of the "Zimbabwean crisis." Anti-ZANU-PF sentiment in Zimbabwe generally flows along the normative construct of ZANU-PF as a party of violence and brutality. This near universal identification of ZANU-PF with violence is ambivalently embraced by ZANU-PF itself, as a party "yeropa" (of the blood) which marks itself as the liberation party that is not afraid to spill blood for "patriotic" reasons. State institutions staffed with ZANU-PF as part of a long-standing policy of cadre deployment are, therefore, seen as an extension of ZANU-PF violent norms. The theme of police and army brutality against activists and citizens is aptly captured by Magamba (2017). Cde Fatso, wearing a summer shirt, introduces himself to the audience with the following words:

> Ladies and gentlemen, Comrades and friends, welcome to "The Week", with me Cde Fatso, where we shoot the news at you like police firing teargas on peaceful protestors.

This broadcast came on the heels of the #ThisFlag and #Tajamuka/Sesijikile protests in 2016, the penultimate year of Robert Mugabe's reign as president of Zimbabwe. The #ThisFlag campaign was fronted by Evan Mawarire, a pastor who used the Zimbabwean flag to signify "noble values such as shared prosperity, democracy and the country's potential in agriculture and mining" (Matsilele, 2019, p.217–218). Since 2016, Evan Mawarire has been incarcerated many times and charged with attempting to overthrow a constitutionally elected government. The protests were triggered by several issues, among them the revelation of the information about the missing US$ 15 billion Diamond Mining Revenue, the introduction of the Bond Notes, the national pledge, and Statutory Instrument 64 of 2016 (Musarurwa, 2016, p.5). Already, the framing of the discourse of the skit is that protesters in Zimbabwe are peaceful and police are violent. Essentially, the skit is counter-hegemonic from the onset, a question which indicates a normative positioning within satiric dissent that regards the establishment with deeply held mistrust.

The same skit is accompanied by a display of #NERA and #Tajamuka on the bottom left screen. The National Electoral Reform Agenda (NERA) describes itself as "a consortium of Zimbabwean political parties fighting for electoral reform in the country" (NERA 2016). It aims at monitoring free and fair elections in Zimbabwe (NERA, 2016). This is against the history of violence and alleged rigging that is used by ZANU-PF against their political opponents (Sachikonye, 2011).

Cde Fatso, addressing the audience in what one can only call a playful tone, states:

> Our police never fail to deliver. I am sure in their meetings they will be like: Commander I got a compliment today from a citizen, and the Commander will be like: Lovemore, you should beat them with a button stick- You know we

don't like being liked! What are we? Facebook? However, here at *The Week* we have devised a way of tracing police and it's called mapuris-ometer. If you look at it, they started off the year as the most annoying African police officers because of their road roadblocks and demands for bribes. The ZRP have ended the year by beating Cde's and hitting Gogo's (The word gogo means an elderly woman or granny). They have beaten previous records held by Iran and South Korea—we call this the "teargas for the people" phase.

The police in Zimbabwe, for instance, are depicted as trigger happy and unprofessional. Hence, Cde Fatso, playing the role of an ironic activist, says, "we will shoot the news to you like the police shoot teargas." The skit presented by Cde Fatso, addresses how the ZANU-PF government routinely deployed the police force to quell dissenting voices in 2016. That year marked a renewed deterioration of Zimbabwe's economy and a steady rise in inflation (Garber, 2016). The violent and undemocratic tendencies of the police are presented as part of an arc that includes corruption and venality. The effect of the skit is to induce, on the one hand, fear of the police and, on the other hand, mistrust and even hostility. This representation of the police is a reaction against the politicization of arms of the state such as the army and the police. At the same time, it is couched as resistance of patriotic discourse, where the army and the police—including the CIO—are seen as the tip of the spear for ZANU-PF's "patriotism" wars. The backstory is that Zimbabwe's endemically corrupt and "unprofessional" police are quick to use riot control equipment and techniques to disperse political activists and ordinary citizens protesting ZANU-PF.

Cde Fatso's statement relates to the 2016 #Tajamuka/Sesijikile and #ThisFlag protests where protesting citizens and political activists where violently dispersed, arrested, and beaten up by the police. Cde Fatso also states, "Commander I got a compliment today from a citizen, and the Commander will be like: Lovemore, you should beat them with a button stick." This sought to show how the Zimbabwean police force is an institution that does not protect citizens, and instead has turned to be violent on them. The same skit uses three insert pictures to demonstrate and further show police violence and brutality. The technique of using insert pictures is prominent throughout most skits by Magamba TV to bring out the intended meaning of specific themes raised by Magamba TV in their episodes. The first insert used in the skit is a picture of an old woman, Lillian Chinyerere Mashumba, whose picture circulated on social media platforms Twitter and Facebook in 2016 after eight anti-riot police officers gathered to beat her up during the #ThisFlag protests. The insert shows police officers carrying guns, protective clothing, and various ammunition where they are violently kicking the old woman. The second insert shows anti-riot police officers dispersing citizens and violently beating them up using sjamboks during the #ThisFlag and #Tajamuka/Sesijikile demonstrations. The last insert by Magamba TV shows police officers who have dispersed protesters after the NERA demonstrations in 2016 by using teargas during these protests.

The same skit also uses infographics to further amplify police violence and brutality. Infographics are "the visual representation of material. They are used to tell stories and convey ideas" (Ferreira, 2014, p.3). I will term this as infographic satire as most skits by Magamba TV use this technique. The infographics used throughout the skits by Magamba TV are laden with ridicule and irony. However, the infographic satire used in this specific skit is titled "Mapuris-o-meter" a portmanteau of Mapurisa (Shona word for police) and a meter (a tool or unit of measurement). Mapuris-o-meter is an innovative way that Cde Fatso uses to not only draw attention to police brutality and corruption but also to set up civic spaces where the performance of the arms of the state can be scrutinized. The infographic satire used by Cde Fatso explains the three stages of "Mapuris-o-meter" which all point to police violence and corruption. Here, Cde Fatso, "physically engages, interrogates, and interacts with the real" (Day, 2011, p.2). Satire, however in this case "both exposes a situation and indicates how it might be changed" (Crithley, 2009, p.16). These tactics of political communication create "ironic juxtapositions" (Day, 2011, p.25) to deconstruct police brutality and violence and create dissonance between how the governments projects itself (and how it wants to be seen) and how people on the street see the government. There is a perpetual deficit between power and the people. Government uses state mouthpieces to try to close this gap, while social media dissidents and ironic activists do the opposite: widen the deficit.

Bustop TV's treatment of the theme of police brutality, albeit during Mugabe's era, is seen in (Bustop, 2017). The skit also follows #Tajamuka/Sesijikile and #ThisFlag protests of 2016 where many citizens and political activists were arrested for taking part in the demonstrations. Maggie condescendingly addresses what seems to be regional and international media regarding the #Tajamuka/Sesijikile protests. The skit also features Gonyeti who plays the role of an ordinary police officer enforcing the law. The skit shows her violently beating protesters using fists, kicks, and a baton stick. Gonyeti is also hurling insults and profanities at the protesting citizens and activists in full view of what seems to be local and international media. The skit also features two male citizens who are political activists.

In the skit, Maggie and Gonyeti are both dressed in what looks like police uniforms. In fact, the skit infamously landed the two satirists in trouble with the police who invoked Zimbabwean law that stipulates that it is illegal to impersonate a police officer: they were arrested and fined 20 USD. The Criminal Law and Codification Act, Chapter 9:23, Section 179, stipulates that impersonating a police officer, peace officer, or public official is illegal. The controversial skit is set in an ordinary high-density suburban setting where, typically, most of the #shutdown events were planned and staged. In the background, ordinary Zimbabwean citizens helplessly watch and pass by, while Gonyeti, playing the role of the police officer, hurls insult and profanities and violently beats up the protesting activists and citizens. The overall effect of the skit by Bustop TV is to brazenly mock and ridicule police officers for appearing to enjoy harassing citizens and political activists. Maggie, identity nabbing the national police spokesperson, vehemently denies that police beat up citizens during the #Tajamuka/Sesijikile and #ThisFlag protests in 2016. Busstop (2017) reads:

> So, like I was saying, those videos that are circulating on social media platforms are not ours. They have been doctored by our detractors from the West just to tarnish our name as the police of this nation. We do not promote violence at all. That is why we do not put those videos on our news. This is because they are not facts. We are a very peaceful police force and we do not promote violence. My fellow officer behind me here is simply doing her duty. She only applies minimal force where necessary. I am sure these two boys here, *vatori nemhosva dza vakapara* (they have committed crimes).

Here the skit uses irony to highlight the subterfuges and spin that attend the brutality of Zimbabwe's police force. The modus operandi of the police seem to be to deny and deflect. Maggie's stern look and continuous officious use of her hands to stress her points, and her insistence that "the videos are doctored by our detractors from the West" portrays syncretic performativity. Statements such as "minimal force," "we are a peaceful force," "we do not promote violence," "we are here to protect the people," are ironic and parodic, showing up government officials as conscienceless spin doctors who will deny, deflect, and justify anything, depending on where their interests lie. Performative irony is central to the meaning of Bustop's Skit. As noted, Gonyeti, playing the role of a violence-prone police officer on set, beats up citizens and protesters with fists and a baton, in full view of citizens who helplessly watch and walk past. While Gonyeti beats up the citizens, hurling insults in English and Shona, such as "Fuck you," "*pamhata*" (which is subsequently muted by Bustop TV as it means buttocks or arse) and "futseke" (voetsak!) or go away Maggie, the police spokesperson, denies that there is police brutality on citizens and activists. Here again is the tactic of identity nabbing and ironic activism familiar from Day's work (2011, p.146–7), which notes that when "participants pretend to be people they are not, appear in public as exaggerated caricatures of their opponents, or ambiguously co-opt some of their power." We see that social media readily "constitutes a fertile ground for practices of identity nabbing. . . . Disembodied and decontextualized, these platforms enable playfulness of identity, providing a comfortable platform for such humorous pranks" (Gal, 2019, p.792).

Another skit, Bustop (2020) *Statutory Instrument of the Evil Servant* proved a defining moment in the relationship between Zimbabwean satire and authority. Set during the "New Dispensation" era, Bustop TV caricature army brutality and suffered consequences for it. The skit addresses the August 1 shootings of 2018 that saw the ZANU-PF government deploy the army and police on the streets of Harare to disperse protesters following inordinate delays by the Zimbabwe Electoral Commission (ZEC) in releasing the election results. Six people were shot and killed in cold blood as a result. Many were injured. The violence led to the Motlanthe Commission of Inquiry led by former South African president Kgalema Motlanthe. The Commission was meant to bring those involved to account. The aftermath of the skit brought things to a head. The satirist, Gonyeti, was subsequently abducted from her home and tortured by suspected government agents. Narrating her ordeal to Sky News, Gonyeti stated that she was warned by her abductors that she was "too young to mock the government." The abductors (the so-called Ferret Team, allegedly composed of members of different security agents in Zimbabwe who consist of the CIO, military, and police (Tshuma et al., 2022) forced Gonyeti to roll around in sewage puddles, drink sewage, undress, and perform mock military drills. They then dumped her out in the open (Alison, 2019). Interestingly, the abductors themselves seemed to be drawing on what I would call the inverted performative to torture the satirist. That is, the "counterhegemonic" appears to acknowledge the success of the satirist's use of the performative register, and so invert it as a way to dissuade such performativity.

The skit shows a conversation between two actors—Gonyeti as a landlady and DRC (Dereck Nzwiyakwi) is a tenant who happens to be a soldier. In the skit, DRC, the soldier-tenant, narrates to his landlady how the army recently beat up civilians gathered to protest the delay in releasing the 2018 presidential election results by the ZEC. During the conversation, the soldier-tenant is carrying a baton while grinning sycophantically, indicating a civil servant's reduced power in the private realm. The soldier takes pleasure in narrating how they beat up civilians, using this mode of address to incorporate his public persona in his private life. DRC says:

> Mai, ndenge ndakamira zvangu ini ndikaudza vanhu kuti simukai apa! Panga paneimwe mbuya yanga yakagara pasi yakaita kunge imimi ndikayiudza kuti imi mai simukayi apo! Ikaramba yakagara maii iya ndobva ndati dhama dhama nayo. Ndobva ndaibata ndikairova! Vakatiza mai vaya, ndikaona kuti varikumhanya and varikufema nemaburi ese epamuviri. Ndakabva ndawona yati

tatara tatara ikadona pasi. Ndikabva ndaitevera ndikairova iripasi zvisingaiti. Mai ini chero imi kana amai vangu dai mangamurimustreet, ndaikupondai mese ndokutsikai musoro.

(Mother, I was on duty, and I told people to disperse since we were instructed by higher authorities to chase away protestors by beating them up. They were demanding the delayed 2018 election results. One of the women who was there, an old woman with a stature like yours refused to disperse and I started beating her up. She ran away, but I caught up with her. She was breathing heavily, and she fell on the ground. I then beat her up because she did not want to listen to me when I told her to move away. Mother, if you or my own biological mother where on the streets protesting, I would have done the same as well—and even trampled your heads too).

This mode of address and lack of remorse draws on irony. The soldier is powerful and full of impunity in his day job but is shown to also be as poor as other ordinary Zimbabweans. Yet the soldier-tenant still brutalizes powerless vendors and street hawkers who have no other choice of livelihood. Vendors in Zimbabwe struggle to make ends meet and are constantly attacked by municipal police, who confiscate their goods. The tenant's address leaves Gonyeti shocked and livid at the same time. She struggles to understand the soldier-tenant's lack of empathy. The soldier tries to justify his actions by saying that "we were instructed by higher authorities," a common defense to justify state-sponsored violence, but also a reflection of the dilemma of the oppressed who often have to do what they have to do to put food on the table. This lack of choice enables those in power to make sub-oppressors out of the oppressed. Sub-oppressors in this case denote institutions used by those in authority such as soldiers and police to oppress ordinary citizens. The use of sub-oppressors is an important element of how ZANU-PF retains power and control. Hence, the soldier-tenant tells the landlady, "Mother, if you or my own biological mother where on the streets protesting, I would have done the same as well." That is, the sub-oppressor takes his official duties seriously.

However, the landlady, like many ordinary Zimbabwean citizens, either retired or retrenched, is making a living in the harsh economic environment by renting out rooms to tenants. In the skit, she is dressed in a headscarf, skirt, a blouse, and slippers—part of ordinary Zimbabwean women's casual at-home dress. Unlike the skit that landed Bustop TV in trouble with the law, where Maggie and Gonyeti were dressed in what looked like police uniforms, here DRC, identity nabbing a soldier, is now careful to dress in costume that is not authentic military camouflage. Instead, he is dressed in blue overalls, green reflector bib, and a blue mining hat, that is "undercover" military gear. DRC's costume is an attempt by Bustop TV to identity nab the military or anti-riot police who wore protective anti-riot gear when dispersing protesters. That is, one can identify a mode of identity nabbing that is "soft" or "weak." This mode of costume is one of many ways of evading arrest and intimidation by police and state security agents. Instead of putting on military costume to signal that he is acting as a soldier, the satirist uses "weak" identity nabbing and innuendo and leaves the rest to the imagination.

Because soldiers and police routinely use excessive force and violence to control and disperse ordinary citizens, activists, and anti-government protesters (Tshuma, 2023; Sachikonye, 2011), the skit uses contrast to make its point about soldiers and police acting tough on their state-sanctioned activities and official roles, but suddenly powerless in the private realm. This is a strong commentary on the dilemmas and contradictions of "just following orders and the schizophrenia of working for an anti-people establishment while living with the people that one brutalizes." The contradiction and schizophrenia are a reality for most civil servants but is most pronounced and inescapable for those working in the repressive state apparatus due to the visibility of the violence. The theme that comes to the fore is that of the important role those sub-oppressors and sub-oppression play in regulating life in the postcolony. In the end, oppression dehumanizes everyone.

Electoral Violence and Propaganda in Zimbabwe

The skit by Magamba (2018) deals with electoral violence and propaganda. The skit is produced closer to Zimbabwe's 2018 elections, using a counternarrative on elections and that stands in contradistinction to the image presented in Zimbabwe's state media. The skit targets the 2018 Zimbabwe elections that saw Mugabe's long-time henchman, Emmerson Mnangagwa, contest the presidential contest for the first time after the 2017 military coup. In the sketch, one of the actors' identity nabs a political editor at state-controlled ZBC who is at a "diary session," brainstorming story ideas with newscasters and reporters. The diary session is centered on adverts, stories, and tactics that the state broadcaster seeks to use to set the electoral agenda in favor of ZANU-PF. The conspirators discuss how to use state media to assassinate the characters of opposition leaders, by associating them in headline stories with witchcraft, promiscuity, and sexual scandals.

One of the conspiratorial "newscasters" in the spoof rehearses what could be a suitable advert to use during election time, parodying adverts from the ZEC. This "rehearsal" represents a mode of presentation that I would call a skit within a skit, whereby the mode of address of the skit is utilized self-referentially within its form. This allows for the spoof not to take itself too seriously, announcing itself as a parody while notifying the authorities that "this is just comedy," thus pre-empting any attempts at censorship. It is akin to a form of aestheticized voluntary self-censorship. In the "rehearsal," the newscaster says:

> The joint election rigging group (J.E.R.G) wishes to advice the nation that the voting season is now open. Those who are deceased and still registered are advised to go and vote within their area of registration. All political parties are advised to desist from violence. However, if you are to beat up someone, make sure it is away from the media or from smart phones which can film and record. To all Zimbabweans, go and vote—dead or alive. We might count your vote, we might not. But your vote still matters to us.

The skit parodies the ZEC adverts often carried by ZBC "encouraging" the electorate to vote in a process that critics see as a shameless attempt to legitimize sham elections. ZEC is not seen, in oppositional circles, but also by many ordinary Zimbabweans, as an impartial player. It is viewed, rather, as a ZANU-PF enabler organization.

JERG, the organization referred to in the skit is in fact the ZEC. Of course, JERC is also meant to rhyme with "jerk," showing the strategy of *kutukirira* (insulting) (Matsilele, 2019) employed in some of the skits. The popular perception, amplified by Magamba TV, is that ZEC colludes with ZANU-PF, state institutions are not to be trusted, and that the establishment is full of hypocrites and corrupt liars. During the Mugabe era, for example, accusations of vote rigging, and manipulation of the voters roll by ZANU-PF were rife. The idea that there is a vast conspiracy denying Zimbabweans their electoral and democratic rights is promoted relentlessly while, interestingly, state media and its functionaries allege a conspiracy *against* ZANU-PF by private media and civic organizations. This offers a parallel to the stance adopted by MAGA (Make America Great Again) Republicans, whose accusations of bias in the "mainstream media" are used as a counterweight to liberal complaints about right-wing intolerance.

The sketch further casts light on how the voters' roll is alleged to have been manipulated, to the extent that non-existent voters could vote for ZANU-PF, how ZANU-PF deliberately delayed election results to facilitate rigging, and how ZANU-PF systematically perpetrated and glorified violence. The episode also raises the issue of polarization of the media, with state media being pro-ZANU-PF and anti-MDC (Movement for Democratic Change), and private media being anti-ZANU-PF and pro-MDC. Finally, the episode highlights the importance of the media and, lately, citizen journalism, in holding power to account and exposing impunity. If those in power would rather commit violent acts away from the glare of journalists and cell-phone-wielding citizens, then the media retains important powers of signification which can cause headaches for the establishment.

CONCLUSION

In this chapter, I have shown how Magamba TV and Bustop TV creates a space in which both dispensations under Mugabe and Mnangagwa can be held to account of social injustices through the power of satire. In a sociopolitical context in which people are free to exercise of freedom of speech, freedom of association and freedom of conscience is for the most part impeded, satire provides an avenue through which to critique the prevailing sociopolitical situation in Zimbabwe. Indeed, satire positions itself as a form of dissent that makes it possible for the emergence of discourses, the themes of which are intended to mock and ridicule the Zimbabwean government and public officials. Satire, as shown, embodies a form of veiled dialogue that takes place between the discourses of the weak, oppressed, and marginalized and the dominant autocratic discourse of the ruling regime. The repressive context gives rise to alternative world narratives outside those of the oppressive regime, mediating the Zimbabwean crisis and offering another framework to the regimes policies. This chapter has also shown how political satire as embodied in Magamba and Bustop TV is instrumental in challenging the rhetoric of newness that the "New Dispensation" has used to describe itself.

REFERENCES

Alison, S. (2019). *"You are too young to mock the government"*: Zimbabwean comedian relives her abduction. Mail and Guardian. Available at: https://mg.co.za/article/2019-12-04-00-you-are-too-young-to-mock-the-government-zimbabwean-comedian-relives-her-abduction (Accessed on 04/11/22).

Ardevol, E., and Gomez-Cruz, E. (2014). Digital ethnography and media practices. In *The International Media of Encyclopedia of Media Studies (Vol. 7), Research Methods in Media Studies*. (pp: 498–518) Oxford: Wiley Black.

Bustop TV. (2020). *Statutory Instrument of the Evil Servant*. Available on: https://www.youtube.com/watch?v=8fysLIhQ3AU&t=156s. (Accessed on 04/11/22).

Bustop TV. (2017). *Order and Law: Special Unit*. [YouTube Video]. Available at: https://www.youtube.com/watch?v=LZJtXQOVUKg. (Accessed on 04/11/22).

Chitanana, T., and Mutsvairo, B. (2019). The deferred 'democracy dividend' of citizen journalism and social media: Perils, promises and prospects from the Zimbabwean experience. *Westminster Papers in Communication and Culture* 14(1): 66–80.

Chiumbu, S., and Musemwa, M. (2012). Perspectives of the Zimbabwean crises. In Chiumbu, S. and Musemwa, M. (eds), *Crisis! What Crisis? The Multiple Dimensions of the Zimbabwean Crisis*(ix–xxi). Cape Town: HSRC Press.

Çoşkun, G.E. (2015). The use of multimodal critical discourse analysis in media studies. *The Online Journal of Communication and Media* 1(3): 40–44.

Day, A. (2011). *Satire and Dissent: Interventions in Contemporary Political Debate.* Indiana: Indiana University Press.

Dery, M. (1993). *Culture Jamming: Hacking, Slashing, and Sniping in the Empire of Signs.* Accessed at: https://www.markdery.com/books/culture-jamming-hacking-slashing-and-sniping-in-the-empire-of-signs-2/ (Accessed on 04/11/22).

Downing, J. (2001). *Radical media: Rebellious communication and social movements.* Thousand Oaks: Sage Publications.

Garber, J. 2015. *Zimbabwe's next move could trigger the return of 'rapid inflation'.* Yahoo Finance. Accessed on: https://finance.yahoo.com/news/zimbabwes-next-move-could-trigger-151500107.html (Accessed on 04/11/22).

Gukumere, S. (2017). #ThisFlag and #ThisGown cyber protests in Zimbabwe: Reclaiming political space. *African Journalism Studies* 38(2): 49–70.

Hammar, A., McGregor, J., and Landau, L. (2010). Introduction. Displacing Zimbabwe: Crisis and construction in southern Africa. *Journal of Southern African Studies* 36(2): 263–283.

Karekwaivanane, G.H. (2019). 'Tapanduka Zvamuchese': Facebook, 'unruly publics', and Zimbabwean politics. *Journal of Eastern African Studies* 13(1): 54–71.

Magamba TV. (2018). *How to Rig and Election.* Available on: https://www.youtube.com/watch?v=hF0BqF-gR08. (Accessed on 04/11/22).

Magamba. (2017). *The Week Season 1 Episode 12.* Available at: https://www.youtube.com/watch?v=Y1TySulxoMw&list=PLXfNIRuwmyVUJaqoLkWZC7-VUgyInucri&index=3. (Accessed on 04/11/22).

Makombe, R., and Agbede, G.T. (2016). Challenging power through social media: A review of selected memes of Robert Mugabe's fall. *Communicare* 35(2): 39–54.

Matsilele, T., and Ruhanya, P. (2020). Social media dissidence and activist resistance in Zimbabwe. *Media, Culture and Society* 43(2): 381–394.

Matsilele, T. (2022). Social media and digital dissidence in Zimbabwe. London: Palgrave Macmillan.

Mhiripiri, N.A., and Mutsvairo, B. (2013). Social media, new ICTs and the challenges facing the Zimbabwe democratic process. In Olorunnisola, A.A., Douai, A., and Hershey P.A. (eds), *New Media Influence on Social and Political Change in Africa*(pp. 1281–1301). Hershey: IGI Global.

Mpofu, S., and Matsilele, T. (2020). Social media and the concept of dissidence in Zimbabwean politics. In Ndlovu-Gatsheni, S., and Ruhanya, Pedzisai, R. (eds), *The History and Political Transition of Zimbabwe from Mugabe to Mnangagwa*(pp. 221–243). New York: Palgrave MacMillan.

Mpofu, S. (2016). 'Toxification of national holidays and national identity in Zimbabwe's post-2000 nationalism'. *Journal of African Cultural Studies* 28(1): 28–43.

Mpofu, S. (2016). Blogging, feminism and the politics of participation: The case of her Zimbabwe. In Mutsvairo, B. (ed), *Digital Activism in the Social Media Era: Critical Refections on Emerging Trends in Sub-Saharan Africa*(pp. 271–294). New York: Palgrave Macmillan.

Msimanga, M.J., Ncube, G., and Mkwananzi, P. (2021). Political satire and the mediation of the Zimbabwean crisis in the era of the "New Dispensation": The case of MAGAMBA TV. In Mpofu, S. (ed), *The Politics of Laughter in the Social*

Media Age: Perspectives from the Global South (pp. 43–56). New York: Palgrave MacMillan.

Moyo, D. (2007). Alternative media, diasporas and the mediation of the Zimbabwe crisis. *Ecquid Novi* 28(1–2), 81–105.

Mujere, J., and Mwatwara, W. (2016). Citizen journalism and national politics in Zimbabwe: The case of the 2008 and 2013 Elections. In Mutsvairo, B (ed), *Participatory Politics and Citizen Journalism in a Networked Africa* (pp. 215–228). New York: Palgrave MacMillan.

Mutsvairo, B., and Rønning, H. (2020). The Janus face of social media and democracy? Reflections on Africa. *Media, Culture and Society* 42(3): 317–328.

Nyaungwa, M. (2021). Laughing at trouble: A multimodal analysis of online economic satire in Zimbabwe. In Mpofu, S. (ed), *The Politics of Laughter in the Social Media Age: Perspectives from the Global South* (pp. 137–155). New York: Palgrave.

Ndlovu-Gatsheni, S. J., and Ruhanya, P. (2020). Introduction: Transition in Zimbabwe: From Robert Gabriel Mugabe to Emmerson Dambudzo Mnangagwa: A repetition without change. In Ndlovu-Gatsheni, S.J., and Ruhanya, P. (eds), *The History and Political Transition of Zimbabwe: From Mugabe to Mnangagwa* (pp. 1–23). London: Palgrave Macmillan.

Ndlovu-Gatsheni, S. (2015). Mugabeism and entanglements of history, politics, and power in the making of Zimbabwe. In Ndlovu-Gatsheni, S. (eds), *Mugabeism? History Power and Politics in Zimbabwe* (pp. 1–29). New York: Palgrave MacMillan.

Ndlovu-Gatsheni, S.J. (2003). Dynamics of the Zimbabwe crisis in the 21st century. *African Journal on Conflict Resolution* 3(1), 99–134.

Rwodzi, A. (2019). Democracy, governance and legitimacy in Zimbabwe since the November 2017 military coup. *Cadernos de Estudos Africanos* 38, 193–213.

Sachikonye, L. (2011). *When a State Turns on its Citizens: Institutionalised Violence and Political Culture*. Auckland Park: Jacana Media.

Siziba, G., and Ncube, G. (2015). Mugabe's fall from grace: Satire and fictional narratives as silent forms of resistance in/on Zimbabwe. *Social Dynamics* 41(3): 516–539.

Tagwirei, C. (2021). The patriotic present: The urgency of now in Zimbabwe's "New Dispensation". In Nyambi, O., Mangena, T., and Ncube, G. (eds), *Cultures of Change in Contemporary Zimbabwe: Socio-Political Transition from Mugabe to Mnangagwa* (pp. 19–37). New York: Routledge.

Tshuma, B.B., Tshuma, L.A., and Ndlovu, N. (2021). Humour, politics and Mnangagwa's presidency: An analysis of readers' comments in online news websites. In Mpofu, S. (eds), *The Politics of Laughter in the Social Media Age: Perspectives from the Global South* (pp. 93–111). New York: Palgrave MacMillan.

Tshuma, L.A. (2023). Heir to the throne: Photography and the rise to presidency by politicians in Zimbabwe and South Africa. *Visual Studies*, 1–10.

Tshuma, L.A., Msimanga, M.J., and Sibanda, M. (2022). "Playing" in the eyes of the ferret team: Examining the use of surveillance strategies by Zimbabwean journalists. *African Journalism Studies* 43(1): 53–69.

Ureke, O. (2021). Aesthetic norms and motivations of subaltern video filmmaking: Comic skits and mobile journalism of the everyday in Zimbabwe. In Valiati, A., and Villarreal, G.Z. (eds), *Ethnographies of "On Demand" Films* (pp. 219–241). New York: Palgrave.

Willems, W. (2010). Beyond dramatic revolutions and grand rebellions: Everyday forms of resistance in the Zimbabwe crisis. *Communicare: Journal for Communication Sciences in Southern Africa* 29(Special Edition 1): 1–17.

Willems, W. (2011). Comic strips and "the Crisis": Postcolonial laughter and coping with everyday life in Zimbabwe. *Popular Communication* 9(2): 126–145.

Zamponi, M. (2005). From social justice to neo-liberalism, to authoritarianian nationalism: Where is the Zimbabwe state going? In Suzanne, D., Zamponi, M., and Henning, M. (eds), *Zimbabwe-The Political Economy of Decline* (pp. 27–43). Discussion Paper 27. Uppsala: Nordiska Afrikainstitutet.

Zimoyo, T. (2016), '*Busstop in breakthrough productions*' in The Herald, 7 April 2016. From https://www.herald.co.zw/bus-stop-tv-in-breakthrough-productions. (Accessed on 04/11/22).

Part III

MEDIA TEXTS PRODUCTION

Chapter 10

Protesting for Change

Ethiopia's Diasporic Media and the Fight for Democracy

Solomon Kebede and Abit Hoxha

This chapter seeks to respond to the question of an alternative public sphere in contexts where normative spaces of engagement are being closed in authoritarian and semi-authoritarian regimes. Tshuma et al. (2022) study explored the state of regulation and censorship in East and Southern Africa and gestured some of the challenges media markets face in semi-authoritarian regimes like Ethiopia more generally, and even more in countries that for long have been considered stable democracies like South Africa. While this study is located within the Ethiopian context, the broader outcomes resonate with other seminal cases (Matsilele and Ruhanya, 2021; Matsilele and Mutsvairo, 2021) that have explored alternative media formats as spaces for counterhegemonic discourses. The works by Msimanga et al. (2022) and Squires (2002) are instructive, especially in conceptualizing the alternative public spheres.

For a long time, Ethiopia has struggled with media freedom and media development (Bonsa, 2000; Levine, 2008; Reta, 2013). In April 2018, Ethiopia experienced a major political transition following a series of mass protests against the Ethiopian People's Revolutionary Democratic Front (EPRDF), which had led the country for twenty-six years. Following the reform within the party itself and the appointment of new leadership, including a new prime minister, Abiy Ahmed Ali, the country has been undergoing a huge political change that has affected all sectors of public life (Dibu and Ahadu, 2020; Fakude, 2019; Fisher and Gebrewahd, 2019; Záhořík, 2017). One of the changes has to do with the liberalization of the media. All journalists who had been in jail during the preceding leadership were freed, and media outlets based abroad for fear of repression were allowed to operate in the country, and new ones were set up. While these changes brought hope among the

Ethiopian population and the media, the country plunged into another cycle of crisis. On the same note, media houses that had started operating under the new regime stopped functioning owing to repression by state and non-state actors as well as financial difficulties (Borkena, 2020; Jima, 2021; Workneh, 2021b).

Besides these difficulties, the mainstream media landscape in Ethiopia is fragmented and ethnicized, which reflects the country's socio-economic and political sphere (Skjerdal, 2011, 2013; Skjerdal and Mulatu, 2021). Diasporic media are a mirror of this ethnicization of media models. Lahneman (2005, p.1) defines a diaspora as "a group that recognises its separateness based on common ethnicity or nationality, lives in a host country, and maintains some kind of attachment to its home country or homeland." Writing on the same topic, with a specific focus on Zimbabwe, Matsilele (2013) used the term diasporic media to refer to the media that was established by journalists who left Zimbabwe due to media repression and the closure of newspapers viewed as anti-ZANU PF and anti-Mugabe. This is the same definition being appropriated for this study.

The chapter is of importance because the media is touted as being central in the continued conflict and protests in Ethiopia. The data is gleaned from interviews with journalists working for the diasporic media to find out more about their political aims, ideology, and networking, along with their social mobilization agenda, which produces social, cultural, and political consequences in Ethiopia. Looking at media organizations from a social movement theory perspective will generate a theoretical model that contributes to the theoretical understanding of diasporic media in a globalized communication context. Therefore, this chapter borrows a theoretical framework from the study of social movements and applies it to journalists working for the diasporic media. This theory assumes that journalists are treated as members of a movement that is unable to work and function as an independent power inside Ethiopia and thus can be treated within the framework of being a movement, although they do not seem to be organized with the same central authority or leadership as classic social movements.

POLITICAL AND MEDIA TRANSITION IN ETHIOPIA

For a long time, the political history of Ethiopia was dominated by monarchical rule until 1974, when a revolution instilled military rule, overthrowing the last king of Ethiopia, Haile Selassie I (1930–1974). This was followed by a new government of army officers that instated military rule for seventeen consecutive years (1974–1991). Since then, the country has been experiencing periodic political turmoil, resulting in a shift of power. The era of the military regime, which removed Haile Selassie I from power, is considered to mark the birth of the Ethiopian diaspora beyond the Horn of Africa region as people started fleeing the new Marxist regime in fear. Before this period, Ethiopians would leave their country on a temporary basis, mainly for study tours (Terrazas, 2007). The military regime was deposed by an armed rebel group that took power in 1991, ending a long, bloody war between the military government and the rebels (Arban, 2019). The rebel group, forming a ruling coalition of ethnic-based political parties named EPRDF (1991–2018), introduced a new form of government organizing the country under ethnic federal states based on language. After twenty-seven years of rule, EPRDF faced another popular protest, leading the country into a power transition and shift of leadership within the ruling circle itself in April 2018 (Dibu and Ahadu, 2020; Fakude, 2019; Fisher and Gebrewahd, 2019; Lyons, 2019; Záhořík, 2017).

The early 1990s began with the design and ratification of the constitution of the land, which to this date has become a source of controversy among the political elites. Some consider it as the source of conflict and political havoc (Milkias and Metaferia, 2005), while others hail it as a cornerstone for the unprecedented respect of the rights of the various ethnic communities in the country (Agegnehu and Dibu, 2017; Mamo, 2017; Smith, 2013b; Van der Beken, 2010). In the context of these two major discourses, when we look at the Ethiopian diaspora media establishment, we can see that freedom is related to the location of the institutions and journalists working there. As per the norm or nature, a change in political leadership brings in a host of new trends and practices that affect the general makeup of society and institutions for a long time. In Africa, in the year 1991 alone, eighty-six waves of mass protests were registered and brought in different changes in thirty-eight countries. These changes brought in the budding of civic associations and private media like never before. These were times of hope for democratic transition (Mozaffar, 1997).

One common trait among these periods of power transitions is the provisional and relative freedom enjoyed by media practitioners and the increase in the diversity and number of media outlets. These situations were usually cut short as the new regimes consolidated their power, followed by the closing of media houses and sending journalists to jail and exile. Between 2010 and 2015, for example, Ethiopia ranked second, following Syria, in the number of journalists fleeing their homeland. During the same period, fifty-seven Ethiopian journalists were officially registered as fleeing their homeland and escaping detention and death threats (Philips, 2015; Schilit, 2014). For some, exile marks the end of their journalism careers, while others continue to engage in some form of journalism, joining the already operational outlets in their new destinations or establishing new ones (Kebede, 2019).

One additional trait observed during the 2018 political transition in the media sector is the invitation by the new government to exiled journalists, including those on death row in absentia, and media houses to return and work at home. During this period, several journalists and media firms that had moved abroad joined the hype of unprecedented levels of media freedom. The news of "no journalist in jail" hit the headlines (Dahir, 2018; Felix, 2018). However, within a span of a year, the much-enjoyed and celebrated media freedom suffered setbacks like attacks against journalists by state and non-state actors, and new provisions on hate speech, war, and ethnic conflict (CPJ, 2020; Dessie et al., 2022; Téwodros, 2021). Assisted by technology, the repression against journalists at home and the new spate of conflicts intensified, which ultimately saw the rise of an unprecedented number of diaspora media platforms.

Until recently, Ethiopians living abroad were living in exile (Gibb, 2002). This idea came from the hope that one day they would return to their country of origin and thrive in a much better context. The issue of contribution to homeland politics among the Ethiopian diaspora is not isolated, as it confirmed some of the findings in earlier studies. There is extensive scholarship that has looked at the political role of diasporic media as an alternative public sphere, especially in conflict states (Georgiou, 2013; Matsilele, 2013; Ogunyemi, 2015; Wolock, 2020; Matsilele et al., 2023). These studies are by no means exhaustive but do give a picture of the kind of scholarly attention that has sought to understand how exiled and ethnic minorities have sought to create bonds with homelands through media artifacts.

Diaspora is the idea of people who imagine themselves as part of the nation but live outside the borders of the original homeland (Matsilele et al., 2023; Kearney, 1995). Safran and Safran (1991) speak about the "idealized return" of diaspora as an idea that keeps this link to the country of origin alive and interest in political, cultural, and social aspects of life alive and strong. In Anderson's (1991, p.6) terms, this "imagined community" is part of the nation in their imagination but operates in a completely different context, often with far better working and living conditions than the country of origin.

In framing diaspora, Butler (2001) defines acculturation and ethnonationalism as intrinsic dynamics in such communities, providing a different angle of understanding diaspora and migration in relation to the country of origin. In today's day and age, one cannot dismiss the views of the influence of technology and development in relation to the amplified communication of diaspora and, to some extent, provision for space or hyperspace, also for the "deterritorialized" where time and space are condensed and compressed (Harvey et al., 1989). In the hyperspaces or spaces as fields of work, journalists operate and create content related to their community back home. Ahmed (2020) concludes that the media provide essential information that can help migrants settle, build local communities, and maintain transnational linkages. Journalists and media in the diaspora are affected by homeland conflict. They try to make sense of conflict in the place of origin, such as in the case of Kurdish media in the diaspora (Smets, 2018). Similarly, other diasporas use media to make sense of conflicts (Smets et al., 2019).

Like the Kurdish diaspora, Eritreans, a diaspora closer to Ethiopia, also engage in similar activities. Bernal (2006) studied the Eritrean diaspora and came to the conclusion that the use of the internet is mostly in the transnational public sphere, where they produce and debate narratives of history, culture, democracy, and identity. They also used internet-based media to mobilize demonstrations, amass funds for war, debate the formulation of the constitution, and influence the government of Eritrea. Bernal also uses the term "internet intellectuals" to explain interpretation and re-articulation of public narratives (Bernal, 2006). But what does this mean for political participation and democracy? One of the answers is given in the innovative work of Tsagarousianou and others in 1999, when e-democracy was starting its foundation. This whole strand of thought, in many ways, led to the expansion of the term "democracy" or what Tsagarousianou calls "cyberdemocracy." He argues that "cyberdemocracy is a study of potential for electronic democracy" (Tsagarousianou et al., 1998), which, in the case of the diaspora, functions well in terms of political participation in the public sphere. Others, such as Kearney, view constructions of narratives to be different, as he claims that "constructions are detached from any local reference" (Kearney, 1995, p.553). Media system in Ethiopia is fragmented anyways and this perhaps is the reason why the diaspora functions well with an already fragmented and thus diverse media system, as mirroring of such.

MIRRORING ETHIOPIAN MEDIA SYSTEM ABROAD

Since April 2018, Ethiopia has been going through an internal conflict, which reflects in the way media productions come into being. It is known that journalists during conflict times adhere to a specific modus operandi (Hoxha and Hanitzsch, 2018) different from generic news production. Moreover, the media and journalists that operate in the diaspora reflect events and conflict from their country of origin, and therefore Ethiopian diasporic media is not an exception as it mirrors the Ethiopian media system. With all its culprits and problems, Ethiopian journalists abroad reflect ethnic cleavages and divisions that exist in the country and employ these divisions in content production. Ethnicization, therefore, does not only happen in Ethiopia itself but also in the diaspora, as ethnic identity of journalists is very important and comes up in questions about belonging and identity during empirical evidence gathering (Ndlovu et al., 2023; Skjerdal, 2021).

The significant political turmoil and endless transition in Ethiopia also present a breeding ground for conflicting views and, therefore, political opportunities for all interested parties in amplifying narratives of conflict and embracing their own kind in emphasis of subjects covered. There is a clear trend in the content and ownership of most media establishments based on their ethnic belonging, and this is also reflected in diaspora activities covered by journalists. Ethiopian journalists in the diaspora nominally perceive their role as mediators of messages and adhere to traditional western roles of journalists and beyond. Beyond, their role is extended to advocating for political change as they see fit. Political developments at home are the main field of interest for them, and the productions they do abroad are mostly dedicated for home audiences distributed through social networks for home as well as throughout Europe and beyond.

Like journalists in Ethiopia, journalists working abroad also have concerns about safety. Concerns regarding the safety and freedom of journalists are contributing to the popularity and growth of diaspora media. A case in point is what happened to the Oromo Media Network (OMN). Until the 2018 political reform, OMN was operating from abroad. Following the change, OMN, along with various media outlets and exiled journalists, moved its operation to its homeland (Lemke and Endalk, 2016). However, the events associated with the assassination of the popular Oromo singer Hachalu Hundesa on June 29, 2020, led to the closure of OMN after its headquarters was searched by the police and some of its journalists detained. OMN then suspended its production and transmission from Ethiopia, resuming its former role as a diaspora media based in the United States. Another case is the escape in December 2022 of a popular journalist and critic of the current government after sustaining detention and harassment by security personnel. Tamerat Negera had been a journalist in exile before the 2018 political change and resumed his journalistic practice after returning home.

THEORETICAL FRAMEWORK

Theoretically, we lean on the social movement model as it is used to explain diasporic media primarily because social movements develop in a context defined by the state and the representation system (Klandermans, 2005). By using the social movement theory, this chapter will analyze cases of Ethiopian diasporic media, focusing on three main aspects of analysis: (a) political opportunity through analyzing the political transition and transfer of power in Ethiopia; (b) resource mobilization, ideology, and framing by looking at the media messages; (c) networking of these social movement-based diasporic media. In her study of social movements, Porta (1999) says that networks of interaction exist between different actors, which may either include formal organizations or not, depending on shifting circumstances. Ethiopian diasporic media falls under these conditions. In addition, the reason for treating diasporic media through the lens of social movement theory is the definition of such by Porta (1999), who opines that social movements are theorized as dense causal networks of communal actors involved in conflictual relations with clearly identified opponents, sharing a distinct collective identity, and using mainly protests as their modus operandi. Gunning's (2007) study of social movements in the Middle East uses the same framework, which is applicable to our focus as well. He uses political opportunity structures, mobilizing structures, and framing processes as a theoretical framework to structure research on movements. Although Ethiopian diasporic media is not a single-issue movement, as Tilly (1978, p.7) argues, with the same big components such as "interest, organisation, mobilisation, opportunity and collective action itself," they can be treated through the frame of social movement theory for the political opportunity they have, framing messages and mobilization. Also, Buechler (2000) argues that "social movements are an extension of politics by other means." Diasporic media, in the case of Ethiopia, is mainly domiciled in the United States and Europe.

METHODOLOGY

There is no sample that would represent diasporas accordingly and do justice in representing the cultural and social factors that make up the identity of diasporas. Functional diasporic media that has roots in Ethiopia is functioning on the basis of a "one-person band" or with a very small number of people. The way these media function is that they are based in private houses and led by individuals who are semi-journalists and semi-activists who produce content following journalistic routines but without the editorial process as such. This complicates the methodology as the names of media could easily be used to trace and find the authors and leaders of these media. In normal circumstances, they would want to be identified. However, to protect them from potential harm or threats, we choose to keep the names of media and journalists as anonymous as possible.

Leaving the country at different times produces different diasporas and, inevitably, also an interest in the political developments of the country. We found journalists operating in Europe, the United States, and Canada who produce various types of media content directed for the Ethiopian audience. The identification of journalists started with a "snowball effect," in which a small number of journalists identified other similar journalists in their network and vouched for the interviewers to ensure access. Ensuring access to diasporic journalists is also a challenge on its own and a real safety concern. We designed an open-ended questionnaire that was filled in together with respondents in a live online interview as a form of an in-depth interview but helped with the questionnaire.

Due to geographical distance and barriers, online interviewing was the only possibility to interview nine journalists who represent the diaspora journalists of Ethiopia. The questionnaires were filled out in English, but interviews were conducted in Amharic as the main language of the respondents. Out of the nine participants, eight are owners and founders of media outlets while only one is an employee. Five of the media are group ownerships while the rest four are owned individually. Four of the respondents live and work in the United States, two in Canada, two in Europe, and one in Africa. All left their homeland due to pressures resulting from their journalistic work. The oldest media was founded in 2005, while the latest was formed in 2021.

The analysis strategy was to follow a simple guideline of three main points of departure of social movement theory and generalize, and compare materials from the interviews. What we found is a representation of views, and perceptions of functioning journalists from the Ethiopian diaspora. These three strands of analysis were followed in order to see how and why journalists working in countries with much better freedom of press and media see the political opportunity for change, how they frame conflict and what the ideology of representation of conflict is, and last but not least, networking and coordination of these journalists among one another vis-a-vis the country of origin. In the end, a narrative and qualitative analysis of these three parts was conducted to ensure a logical flow of overall findings. All questionnaire grids were uploaded in a data analysis software MaxQDA to ensure maximal understanding of all information. Data was coded manually with separate codes to represent concepts of social movement analysis and understanding of political opportunity, framing and ideology, as well as networking of Ethiopian journalists living in Europe and beyond.

FINDINGS

Political Opportunity for Content Production

The situation in Ethiopia leaves much to be desired in terms of respect for human rights and freedom of expression. Freedom House ranks Ethiopia as a hybrid regime (2021), and journalists who fled from the country try to set a political agenda with their media productions. Interviewed journalists speak about political influence back home as if they were living in Ethiopia and see themselves as an extension or mirror of the Ethiopian media landscape. The freedom they enjoy in Europe and elsewhere provides fertile ground for media production of their choice and offers a very good political opportunity for advocating political change and serving as an adversary to power. A journalist living in the United States, who is a former employee of the government in Ethiopia did not want to be identified but claims to understand the system from within. His claim is that there is potential for change, and this is inspired also from abroad.

> I believe the forces behind potential for change are in Ethiopia. Our messages focus on either inspiring or instigating our audiences to move forward and challenge those in power. We carry stories that cannot be aired by media outlets based in Ethiopia. We have insiders who supply us with information. Our job here is to expose and reflect on the events that are taking place there. Then we can see and measure the impact when audiences reach us with their comments. There are times when we see immediate reactions by the state or insurgency or protest by the people who we believe are our audiences (Former government journalist and now running an online media from the United States).

It is common for former government-employed journalists to cross the line and advocate for change after they leave Ethiopia and operate under different circumstances in countries with much more space for work. The political environment provides them with the political opportunity to advocate for political changes or, in other cases, even support government policies, but most oppose current governmental policies. Another journalist who fled from Ethiopia, leaving his job and family behind—unable to work for a network of news or media abroad—uses the opportunity of digital platforms to create content via YouTube as an influence channel for back home. Most of his audience is from Ethiopia, which has not been able to censor the internet entirely.

> We are the result of repressive political systems that are hostile to the media. We are working here as journalists to at least challenge the prevalence of repression against our colleagues and the population as a whole. Unless we work for political change in our homeland what is the point of running away from your country and engaging again in the same profession that inflicted much harm to you and your family? I shouldn't have been here away from my family and friends, had it not been about the regime. So how come I just sit and wait for its (the regime's) natural death to go back to my country? I have to facilitate its demise. (Formerly a radio journalist and now operating a YouTube and satellite aired media jointly with two colleagues from the United States)

Ideology and Framing of Messages

Some of the studies conducted so far (Skjerdal, 2012; Solomon, 2019) on Ethiopian media initiatives in the diaspora found a likely common motive of opposing the incumbent government through disseminating information that counters the dominant state-owned media discourse in the homeland. However, this study evidences diversified and additional motives in the existing diaspora-based media. Following the April 2018 political reform that invited more groups with political and ethnic backgrounds and interests, the media abroad started to reflect the trend in the homeland. As a result, participants admit the media's allegiance to certain political groupings, ethnic interests, or geographical locations.

> Previously I was working towards fighting injustice in my country in wherever part of Ethiopia and to whatever ethnic group that might happen. Recently especially after 2018, I started to observe old colleagues and new ones heralding the grievances of their ethnic groups and ignoring the others. Then I started to question myself for whom I should be a voice and how. Then I left the media I have been working jointly with my colleagues and started my own channel. Getting followers was not a problem as I have already a name (popular). It doesn't mean that I only work for my region. I cover national issues but prioritize when there are matters affecting my region and my people. (Former print journalist in Ethiopia and now running an online media from Canada)

The interest in and operation of diaspora-based media is not only the business of former runaway journalists. The idea behind the establishment of some of the media firms in this study came from individuals or groups in the diaspora who wanted to have a stake in the political discourse back home. A former journalist who currently runs an online platform from the United States recalls how he was approached by a group of individuals wanting him to start a media platform for advocating a cause they affiliate with.

> These are people who came with the resources to finance me and the production process as far as I keep on exposing and bringing the suffering of the people from their ethnic group to the front. They told me that they felt responsible for protecting the rights of their ethnic group members from the abuses of the government and believed that running media is one of the preferred ways to do it. They also mentioned that I should feel responsible for the issue as I belong to the same ethnic group they come from. (A former TV journalist in Ethiopia and currently running a media based in the United States)

Another co-owner of a diaspora media outlet regards the ownership of some media outlets in the diaspora as ethnic-based, which she says are busy heralding the causes of ethnic and geographic groups they affiliate with. In so doing, the media become, for people living in a diaspora, catalysts for reminiscing about other times and places (Drotner, 1998).

> You don't need to do research to see how ethnic-centred some of them are. Look at the names of the individuals owning and working in the media outlet. They all belong to the same ethnic group and at times you find journalists coming from the same village. And when you look at their content it's all about hatred and defamation towards another ethnic group like the one, I belong to. I don't remember a day where they skipped mentioning my ethnic community negatively (Former print journalist in Ethiopia and now running an online media from Canada)

As much as we see polarization in homeland politics, there is observable animosity among the various media practitioners working from abroad. When asked about their potential competitors or views about other diaspora-based media outlets, participants mention platforms they consider to be opposing their views or belonging to a considered "enemy" ethnic group resentfully. For deterritorialized subjects, ethnic media provide points of cultural identification through which they can imagine continuous identities and hence create desirable meanings of their ruptured and shifting identities (Shi, 2005). A journalist working for media advocating the atrocities of the war in Tigray refers to another outlet as sponsored by the federal government of Ethiopia to spread information that justifies the war in Tigray and paints Tigrayans as traitors of the nation.

> If you look at the contents of this media, it is a direct copy of what the government channels are broadcasting to their audiences. People think that this media is established and run by individuals living abroad. But that is not true. I know for sure that journalists are on the payroll of the government. You cannot find a single news or feature story that blames the government for the war in Tigray. (Former Journalist and now running a media after the Tigray conflict)

One interesting development in Ethiopian diasporic media post-2018 is the emergence of media platforms in response to armed conflicts between the government and splinter/opposition groups. Cyberspace has provided the context in which users electronically reconstitute the relationships that existed before migration (Mpofu, 2021; Karim, 1998). Several media platforms abroad have evolved since the eruption in November 2020 of the war between the federal government and the Tigray regional state. A former journalist, who has been engaged in another trade until the outbreak of the war, said it was the conflict and especially the "atrocities committed by the federal army" that forced him to launch a platform advocating the cause of Tigray.

I am not alone in this. There are several former journalists or communications persons who started running media to support the struggle of our region (Tigray) against the invaders. We all have one goal which is to expose the crimes committed by the Ethiopian government and to seek support for the independence of Tigray. Personally, I have these two missions and will not stop journalism until I accomplish them (Former Journalist and now running a media after the Tigray conflict)

We see the conflict at home as the cause of the shifting ideology of media outlets. There are media platforms that were operational before the outbreak of the war but shifted their objectives and focus areas following the conflict. One such media platform is run from the United States with a current subscriber count of 150,000 followers on YouTube. This platform, when established in 2014, announced that it worked for the free flow of information, exposing maladministration, and promoting democratic political discourse throughout Ethiopia. However, with the outbreak of the war in 2020, the founder of the media decided to cover issues that stand against the federal government, which he considers an invader.

With the launch of this war against Tigray, most media outlets sided with the federal government. In the beginning, I tried to do fair coverage of the issue entertaining views from all sides. But this was taken by other diaspora and local media as advocating for my region. As the atrocities committed against civilians in the region intensify, I started focusing on challenging the views of those who blindly support the war. You can brand me in whatever ways you like but my media is against this war. (Owner and producer of a media platform from the United States)

Network and Connections with Home

According to Castells (1997, p.356), diasporan media act as a platform for people resisting economic, cultural, and political disfranchisement, which enables them to struggle and negotiate on behalf of their specific interests/ values. Through time, Ethiopian diasporic media developed three strands of networks that were shaped by the challenges and opportunities of news gathering. The chain of relationships journalists and the media forged with audiences comes first in this regard. Audiences, with their divergent socioeconomic, political, and spatial representations, are basically consumers of news. Simultaneously, they are valid news sources, supplying the diasporic media with tips and interview materials for news production.

During my days as a journalist back home, we don't really take seriously the role of audiences as major sources news. Here we almost rely on them to get tips, to fact check and to reach witnesses on the ground. (Former print journalist in Ethiopia and now running an online media from Canada)

Hence, these diasporic media have been effective in the mobilization of bottom-up redefinition of the power of dispersed groups to form new bonds of cohesiveness and contribute to the ethnic diversity of a multi-ethnic public sphere (Husband, 2000, p. 206). The second line of engagement for the diasporic media evolved as a result of the news gathering challenges faced by journalists sniffing for insider and reliable sources, mainly in government machinery but also in NGO and business establishments at home. These are anonymous sources usually occupying high-profile posts in the systems, supplying/feeding crucial information for starting investigative productions or substantiating developing news packages. According to a former state media journalist who now runs online media from the United States, it usually takes rigorous effort and time to identify and develop trust between the media and the insiders.

> We cannot just take a person for granted for he/she claimed that they hold key and relevant position. We have to crosscheck the authenticity of the information and the position of the person using other networks. Once we developed trust they even lead us to their colleagues with similar statuses in other institutions. As much as we hunt for these sources, there are cases where these individuals look for us to supply us with tips. (A former TV journalist in Ethiopia and currently running a media based in the United States)

The relative freedom to report and work enjoyed by journalists abroad has made diasporic media outlets safe destinations for news items that are unthinkable to be aired or published by journalists in the homeland. This takes us to a third line of network the diasporic media had built over time with individual journalists and news outlets at home. Local journalists, who are in most cases former colleagues of the journalists in the diaspora, feed them with tips for stories that cannot be covered or further investigated by local media outlets. There are cases where local journalists filter news items and pass on those considered as unsafe to report locally to the diaspora platforms. Local journalists, in some cases, are important sources of news stories to the diaspora media.

> I have networks some of them former colleagues who supply me with information. There are times when they have all the information, but they know that it would be dangerous for them to report locally. Then they hand us an almost ready-to-air package. Additionally, we use local journalists for verifying information and finding resource persons. (Formerly a radio journalist and now operating a YouTube and satellite aired media jointly with two colleagues from the United States)

In addition to connections in diaspora—home, journalists operating abroad have an extensive network amongst themselves. Almost all respondents believe that running a media platform from abroad with audiences at home makes a significant contribution to changes in Ethiopia. They argue that though they are far away from their sources, they have the freedom to report on issues that cannot be covered by the media at home. A co-owner of an online platform in the United States who had been a print journalist in Ethiopia until 2009 says the audience's expectation is also to get things that are unaddressed by local journalists.

> We will be flooded with comments of dissatisfaction and even insults the moment we cover a repeat of issues that the local media is handling. We always monitor the local news channels mainly not to echo what they are talking about—we have to at least find out a different angle to the story. (Formerly a print journalist in Ethiopia and now running an online media based in Europe)

Ethiopian journalists operate under heavy conditions in Ethiopia, but diaspora journalists are also not far from it. They are under the impression of being watched, stick together, and try to set the agenda for events at home.

CONCLUSION

This chapter sheds light on Ethiopian diasporic media operating in particular conditions and producing content for a home audience. Della Porta's "network of interaction between different actors" very much applies to Ethiopian diasporic media, considering their horizontal network with one another despite geographical location. Communication technology amplifies this networking among media to also enhance "collective actors involved in conflictual relations" (Diani, 2006, p.30). Despite Ethiopian diasporic media not being a single issue movement with the same social context, the interest in political change and opportunity is present in their framing of messages with the aim of influencing audiences back home. As social movements are an extension of politics by other means (Tshuma, 2023; Buchler, 2000), diasporic media are an imitation of home media, making a case for mirroring the media system abroad.

Ethiopia, being a highly diverse and multicultural country, has its internal fragmentation both in society and in the political landscape, which reflects in the media system. Democratic transition is an ongoing process, and although journalists adhere to Western values of journalism when trying to cover events and report, they remain exposed to non-Western challenges and working conditions. Diasporic media for Ethiopian journalists is the only two-way window to the country because of two-way information circulation that flows from peer to peer. Although Kearney (1995) claims that "constructions are detached from any local reference," this is not the case with Ethiopian journalists in diasporas. Divisions along ethnic lines also define political landscapes and journalistic adherence, thus constructions and news production are very much linked to local references, although produced in the diaspora. This enables the Ethiopian media system abroad to reflect back home for the audiences. The difference in diasporic media from national and local media in Ethiopia is that they are more collaborative and have less culprits of reporting under difficult physical threats and risks.

For Ethiopian diasporic media, the political situation in the home of origin presents a great interest, which also translates into a political opportunity to mostly oppose political developments and be critical towards the system. Fragmentation and ethnicization (Skjerdal, 2011, 2013; Skjerdal and Mulatu, 2021) are also reflected also in sourcing news, as journalists choose sources from their own groups and rarely cross the lines. These divisions are also reflected in the country's socio-economic and political sphere. Journalists living in the diaspora have a vast range of sources from back home who have an interest in having their stories shared and produced due to the lack of internal freedom within Ethiopia. Furthermore, the framing of the messages and professional ideology of diasporic media, although mirrored from home in terms of structure, reflect an advanced understanding of the news production process as well as news values.

Framing of messages is directed for home audiences and has political aims as well, and exactly for that reason, it is part of the ideology for change or further development of the country. Opposing the political elite and government actions is almost an ideological agenda for diasporic media originating from Ethiopia. Finally, the network structure of Ethiopian diasporic media is laid out on two levels, which reflect resource mobilization and availability. First, the network with the home or the origin, which is also the main audience for the media productions. This level is used for both incoming resource mobilization, such as funding and the mobilization of opposition in protests within Ethiopian society. This involves a wide range of sources, leaks, and interest-based network. Second, but no less important, is the diasporic network that functions under a civic identity, mostly but with nuances of ethnic divisions or fragmentation. This is horizontally distributed outside Ethiopia, and interaction among diasporic media is used for sharing information, reaching a wider audience, and overall collaboration.

REFERENCES

Ahmed, R., Rukhsana Ahmed, & Veronis, L. (2020). Creating in-between spaces through diasporic and mainstream media consumption: A comparison of four ethnocultural and immigrant communities in Ottawa. *Canada: International Communication Gazette*, *82*(3), 289–315. https://doi.org/10.1177/1748048519828594.

Bernal, V. (2006). Diaspora, cyberspace and political imagination: The Eritrean diaspora online. *Global Networks-a Journal of Transnational Affairs*, *6*(2), 161–179. https://doi.org/10.1111/j.1471-0374.2006.00139.x.

Bezabih, T., & Tesfaye Bezabih. (2018). Diasporic media use: In participatory politics and citizen journalism: A case in Ethiopia. *International Journal of Research*, *5*(22), 791–811.

Buechler, S. M. (1993). Beyond resource mobilization? Emerging trends in social movement theory. *The Sociological Quarterly*, *34*(2), 217–235.

Butler, K. D. (2001). Defining diaspora, refining a discourse. *Diaspora: A Journal of Transnational Studies*, *10*(2), 189–219. https://doi.org/10.1353/dsp.2011.0014.

Cohen, R. (1997). *Global Diasporas: An Introduction*. London: Routledge.

CPJ. (2019). *Under Abiy, Ethiopia's media have more freedom, but challenges remain*. CPJ. https://cpj.org/2019/04/ethiopia-abiy-ahmed-press-freedom-reform/.

CPJ. (2020). *Melese Diribsa Oromia Media Network (OMN) | Imprisoned in Ethiopia | July 02, 2020* [ANnual Census]. CPJ. https://cpj.org/data/people/melese-diribsa/.

Dahir, A. L. (2018, December 13). For the first time in decades, there are no Ethiopian journalists in prison. Available at: https://qz.com/africa/1494561/ethiopia-has-no-jailed-journalists-in-2018-the-first-since-2004. Accessed on 14 July 2024.

Della Porta, D., & Diani, M. (1999). *Social Movements: An Introduction*. Oxford: Blackwell Publishing.

Dessie, B. A., Ali, A. C., & Moges, M. A. (2022). Ethnic orientation over ethical underpinnings: Emerging trends of the Ethiopian media landscape. *Journalism Practice*, 17(9), 1919–1936.

Gagliardone, I., Pohjonen, M., Beyene, Z., Zerai, A., Aynekulu, G., Bekalu, M. A., Bright, J., Moges, M. A., Seifu, M., Stremlau, N., Taflan, P., Gebrewolde, T., & Teferra, Z. M. (2016). Mechachal: Online debates and elections in Ethiopia—From hate speech to engagement in social media. *Social Science Research Network*. https://doi.org/10.2139/ssrn.2831369.

Gamson, W. A., & Wolfsfeld, G. (1993). Movements and media as interacting systems. *The Annals of the American Academy of Political and Social Science*, *528*(1), 114–125.

Garcia, A. C., Standlee, A. I., Bechkoff, J. R., & Cui, Y. (2009). Ethnographic approaches to the internet and computer-mediated communication. *Journal of Contemporary Ethnography*, *38*(1), 52–84. https://doi.org/10.1177/0891241607310839.

Gebremeskel, S. K. (2019). *Journalistic practice and media production away from home (in exile): The case of Wazema Radio* (Master's thesis).

Georgiou, M. (2013). Diaspora in the digital era: Minorities and media representation. *Jemie*, *12*, 80.

Gunning, J. (2007). *Hamas in Politics: Democracy. Democracy, Religion, Violence.* Oxford. Oxford University Press.

Gibb, C. (2002). Deterritorialized People in Hyperspace: Creating and Debating Harari Identity Over the Internet. *Anthropologica, 44*(1), 55–67. https://doi.org/10.4324/9780203489147-15

Hank Johnston, & Bert Klandermans. (1995). *Social Movements and Culture.* London: Routledge.

Harvey, D., Harvey, D. W., & Harvey, F. D. (1989). *The condition of postmodernity an enquiry into the origins of cultural change.* Oxford: Blackwell Publishing.

Jenkins, J. C. (1983). Resource mobilization theory and the study of social movements. *Review of Sociology.* https://doi.org/10.1146/annurev.so.09.080183.002523.

Jenkins, J. C., & Klandermans, B. (1995). *The Politics of Social Protest: Comparative Perspectives On States And Social Movements.* London: Routledge..

Klandermans, P. G., & Weerd, M. (2000). Group identification and political protest. In S. Stryker, T. Owens, & R. W. White (Eds.), *Social Psychology and Social Movements: Cloudy Past and Bright Future* (pp. 68–92). University of Minnesota Press.

Koopmans, R. (2004). Protest in time and space: The evolution of waves of contention. *The Blackwell Companion to Social Movements,* 19–46.

Lyons, T. (2019). *The Puzzle of Ethiopian Politics.* Lynne Rienner Publishers, Incorporated.

Lahneman, W. J. (2005). Impact of diaspora communities on national and global politics: Report on survey of the literature. Available at: https://cissm.umd.edu/sites/default/files/2019-08/lahneman_diaspora_report.pdf. Accessed 14 July 2024.

Manor, I., Manor, I., Adiku, G. A., & Geraldine Asiwome Adiku. (2021). From 'traitors' to 'saviours': A longitudinal analysis of Ethiopian, Kenyan and Rwandan embassies' practice of digital diaspora diplomacy. *South African Journal of International Affairs, 28*(3), 403–427. https://doi.org/10.1080/10220461.2021.1948915.

Matsilele, T., Mpofu, S., Msimanga, M., & Tshuma, L. (2021). Transnational hashtag protest movements and emancipatory politics in Africa: A three country study. *Global Media Journal: German Edition.*

Matsilele, T., & Ruhanya, P. (2021). Social media dissidence and activist resistance in Zimbabwe. *Media, Culture & Society, 43*(2), 381–394.

Matsilele, T. (2013). The political role of the diaspora media in the mediation of the Zimbabwean crisis: A case study of the Zimbabwean-2008 to 2010. Unpublished MA Thesis. Stellenbosch University.

Matsilele, T., Mpofu, S., & Moyo, D. (2023). Diasporic media and the appropriation of technologies: The case of nehanda radio and Zimbabwean politics. In Matsilele, T. Mpofu, S., and Moyo, D. (Eds), *New Journalism Ecologies in East and Southern Africa: Innovations, Participatory and Newsmaking Cultures* (pp. 251–266). Cham: Springer International Publishing.

Mpofu, S., Ndlovu, M., & Tshuma, L. (2021). The artist and filmmaker as activists, archivists and the work of memory: A case of the Zimbabwean genocide. *African Journal of Rhetoric, 13*(1), 46–76.

Mpofu, S. (2017). *Diasporic New Media and Conversations on Conflict: A Case of Zimbabwe Genocide Debates*. 205–221. https://doi.org/10.1007/978-3-319-56642-9_13.

Msimanga, M. J., Tshuma, L. A., & Matsilele, T. (2022). The why of humour during a crisis: An exploration of COVID-19 memes in South Africa and Zimbabwe. *Journal of African Media Studies, 14*(2), 189–207.

Ndlovu, M., Tshuma, L., & Mpofu, S (Eds). (2023). *Remembering Mass Atrocities: Perspectives on Memory Struggles and Cultural Representations in Africa*. Cham: Springer International Publishing.

Ndlovu, E. (2014). *The Role of Diasporic Media in Facilitating Citizen Journalism and Political Awareness in Zimbabwe*. Unpublished PhD Thesis. University of Salford.

Oberschall, A. (1973). *Social Conflict and Social Movements*. NJ: Prentice-Hall Englewood Cliffs.

Ogunyemi, O. (2018). Introduction: Mediating identity and conflict through diasporic media. *Crossings: Journal of Migration and Culture, 9*(1), 3–12. https://doi.org/10.1386/cjmc.9.1.3_2.

Ogunyemi, O. (2015). Introduction: Conceptualizing the media of diaspora. In *Journalism, Audiences and Diaspora* (pp. 1–14). London: Palgrave Macmillan UK.

Philips, K. (2015). *Faces of Exile*. CPJ.

Schilit, N. (2014). *Mission Journal: Ethiopian journalists must choose between being locked up or locked out* [Mission Report]. Commmittee to Protect Journalists. https://cpj.org/2014/12/mission-journal-in-ethiopia-journalists-must-choos/.

Skjerdal, T. (2011). Journalists or activists? Self-identity in the Ethiopian diaspora online community. *Journalism, 12*(6), 727–744.

Skjerdal, T. (2013). *Competing Loyalties: Journalism Culture in the Ethiopian State Media*. Unpublished.

Skjerdal, T., & Mulatu, M. (2021). The Ethnification of the Ethiopian media. *Fojo Media Institute and International Media Support,* Available at:< Https://Fojo. Se/En/New-Study-Documents-Ethnification-of-the-Ethiopian-Media-2>[Accessed 18 November 2021].

Skjerdal, T. S. (2011). Journalists or activists? Self-identity in the Ethiopian diaspora online community. *Journalism, 12*(6), 727–744.

Skjerdal, T. S. (2012). *Competing loyalties: Journalism culture in the Ethiopian state media* [PhD Thesis]. University of Oslo, Faculty of Humanities.

Smets, K. (2018). Ethnic identity without ethnic media? Diasporic cosmopolitanism, (social) media and distant conflict among young Kurds in London: *International Communication Gazette, 80*(7), 603–619. https://doi.org/10.1177/1748048518802204.

Smets, K., Kevin Smets, & Smets, K. (2019). Doing diasporic media research. *The Handbook of Diasporas, Media, and Culture,* 97–111. https://doi.org/10.1002/9781119236771.ch7.

Snow, D. A. (2004). Framing processes, ideology, and discursive fields. *The Blackwell Companion to Social Movements, 1*, 380–412.

Snow, D. A. (2013). Framing and social movements. *The Wiley-Blackwell Encyclopedia of Social and Political Movements*, 1–3. https://doi.org/10.1002/9781405198431.wbespm434.

Squires, C. R. (2002). Rethinking the black public sphere: An alternative vocabulary for multiple public spheres. *Communication Theory*, *12*(4), 446–468.

Suzanne Staggenborg, Aldon D Morris, Carol McClurg Mueller, & Carol Mueller. (1992). *Frontiers in Social Movement Theory*. London: Yale University Press.

Téwodros. (2021). From state repression to fear of non-state Actors: Examining emerging threats of journalism practice in Ethiopia. *Journalism and Safety* (pp. 267–284). London: Routledge. .

Tsagarousianou, R., Tambini, D., & Bryan, C. (1998). *Cyberdemocracy: Technology, Cities and Civic Networks*. https://doi.org/10.4324/9780203448847

Tshuma, L. A., Matsilele, T., & Msimanga, M. J. (2022). 'Weapons of oppressors': COVID-19 regulatory framework and its impact on journalism practices in Southern Africa. In Dralega, C. A. and Napakol, A. (Eds.), *Health Crises and Media Discourses in Sub-Saharan Africa* (pp. 253–266). Cham: Springer International Publishing.

Tshuma L. A. (2023). Space of loud silences: Digital media start-ups and women's experiences of Gukurahundi atrocities. In Khalid, A., Holmes, G., and Parpart, J. L. (Eds), *The Politics of Silence, Voice and the In-Between* (pp. 202–212). London: Routledge.

Tilly, C. (1977). From mobilization to revolution. https://deepblue.lib.umich.edu/bitstream/handle/2027.42/50931/156.pdf (Accessed on 1 February 2023).

Vliegenthart, R. (2013). Media framing and social movements. *The Wiley-Blackwell Encyclopedia of Social and Political Movements*, 1–3. https://doi.org/10.1002/9781405198431.wbespm474.

Widjanarko, P. (2020). *Media Ethnography in Diasporic Communities*. *32*(2), 124–134. https://doi.org/10.22146/jh.49389.

William Safran, & Safran, W. (1991). Diasporas in modern societies: Myths of homeland and return. *Diaspora: A Journal of Transnational Studies*, *1*(1), 83–99. https://doi.org/10.1353/dsp.1991.0004.

Wogu, J. O., & Ugwuoke, J. C. (2019). Exploring Diasporic Media in Africa within the Framework of Social Identity Theory. *University of Nigeria Interdisciplinary Journal of Communication Studies* *23*(2), 25–39.

Wolock, L. (2020). Diaspora and digital media. In Lopez, L. K. (Eds.), *Race and Media: Critical Approaches* (pp. 190–202). New York: New York University Press.

Workneh, T. W. (2022). Overseas media, homeland audiences: examining determinants of newsmaking in Deutsche Welle's Amharic Service. *Media, Culture & Society*, *44*(2), 323–340.

Chapter 11

Gukurahundi Memory, Subversive Pleasures, and Protest Cultures in Zimbabwe

Mphathisi Ndlovu and Nkosini A. Khupe

Drawing upon the writings of Fiske (1989a, 1989b), this study demonstrates the key role of popular cultural artifacts (graffiti, music, film, social media, paintings, theater, etc.) to express the traumatic experiences of disempowered communities. On the one hand, I argue that the Zimbabwean government is deploying its repressive apparatuses and mechanisms to suppress *Gukurahundi* memories. On the other hand, I demonstrate how the disempowered groups in Matabeleland are creatively using the media and popular cultural artifacts to resist and evade forces of domination. This chapter shows that hegemonic strategies are not absolute because they are met by countervailing forces, or the "fleeting tactics of the weak" (Fiske, 1989a, p. 19). In this form of memory activism, the fleeting tactics of the disempowered groups are akin to "guerrilla warfare," "raiding," and "poaching" (Fiske, 1989a, p.19; De Certeau, 1984, p. xii). In other words, the weak are using *discursive* guerrilla tactics against the strategies of the dominant forces by making "poaching raids against their texts or structures" and playing "constant tricks upon the system" (Fiske, 1989a, p. 32).

GUKURAHUNDI: A HISTORICAL CONTEXT

Gukurahundi is a Shona term meaning the "rain that washes away the chaff from the last harvest, before the spring rains" (CCJP & LRF, 2007, p. xiii). In the political context, it denotes the state-orchestrated violence in Matabeleland and Midlands between 1983 and 1987 that resulted in the deaths of more than 20,000 predominantly Ndebele-speaking civilians.

The ruling party, the Zimbabwe African National Union—Patriotic Front (ZANU-PF), accused the Joshua Nkomo-led opposition party, the Zimbabwe African People's Union (ZAPU), of instigating a "dissident" rebellion and plotting to overthrow the government (Kriger, 2003). The group tagged "dissidents" were former Zimbabwe People's Revolutionary Army (ZPRA) guerrillas who had deserted the national army (Alexander, 1998). ZPRA was an armed wing of ZAPU during the liberation struggle. Nkomo denied any links or association with the activities of the "dissidents."

In 1983, the government deployed a counter-insurgency military unit to the predominantly Ndebele-speaking Matabeleland and Midlands regions under the guise of quashing this "dissident" movement. Matabeleland and Midlands regions were the strongholds of ZAPU. The counter-insurgency military unit, known as the Fifth Brigade, went on to unleash terror in Ndebele-speaking communities and committed atrocities. The Fifth Brigade was comprised of Shona speakers who were former combatants of ZANU PF's military wing, the Zimbabwe African National Liberation Army (ZANLA). Civilians in Matabeleland and Midlands were accused by the Fifth Brigade of aiding and harboring "dissidents." The Fifth Brigade "murdered and tortured thousands of civilians, burned hundreds of villages, and raped and pillaged entire communities" (Cameron, 2018, p. 5). At Bhalagwe camp in Matabeleland South, thousands of *Gukurahundi* victims were detained, tortured, and killed by the government forces (Eppel, 2020; Ndlovu and Mlotshwa, 2022). During the *Gukurahundi*, the Ndebele people were labeled "dissidents" by the Fifth Brigade (Eppel, 2020, p. 260). By the time this violence ended in 1987, at least 20,000 predominantly Ndebele people had been killed by the Fifth Brigade. The Catholic Commission for Justice and Peace (CCJP) and the Legal Resources Foundation (LRF) report (1997) provide detailed accounts of the gruesome killings, abductions, sexual assaults, torture, and other human rights crimes committed against civilians by the government forces.

The massacres halted with the signing of the Unity Accord between ZANU PF and ZAPU in 1987. An amnesty was declared, and both the Fifth Brigade and the "dissidents" were pardoned. However, the official silence surrounding these massacres has been "devastating" (Robins, 1996, p. 73), with affected communities being "forced to live with their silenced memories of horror and fear" (Eppel, 2004, p. 46). Although writers such as Vambe (2012, p. 286) claim that *Gukurahundi* victims have "moved on with their lives," the country remains deeply "wounded" (Rwafa, 2012, p. 323). Ndlovu and Dube (2013, 1) have dismissed Vambe's (2012) work as misleading and lacking "ethical and moral biddings that should be a feature of all academic endeavours." *Gukurahundi* survivors are "still simmering with anger, resentment and frustration" (Rwafa, 2012, p. 323). Memories of the *Gukurahundi* atrocities "heightened the victims' awareness of being Ndebele and at the cost of being Zimbabwean" (Lindgren, 2005, p. 158). Lindgren (2005, p. 156) notes that some *Gukurahundi* survivors "explicitly identify themselves as Ndebele when remembering the atrocities." As a result, traumatic memories of *Gukurahundi* are being recounted and re-animated in various spaces, such as digital media, in ways that promote Ndebele secessionist imaginaries (Ndlovu, 2022; Ndlovu-Gatsheni, 2008).

The current government employs "discourses of silence" to "erase, bury and banish the memories of *Gukurahundi* from the public domain" (Ndlovu, 2018, p. 275). The silencing of victims and the attempts by perpetrators to avoid responsibility are a common features of those traumatized cultures that have undergone extensive repression. In her work on the perpetuation of anti-Semitism in post-war Austria, Wodak defines "discourses of silence" as "explicit denial through justification strategies" (2011, p. 356). Wodak (2003, 2011) identifies the discursive strategies employed by Austrians to justify and deny their involvement in the Holocaust. Such discourses of silence are evident in *Gukurahundi* discourse, which tends to be "rendered taboo" in official spaces (Mpofu, 2015, p. 82). In 1999, at Joshua Nkomo's funeral, Mugabe described the atrocities as a moment of madness. More than a decade later, the now-president Emmerson Mnangagwa, one of the chief architects of *Gukurahundi*, claimed that the traumatic historical episode was a "closed chapter" (Ndlovu, 2018, p. 281). During his inauguration speech in 2018, President Mnangagwa told the people of Matabeleland to "move on" (Mpofu, 2019). Other government officials echoed similar sentiments. In 2020, Obert Mpofu claimed that *Gukurahundi* had been "resolved" by the Unity Accord (Ndlovu and Mlotshwa, 2022, p. 285). A year later, Kembo Mohadi accused those demanding justice for *Gukurahundi* victims of attempting to "divide the nation" (Ndlovu and Mlotshwa 2022, 285). The discourse of unity tends to be invoked by ZANU PF to maintain its hegemony (Mpofu and Moyo, 2017, p. 511). Popular musicians such as Ndux Malax and Black Umfolosi produced pro-unity songs that suggested to the "people of Matabeleland that they had to follow the path of unity or else they would be doomed" (Mpofu and Moyo, 2017, p. 511). Despite this culture of impunity, amnesia, and denialism, there are growing dissenting voices in Matabeleland that are demanding justice, commemoration, and the exhumation and reburial of *Gukurahundi* victims (Eppel, 2020; Mpofu, 2015). This is like "memory movements" in Spain, some of which relate to issues of mass graves and exhumations (Sabido, 2019; Ferrandiz, 2015; Ferrandiz and Robben, 2015). This chapter explores the role and place of popular culture in *Gukurahundi* memory activism and protest.

THEORETICAL REFLECTIONS

This chapter is informed by Fiske's (1989a; 1989b) theorization of popular culture and the everyday lives of people. Fiske's (1989a; 1989b; 1987) work provides a framework for analyzing the ways in which popular culture enables subordinated groups to resist and evade dominant ideologies. The focus is on the popular pleasures and social meanings derived and generated by the subordinates as they seek to disrupt and offend the power bloc (Fiske, 1987, p. 229). Popular culture can be understood as a site of struggle between hegemonic and counter-hegemonic forces. Thus, it is:

> Part of power relations; it always bears traces of the constant struggle between domination and subordination, between power and various forms of resistance to it or evasions of it. (Fiske, 1989a, p. 19)

In essence, popular culture constitutes the "culture of the subordinated and disempowered" (Fiske, 1989a, p. 5). It is made from "below" and involves the struggle to generate meanings and popular pleasures that serve the interests of subordinated groups (Fiske, 1989b, p. 2). In this vein, popular culture is produced or "formed always in reaction to, and never as part of, the forces of domination" (Fiske, 1989a, p. 43). The disempowered groups use the resources provided by the power bloc to construct counter-hegemonic discourses. Fiske uses the term "excorporation" to describe the "process by which the subordinates make their own culture out of the resources and commodities provided by the dominant system" (1989a, p. 15). In this way, the subordinates create their own subcultures out of the resources provided by the hegemonic forces. The disempowered groups operate on a terrain "imposed" and "organized" by the power bloc (De Certeau, 1984, p. 37). Thus, popular culture is produced when subordinated groups "make do" with what is at their disposal (De Certeau, 1984, p. 18). Military metaphors like "guerrilla tactics" and "semiotic guerrilla warfare" (Fiske, 1989a, p. 19; De Certeau, 1984, p. 34) are employed by scholars to describe the constant struggles between forces of domination and subordination. The disempowered groups discursively employ guerrilla tactics against the strategies of the hegemonic forces (Fiske, 1989a). Within these guerrilla's stratagems, there is a certain pleasure in "getting around the rules of a constraining space" (De Certeau, 1984, p. 18) and "avoiding the social discipline of the power bloc" (Fiske, 1989a, p. 47). Thus, the subordinated groups generate social pleasures in the refusal to "finally submit" (Fiske, 1989a, p. 47) and be "subjugated" (Fiske, 1989b, p. 17). Popular pleasures are produced by the "fleeting" and "limited" victories of the disempowered people (Fiske, 1989b, p. 2). In generating these pleasures, the weak employ evasion and trickery to exploit the dominant system (Fiske, 1989a, 1989b).

This chapter is also informed by the concept of collective memory (Halbwachs, 1992). Drawing on this theory, we consider collective memories as social constructs. It is a shared recollection of past events (Edy, 2007; Halbwachs, 1992). These memories are conditioned by sociopolitical and historical conditions. Past events are evoked, appropriated, and used in the context of prevailing needs and circumstances (Halbwachs, 1992; Edy, 2006). The knowledge of the past is preserved and transmitted through sites of memory (Nora, 1989) or vehicles of memory (Confino, 1997), such as films, cemeteries, monuments, and the media. In addition, collective memories are contested as different versions of the past are reproduced (Edy, 2006). As a result, memory struggles are waged by different memory communities as they seek to legitimate their interpretation of the past (Zerubavel, 2003). This chapter considers graffiti, music, film, social media, paintings, theater, etc., as sites of *Gukurahundi* memory. The resurgence of repressed memories in post-dictatorial Spain (Colmeiro, 2011; Faber, 2005).

SILENCING, AUTHORITARIANISM, AND RESTRICTIVE SPACES

Fiske (1989a) posits that the power bloc deploys their "huge, [and] well-organised forces" to reproduce and sustain their domination. In Zimbabwe, the government employs various strategies to restrict democratic spaces. First, repressive state apparatuses such as the army and police are deployed by the power bloc to unleash violence and intimidate journalists, opposition leaders, and human rights activists. In 1997, a public ceremony to commemorate *Gukurahundi* victims in Lupane, Matabeleland South, had to be called off after community members were intimidated and harassed by state security agents (Alexander, McGregor, and Ranger 2000, p. 262). In 2007, *The Good President*, a play by Cont Mhlanga, a theater director, was banned from premiering in Bulawayo (Mlotshwa, 2019). The play invoked memories of the *Gukurahundi*, which are taboo in dominant spaces (Mlotshwa, 2019; Mpofu and Moyo, 2017). Artists in Matabeleland operate in a volatile political environment. Mlotshwa (2019, p. 77) posits that "art produced and performed in Matabeleland is viewed with suspicion by the country's rulers." In addition, *Gukurahundi* memorialization is criminalized. In 2011, Moses Mzila-Ndlovu, an opposition leader, and Father Marko Mkandla, a Catholic priest, were arrested in Matabeleland North for attending a public ceremony to memorialize *Gukurahundi* victims. Pressure groups such as Ibhetshu LikaZulu have been involved in organizing *Gukurahundi* public ceremonies. However, these *Gukurahundi* commemorations at Bhalagwe (October 2017) and in Bulawayo (December 2021) were banned by the police and state security agents. In addition, memorial plaques erected by affected communities at Bhalagwe and Silobela to honor *Gukurahundi* victims have repeatedly been stolen, vandalized, and bombed by suspected state agents. In essence, the government is deploying coercive mechanisms to dispel and suppress dissenting voices.

The state also relies on mechanisms such as draconian laws that stifle freedom of expression and civic engagement. These pieces of legislation, such as the Public Order and Security Act (POSA), which has since been repealed, tend to be used by the state to prohibit public gatherings and muzzle dissenting voices. The Criminal Law (Codification and Reform) Act is another law that has been used to silence government critics. In 2010, this legislation was used to charge an artist, Owen Maseko, for exhibiting a *Gukurahundi* painting at the National Art Gallery of Zimbabwe in Bulawayo (Mpofu, Ndlovu, and Tshuma, 2021). In 2020, Lovemore Zvokusekwa was also charged under the Criminal Law (Codification and Reform) Act for allegedly creating and disseminating falsehoods about COVID-19 on social media. Besides the draconian laws, authoritarian regimes also suppress free speech through "digital authoritarianism" (Mare, 2020, p. 4244). An illustration of digital authoritarian practices is the state-ordered internet shutdowns experienced by Zimbabweans between 2016 and 2019 (Mare, 2020). In addition, the government employs surveillance strategies to track and monitor the activities of the so-called "enemies of the state," such as journalists, activists, and opposition leaders (Tshuma, Msimanga, and Sibanda, 2022, p. 53). This state-sponsored surveillance serves as a strategy of silencing dissenting voices (Tshuma et al., 2022). In this repressive environment, journalists are using digital security technologies to "evade potential surveillance by government authorities" (Tshuma et al., 2022, p. 63). State media, such as *The Herald* and *The Sunday News,* also play a pivotal role in propagating the ideologies of the ruling party. They promote the government's ideology of "patriotic history," which bifurcates citizens into "patriots" and "sell-outs" (Ranger, 2005, p. 13). Within ZANU PF's patriarchal rendition of history and national identity, social actors such as opposition leaders, journalists from the private press, and human rights activists are denounced as traitors and puppets of the West (Ranger, 2005). In addition, the government was reluctant to "democratise the airwaves" (Moyo, 2012a, p. 180). For decades, radio stations such as *Radio Dialogue* were denied broadcasting licenses, with the monopoly of the state-owned Zimbabwe Broadcasting Corporation (ZBC) firmly entrenched (Moyo, 2012a).

MEDIA-DRIVEN ACTIVISM AGAINST AUTHORITARIANISM

Social groups living under repressive regimes have "always come up with alternative forms of communication as tools of subversion" (Moyo, 2007, p. 81).

Alternative media are being creatively exploited by Zimbabweans to "resist state propaganda churned out through the mainstream media" (Moyo, 2007, p. 81). Pirate radio stations such as *Studio 7* are playing a key role in articulating discourses that are countering ZANU PF's hegemonic narratives (Moyo, 2007). The Internet is contributing to challenging "state authoritarianism" (Moyo, 2012b, p. 485). In Zimbabwe's authoritarian environment, diasporic news websites such as *Newzimbabwe.com* constitute "alternative public spheres" (Moyo, 2007, p. 81). These news websites produced content that expressed dissenting views. Online platforms such as *Inkundla.net* enabled Ndebele communities to celebrate their history, culture, and identity (Moyo, 2009). Moreover, *Inkundla.net* enabled *Gukurahundi* survivors to recount and preserve memories of these past crimes (Moyo, 2009). Social networking mailing lists such as the *Forum* enable the people of Matabeleland to discuss the *Gukurahundi* and other issues affecting their communities (Mhlanga and Mpofu, 2014). Thus, digital spaces are seen as "liberating devices" (Mhlanga and Mpofu, 2014, p. 140) that enable communities to articulate sensitive issues that are excluded from mainstream spaces.

Social media-driven protests such as #ThisFlag and #Tajamuka demonstrate the potency of digital spaces in enabling disempowered groups to express their grievances and circumvent state authoritarianism (Mpofu and Mare, 2020; Gukurume, 2017). Digital tools are used by activists to build, mobilize, and coordinate social protests (Mpofu and Mare, 2020, p. 155). In other words, the subaltern groups are using social media to "reclaim their political voices and spaces" (Gukurume, 2017, p. 49). Some scholarly works draw upon the concept of "dissidence" to examine the role of social media (Mpofu and Matsilele, 2020; Matsilele and Ruhanya, 2020) and popular music (Matsilele and Msimanga, 2022) in expressing alternative viewpoints and disrupting authoritarian structures in Zimbabwe. "Dissidents" are seen as "rebels" or "enemies" of the state (Mpofu and Matsilele, 2020, p. 223). They operate by throwing power into "disarray, disorienting it" (Mpofu and Matsilele, 2020, p. 231). As "dissidents," these individuals and groups are painted as "justifiably deserving of violent repression by the state" (Mpofu and Matsilele, 2020, p. 223). Between 2013 and 2019, social media dissidents such as Baba Jukwa, Evan Mawarire, and Tajamuka were instrumental in challenging ZANU PF ideologies (Mpofu and Matsilele, 2020). Digital technologies enable virtual dissidents to "communicate, organise street demonstrations and document human rights violations" (Wessels, 2019, p. 8). In addition, musicians such as Lovemore Majaivana and Thomas Mapfumo acted as "dissident archetypes" resisting ZANU PF dominance (Matsilele and Msimanga, 2022). Other protest musicians, such as Desire Moyo (Ncube, 2022) and Bongani Mncube (Ndlovu and Mlotshwa, 2022), are using songs as a subversive expression of *Gukurahundi* memories.

GUKURAHUNDI COUNTER-MEMORIES AND THE SUBVERSION OF STATE-SANCTIONED COMMEMORATIVE PRACTICES

Commemorations such as national holidays are forms of "cultural nationalism" propagated by the ruling party to sustain its hegemony (Ndlovu-Gatsheni and Willems, 2009). The government is appropriating and using the *Gukurahundi*-related Unity Day holiday to sustain its legitimacy (Mpofu, 2016). It relies on state-owned media to "shape what Zimbabweans know, remember, think and forget about the genocide" (Mpofu, 2016, p. 148). The Unity Day national holiday is a commemoration of the signing of the Unity Accord on December 22, 1987, between ZANU PF and ZAPU, which ended the violence (Mpofu, 2016). However, Unity Day has become a symbol of "silencing" and "forgetting" the *Gukurahundi* atrocities (Mpofu, 2016, p. 153). Discourses on Unity Day are underpinned by an emphasis on "amnesia" and "unity" (Mpofu, 2016, p. 154). In celebrating "unity," state-controlled media like *The Herald* are silent on the "genocide's historical and contextual backgrounds" (Mpofu, 2016, p. 154). In other words, Zimbabweans are not told the "reasons for celebrating Unity Accord or that it came about after the commitment of heinous crimes against humanity in which the state was the aggressor" (Mpofu, 2016, p. 154).

Pressure groups in Matabeleland are using state-sanctioned commemorative practices and public art in their struggles against the dominant system. On December 22, 2021, the police blocked a *Gukurahundi* memorial event at Makokoba township in Bulawayo. The commemorations were meant to start with a march at Joshua Nkomo's statue at the city center. This memorial event coincided with the Unity Day national holiday. An analysis of this incident shows the dynamics of *Gukurahundi* memory activism. First, the disempowered *Gukurahundi* survivors are using cultural resources provided by the government to produce counter-memories. Through a process of excorporation (Fiske, 1989a), *Gukurahundi* survivors are appropriating the Unity Day commemorations to create their subversive memories. While the Unity Day commemoration is one of the strategies deployed by the government to entrench collective amnesia, the subaltern groups are transforming and dismantling this practice. The *Gukurahundi* survivors are pluralizing the meaning of the Unity Day holiday to memorialize their loved ones. Thus, poaching raids (Fiske, 1989a, p. 19) are creatively launched to disrupt and resist state-imposed amnesia. Such memory activism constitutes "guerrilla raids" (Fiske, 1989b, p. 12) as the hegemonic forces are challenged outside the terrain of "open warfare" (Fiske, 1989a, p. 19).

Second, the subordinated people attempted to use Joshua Nkomo's statue as a site of *Gukurahundi* commemorations. Although Nkomo's statue, installed in 2013, serves to promote the ideologies of the ruling party, it has counterhegemonic potential. This state-sanctioned artistic work has come to symbolize a "wounded Matabeleland," and a "reminder of unreconciled hurts" (Ndlovu, 2017, p. 436). In essence, *Gukurahundi* protest cultures manifest in the form of subordinated groups having to "make do" (De Certeau, 1984, p. 18) with the cultural commodities provided by the state, such as the Unity Day commemorations and Joshua Nkomo's statue. Unity Day and Nkomo's statue have become "floating signifiers" (Hall, 1993, p. 111) as their social meanings are contingent, multiple, and contested. Floating signifiers are "elements which are particularly open to different ascriptions of meaning" (Jorgensen and Phillips 2002, p. 28). Cultural artifacts such as Nkomo's public statue assume "chains of signification" (Grossberg, 2005, p. 158), as they can be "disarticulated" from one meaning and "rearticulated" to another (Hall, 1982, p. 80). Street art has become another site of struggle in the process of *Gukurahundi* memorialization.

ON *GUKURAHUNDI* STREET ART AND CREATIVE SUBVERSIVE CULTURES

In January 2022, a "controversial" mural painted by visual artist Leeroy Spinx Brittain appeared on the walls of the Bulawayo City Council Hall. The street art depicted King Lobengula Khumalo carrying a heart-shaped balloon while embracing Mbuya Nehanda. Lobengula was a precolonial Ndebele monarch who led the resistance against colonialism in the 1890s. Nehanda is a revered Shona spirit medium who was also instrumental in the armed struggle of 1896–1897 as she became a "symbol of the resistance to colonial rule in modern Zimbabwe" (Beach, 1998, p. 27). Mbuya Nehanda occupies a central place in the imagination of Zimbabwe. The message inscribed in this Lobengula/Nehanda graffiti was, "Love is greater than Shona and Ndebele, Africans Unite!" The Bulawayo City Council authorities erased the painting but left the inscribed message. The city municipality stated that it was illegal to create graffiti on city council premises without permission. The next day, an unknown artist painted graffiti on the same city council wall with an inscription, "Gukurahundi, we will not forget." This message was a stark reminder of the need to heal *Gukurahundi* scars.

The official narrative on *Gukurahundi* is underpinned by the ideals of unity (Mpofu, 2016; Mpofu and Moyo, 2017). Such ideals are encapsulated in pro-unity songs such as "Unity, unity, unity's number one" by Ndux Malax (Mpofu and Moyo, 2017, p. 511). The theme of unity is also captured in Black Umfolosi's popular song with the lyrics, "One Zimbabwe, no Ndebele, no Shona . . . Unity is ever important" (Mpofu and Moyo, 2017, p. 511). The painting at Municipality Hall became a site of mnemonic struggles. Such is the polysemic nature of cultural texts, as messages are constantly being negotiated, re-appropriated, and contested. On the one hand, the Lobengula/Nehanda mural sought to promote the ideals of unity between the Ndebele and Shona people. Memories of pre-colonial Ndebele raids on Shona communities have shaped these ethnic animosities. During the *Gukurahundi,* the Fifth Brigade claimed to be punishing the Ndebele people for the precolonial "raids" on the Shona communities (Lindgren, 2005, p. 161). Although discourses on peace and unity are noble, they tend to be re-articulated and invoked by ZANU PF to censure *Gukurahundi* survivors for not "moving on." On the other hand, the *Gukurahundi* street art signifies the struggle against collective amnesia. The unknown artist interpreted the Lobengula/Nehanda mural as an attempt to erase *Gukurahundi* memories. As a result, a message, "Gukurahundi, we will not forget," serves to challenge and resist state-imposed amnesia. De Certeau (1984, p. 37) argues that subordinated groups employ tactics such as "poaching," "guileful ruses," and "tricks" to disrupt, resist, and evade forces of domination. The creation of the *Gukurahundi* graffiti captures the tactics of "guerrilla fighters" (Fiske, 1989a, p. 19) as they raid and poach the structures of the powerful. The *Gukurahundi* mural, painted clandestinely by an unknown artist, demonstrates that subversive pleasures are generated through discursive guerrilla tactics. In other words, the subversive pleasures of *Gukurahundi* memory are generated by the disempowered when they avoid "the social discipline of the power bloc" (Fiske, 1989a, p. 47). Given that open discussions on *Gukurahundi* tend to be criminalized in Zimbabwe, popular pleasures arise from the subordinated groups as they evade the dominant system.

The invisible tactical maneuver of the artist in the creation of the *Gukurahundi* mural shows that popular culture is produced by subordinate groups by not challenging the "powerful in an open warfare" (Fiske 1989a, p. 19). In repressive regimes such as Zimbabwe, challenging the powerful in an open warfare "would be to invite defeat" (Fiske, 1989a, p. 19). This is evident in government crackdowns on opposition leaders, artists, and human rights activists who are involved in *Gukurahundi* memorialization efforts (Mpofu et al., 2021; Ndlovu et al., 2019). In such authoritarian contexts, evasion and adaptation are key tactics in the everyday lives of subordinated groups (Fiske, 1989a, p. 34). De Certeau (1984, p. 37) adds that the tactics of the subordinates operate by taking advantage of "opportunities" and "cracks" within the dominant system. Subversive popular pleasures were generated by the artist of the *Gukurahundi* mural, who took advantage of the opportunity presented by the Lobengula/Nehanda painting to recreate and promote memories of the atrocities. Such is the nature of protest art, as it utilizes discursive guerrilla tactics to generate popular resistance. Thus, street art such as this *Gukurahundi* mural articulates the everyday life experiences of subordinated groups as they speak truth to power.

"SPOTTING THE WEAK POINTS": ART EXHIBITION AND MEMORIAL PLAQUES

The tactics of the subordinated groups involve "spotting the weak points in the forces of the powerful and raiding them" (Fiske, 1989a, p. 19). The exhibition of a *Gukurahundi* painting by Owen Maseko in 2010 at the National Art Gallery of Zimbabwe in Bulawayo illustrates the potency of popular culture formation. It captures the practice of subordinate groups spotting weak points in the dominant system and exploiting them. While existing scholarship demonstrates the censorship of Maseko's artistic work and *Gukurahundi* memory (Mpofu et al., 2022; Ncube and Siziba, 2015), this chapter focuses on the subversive cultures that were produced by the artist who used the resources provided by the dominant social order. Fiske (1989a, p. 32) argues that subordinated groups construct their own "spaces" within the "places" where the powerful exercise their hegemony. Popular culture is created when the disempowered occupy the "places" of the powerful and turn them into their own "spaces" (Fiske, 1989a, p. 32). In this vein, Maseko exhibited his *Gukurahundi* paintings at a place that is controlled by the government and turned it into a space for commemorating the Matabeleland atrocities. Thus, disempowered groups "make the places temporarily theirs" and occupy them for "as long as they need or have to" (Fiske, 1989a, p. 32). Maseko's *Gukurahundi* artistic work was showcased temporarily at the art gallery. It was then removed, and the artist arrested and charged with undermining the authority of, and insulting, the president. Popular culture is formed using "imposed systems" (De Certeau, 1984, p. 18) as the subaltern groups must make do with the resources at their disposal.

The theft, vandalism, and bombing of *Gukurahundi* memorial plaques at Bhalagwe and Silobela by suspected state agents constitute an assault on memory. During *Gukurahundi*, Bhalagwe became a "torture and death camp" (Eppel, 2020, p. 216). The plaques to commemorate and honor *Gukurahundi* victims were erected by a Matabeleland-based pressure group, Ibhetshu Lika-Zulu. In January 2022, suspected state agents used explosives to desecrate a *Gukurahundi* memorial plaque at the Bhalagwe mass graves site in Matabeleland South. Two other memorial plaques were vandalized at Bhalagwe in May 2021 and at Silobela (Midlands province) in June 2021. The desecration of these plaques demonstrates the efforts by the government to repress *Gukurahundi* memories. Subversive memory cultures are produced through cultural artifacts that serve to honor and commemorate *Gukurahundi* victims. Memorial plaques serve a counter-hegemonic purpose as they enable *Gukurahundi* survivors to preserve and commemorate the traumatic past. Although the victories of the disempowered are "fleeting or limited" (Fiske, 1989b, p. 2), as is the case with the destruction of the *Gukurahundi* plaques, there are subversive pleasures generated when the victims remember the past against the grain. Bhalagwe constitutes a site of *Gukurahundi* memorialization (Eppel, 2020). With the advent of digital technologies, memories are being transformed and democratized. Images of *Gukurahundi* plaques were circulated in digital spaces such as Twitter in ways that recreated and preserved memories of these historical injustices.

CONCLUSION

This study sought to examine how the people of Matabeleland communities are struggling to appropriate and use popular cultural artifacts to preserve traumatic memories of the *Gukurahundi* genocide. Drawing upon the work of Fiske (1989a), I argue that popular cultural artifacts such as graffiti and paintings are enabling *Gukurahundi* survivors to produce and articulate counter-memories. In the context of *Gukurahundi* forced amnesia, impunity, and denialism in Zimbabwe, disempowered communities are creatively using popular cultural artifacts to challenge and resist state authoritarianism. *Gukurahundi* survivors are utilizing discursive tactics such as guerrilla warfare, raids, and poaching to generate subversive pleasures and protest cultures. Through the process of excorporation (Fiske, 1989a), subordinated groups are "making do" with the resources and structures provided by the power bloc, such as the Unity Day commemorations and the National Art Gallery. The disempowered are using these structures and resources to generate and circulate meanings that disrupt the hegemonic forces. Tactics of guerrilla warfare and poaching (Fiske, 1989a) are being employed by *Gukurahundi* survivors as they utilize cultural artifacts to remember the dead. The art of guerrilla warfare lies in "not being defeatable" (Fiske, 1989a, p. 19).

REFERENCES

Alexander, J. (1998). Dissident perspectives on Zimbabwe's post-independence war. *Africa: Journal of the International African Institute* 68(2): 151–182.

Alexander, J., McGregor, J., and Ranger, T. (2000). *Violence and memory: One hundred years in the 'dark forests' of Matabeleland*. Oxford: James Currey.

Beach, D. N. (1998). An innocent woman, unjustly accused? Charwe, medium of the Nehanda Mhondoro spirit, and the 1896–97 central Shona rising in Zimbabwe. *History in Africa* 25: 27–54.

Cameron, H. (2018). The Matabeleland massacres: Britain's wilful blindness. *International History Review* 40(1) :1–19.

Catholic Commission for Justice and Peace and the Legal Resources Foundation (CCJP & LRF). (2007). *Gukurahundi in Zimbabwe: A report on the disturbances in Matabeleland and the Midlands, 1980–1988*. Johannesburg: Jacana Media.

Chuma, W., Msimanga, M. J., and Tshuma, L. A. (2020). Succession politics and factional journalism in Zimbabwe: A case of the Chronicle in Zimbabwe. *African Journalism Studies* 41(1): 35–48.

Colmeiro, J. (2011). A nation of ghosts: Haunting historical memory and forgetting in post-Franco Spain. *Journal of Theory of Literature and Comparative Literature* 4: 7–34.

Confino, A. (1997). Collective memory and cultural history: Problems of method. *The American Historical Review* 5: 1380–1403.

De Certeau, M. (1984). *The practice of everyday life*. Berkeley: University of California Press.

Edy, J. (2006). *Troubled pasts. News and the collective memory of social unrest*. Philadelphia: Temple University Press.

Eppel, S. (2004). Gukurahundi: The need for truth and reparation. In Raftopoulos, B. and Savage, T. (eds.). *Zimbabwe: Injustice and political reconciliation*. Cape Town: Institute for Justice and Reconciliation. 43–62.

Eppel, S. (2020). How shall we talk of bhalagwe? Remembering the Gukurahundi Era in Matabeleland, Zimbabwe. In Wale, K., Gobodo-Madikizela, P. and Prager, J. (eds.). *Post-conflict hauntings: Transforming memories of historical trauma*. Basingstoke: Palgrave Macmillan. 259–284.

Faber, S. (2005). The price of peace: Historical memory in post-Franco Spain, a review article. *Revista Hispanica Moderna* 58(1–2): 205–219.

Ferrandiz, F. (2015). Mass graves, landscapes of terror. A Spanish tale. In Ferrandiz, F. and Robben, A. C. G. M. (eds.). *Necropolitics, mass graves and exhumations in the age of human rights*. Philadelphia, Pennsylvania: University of Pennsylvania. 92–118.

Ferrandiz, F., and Robben, A. C. G. M. (2015). The ethnography of exhumations. In Ferrandiz, F. and Robben, A. C. G. M. (eds.). *Necropolitics, mass graves and exhumations in the age of human rights*. Philadelphia Pennsylvania: University of Pennsylvania. 1–38.

Fiske, J. (1987). *Television culture: Popular pleasures and politics*. London: Routledge.

Fiske, J. (1989a). *Understanding popular culture*. London: Routledge.

Fiske, J. (1989b). *Reading the popular*. London: Routledge.

Grossberg, L. (2005). History, politics and postmodernism. Stuart Hall and cultural studies. In Morley, D. and Chen, K.-H. (eds.). *Stuart hall. Critical dialogues in cultural studies*. London: Routledge. 151–173.

Gukurume, S. (2017). From Kubatana to #ThisFlag: Trajectories of digital activism in Zimbabwe. *Journal of Information Technology and Politics* 17 (2): 130–145.

Halbwachs, M. (1992). *On collective memory* (Edited, translated and with an introduction by L. A. Coser). Chicago: University of Chicago Press.

Hall, S. (1982). The rediscovery of "ideology": Return of the repressed in media studies. In Gurevitch, M., Bennett, T., Curran, J. and Woollacott, J. (eds.). *Culture, society and the media.* London: Methuen. 56–90.

Hall, S. (1993). What is "black" in black popular culture? *Social Justice* 20(1): 104–114.

Jorgensen, M., and Phillips, L. (2002). *Discourse analysis as theory and method.* London: Sage.

Kriger, N. (2003). *Guerrilla veterans in post-war Zimbabwe: Symbolic and violent politics, 1980–1987.* Cambridge: Cambridge University Press.

Lindgren, B. (2005). Memories of violence: Recreation of ethnicity in post-colonial Zimbabwe. In Richards, P. (ed.). *No peace no war: An anthropology of contemporary armed conflicts.* Oxford: James Currey Ltd. 155–172.

Mare, A. (2020). State-ordered Internet shutdowns and digital Authoritarianism in Zimbabwe. *International Journal of Communication* 14: 4244–4263.

Matsilele, T., and Msimanga, M. J. (2022). Popular music and the concept of the dissident in post-independent Zimbabwe. In Salawi, A. and Fadipe, I. A. (eds.). *Indigenous African popular music. Social crusades and the future.* Cham: Palgrave Macmillan. 59–76.

Matsilele, T., and Ruhanya, P. (2020). Social media dissidence and activist resistance in Zimbabwe. *Media, Culture and Society* 43(2): 381–394.

Mhlanga, B., and Mpofu, M. (2014). The virtual parallax: Imaginations of Mthwakazi Nationalism – online discussions and calls for self-determination. In Solo, A. (ed.). *Handbook on research on political activism in the Information Age.* Pennsylvania: IGI Global. 129–146.

Mlotshwa, K. (2019). Matabeleland and the rulers' political sins: Defining subversive art in Zimbabwe. *Metacritic Journal for Comparative Studies and Theory* 5: 1.

Moyo, D. (2007). Alternative media, diasporas and the mediation of the Zimbabwean crisis. *Ecquid Novi: African Journalism Studies* 28(1): 81–105.

Moyo, D. (2012a). Mediating crisis: Realigning media policy and deployment of propaganda in Zimbabwe, 2000–2008. In Chiumbu, S. and Musemwa, M. (eds.). *Crisis! What crisis? The multiple dimensions of the Zimbabwean crisis.* Cape Town: HSRC Press. 176–198.

Moyo, D. (2012b). Participation, citizenship and pirate radio as empowerment: The case of Radio Dialogue in Zimbabwe. *International Journal of Communication* 6: 484–500.

Moyo, L. (2009). Constructing a home away from home: The internet, nostalgia and identity politics among Zimbabwean communities in Britain. *Journal of Global Mass Communications* 2(1): 66–85.

Mpofu, M., and Moyo, C. (2017). Theatre as alternative media in Zimbabwe: Selected case studies from Matabeleland. *Journal of African Media Studies* 9(3): 507–520.

Mpofu, S. (2015). When the subaltern speaks: Citizen journalism and genocide victims' online voices. *African Journalism Studies* 36(4): 82–101.

Mpofu, S. (2016). Zimbabwe's state-controlled public media and the mediation of the 1980s genocide 30 years on. *Journal of African Media Studies* 8(2): 145–165.

Mpofu, S. (2019). For a nation to progress victims must "move on": A case of Zimbabwe's social media discourses of Gukurahundi genocide silencing and resistance. *African Identities* 17(2): 108–129.

Mpofu, S., and Mare, A. (2020). #ThisFlag: Social media and cyber-protests in Zimbabwe. In Ndlela, M. N., and Mano, W. (eds.). *Social media and elections in Africa, volume 2*. Cham: Palgrave Macmillan. 153–173.

Mpofu, S., and Matsilele, T. (2020). Social media and the concept of dissidence in Zimbabwe. In Ndlovu-Gatsheni, S. and Ruhanya, P. (eds.). *The history and political transition of Zimbabwe. From Mugabe to Mnangagwa*. Cham: Palgrave Macmillan. 221–243.

Mpofu, S., Ndlovu, M., and Tshuma, L. A. (2021). The artist and filmmaker as activists, archivists and the work of memory: A case of the Zimbabwean genocide. *African Journal of Rhetoric: Representations of Genocide in African Cultures* 14(1): 63–93.

Ncube, B. J. (2022). Musicians and political songs in the struggle for freedom in Zimbabwe. In Onyebadi, U. (ed.). *Political messaging in music and entertainment spaces across the globe*. Vernon Press. 184–206.

Ncube, G., and Siziba, G. (2015). (Re)membering the nation's 'forgotten' past: Portrayals of Gukurahundi in Zimbabwean literature. *The Journal of Commonwealth Literature* 52(2): 231–247.

Ndlovu, M. (2017). Facing history in the aftermath of Gukurahundi atrocities: New media, memory and discourses on forgiveness on selected Zimbabwean news websites. *Peace and Conflict Studies* 24(2): 1–22.

Ndlovu, M., Tshuma, L. A., and Ngwenya, S. W. (2019). Between tradition and modernity: Discourses on the coronation of the Ndebele "King" in Zimbabwe. *Critical Arts* 33(2): 82–95.

Ndlovu, M. (2018). New media and Ndebele hiraeth: Memory, nostalgia and Ndebele Nationalism on selected news websites. *African Journalism Studies* 39(4): 109–130.

Ndlovu, M. (2022). Counter-memory, ethno-nationalism and the discursive constructions of Matabeleland in digital spaces. In Mlotshwa, K. and Ndlovu, M. (eds.). *The idea of matabeleland in digital spaces: Genealogies, discourses and epistemic struggles*. Lexington Books. 17–31.

Ndlovu, M., and Tshuma, L. A. (2021). Bleeding from one generation to the next: The media and the constructions of Gukurahundi postmemories by university students in Zimbabwe. *African Studies* 80(3–4): 376–396.

Ndlovu, M., and Mlotshwa, K. (2022). Zimbabwe: Music, performance, and political lyrics as "cure" for post Bhalagwe trauma. In Onyebadi, U. (ed.). *Political messaging in music and entertainment spaces across the globe*. Vernon Press. 279–303.

Ndlovu, T. (2017). Whose Nkomo is it anyway? Joshua Nkomo's statue and commemorative landscape? In Ndlovu-Gatsheni, S. J. (ed.). *Joshua Mqabuko Nkomo of Zimbabwe: Politics, power and memory*. Cham: Palgrave Macmillan. 405–439.

Ndlovu-Gatsheni, S. (2008). Nation building in Zimbabwe, and the challenges of Ndebele Particularism. *African Journal of Conflict Resolution* 8(3): 27–55.

Ndlovu-Gatsheni, S., and Willems, W. (2009). Making sense of cultural nationalism and the politics of commemoration under the third chimurenga in Zimbabwe. *Journal of Southern African Studies* 35(4): 945–965.

Nora, P. (1989). Between memory and history. *Representations* 26: 7–24.
Ranger, T. (2005). The uses and abuses of history in Zimbabwe. In Palmberg, M. & Primorac, R. (eds.). *Skinning the skunk: Facing Zimbabwean futures*. Uppsala. Nordac African Institute. 7–15.
Robins, S. (1996). Heroes, heretics and historians of the Zimbabwe revolution: A review article of Norma Kriger's 'Peasant voices'. *Zambezia* xxiii(1): 73–92.
Rwafa, U. (2012). Representations of Matabeleland and Midlands disturbances through the documentary film Gukurahundi: A moment of madness (2007). *African Identities* 10(3): 313–327.
Sabido, R. S. (2019). Citizens' investigations: Recovery the past in contemporary Spain. In Price, S. (ed.). *Journalism, power and investigation: Global and activist perspectives*. London: Routledge. 117–136.
Tshuma, L. A., and Ndlovu, M. (2020). Immortalizing 'buried memories': Photographs of the Gukurahundi online. *Journal of Genocide Research*. https://doi.org/10.1080/14623528.2020.1850393
Tshuma, L. A., Msimanga, M. J., and Sibanda, M. N. (2022). "Playing" in the eyes of the Ferret team: Examining the use of surveillance strategies by Zimbabwean journalists. *African Journalism Studies* 43(1): 53–69.
Vambe, M. T. (2012). Zimbabwe genocide: Voices and perceptions from ordinary people in Matabeleland and the Midlands provinces, 30 years on. *African Identities* 10(3): 281–300.
Wessels, J. (2019). Authoritarianism, digital dissidence and grassroots media in the Middle East and North Africa. *CyberOrient* 13(1): 4–27.
Wodak, R. (2003). Discourses of silence. Anti-Semitic discourses in post-war Austria. In Thiesmeyer, L. (ed.). *Discourse and silencing: Representation and the language of displacement*. Amsterdam: John Benjamins Publishing Company. 179–209.
Zerubavel, E. (2003). *Time maps: Collective memory and the social shape of the past*. Chicago: Chicago University Press.

Chapter 12

Theorizing Graffiti as a Novel Alternative Public Sphere in Zimbabwe's Contested Politics

Nyasha Cefas Zimuto

Zimbabwe has faced an endless crisis for the past two decades and a half, a result of the chaotic land reform program, corruption, migration of the skilled and productive labor force, and the closure of democratic space. A combination of the above factors saw the companies becoming the most hyperinflationary environment at the close of the first decade of the new millennium, now commonly referred to as the decade of "crises" (Matsilele and Ruhanya, 2024; Matsilele, 2013). It is this crisis that has seen citizens, faced with the closure of independent media, resort to other forms of media artifacts to register discontentment. The emerging forms of protest include humor (Msimanga et al., 2022; Sharra and Matsilele, 2021; Matsilele and Mututwa, 2021), music (Makwambeni, 2017; Matsilele et al., 2023), social media counter-hegemony (Gukurume, 2017; Matsilele, 2022; Matsilele and Mutsvairo, 2022), and lately graffiti (Zimuto, 2021; Zimuto et al., 2023). Essentially, this chapter builds on the above studies, extending on the developing area of protest archetype studies.

As Peteet (1996, p. 142) rightly observes, "as cultural artifacts of resistance, graffiti are not inert . . . as reading is an active kind of behavior, and a text is a 'carrier of relationships'." For this study, the researcher is exploring the communicative aspect between power elites and citizens. Definitionally, this study leans on Baldini (2023, p. 239), who argues that graffiti is "a form of everyday resistance allowing its practitioners to challenge authoritarian power." Baldini further argues, and this researcher concurs, that

> in questioning dominant hierarchies, graffiti is a powerful tool to help correct a specific instance of spatial injustice: the unequal distribution of access to urban

surfaces for self-expression in the city, where corporations and political elites hold an unjustified monopoly over visual communication. (2023, p. 239)

Graffiti takes on many forms, and it serves a purpose beyond being mere vandalism. Studies show the pervasiveness of graffiti as part of human expression (Rahn, 2002; Daly, 2013). It is therefore vital to move from the vandalism aspect of graffiti to looking at the basis that causes people to write different words on the walls "without permission" (Rahn, 2002). Graffiti is a common feature in most human habitat vicinities. However, to the authorities, it is an eyesore.

Daly (2013) posits that graffiti is as old as humans themselves. The argument suggests that graffiti is an essential part of human culture. In modern cities in Zimbabwe, it is rare to find a building that does not have graffiti on it. This presence shows that graffiti is functional, which is why people always make use of it to communicate. Graffiti takes various forms, including words and drawings, which demonstrate the authors' skillful execution of their work. As such, the placement of graffiti is often intentional. These paintings without rules, according to Žuvela (2013), must be labeled as art. The way the work is distributed and the amusing way in which different messages are propelled calls for one to label graffiti as art. Thus, this chapter opines that graffiti as art is inscribed by different artists as a form of protest against the authorities. Scholars have written about protest graffiti, concurring that protest graffiti is a form of art that aims to disrupt the status quo and bring in new dimensions in the viewing of social phenomena (Siham, 2017; Mukhtar, 2015). Graffiti as a public sphere offers the artists anonymity that protects them against victimization (Al-Yassirya, 2020). Consequently, graffiti is used to evade the state and self-censorship that is found in mainstream media platforms. The mainstay of the study is on graffiti because the masses fear speaking and facing authorities to air their views, especially in Zimbabwe, a polarized society. The study, in consequence, lays a potential foundation for the understanding of subtle protest cultures that may be difficult to untangle via direct and conventional means. Considering the idea that there is no art for art's sake in Africa (Achebe, 1988), it becomes imperative to acknowledge that the art on Zimbabwean vicinities is purposeful (Mangeya, 2014; Rahn, 2002).

A GAZE ON GRAFFITI

As already indicated in earlier parts, graffiti is not a new phenomenon but as ancient as human civilization. This view is given weight in the work of Miladi (2018, p. 241), who intimates that "artistic manifestations in the form of written words, scratches, drawings, paintings, symbols and signs on walls date from Ancient Egypt, Greece and the Roman Empire." Graffiti is found on different surfaces in many communities. These range from private property walls to public buildings. In Zimbabwe, it is mainly found on public places' walls as well as on all the other buildings easily accessible to graffiti artists and visible to the audience in urban and rural areas. There are also various writers and reasons for graffiti. Werwath (2013) and Mangeya (2019) list several graffiti writers, including young adults and the misunderstood. To them, these categories are written on the walls because they do not have other ways to express themselves. The abovementioned scholars' postulation becomes relevant in this study as it helps the researcher view graffiti as a communication tool for the oppressed, who do not have other methods of communicating their grievances due to the censorship apparatus found in the Zimbabwean mainstream media. Thus, the chapter focuses on this art without form that results from censorship to show how the Zimbabwean community is negotiating self-identity in a polarized society.

Nicholls (2012) and Reisner (1974) have it that graffiti in many communities under draconian leadership is often conversational. However, they further note that graffiti writing is also triggered by resistance tendencies. This argument leads to the assumption that the Zimbabwean population might be communicating among themselves and with the authorities through graffiti. The graffiti words might be telling a story about the wishes of the masses and their resistance against the ruling elite's dominance. Griffin (2002) concurs aptly by positing that oppression can converge to affect word selection in graffiti. If the proposition by Griffin (2002) is anything to go by, then it is very vital to study graffiti in Zimbabwe to make an exposition of the influence that mainstream media censorship has on the production of graffiti in various communities.

According to Žuvela (2013), South African graffiti communicates opinions not addressed by the powers in totality, and these may also include social grievances. In the same vein, Allen (2011) posits that in Africa, graffiti is two-pronged: it is a communication to the authorities as well as to fellow citizens, and these, in most cases, will be gray areas that citizens would have failed to present through normal communication channels. Thus, their postulations are in tandem with the above arguments, which posit that any form of communication is functional and is triggered by certain forces. These arguments have led to the supposition that in a bid to circumvent censorship and communicate among themselves and to the ruling elites, the masses vent and rant on the walls. The focus of this study is, thus, to highlight the idea that, faced with censorship, the Zimbabwean community is resorting to subtle ways of communication to make themselves visible in a community that disregards public opinions.

Scholars concur that graffiti is a communication channel that people use to converse about issues that they cannot communicate about in other forums (Zimuto et al., 2023; Mangeya, 2018). Moreover, scholars reiterate that people may fail to communicate certain issues, and the only way they can relay their views is through graffiti. For this reason, different walls are part of the informal channels of communication in communities. The researcher has found that Zimbabwean towns' building walls are awash with graffiti writings. A tour around any town in Zimbabwe makes one come to terms with the reality that the masses communicate through writings on surfaces. The argument by the above scholars becomes important as the current study investigates the reasons that are activating the urge to "illegally" communicate. The study takes a step further from what was done by the above-mentioned scholars and focuses on the subtle way Zimbabweans now converse in a community tangled with censorship. It becomes vital for the current study to expose how mainstream media censorship is giving rise to graffiti. The study builds on the argument that graffiti is used when people have no other options and brings to the fore the idea that it is becoming an option for the Zimbabwean masses to converse since all the other avenues of communication are under the control of the ruling elites. This view finds support from the work of Marche (2012, p. 78), and I cite the work extensively to make my point:

> Graffiti is also a vehicle of resistance. In World War Two Spain, inscribing "V" signs on the walls after RAF bombings signified support of the Allied forces, whereas during the Civil War anti-Franco activists wrote the letter "P" as a call to protest, using graffiti as a communication device to propagate censored information. Graffiti on the Berlin Wall from 1961 to 1989, and on the "Security Fence" currently separating Israel from part of the Palestinian territories are on the side opposite the builders', thus expressing resistance to the building.

The above discussion has brought to light the idea that graffiti is functional and serves a purpose worldwide. This chapter argues that the rise of graffiti in Zimbabwe is a result of a need for conversation. The chapter analyzed graffiti found on buildings in Zimbabwe to illustrate that it is a form of protest art. Graffiti, at this juncture, is used to evade censorship and victimization, which are prevalent in Zimbabwe.

THEORETICAL FRAMEWORK

Social movements involve power struggles, and in this chapter, Gramsci's hegemony is used to make sense of the use of graffiti in selected suburbs in Zimbabwe. Gramsci describes two modes of social control. First, there is coercive control, where there is the use of force to subordinate or dominate antagonistic groups. This is direct force that is used when control is low or unstable. It's also used in moments of crisis when fundamental structures are severely threatened. Second is consensual control, where individuals voluntarily assimilate the worldview of the dominant group, that is, hegemonic leadership. Consent is caused by the prestige and confidence the dominant group enjoys because of its position and function in the world of production (Harris, 1991; Hall, 1986). This involves the dominant group persuading other classes to accept its moral, political, and cultural values. However, there are resistant groups that counter such measures that are controlled by the dominant group. For this reason, the media becomes one of the sites of struggle, where power is negotiated. That is, a place of competition between competing social forces. There is competition between the dominant groups and the dominated or subordinated groups, who want to promote their own definitions of reality. There is, therefore, a continuous struggle for dominance between definitions of reality or ideologies (Laclau and Mouffe, 1995). In this case, graffitis are being used by counter-hegemonic forces to challenge the closure of democratic media spaces. Therefore, these institutions (media spaces) are the places where hegemony is constantly fought over, making them sites of struggle between hegemonic and counter-hegemonic ideas (Tshuma and Sibanda, 2024). The media, therefore, don't act simply as instruments for reproducing dominant hegemony. They are also tools for establishing and reinforcing counter-hegemonic ideas. Given the Zimbabwean political sphere, where opposition has been hunted down and critics of the government being harassed by the state, citizens are now using "guerrilla tactics" like graffiti to speak truth to power. Thus, graffiti are street sites of resistance and play a part in political communication. More so, social movements might be recognizable as counter-hegemonic "in a more proactive, visionary sense" (Carroll and Ratner, 1994, p. 6).

METHODS

The researcher made use of the qualitative research methodology, and the camera was used as the major research instrument to gather data for exemplification and illustrations in the discussion. Pictures were gathered from five Zimbabwean towns that were selected purposefully, namely Masvingo, Harare, Bulawayo, Gweru, and Kariba. The sample was chosen purposefully due to its proximity to the researcher and its relevance to the study. Thus, purposive sampling allowed the researcher to gather relevant data from a relevant sample. The chapter used in-depth interviews with purposefully selected language experts from the Midlands State University Languages Department. The department was chosen because the researcher has easy access to intellectuals at the institution as opposed to other higher learning institutions that might have been selected. The data presentation and analysis were done using thematic analysis. This is because it is easy to understand, and it allows for the logical arrangement of data and information (Douglas, 2000). All this was done in a procedural way that helped the researcher decode information from the given data, as propounded by Braun and Clarke (2006). The data was arranged according to different themes that emerged from the proposition as it unfolded. The themes became the sub-headings under the findings section. Graffiti was labeled according to places of origin to show the similarities and commonalities on issues discussed by graffiti protesters regardless of their town of origin.

FINDINGS

The findings were grouped into four main themes, and these are used as sub-headings in the discussion below. Each theme is supported by graffiti data from Zimbabwean platforms and focus group discussion responses pertinent to it.

Protest Poor Governance and Anti-Poor Government Policies

The pictures solicited during the research show that the masses in Zimbabwe protest poor governance through graffiti. Tajamuka is a hashtag that used to trend in Zimbabwe during the Mugabe era in 2017. The saying became widely used to such an extent that resistance against dominance and poor governance endeavors in Zimbabwe is now colloquially referred to as *kujamuka* (to refuse to be dominated). In one of the graffiti, the artist elusively used the word and quoted a Bible verse to show that people no longer want to be led by the current leadership. The artist used the word that is commonly known by the people to show how the masses are trying to shake off the shackles of poor governance and weak government policies that are not pro-poor. Participant 8 reiterated that:

> people are tired of poor governance so by saying Tajamuka in a way they will be saying we are now going to resist poor governance. However, the graffiti producer did not talk about the way they are going to resist poor governance, but the bottom line is he/she used graffiti to talk back to the authorities.

The above postulation points to the fact that graffiti is used to protest poor governance. Participant 21 also said that *whenever one sees this hashtag, he or she knows that the person who used it is referring to the uprising against poor governance.* When probed for more information on graffiti as a public sphere, Participant 29 said that *the founder of #Tajamuka, was once arrested* by the authorities because it was trending on social media, however, this time the masses are using graffiti which is a platform through which anyone can share their views without being identified with the graffiti they produced. The hashtag might now be referring to the resistance against the government's 2024 budget which is seen by the masses as being anti-poor. These propositions have led the researcher to conclude that graffiti in modern-day Zimbabwe is now serving as a public platform, providing a voice to the masses to protest freely through the medium of graffiti as an art form that remains unregulated and beyond the control of the ruling elites (Zaimakis, 2015; Mangeya, 2019).

Thus, this Dada activity, which has no stipulated structure or content, enables the masses to speak back to the authorities in a manner that renders the graffiti producer anonymous in a society where the ruling elites victimize those whom they believe to be against their leadership styles. Graffiti at this juncture becomes part of the protest culture, where topics are often discussed in a variety of media. Second, this forms part of Gramsci's counterhegemony, where the graffiti are used to counter the repressive state and various forces (see Carroll and Ratner, 1994). The words in the picture above are contextualized, and the user and the audience create their meanings out of the commonly used Shona and Ndebele words. *Tajamuka* is used to refer to resistance, which in most cases is intrinsic. The word, contextually used and emanating from the inner emotions of the graffiti producer (Zimuto, Mojapelo, and Mutasa, 2023), is aimed to disrupt the ruling elite's thinking that the masses can only revolt if outside forces influence them. Participant 12 said, *we see what they do and no one has to tell us to resist domination which is rife such that even the young children can see it*. Thus, graffiti are used as an apparatus in Zimbabwean protest culture. The movement primarily rejects the prevailing standards in society through anti-domination cultural works (Streahle, 2011; Allen, 2011). In the Zimbabwean context, good art is mainly defined by the ruling elite and is enjoyed by members of this class as a means of suppressing the masses for easy management. Censorship on all media platforms is rampant as the ruling elites' control even musicians.

The use of graffiti provides a window through which the oppressed can express their thoughts without the influence of the rules that govern the mainstream media. The use of art without rules prompted the notion that art should parallel community experiences and should no longer be separated from the realities of the world (Spiteri and LaCoss, 2003). In Zimbabwe, graffiti inspire people to create art that goes beyond aesthetic pleasure to affect people's lives. Man is an animal that exists within the webs of significance that he has spun. These webs can be loosely defined as culture, and analyzing them is an interpretive search for meaning rather than an experimental search for language structure understanding. Therefore, the concept of protest culture applies to all aspects of society andm at this juncturem to graffiti since everything in society is symbolically mediated (Zaimakis, 2015; Makarati, Mangeya, and Kadenge, 2022). As narrow definitions of culture prevail in social movement research, this broad notion is employed in this chapter in a bid to bring to the fore the idea that graffiti in Zimbabwe is being used to relay messages in a community where censorship is rife. With the help of graffiti, people can express their opinions on government policies and governance without any fear, as evidenced by the deliberate use of taboo hashtags in graffiti. The above findings are in tandem with Al-Yassirya's (2020) proposition that artistic achievements throughout history have been connected to human beings and their fundamental needs. Among the most significant human needs are freedom and the demand for rights. In this context, graffiti art is being used as a tool to resist dominance, public resource looting, and to call for social justice.

Protest Political Violence

The study brought to the fore the fact that the masses in Zimbabwe use graffiti to protest political violence. During the 2023 harmonized elections, cases of political violence were reported in some districts, including Gutu, which is in Masvingo province (The Mirror, November 9, 2022). One of the graffiti is found on a community hall screen guard in Masvingo town. The graffiti read *tozeza baba ndivo vanorova* (we are afraid of the father because he perpetrates violence). People used graffiti to protest the beatings of opposition members. The president is affectionately known as Baba in political circles. Thus, the artist is showing that the father, instead of loving the masses, is afraid of him. The graffiti were written subtly such that it needs great analytical skill to deduce the meaning of the art. When asked about the probable intention of the graffiti artist, Participant 44 said:

> *Zimbabwean media platforms are polarized and even social media is now censored since there is now a law that criminalizes social media content which is deemed anti-government as such the artist protests political violence through graffiti.*

Participant 32 added:

> *the graffiti might have been referring to the fear that the people had during the election time. The artist is thus trying to hide behind a rhetorical statement to bring to the fore their disgruntlement.*

Participant 38 stated that *the fear of being beaten when they speak truth to power results in people writing on the walls as a way of protesting against ill-treatment by the leaders.* Thus, the above findings prove beyond any reasonable doubt the fact that when faced with censorship in the mainstream media, the masses resort to protest graffiti, which aims at speaking back to the authorities about the unhappiness in the country. The authorities use the ideological and repressive state apparatus to make the masses docile; thus, to evade these monitoring agents, the masses in Zimbabwe are using graffiti as a public sphere in which existentialist protests are launched. Ryan (2018) concurs aptly when he posits that when considering the role of art in politics, one may ask whether aesthetics is the battleground of politics or if politics could exist without aesthetics. This clearly shows that the use of protest graffiti in politics is an effective endeavor since art and politics are interwoven, as shown by Ryan's (2018) argument. The masses are subjugated, and thus they decide to use art in a form that is not conventional to share their emotions.

Politically, it is taboo to talk about political violence in Zimbabwe. Participant 28 argued that *it is common knowledge that we are not supposed to talk about violence perpetrated by the ruling elites.* It is an unwritten code of conduct not to speak badly about the ruling elites. Graffiti, as a new public sphere is thus offering an opportunity for the masses to speak about the unspoken realities of their lives (Zaimakis, 2015). According to Spiteri and LaCoss (2003), graffiti is a very vital platform that accords the oppressed a chance to show discontent in an unrestricted manner. Zimbabwean masses are, as a result, utilizing this new phenomenon in a society where political violence is the norm. The masses, through graffiti, have a chance to evade censorship and contextualize their grievances in coded messages that can be easily decoded by the target populations. The unspoken realities are communicated through this subtle form of art and media. It may not be far from reality to conclude that graffiti in Zimbabwe has now taken on a new role and is now being used as an apparatus in protest cultures as media. Matsilele et al. (2021) found that hashtag protests were successful when they were used as a counter-hegemonic strategy in Africa. The study revealed that the hashtag movements had some success in forcing Africa's long-standing dictatorships to make partial concessions of varying degrees.

However, with the advent of cybersecurity laws, many Zimbabweans are now evading the monitoring eye of the ruling elites by resorting to graffiti. There are no rules that govern the production, form, or content of graffiti; as such, this becomes a viable method for the dominated to protest. No one can claim ownership of graffiti as media, and hence it becomes very difficult to control. The emergence of graffiti as a new and influential media platform shows how innovative the oppressed may become in their quest for freedom. Faced with years of denigration and oppressive rule, the masses have thus evolved an art that allows the freedom of expression.

Protest Looting of National Resources

The study has found that the masses protest the looting of natural resources through graffiti. The Chinese are said to be looting natural resources in Zimbabwe, which include gold and diamonds. The graffiti is used by people to show that they are fed up with the looting, and they are warning the foreigners who are looting their resources that time is no longer on their side. The people are always complaining about the looting of resources, which led to the gold mafia heist. Participant 10 said *the country is being looted of its natural resources by foreigners who have links with the political leaders*. Participant 3 concurred, that *if you check in the rural areas and look for those holding mining claims, you will find out that it is the foreigners who are linked to the ruling elite*. Thus, because the main media is controlled by the ruling elites, the masses resort to graffiti as a public sphere through which they discuss and protest the foreign looting of their natural resources. Faced with the threat of being victimized for speaking against the ruling elite's looting, the masses use graffiti art, which is not under the jurisdiction of the rulers and has no rules governing its production, form, or content. In the sections above, graffiti tend to be more critical and against the government and its leadership style. However, as time passes, protesters tend to shift their stance and show more consciousness toward their country and its resources. One of the graffiti pictures incorporates different languages and heavily relies on traditional Zimbabwean cultural discourses that are believed to be shared among both the protesters and the audience in this specific context (Schacter, 2014; Zuvela, 2013). In the Zimbabwean community, it is a norm that a visitor must not overstay their welcome. Thus, the language use and imagery are deliberate because the graffiti producer knows very well that the authorities he/she is speaking back to know the culture of the community, and the community will also be sensitized about the overstaying of the foreigners in the country. Moller (2019) and Werwath (2013) posit that graffiti production is not accidental; hence, the naming of the foreigners and telling them about their overstaying is not accidental but a cautious move that is aimed at making known the emotions of the masses toward foreigners. The elites benefit from the shoddy deals that foreigners are engaged in, and hence, to directly attack them would result in persecution. The masses resort to graffiti writing since this is the only platform that offers them anonymity and protection against detection and victimization.

Protest Mainstream Media Manipulation and Censorship

The exegesis also untangled the fact that the masses in Zimbabwe use graffiti to protest mainstream media dominance by the ruling party. The masses write on government premises in protest of the refusal by the government to give them visibility through state media. The inscription was found in Harare on a dura wall that protects a government premise. Political parties do not receive equal airplay opportunities, causing banned individuals to resort to graffiti protests on government premises. Participant 47 said *the writings are put on government premises to show the ruling elite that although they barred other political parties from advertising on the national broadcaster the walls have become the new public sphere on which the masses can advertise without any censorship.* Thus, the deliberate writing on spaces that are rendered no poster zones is a way of protesting the political domination of the ruling elites. Participant 3 added that *to show the ruling elite that there many ways of spreading political messages and show disdain opposition figures now resort to protest graffiti that is put on government buildings.* Opposition parties often resort to protest graffiti as a means of spreading political messages and showing their discontent toward the ruling party. With the mainstream media playing a role in manufacturing consent and maintaining the status quo (Tshuma et al., 2022), graffiti comes in handy in resisting the status quo without one being harassed. By vandalizing government property, they aim to reinstate their existence and remind the ruling party that they cannot be ignored. This deliberate act of defacing government buildings for a purpose is known as protest graffiti.

Despite the ruling party's attempts to downplay their opposition, they continue to exist and make their voices heard through such acts. Participant 30 has it that *although the ruling party would like to act as if the opposition is non-efficient. The opposition shows its presence by defacing government premises.* Accordingly, faced with censorship, which threatens their existence, opposition parties resort to graffiti writing. The dark spots on the walls in the graffiti are markings generated when the government workers try to erase graffiti from the walls. Nevertheless, protesters keep on writing in disgruntlement. The finding thus points to the fact that political protest graffiti on government premises is a direct response to mainstream media censorship and control by the ruling elite. When discussing censorship, the OpenNet Initiative in 2005 stated that it has become an integral part of the mechanism of distortion, manipulation, and misinformation. It is being used for political, financial, and racial purposes, which are now increasingly affecting the free flow of information worldwide. To evade this dire situation, political players in Zimbabwe, where the mainstream media is censored, have resorted to protesting graffiti. Protest movements have been recognized as significant contributors to the processes of political participation (Wee, 2016). Through graffiti as an apparatus, the masses in Zimbabwe contribute to the political discourse of their country in an elusive manner due to censorship in the mainstream media that hinders them from democratically participating in the political arena of their country.

Graffiti serves to express social protests and cultures of dissent within larger political and sociocultural contexts. It allows the masses to examine the influence of historical trajectories and the responses of various segments of social, political, and legal institutions on both national and international issues. In doing so, graffiti offers a more comprehensive and multi-dimensional view of the transformations of culture and value systems, as well as the development of both national and transnational civil society (Mpofu, 2021; Zaimakis, 2015). Although the masses are forbidden from talking about national issues in mainstream media, graffiti has offered them an avenue through which they can resist hegemonic cultural dominance. Against this setting, the study recognizes graffiti as protest art that gives voice and expression to the masses. Graffiti enables the masses to gain visibility. Thus, the documentation of protest graffiti art is the only way to understand the thoughts and emotions of the masses and their sense of belonging.

Protests Against the Imprisonment of Public Figures without Trial

There is also the finding that the masses protest the unfair incarcerations of influencers in the country. In Zimbabwe, imprisonment is a kind of political punishment, according to 70% of the total sample. People are jailed because of their political affiliations without looking at the gravity of the purported crime. Participant 18 asked, *why is Wiwa in jail?* Participant 30 concurred that *my friend in Zimbabwe you get jailed if you are thought to be on the wrong side. If you are for them, you are lucky no harm will come to you.* Thus, the graffiti above are protesting the continual imprisonment of political activists in general and Job in particular. The common people cannot access the mainstream media due to censorship, and hence they resort to graffiti. Even though the handwriting is spontaneous and improvised, the use of command words was found in the statement by the researcher. The graffiti artist is not asking for but demanding that he be released. The authority shown in this graffiti points to the idea that the masses believe that they have the power to influence the ruling elites. Participant 10 said *we voted them into power so they must respect us we are the bosses.* The sentiments show the authority the masses believe they have.

However, due to the repressive state apparatus, the common people, in most cases, are left without a voice to speak their views, and hence graffiti is emerging as the new public sphere where they discuss issues that affect them without restrictions. The sentence in the graffiti encodes their demands, while the addition of the name Wiwa, an affectionate name for Job, is a contextualized conclusion that aims to show the love people have for the public opinion influencer while at the same time criticizing the grim situation in Zimbabwe. The graffiti show the immoral behavior of the ruling elites and protesters' feelings of being wronged. Be that as it may, the incomplete erasure in the picture shows the struggle and strife between protesters and the ruling elites, and this action negates each other's status as rightful producers of information (Tshuma et al., 2022; Aboelezz, 2014; Zuvela, 2013). The ruling elites believe that the masses are only consumers of popular culture, while the masses believe that they are also supposed to be active creators of information in the community (Flesher, 2010). Accordingly, graffiti give the public a chance to be heard in a community where censorship is the norm. Community members resist and shake off the shackles of domination through graffiti, which is fast becoming a novel public sphere in Zimbabwe. Although graffiti are illegal in Zimbabwe, it has become a means of resistance against the oppressive government. Graffiti provides the masses with a new public space where they can express themselves anonymously and restate their identity. It has become a survival skill for the oppressed, who use it to resist and evade marginalization. Graffiti protest is critical for identity reaffirmation and citizenship because it allows the people to speak back to the hegemonic group. The writings on the walls symbolize the struggle of the Zimbabwean people to reclaim their rights and resist tyranny.

CONCLUSION

The chapter concludes that in Zimbabwe, the masses express their discontent with poor governance through graffiti writing. They use protest graffiti to share their views on government policies and governance without fear. The writing of the Tajamuka hashtag is a prime example of this. The study also revealed that the masses use graffiti as a means of launching existential protests to avoid state monitoring agents and political violence when they stand up in opposition to the ruling elite. Additionally, the research uncovered that the masses protested the looting of resources by the ruling elite. The chapter highlights that the culture of protesting against the ruling elite's looting is prevalent in Zimbabwe. The masses nowadays use graffiti art to express their dissent against the looting of natural resources by foreigners. This form of art is not governed by any rules related to its production, form, or content, and is therefore not under the jurisdiction of the rulers. It has also been revealed that opposition parties often resort to graffiti writing when they face censorship, which could lead to their extinction. This suggests that political protest graffiti on government buildings is a direct response to the control and censorship exercised by the ruling elite over the mainstream media.

REFERENCES

Aboelezz, M. (2014). The Geosemiotics of Tahrir Square: A Study of the Relationship between Discourse and Space. *Journal of Language and Politics* 13(4): 599–622. https://doi.org/10.1075/jlp.13.1.02abo

Achebe, C. (1988). *Hopes and Impediments: Selected Essays.* Doubleday: Anchor Books.

Allen, B. J. (2011). *Difference Matters: Communicating Social Identity, 2nd ed.* Long Grove: Waveland.

Allwood, J. (2003). 'Meaning Potentials and Context: Some Consequences for the Analysis of Variation in Meaning.' In Hubert Cuyckens, René Dirven and John Taylor (eds.), *Cognitive Linguistic Approaches to Lexical Semantics*, 29–66. Berlin: Mouton de Gruyter.

Al-Yassirya. S. (2020). The Social Role of Graffiti of Protesters of 2019. *International Journal of Innovation, Creativity and Change* 13(11): 10–78 www.ijicc.net.

Baldini, A. L. (2023). Graffiti Writing as Creative Activism: Getting Up, Sheeplike Subversion, and Everyday Resistance. *The Journal of Aesthetics and Art Criticism*, kpad001.

Ball, H. (1996). *Flight Out of Time: A Dada Diary. Translated by A. Raimes*. California: University of California Press.

Brain, C., and Clarke. E. (2006). *Steps for Writing a Successful Grant Proposal.* London: University Press.

Carroll, W. K., and Ratner, R. S. (1994) Between Leninism and radical pluralism: Gramscian reflections on counter-hegemony and the new social movements. *Critical Sociology* 20(2): 1–24.

Daly, C. (2013). Graffiti: Art That Plays by Its Own Rules Presented at the 2013 Belmont Undergraduate Research Symposium "Creating A Culture of Discovery: The Excitement and Benefits of Undergraduate Research", Accessed August 06, 2023. www.2013- scarllet.belmont.edu

Douglas, J. D. (2000). *Existential Sociology.* New York: CP Press.

Flesher, F. C. (2010). Collective Identity in Social Movements: Central Concepts and Debates. *Sociology Compass* 4(6): 393–404. https://doi.org/10.1111/j.1751-9020.2010.00287.x

Griffin, Z. -M. (2002). Recency Effects for Meaning and Form in Word Selection. *Brain and Language* 80:465–487.

Hall, S. (1986). Gramsci's Relevance for the Study of Race and Ethnicity. *Journal of Communication Inquiry* 10(2): 5–27.

Harris, D. (1991). *From Class Struggle to the Politics of Pleasure: The Effects of Gramscianism on Cultural Studies.* London: Routledge.

Laclau, E., and Mouffe, C. (1985). *Hegemony and Social Strategy: Towards a Radical Democratic Politics.* London: Verso.

Makarati, P., Mangeya, H., and Kadenge, M. (2022). The Graffiti Subculture: A Culture of Masculine Identity Construction in Zimbabwean Secondary Boarding Schools. *Journal of Research Inovation and implication in Education* 6(2):, 161–167.

Mangeya, H. (2019). Graffiti as A Site for Cultural Literacies in Zimbabwean Urban High Schools. *International Journal of Cultural Studies* 22(3): 334–348. https://doi.org/10.1177/1367877918788577

Mangeya, H. (2014). *A Sociolinguistic Analysis of Graffiti Written in Shona and English Found in Selected Urban Areas of Zimbabwe*. Unpublished Thesis. Unisa.

Marche, G. (2012). Expressivism and Resistance: Graffiti as an Infrapolitical form of Protest against the War on Terror. *Revue française d'études américaines* 1:, 78–96.

Matsilele, T. (2013). *The Political Role of the Diaspora Media in the Mediation of the Zimbabwean Crisis: A Case Study of The Zimbabwean-2008 to 2010* (Masters dissertation, Stellenbosch: Stellenbosch University).

Matsilele, T., and Ruhanya, P. (2024). Media and Democracy: Can the News Media Rightfully Claim Its Role as the Fourth Estate in Zimbabwe Politics? In Barkho, L., Lugo-Ocando, J. A., & Jamil, S. (Eds.). *Handbook of Applied Journalism: Theory and Practice* (pp. 289–300). Cham: Springer Nature Switzerland.

Matsilele, T. (2022). *Social Media and Digital Dissidence in Zimbabwe*. Cham: Palgrave Macmillan.

Matsilele, T., and Ruhanya, P. (2021). Social Media Dissidence and Activist Resistance in Zimbabwe. *Media, Culture & Society* 43(2): 381–394.

Matsilele, T., and Mututwa, W. T. (2021). The Aesthetics of 'Laughing at Power' in an African Cybersphere. In Mpofu, S. (Eds) *The Politics of Laughter in the Social Media Age: Perspectives from the Global South* (pp: 23–41). London: Palgrave Macmillan.

Matsilele, T., Mpofu, S., Msimanga, M., and Tshuma, L. (2021). Transnational Hashtag Protest Movements and Emancipatory Politics in Africa: A Three-Country Study. *Global Media Journal* 11(2): 2–23.

Miladi, N. (2018). Urban Graffiti, Political Activism, and Resistance. In Meikle, G. (Eds.), *The Routledge Companion to Media and Activism* (pp: 241–249). London: Routledge.

Moller, F. S. (2019). Altmetric Articles How Do Sources of Traditional Legitimacy Constrain Popular Uprisings? The Case of the Kingdom of Swaziland. *Small Wars and Insurgencies* 30(2): 392–420.

Mpofu, S., Ndlovu, M., and Tshuma, L. (2021). The Artist and Filmmaker as Activists, Archivists and the Work of Memory: A Case of the Zimbabwean Genocide. *African Journal of Rhetoric* 13(1): 46–76.

Msimanga, M. J., Tshuma, L. A., and Matsilele, T. (2022). The Why of Humour During a Crisis: An Exploration of COVID-19 Memes in South Africa and Zimbabwe. *Journal of African Media Studies* 14(2): 189–207.

Mukhtar, K. (2015). Creativity in the Midst of Crisis. *Danish Centre for Culture And Development, Denmark.* 11.

Nicholls, W. (2012). *Making "Counter Publics" Through the City: Networks, Exchanges and the Creation of Political Discourses. Creative Practice, Activism and Place-identities*, Bristol, UK. www.dol.nz/%5Cpdfs%5Clit-review-work-values.pdf. [Accessed 26-10-18].

OpenNet Initiative. (2005). Internet Filtering in China In 2004–2005: A Country Study. Retrieved November 28, 2023, from http://www.opennetinitiative.net/studies/china/.

Peteet, J. (1996). The Writing on the Walls: The Graffiti of the Intifada. *Cultural Anthropology* 11(2): 139–159.

Rahn, J. (2002). *Printing Without Permission: Hip Hop Graffiti Subculture.* London: Bergin and Garvey.

Reisner, R. (1974). *Graffiti: Two Thousand Years of Wall Writing.* London: Frederick Muller Limited.

Ryan, H. (2018). *Political Street Art: Communication, Culture and Resistance in LatinAmerica.* London: Routledge.

Schacter, R. (2014). The Ugly Truth: Street Art Graffiti and Creative City. *Art & the Public Sphere* 3(2): 161–176.

Sharra, A., and Matsilele, T. (2021). This Is a Laughing Matter: Social Media as a Sphere of Trolling Power in Malawi and Zimbabwe. In Mpofu, S. (Eds), *The Politics of Laughter in the Social Media Age: Perspectives from the Global South* (pp. 113–134). London: Routledge.

Shireen, A. (2021). *Dada and Surrealism, in Brief.* London: Research Gate.

Siham, G. (2017). *Semantics of the murals - semiotic study - Streets of Bejaia Amodel.* Master"s Thesis, Abderrahmane Meera University - Bejaia / Department of Arabic Language and Literature - Linguistics, p. 14

Spiteri, R., and LaCoss, D. (2003). *Surrealism, Politics, and Culture.* Aldershot: Ashgate Publishing.

Streahle, D. A. Z. (2011). Visual Surrealism: A History and Analysis of the Surrealist Image. *The Lehigh Review* 19:22–27. https://preserve.lehigh.edu/cas-lehighreview-vol-19/11 (Accessed: 23 January 2024).

Tshuma, L. A., and Sibanda, M. (2024). The Media and the Commemoration of Robert Mugabe's Death through the Camera's Lens. *Journal of Asian and African Studies* 59(1): 259–273.

Tshuma, B. B., Tshuma, L. A., and Ndlovu, M. (2022). Twitter and Political Discourses: How Supporters of Zimbabwe's Ruling ZANU PF Party Use Twitter for Political Engagement. *Journal of Eastern African Studies* 16(2): 269–288.

Wee, L. (2016). Situating Affect in Linguistic Landscapes. *Linguistic Landscape* 2(2): 105–126. https://doi.org/10.1075/ll.2.2.01wee

Werwath, T. (2013). *Urban Assault: The Culture and Politics of Urban Graffiti.* London: University Press.

Zaimakis, Y. (2015). Welcome to the Civilization of Fear: On Political Graffiti Heterotopias in Greece in Times of Crisis. *Visual Communication* 14(4): 373–396. https://doi.org/10.1177/1470357215593845

Zimuto, N. C., Mojapelo, M., and Mutasa, D. (2023). Emotive Art: An Analysis of Graffiti from Selected Secondary Schools in Bikita-Matsai District, Zimbabwe. *Critical Arts* 37: 1–15. 10.1080/02560046.2023.2212747.

Žuvela, S. (2013). Graffiti: A Form of International Communication. *Journal of Social Psychology* 4(133): 589–590.

Chapter 13

Publishing as Revolutionary Tools from Pre-independence to Post-independence Kenya

Job Mwaura

Diverse media forms and technologies play an unequivocal role in the vast sociopolitical and cultural contention landscape. They stand not merely as passive conduits but as active catalysts, articulating dissent and magnifying the often-muted voices engaged in these struggles, bridging the chasm between obscurity and recognition. This has been the case since the pre-independence period. For instance, the radio, newspapers, and other publications were important in the anti-colonial struggle in various parts of Africa. Radio became a revolutionary tool in some African nations during the fight for independence. *Radio Freedom*, the oldest liberation radio in Africa, served South Africa's African National Congress (ANC) as a propaganda tool during the Apartheid era. Since *the apartheid regime banned Radio Freedom*, it broadcast from other African nations, including Zambia, Angola, Ethiopia, Madagascar, and Tanzania (Lekgoathi, 2010; Wa'Njogu, 2004; Simpson, 2009). Elsewhere, Berg (2008) notes that in the Horn of Africa, *Radio Mogadishu* broadcast the voices of the liberation front of Western Somalia, the Abo region, and those of Eritreans. He further noted that *Radio Halgan,* which operated until 1988 in Ethiopia, carried an anti-Somali broadcast of Radio Kulmis (Radio Unity). While unique in their contexts, these instances embody the broader theoretical framework of media as a conduit of dissent. They underscore the profound impact of these alternative media forms in shaping liberation narratives, fostering unity, and challenging dominant discourses.

Apart from radio, colonial literature from African authors also emerged across the continent, documenting various forms of colonial atrocities that were taking place. For instance, in the late 1700s, Nigerian author and abolitionist Olaudah Equiano documented his experience as an enslaved person in a nine-ed memoir widely read in Europe and America (Lovejoy, 2005). In the early 1910s, authors such as Ghanaian activist Ekra-Agiman wrote one of the first African novels on racial emancipation and advocated for pan-Africanism (Tylor, 2018). Later, African plays emerged from authors like South African author Herbert Dhlomo in 1935 and Ngũgĩ wa Thiong'o in the 1960s in Kenya, among others. Between the 1900s and 1960s, other pan-African authors emerged and published in missionary, Indian, and Arabic publications. Most of these literary works and media productions were revolutionary and inclined toward themes such as racial segregation, anti-colonialism, land rights, and slavery.

The chapter takes a historical perspective on alternative publications/press and media productions in Kenya that were instrumental in the liberation struggles in pre- and post-independence regimes in Kenya. These include newspaper articles, magazines, songs, theater shows, radio, pamphlets, journals, books, and other protest literature. I argue that these pre- and post-independence media productions, literature, and other alternative publications used purposely for activism and other forms of struggle played an essential role in establishing the current culture of using digital media platforms for activism. It is also important to note that the vibrant and relatively free media ecosystem in Kenya stems from decades of struggle for freedom of expression and freedom of the media. Kenya is one of the most dynamic digital ecosystems on the continent, with a large and active population on social media. According to a 2023 report by the We Are Social Data Portal, Kenya had 17.86 million internet users, representing 32.7 percent of the population. Of these, 10.55 million were active social media users. The most popular social media platforms in Kenya are Facebook (7.2 million users), Twitter (3.2 million users), and Instagram (2.8 million users). The media landscape in Kenya is also vibrant and diverse. A report by the Media Council of Kenya titled "State of the Media in Kenya 2022" found 1,018 media outlets in Kenya, including 929 radio stations, 55 television stations, and 34 newspapers. Most media outlets in Kenya are privately owned. The chapter begins by highlighting how missionary and Indian-led publications inspired members of nationalist and pan-African movements to use them for anti-colonial liberation struggles. The chapter also discusses three generations of authors and media producers—the pre-independence and post-independence authors and media producers—and the contemporary digital media producers and how they used or have been using the media for activism.

MISSIONARY /CHURCH-LED PUBLICATIONS

Essentially, missionary-led and church-sponsored publications were some of the earliest forms of media to be established in Kenya. Wa'Njogu (2004) documents the history of the first newspaper in Kenya and mentions that *Taveta Chronicles* was the first to be published in 1895 by the Reverend

Albert Stega of the Church Missionary Society—(CMS), and it targeted the British settlers in Kenya. It was published in 1901 and closed due to financial difficulties. Other publications by CMS included—*The Weekly East African, Lenga Juu,*[1] and the *Ugandan Mail,* both in 1899. The Taveta Chronicle published articles on various stories, such as education, health, and agriculture. The newspaper also reported on the arrival of new British administrators in the area, and some articles advocated for fair treatment of everyone by the colonial masters, such as an article appearing in March 1922 calling on the British administrators to treat everyone fairly regardless of their race or ethnicity (Sifuna, 1977).

The church used such media publications to spread the gospel and inform people of current events. In later years, missionaries from other groups also owned publications such as *Mombasa Diocesan Magazine* (1903), *Kikuyu News*[2] (1908), *Wathioma Mukinyu*[3] (1916), *Kenya Church News* (1929), *Catholic Times of East Africa* (1937), and Mombasa Diocesan Gazette (1922). These publications tended to be somewhat neutral in their content, though sometimes leaning toward the ideologies of the local population to gain their interest and support. But Pugliese (1995) notes that while other European and missionary writers/publishers depended on Kenyans to provide materials, labor, and essential information for their writings and publications, the Kenyans remained unacknowledged.

In the post-independence period, church publications increased in number, and some transformed from a focus on spreading the gospel to a focus on other emerging societal issues like poor governance. Mukhongo (2015) notes that although the church was cautious of conflicting with the government during the colonial period and a few years after independence, a church-sponsored publication named *Target,* which Rev. John Schofield sponsored, had managed to publish articles that included social and political commentaries. In later post-independence years (1968–1971), Rev. Henry Okullu became the assistant editor, and together, they continued to publish articles about the oppressive ideologies of Kenyatta's government. These publications were the first activism tools in Kenya, which happened in 1894 when Kenya was declared one of the East African protectorates of the British government. The invasion of the British colonialists brought about sociopolitical, cultural, and economic changes in Kenya—which was the beginning of an oppressive regime directed against the African natives.

INDIAN PUBLICATIONS

Indians first came to Kenya in the 1890s to work as security forces for the British administration, which had established the East African Protectorate

(Murunga and Nasong'o, 2007). In the same period, the British administration, through an Indian contractor, Alibhai Mulla Jeevanjee, began constructing the Kenya Uganda Railway from 1896 to 1901 (Brennan, 2001). Sowell (1997) further adds that it was at this time that the Indians migrated to East Africa in large numbers to construct the railway. Some Indians were politically ambitious and involved in the nationalist movement in Kenya and East Africa. For example, in 1900, the East African Indian National Congress was formed to advocate for the rights of Indians in East Africa (Gopal, 1972). In 1920, the Indian Association of Kenya was created to represent the interests of Indians in Kenya. These organizations played a significant role in the struggle for independence in Kenya and East Africa (Ogot, 1972). But it is important to note that not all Indians were politically ambitious. Many Indians were content to live and work in Kenya and East Africa without getting involved in politics. It is also important to note that not all Indians were involved in the nationalist movement. Some Indians supported the British colonial government.

Indians first came to Kenya in the 1890s to work as security forces for the British administration, which had established the East African Protectorate (Murunga and Nasong'o, 2007). In the same period, the British administration, through an Indian contractor, Alibhai Mulla Jeevanjee, began constructing the Kenya Uganda Railway from 1896 to 1901 (Brennan, 2001). Sowell (1997) further adds that it was at this time that the Indians migrated to East Africa in large numbers to construct the railway.

Some Indians were politically ambitious and involved in the nationalist movement in Kenya and East Africa. For example, in 1900, the East African Indian National Congress was formed to advocate for the rights of Indians in East Africa. In 1920, the Indian Association of Kenya was created to represent the interests of Indians in Kenya. These organizations played a significant role in the struggle for independence in Kenya and East Africa. It is important to note that not all Indians were politically ambitious. Many Indians were content to live and work in Kenya and East Africa without getting involved in politics. Not all Indians were involved in the nationalist movement, and some Indians supported the British colonial government.

Since the missionary publications targeted the European settlers in Kenya and abroad, the Indians and Africans needed space where their voices could be articulated (Wa'Njogu, 2004). Soon after the completion of the Kenya Uganda railway in November 1901, an Indian merchant called Alibhai Mulla Jeevanjee founded three newspapers named *The African Standard, Mombasa Times,* and *Uganda Argus* (Durrani, 2016). These publications became the second wave of media in the country after the earlier material published by missionaries. Jeevanjee had begun to take an interest in politics, and this newspaper served as a platform where individuals could express their views against the oppression of the colonial administration. Hawley (2008) states that:

> leading Indian professionals and merchants began formulating collective opposition to discriminatory policies. . . . the Europeans had reserved the agriculturally and climatically desirable Kenya highlands solely for European occupation.

Such protests by the Indians reignited African nationalists to put more questions on the activities of the white settlers who displaced them from their land. The Indian activists also questioned why white settlers had allocated themselves land in the highlands of Kenya while they were not allowed to own land, even when they could afford to buy it. Durrani (2016) describes Indian dissent and political activity as follows:

> the Asian African community had long been involved in dissent and political activity against oppression in Kenya . . . A.M. Jeevanjee and M.A. Desai continuously and successfully challenged and controlled settler ambitions for their self-rule in Kenya on the apartheid model of South Africa.

In later years, most of the newspapers started by the Indians were radically opposed to British colonial rule. The *Daily Chronicle*, published between 1947 and 1962, was created by a small group of young Indian militants (Durrani, 2016). Pio Gama Pinto and Pranlal Shethi, the editors of the *Daily Chronicle*, led these individuals. Durrani (2016) adds that other notable publications by the Indian community included the *East African Chronicles* (1919–1922), whose editor was Manilal A. Dasai. This paper supported African nationalists like Harry Thuku in publishing their articles against colonialism. Newspapers became a valuable tool for activism. Durrani (2016, p. 37) mentions that:

> Desai also made available his office to [Harry] Thuku and gave him clerical and financial support. An outspoken critic of colonial rule, Desai turned the offices of *East African Chronicle* into a meeting place for South Asian and African political activists. His defence of humanity encouraged many young men like Jomo Kenyatta of the Kikuyu Central Association (KAU) to do likewise. Desai inspired and helped other Africans to publish their papers, including Harry Thuku, who published *Tangazo* with Desai's support.

The contributors used newspapers like the *East African Chronicles* to express dissent and fight for equal rights. Others, such as *Hindi Prakash* (1911–14) and *Indian Voice* (1911–14), were purposely established to express their grievances about the colonial government. However, such radical moves made by the Indian community made the British authorities to begin repression against the newspaper owners and editors. Haron Ahmed and Pranlal Purshotam, the editors of the *Daily Chronicle*, were jailed for six months by the British government for expressing sympathy with Mombasa Dock Workers, who went on strike in 1947 (Durrani 2016). In the same year, the British government in Kenya dissolved their printing press, *The Express Printing and Publishing Company* (Government of Kenya, 1947).

A critical point to note is the role of Asian communities in helping the Kenyan nationalists publish their presses. Pugliese (1994) indicated that since Africans could not afford to buy printing equipment and European printers would not print African newspapers, they had to rely on the presses owned and supported by Indian radicals trying to form a united non-European front against the colonial government. However, the British Colonial administrators were not pleased with how Asian communities helped the Kenyan nationalists establish their presses. Pugliese (1994, p. 57) adds that:

> in the early 1950s, the authorities became aware of it and took a series of measures against the printers. The government tried to discourage them from printing African newspapers by giving them heavier sentences than the editor in the sedition cases. V. G. Patel (Who later sold his printing equipment to Muoria) went to jail for producing *mumenyereri (Caregiver)*, as did G. L. Vidyarthi for printing *Sauti ya Mwafrika*.

The Indian publications were thus crucial to the Kenyan nationalists, who saw them as a foothold in publishing their media. Their support for the African nationalists in publishing their voices was essential in forging a united front against the European settlers in Kenya.

PRE-INDEPENDENCE NATIONALIST PUBLICATIONS

The quest for self-rule by indigenous Africans from the mid-1920s led to the establishment of local publications across the African continent. In Kenya, the nationalists published articles, songs, poems, and pamphlets to communicate messages mainly in vernacular languages, which was also a form of resistance against the colonial administration. The nationalists used their languages, so the colonial administration could not easily understand them (Pugliese, 1994; Wa Wanjau, 1988). The most successful use of vernacular "media" for resistance was through the songs written and sung by nationalists, such as Gikuyu militants, while serving sentences in various detention camps in Kenya. The songs were political and regularly sung by members of political parties such as KAU to spread anti-government sentiments. Pugliese (1994) noted the following concerning political songs and hymns during the colonial period:

> the political messages in the songs were set to well-known church tunes ... and they could be sung freely in the presence of all but a very few Europeans since the vast majority could not understand a word of Gikuyu.

Using songs as a strategy for resistance was significant because illiterate individuals learned them through word of mouth, and literate individuals read the written songs and taught others. Songs such as *Nyimbo cia kwarahura ruriri* (songs to awaken communities) by Kinuthia Mugia, *Nyimbo cia matuko maya* (current songs) by Muthee Chege, *Nyimbo cia Gikuyu na Mumbi* (songs of Gikuyu and Mumbi), and *Nyimbo cia ciana cia Gikuyu na mumbi* (songs of the children of Gikuyu and Mumbi) were the most popular songs in 1951 and 1952 (Wa Wanjau, 1988). The songs urged the Agikuyu community to revolt against colonial injustices.

However, the enormous influx of these African-led publications began in the 1940s and 1950s. Several reasons could have resulted in this influx of vernacular publications. First, in the middle of World War II, Kenyan soldiers, the majority of whom were volunteers led by British officers, participated in the war in distinct parts of Africa. When the soldiers returned home and interacted with other African nationalists during the war, they began pushing for the end of colonialism to address social, political, and economic injustices. Second, by this time, Africans had already gained literacy skills after attending missionary schools. Therefore, they could read and write in their vernacular and some in English. Thirdly, Africans gained skills to operate printing works. These skills were achieved through the workforce they provided in British, Asian, and missionary presses. Lastly, Africans had gained enough capital to afford to buy printing machines. Gakaara Wanjau, in his prison diary, states that he first operated a publishing company without owning any printing machine. He would edit and take manuscripts to an Indian-owned printer for printing and distribution.

NOTABLE PRE-INDEPENDENCE AUTHORS: GAKAARA AND KENYATTA

Gakaara wa Wanjau was perhaps the most prolific vernacular author in East Africa in the pre-independence period. He began writing in the Gĩkũyũ language in the 1940s, when African politics had become increasingly militant (Pugliese, 1994). His writings, and those of other nationalists, challenged the European invasion and colonial control. Some of his known works include

Riũa Rĩtaanathũa (Before the sun sets), *Mageria Nomo Mahota* (You only win after trying), *Ngwenda Ũũũnjurage* (I want you to kill me), *Mwandiki wa Mau Mau Ithaamirio-ini* (A Mau Mau writer in concentration camps), *Nyĩmbo cia Mau Mau: iria ciarehithirie wiyathi* (The songs of Mau Mau that brought self-rule), *Waigwa atia* (What is the news), and *kiume na Bidii kwa Mwafrika* (The spirit of adulthood for an African). Gakaara's works were radical and spoke directly to the Agikuyu speakers, especially those fighting colonial injustices. In his writings, he protested British colonial rule in Kenya.

Jomo Kenyatta was another pre-independence writer and editor of *Mwigwithania,* the Kikuyu Central Association (KCA)[4] publication. He moved to Britain in the early 1930s to further his education and stayed on until 1946. Among the institutions he attended while in Britain was the London School of Economics, where he graduated with a Diploma in Anthropology and published his thesis—*Facing Mount Kenya*. During his stay, he participated in various activities to end British colonial rule in Africa and other parts of the world, such as India and the Caribbean. At that time, the British government conducted surveillance to establish his ideological orientation, monitor his political activities, and identify his social and political contacts in Britain and Kenya (Maloba, 2017). Maloba (2017, p. 61) further noted that:

> Beyond the book [*Facing Mount Kenya*], Kenyatta also published articles in newspapers and periodicals throughout his stay in Britain. The intelligence services noted each contribution. In the case of newspaper publications, clippings of the paper were attached to reports in the many files maintained on his activities. In March 1930, on his first trip, Kenyatta wrote a letter to *The Times*, in which he reiterated many of the major points contained in the petition he had brought to the Colonial Office.

Throughout his stay in Britain, he published newspaper articles and various periodicals. Kenyatta's most radical publication was an article for Nancy Cunard's *The Negro Anthology*, titled *Kenya*. Maloba (2017) reports that, in the article, he lamented how Africans had been robbed of their land and were reduced to enslaved people. Between 1931 and 1937, Jomo Kenyatta also published in George Padmore's collection titled *The Negro Worker*. He published articles such as *An African Looks at British Imperialism* and *British Slave Rule in Kenya. The Negro Worker* became one of the most controversial and radical publications that dealt with black issues during that era (Ballantyne, 2002; Maloba, 2017).

Having had experience with the media while working at KCA's *Mwigwithania*, Kenyatta found the tool crucial in pushing for social and political change. On his return to Kenya, the colonial government was aware of his radical abilities and the influence gained from his education in Britain and Russia, his writings and speeches, and his interaction with scholars and nationalists from various African nations, India, and the Caribbean.

MEDIA ACTIVISM IN POST-INDEPENDENCE KENYA

Kenyatta's attitude toward the opposition leaders and parties affected how the media operated in the post-independence era. Hornsby (2012, p. 76) observed the following about the way the independent leaders viewed the press:

> The freedom of the press was far from guaranteed at independence. Legislation from 1960 gave the government significant powers over the media. The new elite warned the press to respect the government and cease exposing its internal divisions.

Repression of the media was therefore carried forward to the independent government from the colonial government. The press was a vital tool for development but also a potential threat to the new government (Mukhongo, 2015). Mbeke (2010) observed that Jomo Kenyatta and his nationalist colleagues were keenly aware of the might of the press, and they set out to manipulate and control the media for propaganda purposes. In the 1970s, there seemed to have been a general frustration from the Kenyan citizens since their expectations after *Uhuru* (freedom) had not been met. There was a feeling that Jomo Kenyatta's government was returning the citizens to the darker days of colonialism rather than a progressive and equal country. This pent-up frustration ignited another era of writing among a new crop of writers drawn from the University of Nairobi. This new generation of writers began to look for ways to express themselves and give a political opinion, even in a political environment that had become repressive.

Ngũgĩ wa Thiong'o

Ngũgĩ wa Thiong'o was one of the post-independence era's most prominent political and fictional authors. In 1963, he produced his first play, *The Black Hermit*, a version staged at Makerere University. The same year, he began writing a column in the *Nation* newspaper entitled "As I see it." Initially, he commended President Kenyatta for his stance on nationalism. Munene (2015) states that by September 1963, Ngũgĩ was no longer praising Kenyatta but instead had begun asking tough questions about the policies the independence government was adopting. From that point on, he never turned back.

In 1964, Ngũgĩ authored his first fictional novel, *Weep Not* Child.[5] This novel explored the adverse effects of British imperialism in Kenya. In the book, Ngũgĩ was highly critical of the colonial rule in Kenya. His second novel, *The River Between,* was set during the colonial period, and it tells the story of a young leader called *Waiyaki,* who was struggling to unite two villages (*Kameno* and *Mukuyu*) where differences in faith had separated. This story is also a premonition of what was to happen in post-colonial Kenya—the problems caused by deep-rooted ethnic and political divisions.

Ngũgĩ adopted several ways of resisting. First, he changed his name from James Ngũgĩ to Ngũgĩ wa Thiong'o and denounced all colonial practices. He also began writing in his native language. Some of the books he authored in the Gikuyu language included *Caitaani mutharaba-Ini* (Devil on the Cross, 1980), *Ngaahika Ndeenda: Ithaako ria ngerekano* (I Will Marry When I Want, co-authored with Ngugi wa Mirii, 1982), *Matigari ma Njiruungi* (The remains of Njiruungi, 1986), and *Mũrogi wa Kagogo* (Wizard of the crow, 2004). Ngũgĩ's writings in the post-independence era focused on or had an overriding theme of challenging colonial attitudes and ways of thinking, as well as offering a representation of Africans at a crossroads in the aftermath of colonial rule. To date, Ngũgĩ remains active as a writer in the tradition and spirit of decolonization. His writings include novels, plays, memoirs, essays, non-fiction, and short stories. Equally important, in 1976, he was crucial in setting up *Kamiriithu Community Education and Cultural Centre. This community centre* also had a traveling theater club inclined to celebrate African languages in theatrical performances. The group also performed plays with themes on pressing issues of that era. One year after establishing the community center, Ngũgĩ was detained for a year without trial. His play *Ngaahika Ndeenda* provoked the then-vice-president Daniel Moi, and his novel *Petals of Blood* (1977) discussed the post-independence issues in Kenya. The group was consequently banned in early 1982, and government forces torched the center's structures.

Ngũgĩ's writings drive several ideologies, such as decolonization, cultural revitalization, linguistic reclamation, and resistance against neocolonialism, which are still relevant in today's post-colonial studies. In this context, Ngũgĩ uses the media (literary works) to push for change within African societies, and he regards literature as a valuable tool for activism. In his non-fictional essay—*Decolonising the Mind*, Ngũgĩ advocated for a shift from the colonial mentality and a return to our African way of doing things, including using African languages. He was against cultural imperialism and regarded it as a form of enslavement (Amoko, 2010; Wa Thiong'o, 1981).

Koigi wa Wamwere

Another prominent post-independence writer was Koigi wa Wamwere,[6] a politician and a member of parliament in the 1970s. In an interview with him for this research, he mentions that he left his studies at Cornell University in the United States and returned to Kenya when he became convinced that, despite independence, Kenya had not earned democracy and freedom, and he wanted to fight for that. He went further to say that:

> When I arrived here, I asked myself what platform I would use to realise my goals. And I remember taking a journalism course as one of my humanities. So, I decided that I was going to look for a position in one of the newspapers as a columnist. I was lucky that I was given this position by *Sunday Post,* whose editor by then was Salim Lone. The paper had a very progressive outlook. Every weekend, I would have an article in the *Sunday Post,* and it would cause many controversies. Many people thought that it was too much for human rights, some government officers also felt that I was too much for workers' rights, and of course, the police thought that I was using the platform to make trouble. So, every time the article appeared, the police would visit me. And it reached a point where I knew for sure that the police would come for me. So, I would go to the police station before they approached me. And I would tell them that they needed not to go for me, and I would explain to them what I meant to say in the article.
> [Koigi wa Wamwere, interview, January 7, 2019]

Koigi was arrested several times based on false allegations of owning weapons and subversive publications, illegally entering a security zone, and attempted robbery with violence (wa Wamwere, 1988). Unlike Ngugi, his writings are non-fictional but political, agitating for sociopolitical change in Kenya. Some of his publications include *A Woman Reborn* (1980), *Conscience on Trial: Why I Was Detained: Notes of a Political Prisoner in Kenya* (1988), *People's Representative and the Tyrants* (1992), *Dream of Freedom* (1997), *Tears of the Heart: A Portrait of Racism in Norway and Europe* (2000), *I Refuse to Die: My Journey for Freedom* (2003), *Negative Ethnicity: From Bias to Genocide* (2003), and *Towards Genocide in Kenya: The Curse of Negative Ethnicity* (2008). Just like Gakaara wa Wanjau's detention diary—*Mwandiki wa Mau Mau Ithaamirio-ini (Mau Mau Author in Detention)*, and Ngugi's book *Detained: A Writer's Prison Diary*, which he wrote while in Kamiti Maximum Prison,[7] Koigi documents brutal treatment and other experiences while in prison in *Conscience on Trial: Why I Was Detained: Notes of a Political Prisoner in Kenya* (1988).

Gitobu Imanyara

Just as the alternative press grew before independence (the 1940s), a similar phenomenon developed in the 1980s/90s. Njogu and Middleton (2009) note that, with some external support, certain sections of the elite (referring to influential individuals or groups in society) took the initiative to establish an alternative press. It is essential to clarify that these elites, typically associated with positions of power and privilege, are not commonly known for their deep attachment to social justice. However, their motivation for founding the alternative press was twofold: to counter the complacent local mainstream media and to combat the injustices perpetuated by the government. Gitobu Imanyara was one of the prominent writers, editors, and publishers of this era who is still an active writer and publisher in the current liberation struggles. He is also a human rights lawyer, journalist, and politician. He founded the *Nairobi Law Monthly* in 1987, a publication that crusaded to restore democracy (Imanyara, 1992). Initially, this publication catered to a small group of Kenya's legal fraternity. Imanyara (1992) stated that the idea of starting *Nairobi Law Monthly* sprang up when he was serving a prison sentence at Kamiti Maximum Prison in 1983. In an interview for this research study, he said.

> I did not train as a journalist. I trained as a lawyer, and as a practising lawyer, I experienced how the law was being used negatively to settle scores to achieve a political purpose and as a tool of control. [. . .] I was imprisoned for two years. During that time, the courts-martial jailed many of the officers wrongfully. I also met many prisoners who were in prison for no offence at all. They had disagreed with somebody, or some political person had engineered their arrest and had them imprisoned with fixed charges. The legal process and the law were being abused. That is how *Nairobi law monthly* was born. I promised myself that if I did get out of prison, I would start a publication that championed human rights abuses through the enlightenment of others...
> [Interview with Gitobu Imanyara, January 15, 2019]

In early 1990, Gitobu was arrested again after authoring an article titled "The Historical Debate: Law, Democracy and Multiparty Politics in Kenya." The government accused him of engaging in subversive activities aimed at undermining and overthrowing the government (Imanyara, 1992, p. 22). After his release, Gitobu continued to use the media to push for sociopolitical change. He fought for the return of multiparty democracy in Kenya in the 1990s. Together with other members of the Law Society of Kenya (LSK), Gitobu remained steadfast in the struggle for democracy in Kenya. *Nairobi Law Monthly*, which he later renamed *African Law Review*, became an essential platform for expressing resistance and dissent against Daniel Moi's government. In later years, Gitobu founded another magazine, *The Platform*, which acts as a platform for alternative voices and focuses on contemporary issues of law, justice, and society.

Other examples of the alternative press in the 1980s and 1990s that championed democracy included *Finance*, which was owned and edited by Njehu Gatabaki, and *Society*, held by Pius Nyamora. In 1985, the National

Council of Churches of Kenya (NCCK) founded *Beyond*, which Bidan Mbugua edited. Bidan Mbugua's publication called for promoting religious life and condemned ungodly behavior such as tribalism, injustices, and social immorality. He was particularly critical of the March 1988 elections in Kenya, where there was massive vote rigging. Press (2015, p. 214) noted the following about Bidan Mbugua's magazine:

> The magazine sold out quickly as Kenyans, not used to seeing government fraud so boldly exposed, rushed to grab even the additional copies printed before the government banned the sale later the day of publication. Many were being arrested for carrying the Beyond magazine. So, it was enormous—the magazine created a massive crisis in the country. And with that reaction, it is like the tide [of resistance to the regime] that you could not stop was born.

Mbugua was jailed for this, and the publication was banned. Njogu and Middleton (2009) note that the banning of *Beyond* made the *Financial Review*, founded in 1987 and edited by Peter Kareithi, emerge from the shadows. Initially, it had been an occasional supplement to Hillary Ng'weno's Weekly Review. Amid government censorship, these alternative presses became important in repealing Section 2(a) of the Constitution, which allowed for the reintroduction of multiparty politics in Kenya. The dissolution of Section 2(a) also set the pace for the fight for a new Constitution, which was realized in 2010. Gitobu Imanyara credits the alternative press and the resilience of the second liberation nationalists with the freedom of expression that Kenyans enjoy today. He mentions that:

> The media as a medium of expression and communication is crucial; it is critical not only at that time but even now because it is a communication that enables people to enjoy that inherent values as human beings without the ability to communicate. And not just print media but electronic and other forms of media. If you limit the human person to communicate and express themselves, you restrict the inherent value of a human being. There are significant challenges that the internet has brought, particularly regarding fake media, criminal activities, and terrorism, so these are challenges that we must face. We do not fix them by banning them because you cannot suppress an idea whose time has come.
> [Interview with Gitobu Imanyara, January 15, 2019]

It is also important to note here that there were a host of other publications that were considered seditious for exposing the injustices of the Kenyatta and Moi governments in the 70s, 80s, and 90s. For instance, a magazine named *Pambana* (Swahili for struggle), owned by the December 12 movement,[8] was banned, and its editor, journalist Wangondu Kariuki, was arrested and charged with four and a half years. According to Index on Censorship 6/82, it noted:

> Weeks before the hearing of Kariuki's case, the President of Kenya (President Moi) and other members of the government had made public statements calling for the conviction of those found in possession of underground papers like *Pambana*. (p. 34)

Wa Kinyatti (2019) also noted that other revolutionary documents clandestinely printed and distributed both within Kenya and abroad encompassed a range of themes exposing the oppressive nature of Moi's regime. Examples of such papers included titles like *Moi's Reign of Terror* (1983), *University Destroyed, Moi Crowns Ten Years of Government Terror in Kenya* (1983), *Kenya: Register of Resistance* (1986), *Struggle for Democracy in Kenya*(1987) among others. These publications courageously shed light on human rights abuses, suppression of dissent, state-sponsored violence, and the ongoing struggle for democracy within Kenya.

CONTEMPORARY ASPECTS OF THE MEDIA AND ACTIVISM

While the use of the media for activism has been a common trait of many liberation movements and political formations advocating for change, the development of media technology has also meant a difference in how activism is conducted. For instance, before the advent of digital media, radio and paper publications were the main tools of change. Currently, digital media has redefined and transformed activism. Murthy (2018) discusses how social media has fundamentally changed the landscape of organizational communication, from mobilizing resources to even making grassroots activism more feasible. For instance, Mutsvairo´s (2016) research extensively delves into the phenomenon of digital activism in the social media era, shedding light on its multifaceted dimensions and implications. Through thorough analysis, Mutsvairo uncovers this form of activism´s diverse aspects and consequences, providing a comprehensive understanding of its dynamics. These include the ways in which digital platforms enable quicker and more widespread dissemination of activist messages, the role of social media in facilitating the organization of protests and mobilization with minimal resources, and the impact of online networks in creating global solidarity for local causes.

Moreover, Akpojivi´s (2018) work focuses on the #ZumaMustFall movement, offering a case study that provides valuable insights into the euphoria, delusion, and complex dynamics surrounding digital activism. By examining this specific campaign, Akpojivi highlights the intricacies and challenges digital activists face and the potential limitations of their efforts. Moreover, Akpojivi's (2018) work focuses on the #ZumaMustFall movement, offering a case study that provides valuable insights into the euphoria, delusion, and complex dynamics surrounding digital activism. By examining this specific campaign, Akpojivi highlights the intricacies and challenges digital activists face, such as the difficulty in translating online enthusiasm into substantial offline action and the ease with which such movements can be co-opted or diluted by diverse interest groups. Furthermore, Akpojivi discusses the delusion that can arise when the perceived strength of a digital campaign does not match its real-world impact. In line with the interplay of class dynamics in social activism, Mwaura´s (2019) research, on the other hand, explores how digital platforms intersect with socioeconomic factors in Kenya. By investigating the role of social media in activism, Mwaura offers valuable perspectives on the influence of digital platforms on class constructs and social participation.

Media forms have been a driving force in transforming human interaction, both positively and negatively, over the years. The evolution of various media technologies has changed how we perceive and define media and shaped our social dynamics. A 2019 study published by the Pew Research Center demonstrated the significant impact of social media on human interaction. The study revealed that social media platforms have facilitated connections between geographically distant individuals, allowing them to maintain relationships with friends and family. Moreover, social media has provided a means for individuals to discover and connect with like-minded individuals who share their interests (Silver and Huang, 2019). However, it is essential to acknowledge that social media can also contribute to conflicts, stress, and issues related to self-esteem and mental health (Pew Research Center, 2019). Different forms of the press act not only as informative and educative tools but also as platforms that provide citizens with avenues to express themselves—to critique various ideologies on sociopolitical and economic issues, and to express dissent to multiple ideologies. The media, for several decades now, has been used to speak truth to power, for power to manipulate people, to radicalize individuals, and to foster critical thinking about personal circumstances and societal trajectories. The media has evolved and revolutionized the way people communicate. It is important to note that when early forms of technology were invented, such as the radio and newspapers, the media was taken away from ordinary individuals. However, with new technologies like the internet, the media has become more accessible to ordinary people. This has led to a more democratic media landscape where regular people can have a voice (Kperogi, 2022; Mutsvairo and Ragnedda, 2019).

However, the current development in media technology has taken back the media to ordinary individuals, thus advancing aspects of media and democracy (Akpojivi, 2018; Salawu and Chibita, 2016). Social media platforms have become spaces where ordinary citizens can create and share their media. The downside of this is that the algorithmic power of technology companies has been used to profit from users' interactions in online spaces (Digital Capitalism). In addition, Moyo (2009) observed that various digital divides in the global south epitomize severe information poverty that affects billions of people in the supposed age of the information society.

In the last few years, digital media have become spaces of public debate. In a paper on how the youth use the press, Vromen et al. (2015) argue that young people from a broad range of existing political and civic groups use digital media for sharing information and mobilizing, which becomes a way of redefining political action and political spaces. However, this is not a new thing—but the size at which it is happening makes it unique. Letters to the editors, commentaries in mainstream media, radio talk shows, call-in sessions, etc., have become spaces of political debate for ordinary citizens and areas for expressing defiance of oppressive government decisions. Although, for several years, the Kenyan government repressed individuals and media organizations that were critical of them, citizens still found a way to publish their concerns in alternative media such as gutter presses, pamphlets, magazines, novels, and music and dance.

Further, the similarity is very striking when looking at the concerns of ordinary citizens in post-colonial Kenya and those of the same citizens during the colonial period from the late 1880s to the 1960s. The primary concern of the nationalists during the colonial period was fighting for social justice. Specifically, they were enraged by the decision of the colonial administration to displace them on their land. These concerns were expressed in many ways, but one was through the media. Some notable individuals who have consistently used social media for political change include Boniface Mwangi, Khelef Khalifa, Okiya Omtatah, Hussein Khalid, and Jerotich Seii. These individuals' consistent use of social media has enabled them to reach a broader audience and spark meaningful conversations, mobilize communities, and pressure authorities to address pressing social and political issues. Their active engagement on social media platforms has been instrumental in driving political change and advocating for social justice in Kenya.

CONCLUSION

This chapter traced the trajectory of media forms and activism in Kenya. The discussion in this chapter revolved around the alternative press and its role in socio-political change in pre- and post-independence Kenya. As noted in this chapter, missionary and Indian-owned publications established the media as tools for driving change (activism) in Kenya in pre-independence. Their support for the African nationalists in publishing their voices was essential in forging a united front against the colonial administration in Kenya. It is important to note that despite the repression these media producers and authors faced (and continue to face) from various regimes, they did not stop producing dissenting media. This historical review is, therefore, essential in understanding the current wave of digital activism in Kenya. First, it highlights the importance of the media as a tool for sociopolitical change. Secondly, digital activism is pegged on the ideologies of alternative media—where alternative media represents the interests of the oppressed. Jeppesen (2015) stated that alternative media share an anti-authoritarian ideology and emphasize collective autonomy, supporting the idea that one person's liberation is liberation for all. Therefore, alternative media are organized and rooted within "decentred liberatory social movements," emphasizing values such as collective decision-making and "horizontalism." Lastly, this chapter was essential in understanding that a culture of resistance in Kenya started pre-independence and has continued into the current era. While the current generation of resistance uses sophisticated media tools for social change, some of the grievances by citizens, such as poor governance, government repression, and corruption, have remained the same.

NOTES

1. *Lenga Juu* is Swahili for "Aim higher" a CMC publication that was published in 1911.
2. Kikuyu News was published by Church of Scotland Mission in English every month.
3. Wathioma Mukinyu is kikuyu for "Great Friend," a publication of the Consolata Catholic Missionaries in Nyeri, Kenya.
4. The Kikuyu Central Association (KCA), led by James Beauttah and Joseph Kang'ethe, was a political organisation in colonial Kenya formed in 1924 to act on behalf of the Gĩkũyũ community by presenting their concerns to the British government.
5. Weep Not, Child integrates Gikuyu mythology and the ideology of nationalism that serves as a catalyst for much of the novel's action. The novel explores the negative aspects of colonialism and imperialism.
6. He was an MP for Nakuru North (Now Subukia Constituency). In the informed consent for this research, Mr. Koigi gave permission for his name to be used in the final research report.
7. Kamiti maximum prison is a Maximum-security prison located near Nairobi in Kenya for hardcore criminals.
8. December 12 was the date in 1963 when Kenya achieved formal independence from Britain.

REFERENCES

Akpojivi, Ufuoma, (2018) *Media Reforms and Democratization in Emerging Democracies of Sub-Saharan Africa*. Cham: Springer International Publishing.

Amoko, Apollo Obonyo, (2010) *Apollo Obonyo Amoko (Auth.)-Postcolonialism in the Wake of the Nairobi Revolution_ Ngugi Wa Thiong'o and the Idea of African Literature*. New York: Palgrave Macmillan.

Aiyar, S., (2011). 'Empire, race and the Indians in colonial Kenya's contested public political sphere, 1919–1923.' *Africa 81*(1), 132–154.

Ballantyne, Tony, (2002) *Orientalism and Race: Aryanism in the British Empire*. Cambridge Imperial and Post-Colonial Studies Series. Basingstoke, Hampshire: Palgrave.

Berg, Jerome S., (2008) *Broadcasting on the Short Waves, 1945 to Today*. Jefferson, North Carolina, and London: McFarland & Company Inc.

Brennan, J. R. (2015) 'A History of Sauti ya Mvita (Voice of Mombasa): Radio, Public Culture, and Islam in Coastal Kenya', 1974-1966. In R. I. Hackett & B. F. Soares, eds., New Media and Religious Transformations in Africa, Bloomington, IN: Indiana University Press. 19–38.

Durrani, Shiraz, (2016) *Never Be Silent: Publishing and Imperialism 1884-1963*. Vita Books. Government of Kenya. (1947) '*Kenya Gazette*,' June 10, 1947.

Hawley, John C., (2008) *India in Africa, Africa in India: Indian Ocean Cosmopolitanisms*. Indiana University Press.

Hornsby, Charles. (2012) *Kenya: A History since Independence*. London; New York: I. B. Tauris.

Imanyara, Gitobu, (1992) 'Kenya: Indecent Exposure.' *Index on Censorship* 21(4): 21–22.

Lekgoathi, Sekibakiba Peter, (2010) 'The African National Congress's Radio Freedom and Its Audiences in Apartheid South Africa, 1963–1991.' *Journal of African Media Studies* 2(2): 139–153.

Jeppesen, Sandra, (2015) 'Understanding Alternative Media Power: Mapping Content & Practice to Theory, Ideology and Political Action.' *Democratic Communique* 27: 54–77.

Kperogi, F. A. (Ed.). (2022). *Digital Dissidence and Social Media Censorship in Africa*. London: Routledge.

Lovejoy, Paul E. (2006). 'Autobiography and Memory: Gustavus Vassa, Alias Olaudah Equiano, the African.' *Slavery & Abolition* 27 (3): 317–347. https://doi.org/10.1080/01440390601014302. Accessed on August 8, 2022. NY: Springer Berlin Heidelberg.

Manji, A. (2020). *The struggle for land and justice in Kenya* (Vol. 49). Martlesham: Boydell & Brewer.

Mbeke, P. O., (2010) *Mass -media in Kenya: Systems and practice*. Nairobi: The Jomo Kenyatta Foundation.

Moyo, Last, (2009) 'The digital divide: Scarcity, inequality and conflict.' In *Digital cultures: Understanding new media*, eds G. Creeber and M. Royston, pp. 122–130. Berkshire: Open University Press.

Mukhongo, Lusike, (2015) 'Friends or Foes? A Critique of the Development of the Media and the Evolving Relationship between Press and Politics in Kenya.' *Critical Arts* 29(1): 59–76.

Munene, Macharia (2015). *Historical reflections on Kenya: Intellectual adventurism, politics, and international relations.* University of Nairobi Press.

Murthy, Dhiraj, (2018) 'Introduction to Social Media, Activism, and Organizations.' *Social Media + Society* 4(1): 205630511775071.

Murunga, Godwin R., and Shadrack W. Nasong'o, (2007) *Kenya: The Struggle for Democracy.* London; New York: Zed Books.

Mutsvairo, B., (2016). *Digital activism in the social media era.* Switzerland: Springer Nature.

Mwaura, J. (2019). Class interplay in social activism in Kenya. In Polson, E., Clark, L. S., and Gajjala, R. (Eds.), *The Routledge Companion to Media and Class* (pp. 280–292). Routledge.

Njogu, K. and Middleton, J. (Ed.), (2009). *Media and identity in Africa.* Edinburgh: Edinburgh University Press.

Nyaundi, Lewis, (2017) 'Fearless Voice of the Legal Fraternity: AfBA Rekindled to Protect Rule of Law.' *The Star, Kenya*, July 5, 2017.

Press, Robert M. (2015) *Ripples of Hope: How Ordinary People Resist Repression without Violence.* Protest and Social Movements 4. Amsterdam: Amsterdam University Press.

Pugliese, Cristiana, (1994) *Author, Publisher, and Gikuyu Nationalists: The Life and Writings of Gakaara Wa Wanjau.* Nairobi: Bayreuth African Studies 37.

Salawu, Abiodun, and Monica B. Chibita, eds., (2016) *Indigenous Language Media, Language Politics and Democracy in Africa.* London: Palgrave Macmillan UK.

Shiundu, Alphonce (2011) 'MP Condemns Raid on Publishing Firm.' *Daily Nation*, September 9, 2011, Friday Nation edition.

Sifuna, D. N., (1977). 'The Mill Hill Fathers and The Establishment Of Western Education In Western Kenya 1900–1924: Some Reflections.' *Trans-African Journal of History* 6: 112–128.

Simpson, Thula, (2009) 'Umkhonto We Sizwe, We Are Waiting for You': The ANC and the Township Uprising, September 1984 – September 1985.' *South African Historical Journal,* 61(1): 158–177.

Silver, L., and Huang, C., (2019, August 22). *Social media users are more likely to interact with people who are different from them.* Pew Research Center. Retrieved August 2022, from https://www.pewresearch.org/internet/2019/08/22/social-media-users-more-likely-to-interact-with-people-who-are-different-from-them/

Sowell, Thomas (1997). *Migrations and cultures: A world view.* New York: Basic Books.

Taylor, Mildred Europa, (2018) 'The First African Novel Written in English Was Authored by This Prolific Ghanaian Writer in 1911.' Blog. *Face of Africa* (blog). December 3, 2018. https://face2faceafrica.com/article/the-first-african-novel-written-in-english-was-authored-by-this-prolific-ghanaian-writer-in-1911.

Vromen, Ariadne, Michael A. Xenos, and Brian Loader (2015). 'Young People, Social Media and Connective Action: From Organizational Maintenance to Everyday Political Talk.' *Journal of Youth Studies* 18(1): 80–100.

We Are Social. (2023, February 13). Digital 2023: Kenya. Datareportal. Retrieved February 15, 2023, from https://datareportal.com/reports/digital-2023-kenya

Wa Kinyatti, Maina, (2019) *History of Resistance in Kenya 1884-2002*. Kenya: Mau Mau Research Center (MMRC).

Wa Thiong'o, Ngugi, (1981). *Decolonising the mind*. Harare: Zimbabwe Publishing House.

Wa Wanjau, Gakaara, (1988) *Mau Mau Author in Detention*. Nairobi: Heinemann Kenya Limited.

Wa'Njogu, J. Kiarie, (2004) 'Language and Multiparty Democracy in a Multiethnic Kenya.' *Indiana University Press* 50(3): 20.

Chapter 14

Photographs, Protest, and Memory
A Case of #BlackLivesMatter in South Africa
Lungile Tshuma

Protests appearing under the X (formerly Twitter) hashtag #BlackLivesMatter (BLM), which has its roots in the United States stemming from police brutality, have also become popular in the global South as many black activists in the global South argued that black people were being undermined by the economic and political system, which appears to favor white people. The fight to improve the plight of black people in the United States also became significant in South Africa, as black South Africans felt they were economically and socially disadvantaged by a system that was ultimately a product of the apartheid regime. The starting point of these debates is the "movement frame," which denotes the way activists define problems to encourage movement participation. South Africa is regarded as a "miracle nation," which came about through a smooth transition that some felt could well have led to a bloodbath (Jacobs, 2007). According to Chasi and Rodney-Gumede (2016, p. 731), "the magical transformation that South Africans envision entails moving from colonial and apartheid rule, based on inequity and injustice that worked to secure white prosperity at the expense of the colonised masses." As such, the transition has been a subject of debate, with several movements challenging the hegemonic narrative, which is mainly camouflaged under the concept of the "rainbow nation." Thus, the South African political transition is ongoing, despite the move from the apartheid system of institutionalized racism to a liberal democracy. Bosch (2017) argues that while the country's first democratic elections were held in 1994, South Africa could still be considered a transitional democracy as it still shows signs of incomplete democratic consolidation. Writing on democratic transitions, Boix and Stokes (2003) argued that glaring inequalities are a hindrance to transitions to democracy because in highly unequal societies, "democracy would empower the poorer masses to push strong redistributive demands, elites would block transitions or undermine democracy where it had emerged" (Weyland, 2017, p. 387). Haggard and Kaufman (2021) developed these earlier views and indicated that drivers of democratic transitions include the capacity of the opposition to effect change, and the role of international players. Against these views, countries such as Zimbabwe have been characterized as having an "unfinished business," owing to failed democratic transitions from the colonial era to post-independence (Ndlovu-Gatsheni, 2011, p. 20). Therefore, criticism of South Africa's democracy might not be surprising as (Ezrahi, 2012, p. x) argues that while contemporary democratic states have delegitimized naked force, "institutionalizing the vision of popular sovereignty or 'government by the consent of the people' has been only partial and deeply flawed in many democracies." It is against this background that South Africa, to date, keeps experiencing bloody uprisings as citizens, especially the black majority, who believe that the country witnessed a "change without change" since they are still poor.

Against this background, Zelizer (2010, p. 3) argues that images have not been incorporated into academic research because researchers continue to perceive the "verbal record . . . as arbiters of the real world takes precedence over the visual counterpart." However, with contemporary industrial societies having turned their citizens into "image junkies" and creating "the most irresistible form of mental pollution" (Sontag, 1993, p. 45), it is important to understand the use of photographs in protest movements. This chapter examines the use of protest photographs by the #BlackLivesMatter movement in South Africa, specifically examining the rearticulation of apartheid used to highlight the present struggle in South Africa. Although the causes of the #BlackLivesMatter movement are similar across the globe, as they all fight for the inclusion and importance of black lives in society, there are nonetheless significant differences across societies based on diverse histories, politics, and overall context. Given that photography constitutes a mirror with a memory, I argue that photographs are being used to invoke and trigger apartheid memories to make sense of the contemporary needs of society and to serve the future.

The basic framing of the movement, Black Lives Matter, helps us understand several issues that affect the majority black population in South Africa, ranging from racial inequality to police violence to healthcare. Protests have been common in South Africa, with the well-known social media protests being on #FeesMustFall and #RhodesMustFall where the former was led by students, especially from the previously marginalized black population, who demanded that they receive free education, while the latter was a decolonial move to remove all the colonial symbols, as Cecil John Rhodes statues still symbolized the colonial system, which is yet to be removed (see Mpofu, 2017). Both protests were mainly initiated by university students, and these emerged within this broader context of growing social discontent (Bosch, 2016). At the height of the student protests in 2015, Twitter played a key role in disseminating information, which included photographs, to participants, garnering support for protest activities, and acting as a "choreography of assembly" (Gerbaudo, 2012, p.5). With this in mind, "any photograph is dependent on a series of historical, cultural, social and technical contexts which establish its meanings as an image and an object" (Clarke, 1997, p. 19).

THE PLACE OF PHOTOGRAPHS IN COMMUNICATION

This chapter recognizes the debates on the use of photographs in communication. The debate has been between the positivists, who are adamant that meaning lies in the photograph, which mirrors reality and authentically represents events (Wells, 2003). On the other hand, constructivists contend that photographic representation and its power are contextual because its meaning is "dependent on a series of historical, cultural, and technical contexts" (Clarke, 1997, p. 19). This chapter supports the latter perspective. Based on the former, the power of photographs in communication lies in them being recognized as an effective tool for framing in a less obtrusive manner than written text (Messaris and Abraham, 2001). From a viewer's perspective, photographs' effectiveness as a framing vehicle comes from their ability to capture events and reflect what existed in front of the camera (Greenwood and Jenkins, 2013, p. 249). To add more, photographs are key in communication because people remember and believe what they see more than what they hear (Khan and Mazhar, 2017, p. 2). Therefore, photographs are, arguably, important tools in communication because they have a higher degree of believability. When taken in protest and memory studies, a photograph can work as evidence of the brutality that took place during the apartheid era, and such an incident might be hard to deny as it is captured on camera. Furthermore, photographs function as concrete and vivid cues, exemplars, which provide context that adds to and enhances the understanding of an issue being discussed (Abraham and Appiah, 2006). Therefore, the ability of photographs to depict realism and provide direct evidence of events makes them powerful communication tools that engage and move viewers more than text.

The power of photographs as a communication tool also lies in the fact that audiences process visuals faster and more efficiently than written text, and visuals contain more information than other symbol forms (Graber, 1996; 2001; Paivio, 1979). Similarly, brain-imaging studies indicate reactions to photographs are stronger and more persistent than reactions to text (Shapiro, 2004). In newspapers, Moses (2002) noted that graphics, photographs, and headlines get far more attention from readers than written text does. Readers may focus on photographs because they are memorable and aid in information recall (Berry and Brosius, 1991), and photographs may not just enhance memory for verbal themes; they provide a contextual framework in which semantic comprehension of the narrative takes place (Cieplak, 2017). Visuals drive us toward memorization, retention, and understanding about anything by providing us with prior knowledge about subjects and phenomena (Khan and Mazhar, 2017, p. 2). Similarly, Robert Sternberg (2006), in his study of the effects of photographs on memory, concluded that images could build our concepts and strengthen already-held concepts in our minds. Such work by photographs illustrates their power as a communicative tool that can engage and influence people. Schill (2012), in his review of the impact of visuals in political communication, identifies ten functions of images that make them a central component of communication. Thus, images serve as arguments, have an agenda-setting function, dramatize policy, aid in emotional appeals, build the candidate's image, create identification, connect to societal symbols, transport the audience, and add ambiguity (Schill, 2012). People interpret meaning and act upon images based on pre-existing knowledge and beliefs (Greenwood and Jenkins, 2013).

However, it is crucial to understand the cultural approach to photography. As highlighted earlier, images do not function independently; rather, they tap into existing cultural and historical knowledge within the viewers and typically operate in conjunction with linguistic or textual arguments (Schill, 2012, p. 122; Mpofu et al., 2021). For this reason, photographs can have multiple connotations, making them complex communicative tools. This means that photographs of protest cultures in South Africa can only be understood within the context in which they are circulating. As such, this study argues that there is a need to understand the socio-economic factors that are at play in photographic meaning making. Images act as enthymemes, or implied arguments, with the audience filling in a portion of the evidence, reasoning, or claim to complete the argument (Blair, 2004). As Domke, Perlmutter, and Spratt (2002, p. 147) note, "people react in complex ways to news images." Therefore, socioeconomic backgrounds play a role in understanding the work of photographs. Kuhn (2007) reminds us that photographs are social objects that can be changed by the context in which they are read or seen. In relation to this view, it is also crucial to acknowledge the mobility of photographs, especially in the digital age. Hence, the study will appreciate the source of photographs and when they were taken before making sense of their new lease on life on Twitter. It is at the heart of this study, through context, to understand how photographs are being reused in the contemporary era. The next section discusses protest cultures in South Africa. The main thrust of the section is to highlight the work that has been done on protests, which, as indicated above, has largely neglected the use of photographs in protests.

PROTEST CULTURES IN SOUTH AFRICA

South Africa's transition from the apartheid era has been the subject of discussion owing to growing dissident voices resulting in various forms of protest. One of the major reasons for the continual use of protest as communication has arguably been due to the country's elite transition. Sparks (2011), for instance, compares South Africa to other transitional democracies when he states that only economic and political elites were empowered through democratization, not ordinary citizens and their organizations. Therefore, these protests can be read within the evils of the apartheid era and further "best understood not as a miraculous historical rupture, but as a dramatic phase in an ongoing struggle to resolve a set of political, economic and social contradictions that became uncontainable in the 1970s" (Marais, 2011, p. 2). Despite the entrenched and mature democracy that is enjoyed in South Africa as opposed to countries in the region, Wasserman et al. (2018, p. 1) argue that "dissent about the dividends of democracy for the majority of the country's citizens, together with widespread perceptions of government corruption, has resulted in ongoing protests." Some of the causes or reasons for protest include high levels of unemployment, housing, water and sanitation, electricity, corruption and municipal administration, health, and crime. These protests, which started in the early 2000s, have since become "a daily occurrence" (Pieterse and Van Donk, 2013, p. 109).

The ANC-led government inherited an uneven economic and social setup with a severe backlog of service delivery as the apartheid government neglected and disadvantaged the majority of black South Africans. According to Zwelibanzi Mpehle (2012), of 284 municipalities, 71 percent were unable to offer sanitary services to 60 percent of their residents, 64 percent failed to remove refuse from 60 percent of homes, 55 percent could not provide water for 60 percent of properties, 43 percent could not provide electricity for 60 percent of homes, and 41 percent could not provide housing for 60 percent of their residents. Furthermore, while the majority black population was enjoying new rights in the form of voting, they remained marginalized, as access to economic opportunity coupled with the failed promises of the ANC-led government of jobs and housing pushed them further into poverty. This then resulted in dissident voices that kept using protest as a form of communication since the mainstream media had remained elitist. Wasserman et al (2018, p. 4) add that the protests that have been occurring in South Africa "are not only about the delivery of services but express a deeper discontent with the fruits of democracy, more than twenty years after the end of apartheid." Thus, protests can be a strategy in what Brown (2015, p. 61) refers to as "repertoires of disruption' that citizens can make use of to 'enmesh notions of status into ongoing practices of empowerment and self-realisation" (Brown, 2015, p. 59).

The growing use of social media has also resulted in the increase of online protests. The role of social media and mobile technologies in protests and revolutions has been contested, with examples including the Arab Spring and other African countries like Zimbabwe and Swaziland (Matsilele et al., 2021; Matsilele and Ruhanya, 2021; Bodunrin and Matsilele, 2023). Despite such views, Bosch (2017, p. 224) contends that "what is clear is that social media has facilitated protest participation by increasing opportunities for engagement in collective action." X, formerly Twitter, has recently become the focus of scholarly attention, with increased research on how it can be used to facilitate communication, to inform and mobilize during social unrest, to inform political discourse, and to precede revolutionary events on the ground (Bosch, 2017; Gleason, 2013). Paolo Gerbaudo (2012) argues that social media has resulted in the emergence of new forms of protest.

In South Africa, different social media protests have been emerging, with the significant ones being #BlackLivesMatter, #RhodesMustFall, and #FeesMustFall. Twitter discussions around #RMF played a key role in challenging memories around Cecil John Rhodes. The protest was mainly about racism and decolonizing memory and curriculum in South Africa. Decolonizing memory, this paper argues, entails that institutions churn out memories that celebrate black African histories and further do away with memories that evoke colonial legacy. In South Africa, this meant removing statues that either celebrate, evoke, or commemorate colonialists like Cecil John Rhodes. The movements were mainly spearheaded by youths, and, as argued by Katharyne Mitchell (2013, p. 443), "each age attempts to refashion and remake memory to serve its own contemporary purposes." Thus, the #RhodesMustFall protest movement

> could be framed as a collective project of resistance to normative memory production, creating a new landscape of "minority" memory and bringing to the fore the memory of groups who have been rendered invisible in the landscape, thus speaking to an alternate interpretation of historical events. (Bosch, 2017, p. 222)

Two key issues emerge from these protests. First, the protests were in response to ongoing inequalities that the ANC-led government had failed to address or correct decades after gaining power. Secondly, social networking sites became key enablers for students and other social media users to engage in and promote participation in protest cultures.

VISUAL MEMORIES AND PROTEST IN THE DIGITAL SPHERE

Photographs have been appropriated by many as agents of protest. Social media movements depend heavily on photographs, which they produce and disseminate to their wider network as evidence of what will take time at a given place. However, the use of photographs is not innocent, as they are produced and used for certain ideological reasons. Photographs are "fragile objects" (Sontag, 1997, p. 4), measured by the clarity and interest of the information that they communicate as symbols, or preferably, as an allegory (Bourdieu, 1990, p. 92). The meaning they produce is bound to be "up for grabs" (Hall, 1997). When applied to both protest and memory, photographs have a voice. According to Zelizer (2010, p. 13), a visual voice is an "image's orientation to the imagined, emotional and contingent cues in its environment, which facilitates its relationship with a broad range of contexts events, people, practices, and other things." Thus, photographs of protest should be read within the context of production and circulation so that one can see the discourses that protesters are producing. Furthermore, photographs have a voice that refers to "the ways in which an image's meaning is used for a wide variety of strategies and objectives all of which increase over time and space" (Zelizer, 2010, p. 13). Thus, through the voice of the visual, the study goes beyond looking at what is being framed and its representations to broader issues that are evoked by visuals in mediating contemporary issues and the future.

The politics around protest can also be best explained by the theory of counter-memory, as explained by Michel Foucault (1977). Social media networks like Twitter enable different communities, especially the marginalized, to produce counter-memories online that challenge the status quo (Msimanga et al. 2022; Tshuma and Phiri, 2022; Matsilele and Mutsvairo, 2021; Ndlovu et al., 2019). In reference to South Africa, the key discourse has been that the country is a "rainbow nation," yet the black majority are mostly poor and economically marginalized. Counter-memory, according to Foucault, is a resistance against hegemonic narratives that tend to silence marginalized views. Thus, as the findings will demonstrate, it is through the #BlackLivesMatter movement that we will be able to show the selective use of South Africa's historic past by others to "speak" and mediate upon the country's situation, creating "an unstable assemblage of faults, fissures, and heterogeneous layers that threaten the fragile from within or underneath" (Foucault, 1977, p. 146). As a result, the movement represents a counter-discourse and campaign of "undermining power where it is most invisible and insidious" (Foucault, 1977, p. 208). Therefore, discourses on Twitter around the #BlackLivesMatter movement make visible the power relations in place and call into forum the discussion about the country's democracy.

METHODOLOGY

This study analyzes photographs taken from X, formerly Twitter. The tweets were gathered through an open-access tool called Mecodify, which is an open-source and feature-rich tool created through the MeCoDEM project primarily to extract, analyze, and present Twitter data.

The tool works by searching for a specific inquiry and producing results by identifying certain tweet IDs. In this study, Black Lives Matter in South Africa is the key phrase that was used to search for material. I managed to get over 120 images. However, not all these images were related to the study. The study selected images that evoked memories of the liberation struggle. The study, for ease of gathering data, used hashtags that were running under the name Black Lives Matter. Hashtags were useful in that they helped in following the conversation and debates around the ongoing issue. The other important element of Twitter is the use of retweeting.

While retweeting can simply be seen as the act of copying and rebroadcasting, the practice contributes to a conversational ecology in which conversations are composed of a public interplay of voices that give rise to an emotional sense of shared conversational context. (Boyd et al. 2010, p.1)

For analysis, this study used visual content analysis, which is "a systematic, observational method used for testing hypotheses about the ways in which the media represent people, events, situations and so on" (Bell, 2001, p.14). This method was used to assess a range of discourses produced by people and memories evoked by people, as well as the use of visuals to assess the ongoing socio-economic situation in the country.

ANALYSIS

The next section discusses the study's findings. The section has three themes, which were all developed through qualitative content analysis of photographs that were shared under the #BlackLivesMatter movement in South Africa. The themes are #BlackLivesMatter and race; Not yet Uhuru: A case of liberation with no economic empowerment and challenging the "rainbow nation."

#BLACKLIVESMATTER, MEMORY, AND RACE

One of the key issues central to the #BlackLivesMatter movement is racial inequalities, where whites are accused of enjoying more benefits compared to the black race. Such discourse is also common in the South African movement, where protesters under the movement registered their displeasure over the way they were treated in a supposedly liberated country. One of the images captures the Soweto Uprisings, where school students were shot dead by the Apartheid regime. The Soweto Uprising was a series of demonstrations and protests led by black school children in

South Africa under apartheid that began in June 1976. The students were unhappy because schools in the townships of Soweto were forced to use the Afrikaans language for teaching certain subjects. Two photographs were circulated on Twitter. The first photograph shows the dead bodies of pupils, while the other photograph shows injured pupils lying in a pool of blood. According to Katherine Verdery (1999, pp. 28–29), "dead people come with a curriculum vitae or resume—several possible résumés, depending on which aspect of their life is being considered." Considering that photographic meaning is contextual (Tshuma et al., 2023; Ndlovu et al., 2023; Clarke, 1977), photographs were used to remember the sacrifices that the deceased made and challenge the current ANC government for failing to deliver or fulfill the ethos of the struggle that other people sacrificed their lives for. Photographs are used by protesters to show that there is "change without change" in South Africa. Photographs have enabled protesters to "argue" that while the country is liberated, the apartheid system is still in place. One of the photographic discourses is closely related to #FeesMustFall movement, where the poor are unable to complete their studies due to financial challenges. Therefore, Twitter has played a huge role in facilitating "access to large numbers of contacts enabling movements to reach critical mass, they promote the construction of group identities that are key features of protest" (Bosch, 2017, p. 224). Racial inequalities are evoked by commemorating liberation icons hence, "the dead are not dead; they are alive" (Zertal, 2005, p. 55). Meaning that the "dead" are being used to guide and inspire the current generation of fighters. Therefore, by showing images of the Soweto youth uprising and liberation icons like Nelson Mandela and Oliver Tambo, protesters benefit from the already held view about photographs whose evidence can't be questioned. The grammar of the visual design indicates that by looking into the camera, the constructed icons are authoritatively looking at people and addressing them emotionally, as "eyes are the windows to the soul" (Bowen, 2018, p. 54; Kress and Van Leeuwen, 1996). Pierre Bourdieu (1990, p. 73) supports this school of thought by noting that the "photograph can be seen as the model of veracity and objectivity . . . its (photographic) plate does not interpret it. It records. Its precession and fidelity cannot be questioned." Therefore, protesters are engaged in subactivism, which is explained by Maria Bakardjieva (2010, p. 134) as "not about political power in the strict sense, but about personal empowerment seen as the power of the subject to be the person that they want to be in accordance with [their] reflexively chosen moral and political standards." Therefore, despite celebrating the health of the country's democracy, through photographic representation under #BlackLivesMatter, "the country still finds itself in a period of historical juncture, reflected by growing socio-economic inequality and citizen discontent, together with frequent public sphere debates around collective memory and recollections of history" (Bosch, 2017, p. 222).

NOT YET UHURU: A CASE OF LIBERATION WITH NO ECONOMIC EMPOWERMENT

South Africa treasures herself as one of the developed countries in Africa. However, Twitter users under #BlackLivesMatter are challenging the country's liberation, which, to the majority, has not yet ushered in any economic benefits for them. Online protesters shared photographs showing their living conditions, which they argue hasn't changed. In one of the photographs, squatter camps are captured with raw sewage flowing. Thus, the "arguments" that are being advanced through photography are that the independence that is being celebrated is a fallacy, as black lives haven't changed. Second, an analysis of many images that were circulated around Youth Day and Freedom shows that users used the hashtag to protest the poor state of their financial and economic status. In one of the photographs, blacks are juxtaposed with whites. Blacks are captured owning taverns—small shops in their home—while whites are shown owning land and companies. Such a comparison shows the economic inequalities that exist in South Africa. To the users, liberators fought to liberate the country, but their efforts are in vain as the economic power is still in the hands of the white minority. Photographs are used in protest "mainly as a social rite, a defense against anxiety, and a tool of power" (Sontag, 1997, p. 8). Furthermore, Howard Becker (2002, p. -11) argues that "photos are valuable too far the way they reveal real, flesh and bloodlife." With collective memory being "a tool not of retrieval but of reconfiguration (that) colonises the past by obliging it to conform to present configuration" (Zelizer, 1998, p. 3), Twitter users have been protesting under #BlackLivesMatter by appropriating their own memories or understanding of the liberation war to thwart and challenge the hegemonic narrative that the country is progressing well.

Furthermore, while some of the photographs are used to show brutality under the apartheid regime, their contemporary use is restructured to "argue" for economic gains that the fighters and departed heroes and heroines fought for. Such use of photographs, mainly depicting moments of the apartheid era, shows that they (photographs) can be easily altered and are "subject to a continuous state of transformation and metamorphosis. Each change of context changes it as an object and alters its forms of reference and value" (Clarke, 1997, p. 19). Therefore, visuals have been used to "legitimise the grounds upon which some interpretations can be favored, and others impeded" (Rodriguez and Dimitrova, 2011, p. 51). As such, photographs are being used by protesters to call for economic empowerment and register their displeasure because they are languishing in poverty, yet one of the key cornerstones of the struggle was for economic empowerment. Against this background, the contextual reading of photographs shows that they are being used to "furnish evidence. Something we hear about, but doubt, seems proven when we're shown a photograph of it" (Sontag, 1977, p. 4).

Friedman and Kenney (2005, p. 1) remind us that "histories produced with an immediate goal in mind: they are partisan histories, narratives about the past designed to help win arguments and political struggle." Against this view, the protest movement, by and large, seeks to challenge the hegemonic narrative. To them, their lives matter, and they need to enjoy economic and political rights like their white counterparts. Key to this argument is their challenge of the hegemonic narrative that portrays the country as progressive, yet the black majority is not part of that progress. Thus, protesters selectively disregard the progress that has been made to uplift the previously marginalized black community. Such a selective use of memories shows that the act of remembering or re-creating the past through sites of memory like photographs is not simply "the retrieval of stored information, but the putting together of a claim about the past states of affairs by means of a framework of shared cultural understanding" (Halbawachs, 1992, p. 43).

CHALLENGING THE "RAINBOW NATION"

The media in South Africa usually frames the country as a "rainbow nation" to denote the coexistence of different races, tribes, and ethnic groups who all coexist in peace. Bennet Anderson (1991, p. 6) argues that the nation is imagined as "sovereign" and "limited." This study argues that protest movements use photographs to challenge the hegemonic narrative of a nation. Photographs are key vehicles in constructing identities as they foster "coherence in the imagined discourse of a nation, legitimizing, validating, and authenticating a sense of national identity" (Edwards 2015, p. 321). By depicting the failed promises by the African National Congress (ANC) government, including the abandonment of those students who did not finish their higher education studies, the #FeesMustFall movement argues the nation is fragile as there are some who are not enjoying the benefits of being in a nation. The rainbow nation is treated as a fallacy, with protesters using photographs to argue that there are many nations in South Africa. First, protesters used photographs of squatter camps in Alexandra Township in Johannesburg and juxtaposed them with photographs of low-density suburbs in Sandtown, which are largely occupied by whites. This study argues that photographs are producing knowledge on national identity, but such knowledge should not be seen as innocent, instead, it is structuring power relations that are closely tied to identity politics. Therefore, "like all forms of photographic representation, it is not simply a record of a given moment, for it cannot be innocent of the values and ethics of those who worked with it" (Hamilton, 1997, p. 76). Thus, the analysis shows that selected photographs are framed so "to make known, to confirm, and to give testimony" to a nation (Hamilton, 1997, p. 85).

To add more, as a form of communication, photographs have the capacity to reflect social contexts, depict specific events, and provide a visual link that influences the concept of national identity (Albers, Frederick and Cowan, 2009). Therefore, through the selective use of the past, the state of poverty and underdevelopment among the black community enables protesters to construct their own imagined nation. The value of using photographs to construct such a nation is based on the view that they "encode an enormous amount of information in a single representation" (Grady, 2004, p. 20). Based on the view that "knowledge is always working in the interest of a particular" (Mills, 2003, p. 76), the #BlackLivesMatter movement is structuring its own narrative to confirm and affirm that they oppose the hegemonic narrative of a contented nation. Thus, protesters have decided to value some histories more than others and "provide narrative patterns and examples of how individuals can and should remember and stimulate memory" (Olick, 1995, p. 225). There have been various initiatives empowering the black community, like the BEE (Black Economic Empowerment), but such important issues are not highlighted. Moreover, some of the freedoms that are enjoyed by South Africans are rare on a continent that is ruled by dictators. Hence, the nation that is being constructed is based on selected historical and present moments designed to challenge the hegemonic view.

DISCUSSION

One of the key issues emanating from the study is that the movement makes use of social media (in this case, Twitter) to circulate photographs that evoke memories of the apartheid era and yet also help to make sense of their current predicament. One of the key takeaways from the study is the centrality of photographs in memory and protest. Such a relationship between photograph and memory is rightly captured by Eco (2003, p. 126), who writes that "it is the visual work . . . that is now a part of our memory," while Zelizer (1998, p. 5) argues that "much of our ability to remember depends on images." Protest needs something concrete to justify its actions and influence others to join the bandwagon. As such, photographs are the appropriate tools because they have been sanctioned as "accurate," "truthful," and "authentic" and carry "an implicit guarantee of being closer to the truth than other forms of communication" (Messaris and Abraham, 2001, p. 217). Therefore, protests under #BlackLivesMatter also benefit from its use of social media.

This chapter also highlighted the value of photographs in communication, coming against a background where "within media and communication studies, the role of the visual image in news discourse has traditionally received rather notional or secondary attention" (Parry, 2010, p. 418). Protest movements are gaining more power and visibility online and empowering the previously marginalized to take part in debating and putting across their views on socioeconomic affairs in South Africa. Thus, the growth of social media "signals the advent of a new way of mobilising and organising student political power" (Luescher and Klemenčič, 2017). Photographs are also being used as a "tool of power" by protesters to exercise their democratic right, that is, to participate in deliberations related to the state of life for marginalized black people. Castels (2015, p. 316) also argues that the network society fosters democratic potential on the basis that "these networked social movements are new forms of democratic movements, movements that are reconstructing the public sphere in the space of autonomy built around the interaction of local places and Internet networks." Therefore, protest movements online, as seen in the #BlackLivesMatter allow people to form online communities as they constitute "networks of individuals and groups, based on shared collective identities' which engage in collective actions of political and social conflict" (Rochon in Gill and DeFronzo, 2009, p. 208).

The #BlackLivesMatter captures the essence of black lives, who argue that they are yet to enjoy equal economic and social rights with their white counterparts in South Africa, and this shares a similar cause with the movement in the United States. Thus, black population still feels that it is playing a secondary role to the white population, which controls the means of production. According to Gill and DeFronzo (2009, p. 208), "the political terrain engaged with movement activity is cultural and political, and particularly socially and politically marginal groups have been noted to participate in social movements." Through the protest movement, people can understand the key discourses prevailing in South Africa. In this case, what is common is a clear challenge to the hegemonic memories that sought to paint South Africa as a rainbow nation. This era of the network society has also managed to assist communities in coming together and thus " . . . creating a permanent forum of solidarity, debate, and strategic planning" (Castels, 2015, p. 172). In addition, Castells' (2015, pp. 169–171) empirical theory of internet-age networked movements suggests that they are:

> successful in mobilizing a greater diversity of activists and participants (issuing in truly multi-cultural, multiracial, multi-gender, multi-class, and multi-partisan

movements), and that they are characterised by spontaneity, a lack of clearly defined leadership and an attempt at a new active democratic practice.

Therefore, photographs that evoke memories of the struggle are brought to the fora to "incite" other protesters to challenge hegemonic narratives of the past and mediate on the present and the future.

CONCLUSION

The movement is also being used to construct collective memories. Aleida Assmann (1995, p. 181) defines collective memory "as the shared representation of the past," and a similar definition is given by Zelizer (1995, p. 214), who defines "collective memory as the recollections that are instantiated beyond the individual by and the collective." This study, therefore, concludes by arguing that photographs play a crucial role in identity construction. The key issues that are being depicted through photography include the use of movement to address racial inequalities, challenge hegemonic memories, and further show that the country is yet to enjoy economic freedom. In this study, "stories" of marginalization and economic disempowerment are being "testified" through photographs, which then help to produce discourses that are appropriate for the collective. Photographs have a "universal language" that can be read by people from different cultures and can reveal unseen things. They depict what people saw and indicate that this cannot be disputed. Thus, photographs "bear witness" to the suffering, neglect, and state of despair that the black community has endured, leading them to argue and bring to the attention of the elite that their lives matter. As such, photographs are used to construct a nation based on marginalization. The study further concludes that the meaning and the communication power of photographs lie within a context.

REFERENCES

Abraham, L. (2003). *Media stereotypes of African Americans. Images that injure: Pictorial stereotypes in the media,* Westport, CT: Praeger.

Abraham, L., & Appiah, O. (2006). Framing News Stories: The Role of Visual Imagery in Priming Racial Stereotypes, *The Howard Journal of Communications,* 17(3): 183–203.

Albers, P., Frederick, T., & Cowan, K. (2009). Features of Gender: A Study of the Visual Texts of Third Grade Students, *Journal of Early Childhood Literacy* 9(2): 243–269.

Anderson, B. (1991). *Imagined Communities: Reflections on the Origin and Spread of Nationalism*, London: Verso.

Ansell, B., & Samuels, D. (2014). Introduction. In Ansell and Samuels (Eds.), *Inequality and Democratization: An Elite-Competition Approach* Cambridge: Cambridge University Press, pp. 1-16.

Assmann, A. (2008). Canon and Archive. In Gruyter, W. (ed) *Cultural Memory Studies: An International and Interdisciplinary*. Berlin: Handbook.

Bakardjieva, M. (2010). *The Internet and Sub-activism: Young People, ICTs and Democracy,* Gothenburg: Nordicom.

Becker, H. (2002). Visual evidence: A Seventh Man, the specified generalization, and the work of the reader, *Visual Studies* 17(1): 3–11.

Ballenger, H. B. (2014). Photography: A Communication Tool. Thesis, Georgia State University, 2014. [Online] Available at: https://scholarworks.gsu.edu/art_design_theses/147. (Accessed: 28/10/2020).

Barthes, R. (1982). *Camera lucida: Reflections on photography*, London: Vintage.

Berry, C., & Brosius, H.-B. (1991). On the multiple effects of visual format on TV news learning, *Applied Cognitive Psychology* 5: 519–528.

Berger, J. (1982). *Ways of seeing*, London: Penguin Books.

Berger, P. L., & Luckman, T. (1966). *The social construction of reality*, California: Pegnum.

Bodunrin, I. A. and Matsilele, T. (2023). Social media and protest politics in Nigeria's# EndSARS campaign, *Handbook of Social Media in Education, Consumer Behavior and Politics: Volume 1* 111(114): 109.

Bourdieu, P. (1990). *Photography*. Oxford: Polity Press.

Bosch, T. (2017). Twitter activism and youth in South Africa: the case of #RhodesMustFall, *Information, Communication & Society* 20(2): 221–232.

Castells, M. (2007). Communication, Power and Counter-Power in the Network Society. *International Journal of Communication* 1(1): 238–266.

Chasi, C., & Rodny-Gumede, Y. (2016). Ubuntu journalism and nation building magic, *Critical Arts* 30(5): 728–744.

Cieplak, P. (2017). *Death, Image, Memory. The Genocide in Rwanda and its Aftermath in Photography and Documentary Film*, London: Macmillan.

Clarke, G. (1997). *The Photograph*, Oxford: Oxford University Press.

Didi-Huberman, G. (2008). *Images in spite of all*, Chicago: Chicago University Press.

Edward, E. (2015). Photographs as Strong History. In Costanza, C and Serena, T (ed). *Photo Archives and the Idea of Nation*, Berlin and Boston: Walter de Gruyter. 321–329.

Ezrahi, Y. (2012). Imagined Democracies: Necessary Political Fictions. New York. Cambridge University Press.

Foucault, M. (1980). 'Prison Talk', trans. Colin Gordon. In Colin Gordon (ed.) *Power/Knowledge: Selected Interviews and Other Writings 1972–1977*. New York: Pantheon. pp. 37–54.

Gerbaudo, P. (2012). *Tweets and the Streets: Social Media and Contemporary Activism*. Pluto Press. https://doi.org/10.2307/j.ctt183pdzs

Graber, D. (1996). Say it with Pictures. *Communication Studies* 545(1): 56–73 Photography'. In Hall, S. (ed) *Representation: Cultural Representations and Signifying Practices*, London: Sage Publication, pp. 77–150.

Haggard, S. and Kaufman, R. (2016). *Dictators and -Democrats: Masses, Elites, and Regime Change*, Princeton: Princeton University Press.

Halliday, M. (1985). *An Introduction to Functional Grammar*, London: Arnold.

Halbwachs, M. (1992). *On Collective Memory (Edited, translated and with an introduction by Lewis A. Coser)*, Chicago: University of Chicago Press.

Hamilton, P. (1997). 'Representing the Social: France and Frenchness in post-war humanist Photography'. In Hall, S. (ed) *Representation: Cultural Representations and Signifying Practices*, London: Sage Publication, pp. 77–150.

Hodge, R. and Kress, G. (1993). *Language as Ideology,* London: Routledge.

Jacobs, S. (2007). The media picture: Mapping the contemporary media scene in South Africa. In G. Gunnarsen, P. MacManus, M. Nielsen and H. E. Stolten (ed). *At the End of the Rainbow? Social Identity and Welfare State in the New South Africa*, Copenhagen: Africa Contact, pp. 153–163.

Jones, S. R., Torres, V. and Arminio, J. (2006). *Negotiating the Complexities of Qualitative Research in Higher Education: Fundamental Elements and Issues,* New York: Routledge.

Kress, G. and van Leeuwen, T. (2006). *Reading Images: The Grammar of Visual Design,* New York: Routledge.

Matsilele, T. and Mutsvairo, B. (2021). Social media as a sphere of political disruption. In Karam and Mutsvairo (Eds.), *Decolonising Political Communication in Africa* (pp. 179–190). London: Routledge.

Matsilele, T. and Ruhanya, P. (2021). 'Social media dissidence and activist resistance in Zimbabwe.' *Media, Culture & Society* 43(2): 381–394.

Matsilele, T., Mpofu, S., Msimanga, M. and Tshuma, L. (2021). Transnational hashtag protest movements and emancipatory politics in Africa: A three country study. *Global Media Journal: German Edition* 11(2): 1-23.

Mitchell, K. (2013). 'Monuments, memorials, and the politics of memory.' *Urban Geography* 24(5): 442–459.

Mpehle, Z. (2012). 'Are service delivery protests justifiable in the democratic South Africa?' *Journal of Public Administration* 47(si-1): 213–227-.

Mpofu, S., Ndlovu, M. and Tshuma, L. (2021). 'The artist and filmmaker as activists, archivists and the work of memory: A case of the Zimbabwean genocide.' *African Journal of Rhetoric* 13(1): 46–76.

Moses, M. (2002). *Readers consume what they see*. Poynter Report. Retrieved from: poynterinstitute.org.

Msimanga, M. J., Tshuma, L. A. and Matsilele, T. (2022). 'The why of humour during a crisis: An exploration of COVID-19 memes in South Africa and Zimbabwe.' *Journal of African Media Studies* 14(2): 189–207.

Ndlovu, M., Tshuma, L., ānd Mpofu, S (Eds). (2023). *Remembering Mass Atrocities: Perspectives on Memory Struggles and Cultural Representations in Africa*. Cham: Springer International Publishing.

Ndlovu, M., Tshuma, L. A., and Ngwenya, S. W. (2019). Between tradition and modernity: Discourses on the coronation of the Ndebele "King" in Zimbabwe. *Critical Arts* 33(2): 82–95.

Philipps, A. (2012). "Visual protest material as empirical data.' *Visual Communication* 11(1): 3–21. https:// doi.org/10.1177/1470357211424675

Saukko, P. (2003). *Doing Research in Cultural Studies; An Introduction to Classical and New Methodological Approaches Introducing Qualitative Methods,* London: Sage.

Sontag, S. (2003). *Regarding the Pain of Others,* New York: Picador.

Sontag, S. (1977). *On Photography,* Harmondsworth: Penguin Books.

Sontag, S. (1978). *On Photography,* London: Penguin Books.

Schill, D. (2012). The Visual Image and the Political Image: A Review of Visual Communication Research in the Field of Political Communication, *Review of Communication* 12(2): 118–142-. https:// doi.org/10.1080/15358593.2011.653504.

Sparks, C. (2011). 'South African media in comparative perspective.' *Ecquid Novi: African Journalism Studies* 32(2), 5–19. https:// doi.org/10.1080/02560054.2011.578873.

Sternberg, R. J. (2006). Stalking the elusive creativity quark: Toward a comprehensive theory of creativity. In P. Locher, C. Martindale, L. Dorfman, V. Petrov, and D. Leontiev (eds.). *New Directions in Aesthetics, Creativity, and the Arts,* Amityville, NY: Baywood, pp. 79–104.

Tshuma, L., Ndlovu, M. and Mpofu, S. (2023). Mass Atrocities and Memory Struggles in Africa and the Global South. In M. Ndlovu, L. Tshuma and S. Mpofu (eds). *Remembering Mass Atrocities: Perspectives on Memory Struggles and Cultural Representations in Africa,.* Cham: Springer International Publishing, pp. 1–14.

Tshuma, L. A. and Phiri, L. (2022). '*Photographing the "nation" in the digital age: A case of matabeleland discourses on social media platforms.*' The Idea of Matabeleland in Digital Spaces: Genealogies, Discourses, and Epistemic Struggles, 241.

Tshuma L. A. and Ndlovu, M. (2020). 'Immortalizing "Buried Memories": Photographs of the Gukurahundi Online.' *Journal of Genocide Research.* https://doi.org/10.1080/14623528.2020.1850393.

Tshuma, L. A. (2019). 'Political billboards, promise, and persuasion: An analysis of ZANU-PF's 2018 harmonized elections political campaign.' *Journal of Marketing Communications.* https://doi.org/10.1080/13527266.2019.1683057.

Van Leeuwen, T. (2005). *Introducing Social Semiotics,* London/New York: Routledge.

Verdery, K. (1999). *The Political Lives of Dead Bodies: Reburial and Post-socialist Change.* New York: Columbia University Press.

Weyland, K. (2017). 'Dictators and democrats: masses, elites, and regime change, by Stephan Haggard and Robert Kaufman.' *Democratization* 24(2): 386–388.

Wright, T. (2004). *The Photographic Handbook,* London. Routledge.

Zelizer, B. (2010). *About to Die: How News Images Move the Public,* Oxford: Oxford University Press, Chicago: University of Chicago Press.

Index

African National Congress (ANC), 7, 17, 71, 76, 235, 265
Arab Spring, 3–5, 71, 72, 88, 89, 108
authoritarian regimes, 5, 56, 73, 89, 116, 139, 183, 208

Buhari, Muhammadu, 58, 61, 63, 92, 94

carnivalesque, 76, 77, 79, 82, 163
citizen journalism, 163, 175
collective memory, 207, 264, 268
colonial era, 19, 110–113, 256
corruption, 1, 17, 18, 49, 70, 71, 78, 79, 121, 122, 144, 145, 159, 169, 170, 218, 259
counterhegemonic, 43, 48, 73, 172

decolonized/decolonization, 2, 4, 13, 14, 16, 20–25, 27, 72, 89
diasporic media, 8, 183, 184, 186, 189, 195
digital activism, 21, 32, 76, 161, 248, 251
disenfranchised, 35, 164
dissidents, 89, 112, 170, 204

Eswatini, 12, 17, 18, 19, 20, 27
Ethiopia, 8, 26, 182, 184, 185, 188

fake news, 6, 54–59, 61, 113
FRELIMO, 123–125

Global South, 2, 108, 110, 145, 250, 254
graffiti- 4, 8, 148, 161, 203, 211
Gukurahundi, 8, 112, 202–205, 207, 210, 212

hashtag movements, 4, 5, 35, 36, 72, 73
hip hop, 134, 140

injustice, 8, 13, 20, 130, 134, 138, 160, 214, 241
internet shutdowns, 7, 16, 26, 115, 208

Mawarire, Evan, 17, 35, 36, 41, 43, 168, 209
media freedom, 183, 186
Movement for Democratic Change (MDC), 38, 39, 107, 113, 175
music, 7, 8, 77, 133, 139–141, 145, 207

national symbols, 6, 39, 40, 41, 47, 50

oppressive, 2, 15, 16, 21, 27, 50, 111, 231, 237

photographs, 8, 256–258, 260
protest movements, 4, 5, 21, 74, 89, 265

public sphere, 2, 21, 50, 72, 77, 81
publishing, 235

rebel, 2
repressive, 2, 114, 115, 134, 176

satire, 2, 8, 55, 145, 147
social media activism, 73, 162, 163
social movements- 6, 13, 17, 21, 25, 88, 122

Third Chimurenga, 39, 40
trolling, 74, 75, 78

Ubuntu, 2, 27

violence, 28, 29, 110, 112, 163

Zanu-PF, 5, 35, 37, 39

About the Editors and Contributors

EDITORS

Lungile Tshuma is Researcher in the Center for Communication and Culture, Universidade Catolica Portuguesa, Portugal. He holds a PhD in journalism studies from the University of Johannesburg, South Africa. Lungile's research interests are in photography, memory, journalism, and political communication. He has published in several peer-reviewed journals, such as *African Journalism Studies, Nations and Nationalism, Media Culture and Society,* and *Journal of Communication Inquiry.*

Trust Matsilele is Senior Lecturer at Birmingham City University. Matsilele holds a doctorate degree from the University of Johannesburg and a Master of Philosophy in Journalism from Stellenbosch University. Dr. Matsilele publishes in areas of social media and protest cultures, journalism studies, and digital humanities. His research has been published in D*igital Journalism, Media Culture and Society, Journal of Science Communication (JCom)* among others.

Shepherd Mpofu is an associate professor of Media and Communication at the University of South Africa, South Africa. He has published several articles on communication, media, and journalism in Africa. His body of work covers social media and politics; social media and identity; and social media and protests. He is the coeditor of *Mediating Xenophobia in Africa* (Palgrave 2020) and editor of *The Politics of Laughter in the Social Media Age: Perspectives from the Global South* (Palgrave Macmillan 2021) and *Digital Humor in the COVID-19 Pandemic: Perspectives from the Global South* (Palgrave Macmillan 2021).

Mbongeni Msimanga holds a PhD in Communication from the University of Johannesburg. Now, he is a postdoctoral fellow at the Johannesburg Institute of Advanced Study (JIAS), South Africa. He completed his PhD in 2022. Previously, Mbongeni was a recipient of the Canon Collins Sol Plaatje scholarship. His research interests are in digital cultures, satire, identity constructions, and political communication.

CONTRIBUTORS

Kunle Adebajo is the investigations editor and head of internal fact-check at HumAngle and a former investigative reporter at the International Center for Investigative Reporting (ICIR). He is a 2019 fellow of Africa Check, 2020 fellow of Dubawa, and an alumnus of the British Council's Future News Worldwide program. He is passionate about human rights and educational reform, as well as how human-centered storytelling can help bring attention to related issues. Kunle has won a number of journalism awards, including the 2018 Alfred Opubo Prize for Opinion, 2018 Budeshi Datathon Writers' Challenge, 2019 West Africa Medica Excellence Award for Best Telecommunications Report, and 2020 Diamond Media Award for Education Reporting. He was also a 2020 finalist for the Isu Elihle Awards on child-centered reporting and a top entrant for the 2020 PwC Media Excellence Awards. He can be reached at adekunlebaj@gmail.com.

Raheemat Adeniran teaches journalism at the School of Communication, Lagos State University, Lagos, Nigeria. She holds a PhD in Communication Studies (2018) from Lagos State University. She has research interests in journalism studies, health communication, fact-checking, and misinformation studies. She was a 2020 fact-checking research fellow with Dubawa, Nigeria's first indigenous fact-checking organization. She is a team player who is well-published and regularly collaborates with other researchers. She can be reached at raheemat.adeniran@lasu.edu.ng.

Lorenzo Dalvit is an associate professor of Digital Media and Cultural Studies at Rhodes University in South Africa and the former MTN Chair of Media and Mobile Communication at the same institution. His main areas of academic interest are digital inequalities (e.g., in terms of gender, language, geographical location, (dis)ability) through a critical and/or decolonial lens. He (co)authored more than 150 publications across disciplines ranging from Sociology to Education, Linguistics, and Media Studies.

Temitope Opeyemi Falade is a PhD candidate at the School of Media and Communication, Pan-Atlantic University, Lagos, Nigeria. A graduate of

Computer Science and Digital Media, her research focuses on social media and its impact on society. She teaches Introduction to Social Media Networks and Introduction to Computer-Aided Design to undergraduate students of Pan-Atlantic University. She has facilitated different training programs targeted at managers, journalists, and communications officers in the public and private sectors. She is also the communications manager for Pan-Atlantic University, Lagos, Nigeria.

Abit Hoxha is an assistant professor and researcher at the Department of Nordic and Media Studies, University of Agder. He is pursuing his PhD on "Comparing conflict news production" at LMU Munich. His research interests are journalism and news production in conflict, declining democracies, dealing with troubled pasts, and media and democracy. His research extends from Africa to the Middle East, Western Balkans, as well as Europe. His current research focuses on the media and democracy relationship, emphasizing democratic decline throughout Europe. Abit is also involved in training journalists on sensitive reporting.

Solomon Kebede is a PhD fellow at the Department of Global Development and Planning, University of Agder, Norway. He has been practicing journalism in Ethiopian local media and freelancing in international outlets. His research topics include diaspora media, international public broadcasting, media systems, and conflict.

Nkosini A. Khupe is a lecturer in journalism and media studies, and his research interests are in media, democracy, and safety of journalists. Khupe is pursuing his PhD in journalism studies at Stellenbosch University, South Africa.

Tânia Machonisse is a PhD candidate in Cultural Studies at the University of Trás-os-Montes e Alto Douro, Portugal. She holds an MA degree in communications from the University of Southern Indiana, USA; a postgraduate degree in gender studies from the University of Iceland; and a BA in journalism from Eduardo Mondlane University, Mozambique. She is a former Fulbright Scholar in the USA and a former UNESCO Scholar in Iceland. Tânia Machonisse is a lecturer at the School of Communications and Arts at Eduardo Mondlane University.

Blessing Makwambeni is Senior Lecturer and Masters convenor in the Media Studies department at the Cape Peninsula University of Technology in South Africa. He also serves as the Faculty of Informatics and Design Research Ethics Chair. Blessing holds a PhD in Communication from the

University of Fort Hare, South Africa, and has previously taught Journalism and Media Studies at the National University of Science and Technology in Zimbabwe. His research interests lie in the broad areas of political communication, audience studies, digital politics, development communication, and strategic communication.

Tawanda Mukurunge is Lecturer of media and communication studies at Limkokwing University of Creative Technology in Lesotho. He is also a PhD candidate in journalism at Rhodes University in South Africa. Holder of a Master of Arts degree in Media and Communication Studies from the University of Zimbabwe. Email: tawanda75mukurunge@gmail.com

Job Mwaura is Postdoctoral Research Fellow at the Wits Centre for Journalism at the University of the Witwatersrand. He was previously a researcher in the Department of Journalism at Stellenbosch University and at the University of Cape Town, in the Institute for Humanities in Africa (HUMA). Dr. Job Mwaura completed his doctoral studies in the Department of Media Studies at the University of the Witwatersrand (Wits), South Africa. He holds an MSc in Communication and Journalism from Moi University, Kenya. He researches and publishes on digital media in Africa, African studies, digital culture, activism, and social justice.

Mphathisi Ndlovu is a research fellow at Stellenbosch University and an Alliance for Historical Dialogue and Accountability (AHDA) fellow at Columbia University's Institute for the Study of Human Rights. He holds a PhD in journalism from Stellenbosch University and is also a research fellow at the same institution. Mphathisi is also a research fellow at Africa No Filter, a South African-based initiative that seeks to change the harmful narratives about Africa. His research interests are in collective memory, identity politics, and digital cultures. Mphathisi is also an associate professor in the Department of Journalism and Media Studies at the National University of Science and Technology (Zimbabwe). His works have been published as book chapters and peer-reviewed articles in journals such as *Digital Journalism*, *African Cultural Studies*, *Journal of Genocide Research*, and *Nations and Nationalism*. Mphathisi is coediting a book titled *The Idea of Matabeleland in Digital Spaces: Genealogies, Discourses and Epistemic Struggles* which is in press at Lexington Books.

Ruth Karachi Benson Oji (PhD) is a senior lecturer at the English Unit, Pan-Atlantic University, Lagos and she is interested in interrogating issues of language use in media discourse, especially from a critical discourse perspective. Email: roji@pau.edu.ng

Nyasha Cefas Zimuto is currently an English and Communication Lecturer at Gacuba Teacher Training College in Rwanda. He holds a PhD in Languages, Linguistics, and Literature from the University of South Africa, obtained in 2022. He completed his MA in African Languages and Culture in 2013 at Midlands State University, Zimbabwe, and a Post Graduate Diploma in Education from the Zimbabwe Open University in 2017. His areas of interest include sociolinguistics, communication, African languages, media, and cultural studies.

Milton Keynes UK
Ingram Content Group UK Ltd.
UKHW042050150824
447006UK00004B/30